Preface

The title of this book is self-explanatory: it is, broadly, about military training concerning children in armed conflict. It is also a book that explicitly attempts to link theory with practice—and it addresses a topic that engages a range of different organisations and individuals.

The book is therefore intended to be read and used by those involved in the training of national armed forces, including military personnel, government representatives and policy-makers, and members of non-governmental and inter-governmental organisations. It is hoped that it will also be of interest to academics, lawyers and others concerned with 'child rights' and related law and policy more generally.

Accordingly, the book is structured for ease of reference by these various categories of reader, so that it can accommodate those with specialised interests who may wish to read only some chapters, or indeed some sections of some chapters. For those concerned only with the main child-related rules pertinent to military training, these rules are highlighted in the text, marked with *, and they are also summarised as self-contained training notes in Appendix Six. For other specialised readers, there follows a brief guide to the ten chapters, highlighting areas that may be of interest.

Chapter One *(Introduction)*—the final section, particularly the 'Definitions' and 'Outline': relevant for all readers;
Chapters Two-Five *(Law and Policy: Content of Rules Relevant to Officer Training)*: particularly relevant for those involved in military training (eg, officers and other military personnel, government representatives and representatives of international organisations);
Chapter Six *(Law and Policy: Obligations of Governments)*: particularly relevant for members of governments, policy-makers, representatives of international organisations and others engaged in dialogue with states concerning child-specific military training;
Chapter Seven *(Impact of Law and Policy)*: particularly relevant for those involved in military training (as above, Chapters Two—Five). However, it is likely that experienced trainers will already be familiar with this material;
Chapters Eight-Nine *(Country Studies and the ICRC)*: relevant for general readership—those with an interest in military training practice 'on the ground';
Chapter Ten *(Conclusion)*: relevant for all readers.

The Appendices (One to Six) supplement the text, and readers will be referred to the pertinent Appendix by information set out in the related chapters. Appendices Five and Six contain examples of actual training materials that can be adapted for use in a variety of military courses.

The endnotes after each chapter are likely to be of interest primarily to those with a more detailed academic interest in the subject-matter of this book.

Military Training and Children in Armed Conflict

Law, Policy and Practice

Military Training and Children in Armed Conflict

Law, Policy and Practice

Jenny Kuper

MARTINUS NIJHOFF PUBLISHERS
LEIDEN • BOSTON

A C.I.P. Catalogue record for this book is available from the Library of Congress.

Printed on acid-free paper.

ISBN 90 04 13673 8
© 2005 Koninklijke Brill NV, Leiden, The Netherlands.
Cover photograph © ANP, The Netherlands.

Koninklijke Brill NV incorporates the imprints Brill Academic Publishers, Martinus
Nijhoff Publishers, and VSP.
http://www.brill.nl

Printed and bound in The Netherlands.

Dedicated, once more, to Sam Pablo, Joe, and Ellie. Dedicated also to the children of Gulu, Uganda, and those in all the other many zones of armed conflict, who have no choice but to live in the presence of extraordinary horror and instability—in the hope, still, that change will come, and that it will be for the better.

Acknowledgements

It would be impossible to thank adequately all those whose advice, encouragement and support have helped in the writing of this book. This impossibility is, in part, because so many have been involved. Further, some of those involved have requested anonymity (due to their official positions, e.g. in government or in the armed forces). The latter will, I hope, know that I am most grateful for their contributions.

In any event, it is a great pleasure to express publicly my appreciation of those who do not require anonymity.

These are, firstly, my funders, the Nuffield Foundation, without whose assistance this work would not have been possible. I am particularly indebted to Sharon Witherspoon (Deputy Director) and others connected with this Foundation, whose perceptive comments helped to narrow the focus of what was, initially, an even more ambitious project! I am also grateful to Save the Children Sweden, and to the John D and Catherine T MacArthur Foundation for providing a substantial part of the funding for my earlier, related work on child civilians.

Next, I would like to thank my colleagues at the London School of Economics (LSE), and particularly the Law Department and the Development Studies Institute, both of which provided me, at different times, with an office, equipment, secretarial assistance, and the stimulus of a lively intellectual environment. I owe thanks, too, to a number of the LSE librarians, individual secretaries and students, who all helped with various tasks on occasion.

In the course of this project, I was fortunate to work consecutively with three very able Research Assistants, all PhD students. These were: Monica Feria-Tinta, Chitra Massey and, most recently, Claire LaHovary. I am particularly grateful to the latter, who assisted me for the longest period, and with great competence throughout.

Invaluable assistance was also provided by the 12 individuals, with a wide range of relevant experience, who agreed to act as my Advisory Committee for this work. These were, in the UK: Dr Liz Barnett, Dr Chaloka Beyani, Professor Christine Chinkin, Professor Christopher Greenwood, Dr James Putzel (all based at LSE), Major General (Retired) Tony Rogers, and Sarah Uppard (Save the Children-UK). Other members were: Patrick Brugger (Head of the Unit for Relations with Armed and Security Forces, International Committee of the Red Cross), Ilene Cohn (former staff member for the Special Representative of the UN Secretary General on Children and Armed Conflict), Una McCauley (former West Africa Regional Advisor on Children in Armed Conflict and Displacement, Save the Children Sweden), Major Bruce Oswald (Australian Defence Force), and Professor Katarina Tomasevski (UN Special Rapporteur on the Right to Education).

Certain Advisory Committee members were, inevitably, more actively involved in this project than others, but the support of all 12 was much appreciated. In particular, I welcomed the occasionally challenging contributions of some Committee members from a military background, who from time to time had to temper my 'child-friendly' approach with reminders of the harsher realities of military life. It is also worth noting here that, although I was guided by the Committee members, they did not have a veto on the final manuscript (and in any event they sometimes had divergent views, so that it was difficult to ascertain even a majority opinion on certain points). Their role was purely advisory, and any errors of judgement, fact or law in this book remain my responsibility.

In addition, I wish to express sincere thanks to the members of the UN Committee on the Rights of the Child, and representatives of the San Remo International Institute of Humanitarian Law, the International Committee of the Red Cross and the office of the Special Representative of the UN Secretary General on Children and Armed Conflict (see Chapter Eight).

Many thanks are also due to my hosts in Uganda, the family of Flora Nkurukenda, to the Uganda office of Save the Children Denmark (especially Sandra Oder) and to the children, and members of the Ugandan People's Defence Forces, whom I met in Gulu (again, see Chapter Eight).

A debt of gratitude is owed, as well, to the various experts who commented on the 'Background Notes' for the 11 country studies (see Appendix Four), and to Colonel Charles Garraway (retired), Yuval Ginbar, Professor Adam Kuper and Nicole Wyld, for their helpful suggestions on aspects of the manuscript.

Thanks, too, to my publisher Lindy Melman of Martinus Nijhoff, whose enthusiasm for this project never flagged, to my former publisher Richard Hart (then at Oxford University Press) for his informal help and advice, and to my copy-editor, Melanie Hamill.

Last but definitely not least, I acknowledge the tremendous support and warmth of friends and family, which greatly sustained me. My loving thanks to you all, and particularly to my son, Sam Pablo—still uniquely true to himself.

Contents

Preface   vii

Acknowledgements   ix

Contents   xi

Abbreviations   xiii

Table of Treaties and Other Selected Legal Instruments   xvii

1.   Introduction: Context, Questions and Framework   **1**

Part 1 Law and Policy Relevant to the Training of Officers of National Armed Forces as Regards the Treatment of Children at the Outset, During, and Shortly After Situations of Armed Conflict   **19**

2.   Part I(A)(1)—Law and Policy: Content of Rules Relevant to Officer Training —Parameters and Basic Principles   **21**

3.   Part I(A)(1)—Law and Policy: Content of Rules Relevant to Officer Training Regarding Children—Child Civilians   **33**

4.   Part I(A)(1)—Law and Policy: Content of Rules Relevant to Officer Training Regarding Children—Child Soldiers   **45**

5.   Part I(A)(1)—Law and Policy: Content of General Rules Relevant to Officer Training Regarding Children—Landmines, Culpability/Command Responsibility, and Selected War Crimes Trials (1998-2001)   **59**

6.   Part I(A)(2)—Law and Policy: Obligations of Governments—Treaty Law, 'Soft Law', and the Committee on the Rights of the Child   **81**

7.   Part I(B)—Impact of Law and Policy: Methodology   **99**

Part II Practice: Training for Officers of National Armed Forces on the Treatment of Children—Country Studies and the ICRC   **119**

8.   Part II—Introduction and Country Studies (Category A)   **121**

9.   Part II—Country Studies (Category B) and the ICRC   **151**

Part III Summary and Recommendations   **167**

10.   Conclusion   **169**

Appendices   **177**

1.   Captured Child Soldiers in Non-International and in International Armed
          Conflict   **179**

2.   Civil-Military Cooperation: Save the Children, West Africa   **187**

3.   Charts: I) Child-Related Training Materials—Eleven Selected Countries, and
          II) Summary of Comments—San Remo Institute   **191**

4.   'Background Notes' to Country Studies—Category (A) and Category
          (B)   **215**

5.   Sample Training Materials   **239**

6.   Summary: Key Rules Regarding Child Civilians and Child Soldiers   **263**

Bibliography   **271**

Index   **289**

Abbreviations

Selected Abbreviations—Treaties

GCs:	1949 Geneva Conventions
GPs:	1977 Geneva Protocols
1907 Hague Convention IV:	1907 Hague Convention IV Respecting the Laws and Customs of War on Land
1948 Genocide Convention:	1948 Convention on the Prevention and Punishment of the Crime of Genocide
1948 UDHR:	1948 Universal Declaration of Human Rights
1949 GC I:	Convention (I) for the Amelioration of the Condition of the Wounded and Sick in Armed Forces in the Field
1949 GC II:	Convention (II) for the Amelioration of the Condition of Wounded, Sick and Shipwrecked Members of Armed Forces at Sea
1949 GC III:	Convention (III) Relative to the Treatment of Prisoners of War
1949 GC IV:	Convention (IV) Relative to the Protection of Civilian Persons in Time of War
1966 ICCPR:	1966 International Covenant on Civil and Political Rights
1966 ICESCR:	1966 International Covenant on Economic, Social and Cultural Rights
1977 GP I:	Protocol Additional to the Geneva Conventions of 12 Aug 1949 and relating to the Protection of Victims of International Armed Conflicts (Protocol I)
1977 GP II:	Protocol Additional to the Geneva Conventions of 12 Aug 1949 and relating to the Protection of Victims of Non-International Armed Conflicts (Protocol II)
1980 Weapons Convention:	1980 UN Convention on Prohibitions or Restrictions on the Use of Certain Conventional Weapons Which May be Deemed to be Excessively Injurious or to Have Indiscriminate Effects
1984 CAT:	1984 Convention Against Torture
1989 CRC:	1989 Convention on the Rights of the Child

1998 Statute of the ICC: 1998 Rome Statute of the International Criminal
                                Court
1999 ILO Convention No 182:   1999 Convention Concerning the Prohibition and
                                Immediate Elimination of the Worst Forms of
                                Child Labour (No 182)
2000 Optional Protocol on   2000 Optional Protocol to the Convention on the
Child Soldiers: Rights of the Child on the Involvement of Children
                                in Armed Conflict
2002 Optional Protocol on   2002 Optional Protocol to the Convention on the
the Sale of Children: Rights of the Child on the Sale of Children, Child
                                Prostitution and Child Pornography

Selected Abbreviations—Bibliography

AI: Amnesty International
BIICL: British Institute of International and Comparative
                                Law
B'Tselem: The Israeli Information Center for Human Rights
                                in the Occupied Territories
CICC: Coalition for an International Criminal Court
CMA: Community Media Association
CSC: Coalition to Stop the Use of Child Soldiers
CUP: Cambridge University Press
DCI: Defense for Children International
DESTIN: Development Studies Institute
HDIP: Health Development Information and Policy Insti-
                                tute
HRW: Human Rights Watch
ICRC: International Committee of the Red Cross
ICHRP: International Council on Human Rights Policy
ISS: Institute for Security Studies
LSE: London School of Economics and Political Sci-
                                ences
OUP: Oxford University Press
NIOD: Netherlands Institute for War Documentation
SC: Save the Children
SC S: Save the Children Sweden
SC D: Save the Children Denmark
SCSI: Strategic and Combat Studies Institute
WCRWC: Women's Commission for Refugee Women and
                                Children

Journals

California L Rev:	California Law Review
Harv Hum Rts J:	Harvard Human Rights Journal
Harv Int'l LJ:	Harvard International Law Journal
Int'l J Refugee L:	International Journal of Refugee Law
IRRC:	International Review of the Red Cross
Military L Rev:	Military Law Review
Netherlands Int'l L Rev:	Netherlands International Law Review
Psychol Rev:	The Psychological Review
Sydney L Rev:	Sydney Law Review

Selected Abbreviations—General

ARC:	Action for the Rights of Children
ICC:	International Criminal Court
ICTR:	International Criminal Tribunal for Rwanda
ICTY:	International Criminal Tribunal for the Former Yugoslavia
IHL:	International Humanitarian Law
LOAC:	Law of Armed Conflict
NGO:	Non-governmental Organisation
POW:	Prisoner of War
San Remo Institute:	San Remo International Institute of Humanitarian Law
SRSG/CAC:	Special Representative of the UN Secretary General on Children and Armed Conflict

Table of Treaties and Other Selected Legal Instruments

1907 Hague Convention IV Respecting the Laws and Customs of War on Land   82, 92n, 270n
  Article 1   82
  Article 2   184n
  Article 22   23, 264

1924 Declaration on the Rights of the Child   35

1945 Charter of the United Nations
  Article 25   93n

1945 Statute of the International Court of Justice   13n
  Article 38   13n

1948 Convention on the Prevention and Punishment of the Crime of Genocide   26, 31n, 93n
  Article 2   26
  Article 5   83, 93n

1948 Universal Declaration of Human Rights
  Article 3   26
  Article 5   27
  Article 9   56n
  Article 10   56n
  Article 11   56n
  Article 25(2)   25

1949 Geneva Convention (I) for the Amelioration of the Condition of the Wounded and Sick in Armed Forces in the Field   2, 9, 11n, 29n, 34, 37, 41n, 46, 54n, 63, 77n, 82, 92n, 125-126, 130, 132, 134, 136, 138, 149n, 151, 153, 155, 157, 162, 170, 172-173, 181,192, 196, 199, 210, 243, 265
  Article 1   82
  Article 2   76n
  Article 3   12n, 27, 29n, 34, 40n, 54n, 73, 76n, 179-180, 193, 202, 260, 265
  Article 9   92n
  Article 15   196
  Article 23   196
  Article 49   63
  Article 50   63

1949 Geneva Convention (II) for the Amelioration of the Condition of Wounded, Sick and Shipwrecked Members of Armed Forces at Sea   70, 2, 9, 11n, 29n, 34, 37, 41n, 46, 54n, 63, 70, 77n, 82, 92n, 125-126, 130, 132, 134, 136, 138, 149n, 151, 153, 155, 157, 162, 170, 172-173, 181, 192, 196, 199, 210, 243, 265
  Article 1   82
  Article 3   12n, 27, 29n, 34, 40n, 54n, 73, 76n, 179-180, 193, 202, 260, 265
  Article 9   92n
  Article 18   196
  Article 50   63
  Article 51   63

1949 Geneva Convention (III) Relative to the Treatment of Prisoners of War   2, 9, 11n, 29n, 34, 37, 41n, 46, 54n, 63, 77n, 82, 92n, 125-126, 130, 132, 134, 136, 138, 149n, 151, 153, 155, 157, 162, 170, 172-173, 181-184n, 192, 196, 210, 243, 265
  Article 1   82

Article 3   12n, 27, 29n, 34, 40n, 54n, 73, 76n, 179-180, 193, 202, 260, 265
Article 4   184n
Article 5   184n
Article 9   92n
Article 12   182, 185n
Article 13   182, 185n, 202
Article 14   182, 185n, 202
Article 15   182, 185n
Article 16   182, 184n, 260
Article 41   92n
Article 45   184n
Article 49   182, 184n
Article 82   56n
Article 87   53, 184n
Article 109   182
Article 109(3)   183
Article 111   183
Article 117   183
Article 118   183, 203
Article 119(5)   183
Article 129   63
Article 130   63
Section IV, Chapter III   182

1949 Geneva Convention (IV) Relative to the Protection of Civilian Persons in Time of War   2, 9, 11n, 29n, 33-35, 37-39, 40-41n, 46-47, 54n, 63, 70, 77n, 82, 92n, 125-126, 130, 132, 134-136, 138, 149n, 151, 153, 155, 157, 162, 170, 172-173, 181, 192, 196, 199, 210, 243, 265270n
Article 1   82
Article 3   12n, 27, 29n, 34, 40n, 54n, 73, 76n, 179-180, 193, 202, 260, 265
Article 5   184n
Article 10   92n
Article 14   35, 39, 40n, 196, 202, 266
Article 15   35, 40-41n, 202, 266
Article 16   39, 40n
Article 17   36, 40n, 196, 202, 266

Article 18   39, 40n, 201
Article 19   40n, 201
Article 20   40n, 201
Article 21   39, 40n
Article 22   29n, 39, 40n
Article 23   35, 39, 40n, 196, 266
Article 24   36, 39, 40n, 183, 185n, 195, 201, 260, 266
Article 25   36, 40n, 196, 202
Article 26   36, 40n, 196, 202
Article 27   27, 33, 36, 40n, 265-266
Article 38(5)   39
Article 49   36, 266
Article 50   37-38, 39
Article 51   38
Article 68   37, 47, 53, 266, 268
Article 81   43n
Article 82   36, 43n, 181, 266
Article 85(2)   181
Article 89(5)   181
Article 91   39
Article 92   181
Article 94   181
Article 99   92n
Article 119   181
Article 127   39
Article 132(2)   183, 185n
Article 133   183
Article 136   37-38
Article 144   82, 92n
Article 146   63
Article 147   63
Annex 1   196
1954 Convention Relating to the Status of Refugees   40-41n

1959 Declaration on the Rights of the Child   35, 41n

1966 International Covenant on Civil and Political Rights   25, 38, 43n, 52, 56n, 84, 270n
Article 2   83
Article 2(1)   93n
Article 2(2)   93n

Article 2(3)   93n
Article 4   84
Article 4(1)   83
Article 4(2)   93n
Article 6   26, 28n
Article 6(5)   37, 47, 266, 268
Article 7   27, 49, 53, 57n, 270n
Article 10(2)(b)   43n, 52, 262
Article 14(1)   52
Article 14(2)   52
Article 14(3)   57n
Article 14(3)(a)   52
Article 14(3)(b)   53
Article 14(3)(f)   52
Article 14(4)   52
Article 14(7)   52
Article 15(1)   52
Article 23   25, 36, 266
Article 24   61
Article 24(1)   25

1966 International Covenant on
Economic, Social and Cultural
Rights   270n
Article 10   36, 266
Article 10(1)   25
Article 10(2)   39
Article 10(3)   25, 49
Article 12   25
Article 13   25

1977 Protocol Additional to the Geneva
Conventions of 12 August 1949 and
Relating to the Protection of Victims of
International Armed Conflicts (Proto-
col I)   2, 9, 11n, 23-24, 29n, 33, 35,
37-38, 41n, 46, 47, 54n, 63, 92n, 114n,
125-126, 130, 132, 134, 136, 138, 151,
153, 155, 157, 162, 172, 182, 184n, 193,
199, 264
Article 1(4)   12n
Article 6   82
Article 8(a)   39
Article 11   182
Article 35(1)   23, 264

Article 35(2)   23, 59, 264
Article 42   184n
Article 43(1)   63, 67
Article 43(2)   184n
Article 45(3)   181
Article 48   24, 40n, 265
Article 51   40n, 265
Article 51(4)   24
Article 51 (5)(b)   24, 264
Article 52(3)   34
Article 57(2)   30
Article 59   35, 41n, 202, 266
Article 60   35, 41n, 202, 266
Article 70   196
Article 70(1)   35, 266
Article 71   201
Article 74   36, 196, 202
Article 75   56n, 181
Article 75(2)   34
Article 75(5)   43n
Article 76   43n
Article 77   157, 184n, 192, 195,
197-198, 201, 260
Article 77(1)   31n, 34-35, 66, 198,
201, 265
Article 77(2)   46-47, 54n, 181, 267
Article 77(2)(c)   54n, 267
Article 77(3)   46, 157, 267
Article 77(4)   43n, 157
Article 77(5)   37, 47, 53, 56n, 266,
268
Article 76   43n
Article 78   36, 42n, 183, 201, 266
Article 81   82
Article 82   82
Article 83   82
Article 85   43n, 63
Article 86(1)   63
Article 86(2)   67
Article 87   67
Article 87(1)   63
Article 87(2)   63, 76n
Article 87(3)   63
Article 89   43n
Article 94   43n

Article 96(3)   12n
Article 119   43n
Article 132   43n

1977 Protocol Additional to the Geneva
Conventions of 12 August 1949 and
Relating to the Protection of Victims of
Non-international Armed Conflicts
(Protocol II)   2, 9, 11n, 12n, 29n, 34,
46, 54n, 70, 73, 114n, 125-126, 130,
132, 136, 138, 151, 153, 155, 157, 161,
172, 184n, 193, 199
    Article 4   56n, 76n, 179, 192
    Article 4(1)   180
    Article 4(3)   34-35, 46, 66, 180, 261,
    265, 267
    Article 4(3)(b)   36
    Article 4(3)(c)   46, 54n, 267
    Article 4(3)(d)   46, 267
    Article 4(3)(e)   36, 266
    Article 5   56n, 180
    Article 5(1)   184n
    Article 5(2)   184n
    Article 6   56n, 180
    Article 6(4)   37, 47, 53, 266, 268
    Article 19   82

1979 Convention on the Elimination of
All Forms of Discrimination Against
Women   40n
    Article 10   40n

1980 Convention on Prohibitions or
Restrictions on the Use of Certain
Conventional Weapons Which May be
Deemed to be Excessively Injurious or
to Have Indiscriminate Effects   59-60,
74n
    Article 6   82
    Protocol II   75n
        Article 3(2)   61
        Article 3(3)   61
        Article 3(4)   61
        Article 6(1)(b)(v)   61

Amended Protocol II (adopted 3 May
1996)   75n
    Article 3(7)   61
    Article 3(8)(a)   61
    Article 3(10)   61
    Article 3(11)   61

1984 Convention against Torture and
other Cruel, Inhuman or Degrading
Treatment or Punishment   27, 32n,
38, 49, 53, 270n
    Article 2(2)   55n
    Article 10(1)   83
    Article 10(2)   93n
    Article 14   57n

1985 United Nations Standard
Minimum Rules for the Administra-
tion of Juvenile Justice (the Beijing
Rules)   56n, 165n, 262
    Rule 10.1   262
    Rule 10.3   262
    Rule 13   262
    Rule 13.4   262
    Rule 19   262

1989 Convention on the Rights of the
Child   3, 13-14n, 17n, 25-26, 28-29n,
31n, 38-39, 43n, 48, 54-56n, 70, 82-87,
90-91, 125-126, 130, 132, 134, 136, 138,
151, 153-155, 157, 160, 165, 169, 172,
179, 180, 182, 184n, 192-193, 213, 242,
243, 245, 252, 255, 257, 258, 270n
    Article 1   9, 262
    Article 2   83
    Article 3   49
    Article 3(c)   262
    Article 3(3)   38
    Article 4   61, 83
    Article 5   36, 266
    Article 6   26, 32n, 35, 61, 263, 265
    Article 7   36, 266
    Article 8   36, 266
    Article 10   36

Article 12   17, 36, 42-43n, 52, 183, 266

Article 16   36, 266

Article 19   32n, 35, 38, 49, 54n, 265

Article 24   35, 38, 49, 61, 266

Article 34   32n, 35, 38, 41n, 48, 54n, 245, 265, 269

Article 37   39, 56n, 61, 262, 269

Article 37(a)   27, 35, 37-38, 47-48, 53, 57n, 264-266, 268-269

Article 37(b)   51

Article 37(c)   38, 52, 57n

Article 38   3, 32n, 34, 47, 61, 83, 199, 265

Article 38(1)   35, 47, 54n, 265

Article 38(2)   46-47, 54n, 267

Article 38(3)   47, 244, 267

Article 38(4)   35, 39, 243, 265-266

Article 40   56n, 262

Article 40(1)   52, 57n

Article 40(2)(a)   52

Article 40(2)(b)(i)   52

Article 40(2)(b)(ii)   52

Article 40(2)(b)(iii)   52

Article 40(2)(b)(iv)   57n

Article 40(2)(b)(vi)   52

Article 40(2)(b)(vii)   52

Article 40(4)   52

Article 41   29n, 50, 57n, 180, 185n

Article 42   83

Article 43   14n

Article 43(2)   95n

Article 43(3)(b)   51

Article 44   14n

Article 44(1)   89

Article 44(6)   92n

Article 45   14n

Article 45(b)   89

1989 Second Optional Protocol to the International Covenant on Civil and Political Rights, aiming at the abolition of the death penalty   26, 31n

1990 African Charter on the Rights and Welfare of the Child   17n, 193, 195
   Article 22   17n, 54n

1990 Rules for the Protection of Children Deprived of their Liberty, 38, 56n
   Rule 11(a)   262
   Rule 17   262
   Rule 22   262
   Rule 29   262

1993 Statute of the International Criminal Tribunal for the Former Yugoslavia   10-12n, 26, 64, 76n
   Article 7   64
   Article 7(1)   63
   Article 7(2)   64
   Article 7(3)   64
   Article 7(4)   64
   Rules of Procedure and Evidence
   Rule 90(b)   65

1994 Statute of the International Criminal Tribunal for Rwanda   26, 64-65, 76n
   Article 4   73
   Article 6   64
   Rules of Procedure and Evidence
   Rule 90(c)   65
   Rule 96(i)   65

1997 Convention on the Prohibition on the Use, Stockpiling, Production and Transfer of Anti-Personnel Mines and their Destruction (the 'Ottawa Convention')   60-62, 74n, 125, 127, 130, 132, 134, 138, 151, 153, 155, 157
   Article 1(1)   62
   Article 4   62
   Article 5(1)   62

1998 Statute of the International Criminal Court   26, 29n, 48, 64-65, 77n, 125, 127, 130, 132, 134, 136, 138, 147n, 151, 153, 155, 157, 193, 268

Article 5(1)(d)   76n
Article 5(2)   76n
Article 6   76n
Article 6(e)   76n
Article 7   76n
Article 7(1)(g)   76n
Article 7(2)(c)   76n
Article 8   76n, 145n
Article 8(2)(b)(ix)   76n
Article 8(2)(b)(xxii)   76n
Article 8(2)(b)(xxvi)   47, 76n, 268
Article 8(2)(c)   12n
Article 8(2)(e)   12n
Article 8(2)(e)(iv)   76n
Article 8(2)(e)(vii)   47,76n, 268
Article 25(3)   64
Article 26   64
Article 28   64
Article 28(a)   64
Article 28(b)   64
Article 33   64
Article 36(8)(b)   65
Article 42(9)   65
Article 54(1)(b)   65
Article 68(1)   65
Article 68(2)   65
Article 124   145n
Rules of Procedure and Evidence
Rule 17(3)   65
Rule 19(f)   65
Rule 75(1)   77n
Rule 86   65
Rule 88   77n
Rule 89(3)   77n
Rule 112(4)   77n

1999 International Labour Office
Convention Concerning the Prohibi-
tion and Immediate Elimination of the
Worst Forms of Child Labour   29n, 55,
125, 127, 130, 132, 134, 136, 138, 151,
153, 155, 157, 193, 270n
Article 2   48, 268
Article 3(a)   48, 268

2000 Optional Protocol to the Conven-
tion on the Rights of the Child on Child
Soldiers   9, 29n, 47-49, 91, 125, 127,
130, 132, 134, 136, 138, 151, 153, 155,
157, 165n, 223, 270n
Article 1   47, 55n, 268
Article 2   47, 55n, 268
Article 3(1)   47, 268
Article 3(2)   47, 268
Article 3(3)   47, 268
Article 3(4)   47
Article 4   268
Article 6   83, 93n
Article 7   83, 93n
Article 8   83, 93n
Article 8(1)   88
Article 10   55n

2002 Optional Protocol to the Conven-
tion on the Rights of the Child on the
Sale of Children, Child Prostitution and
Child Pornography   35, 41n, 54n, 265,
270n
Article 1   35
Article 3   35

1

Introduction: Context, Questions and Framework

Introduction

What are the legal and quasi-legal obligations of military personnel as regards their treatment of children? In particular, what are the obligations of officers of national armed forces in relation to children, either civilians or combatants, whom they or those under their command may encounter while participating in situations of armed conflict? How realistic and achievable are these obligations? How can compliance with them be encouraged, monitored, and/or enforced?

This book aims to address these questions in the context of military training. In doing so, it has another, inextricably-linked aim: to see if there are ways in which the training of officers can improve the protection of children in armed conflict situations, in accordance with international law and policy.

The book is intended for use particularly by those involved in training of national armed forces, including officers themselves, and members of governments, non-governmental organisations (hereafter NGOs) and inter-governmental organisations. It is hoped that it will also be of interest to lawyers, academics and others concerned with 'child rights' and related law and policy. As already emphasised in the Preface, the book is structured for ease of reference by these various categories of reader, so that it can be read in different ways according to their requirements.[1]

There are many reasons for undertaking the research on which this book is based. These include, first, that all children, especially young children, are particularly vulnerable, and are often subject to abuse in situations of armed conflict. Second, there is a large body of law relating to the protection of children in such situations, but little information as to how, or even if, military training addresses this body of law. This book will, among other things, provide such information as regards selected countries.

a)   The Changing Context: Armed Conflict

That said, the questions in the first paragraph above must be both asked and answered in a context where the nature of armed conflict has undergone profound changes since the major international treaties were drafted—ie treaties such as the 1949 Geneva Conventions (hereafter GCs) and the 1977 Geneva Protocols (hereafter GPs).[2] These changes extend to international armed conflicts, which now constitute a minority of the conflicts that have raged fiercely in almost every part of the globe in the last few decades. Change is also evident in non-international armed conflicts, which are increasingly conducted in ways not foreseen by those drafting the post-WW II international humanitarian law (hereafter IHL[3]) treaties.

Modern armed conflicts are also conducted in ways that have a profound impact on children, both as civilians[4] and as combatants. According to a 2001 UNICEF publication,

> in the last decade, 2 million children were killed by conflict,[5] 12 million children were made homeless, 6 million children have been injured or disabled, at least 300,000 at any given time are actively involved in armed conflict, 8-10,000 are killed every year by landmines, and 500 million small arms and light weapons' (widely regarded as facilitating the use of child soldiers[6]) 'are in circulation'.[7]

So, on the one hand, how does international law apply to, and how must soldiers and officers be trained to participate in, non-international armed conflicts that do not conform to earlier IHL models? This question arises, eg, in conflicts in which non-governmental forces—which are increasingly regarded as bound by IHL rules[8]—blatantly flout this body of law (as has happened in a wide range of countries in Africa, Asia, Latin America and Europe); it arises where violations of international law are committed by paramilitary forces, often with covert government support (eg Peru, Colombia, Serbia and Croatia[9]); where soldiers have been drugged to the extent that they are barely conscious of their actions (eg Sierra Leone[10]); where child soldiers have been as young as eight (eg in Liberia and Sierra Leone[11]) or 10 years old (Cambodia and Guatemala[12]); and it arises where the very aim of the conflict has been the genocidal annihilation of an ethnic group, including its children (as in Rwanda and in the former Yugoslavia).

On the other hand, how does this body of law apply to international armed conflicts, particularly when the more industrialised countries are involved? How does it apply, in these armed conflicts, eg, if such countries choose in future to conduct hostilities almost entirely by computer,[13] or by the use of nanotechnology?[14] Or (more pertinent at the time of writing), where the aim of these governments is, *inter alia*, to use such strategies to prevent casualties among their own forces—although this may result in disproportionate damage to their opponents (as was alleged, eg, in relation to certain NATO actions in Kosovo[15])? Or where such governments subcontract their military obligations to private companies like Sandline International or Dyncorp (eg the US in Kosovo[16])? How can law and soldiers respond legitimately to commanders of armed groups dressed in civilian clothing who conduct operations from civilian buildings or vehicles (eg arguably Israel/Palestine[17])?

And do existing IHL rules and principles continue to have validity in a world where massive terrorist attacks—such as the 11 September 2001 attacks on New York and Washington—may increasingly occur?[18]

Indeed, at the time of writing, the Swiss government and others were organising an 'informal, high-level expert meeting' (to be held in 2003) 'to promote a better understanding of the legal challenges arising in contemporary conflicts'. In particular, the meeting aimed to initiate discussions and research that would 'clarify existing ... IHL principles and obligations, and, thereafter, strengthen their application.'[19]

Further, despite the large numbers of conflicts that have been waged in the last few decades, recent research has indicated that armed conflict is actually on the decline.[20] There is evidence that this is the case, although there is also evidence to the contrary.[21] If indeed armed conflicts are on the decline, the implications are, among other things, that there may in future be less need either for conventional armed forces or for military training as currently conducted.

All these trends must be borne in mind by those concerned with the conduct of armed conflict, including military training. The landscape of armed conflict is constantly changing. (Indeed, these changes have led to the characterisation of certain recent armed conflicts as 'new wars'.[22])

In this context, it may be that the most effective training as regards the treatment of children in armed conflict will prove to be the simplest: clear, basic rules that can be adapted to a range of situations, some foreseen and foreseeable, while others currently exist only in the realm of imagination (or nightmare).

In any event, this book takes as its starting point the position that basic principles of IHL and human rights law applicable to armed conflict in general, and to children in particular, have not changed, and are not likely to change in the foreseeable future, despite all of the above. These principles (many of them considered to be customary law[23]) underpin detailed rules, set out in international conventions and in other legal materials, which remain valid and relevant, as will be discussed below.

b)   The Changing Context: Children in Armed Conflict

Another fairly recent phenomenon—particularly since 20 November 1989, when the Convention on the Rights of the Child (hereafter 1989 CRC)[24] was adopted by the UN General Assembly—has been a proliferation of interest and activity in law and policy relating to children. Shaped by the wide-ranging provisions of the 1989 CRC, the resulting legal and policy initiatives have covered child trafficking, labour, prostitution, abduction, imprisonment, health, education, discipline, family relations and freedom of expression, to name but a few. The impact of these initiatives has, however, been uneven and sometimes disappointing, inevitably affecting some countries more than others and some children more than others.[25]

In this context, attention has increasingly focussed on children (generally defined as those under 18, as discussed below) involved in armed conflict, and much has now been written on the devastating effects of such conflict on children.[26] This issue was also significant in the early years of the 1989 CRC. The Working Group drafting Article 38 of this Convention, on children in armed conflict, nearly brought the whole drafting process to a standstill when it failed to reach agreement on certain key points, and especially on the age at which children could legitimately become combatants.[27]

In the last few years certain initiatives have particularly brought into the limelight the issue of children in armed conflict. Central among these was the 1996 'Machel Report',[28] which resulted from the Committee on the Rights of the Child's[29] first 'Day of Discussion', (5 October 1992), that had as its topic 'Children in Armed Conflict'. This report recommended, *inter alia*, establishment within the UN of an office dedicated to the protection of children in armed conflict (para 266), and in August 1997 the UN Secretary-General appointed Olara Otunnu (as 'Special Representative of the UN Secretary General on Children and Armed Conflict' (hereafter, SRSG/CAC)) to fulfil this role.[30]

c)   *The Changing Context: Military Training Concerning Children*

The above initiatives will be referred to again in the course of this book. At this point, suffice it to say that one of their outcomes has been an upsurge of interest in the training of military (and other) personnel on the treatment of children in situations of armed conflict. Such training is being planned or conducted by governmental, non-governmental and inter-governmental bodies. A great deal of the training focusses on peace support (peace-keeping, peace-making, peace-building)[31] forces. This is understandable, since such forces are normally relatively accessible, and the number of UN peace support operations has doubled since 1991.[32]

The reason behind the increasing interest in military training regarding children has been explained in part by one NGO involved in such training as follows:

> In some countries the military is arguably the most important state institution …, the ultimate guarantor of sovereignty and liberty but it also has the potential to overthrow civil authority and destroy good governance. Equally the ever-changing nature of conflict means that the military is perhaps one of the most important institutions in child protection, members of armed forces are often 'front line' both in conflict and in non-conflict duty. They serve as soldiers and as community members, and are often those with the first contact with children in conflict-affected situations. At times members of armed forces play key protection roles and at other times they play the role of abuser.[33]

Further, military training on international law in general rests partly on the following assumption: that, without such training, military personnel are likely to remain ignorant of their legal obligations, which is clearly one factor that can lead to violations of these obligations. Ignorance can also lead to misperceptions by military personnel of both guilt and innocence in relation to acts they have committed in the course of their duties.[34] The International Committee of the Red Cross (hereafter ICRC) argues that '[w]hat is needed therefore is a situation in which no one—neither those who give the orders, nor those who carry them out, nor those who let the violence happen—can say: "I didn't know"'.[35]

Basic Questions

It may be useful at this point to pose a few rather basic questions, which can be too easily dismissed as naive or self-evident. One such question is whether rules requiring military personnel to treat children with particular care may have the effect of sanitising armed conflict, of making it at least appear to be more acceptable, a polite game with rules. This question of course applies to IHL as whole, and it is a question that rightly perplexes many.[36]

There is also the question of the morality of spending large amounts of money on military training initiatives, and providing substantial salaries for those engaged in this work in some of the most destitute places on this planet. Does military training—particularly regarding international law—actually serve its intended purpose? How can its effectiveness be demonstrated and monitored? Why are so many different international organisations, governmental and non-governmental, involved in military training? Do they collaborate with each other, or compete?

That said, there is a real, pragmatic issue to be addressed, which is: how should military personnel (in this context, officers of national armed forces) be trained? The importance of this question cannot be over-emphasised. Officers and armed forces as a whole have to confront this issue on a daily basis. Whatever academics and others may think about the nature and future of armed conflict, and/or of international law, military training continues 'on the ground'. Should it consist only of, eg, weapons training and tactics? Or should it take account of relevant international law—and, specifically, international law that addresses the reality that children are ever-present in situations of armed conflict?

Then, too, there is the question of whether the body of international law that applies to armed conflict is an attempt to impose largely 'Northern' values on countries 'in the South'. A simple—and positivist—answer is that countries are bound by the international treaties they have ratified, whatever their cultural values. This answer is open to challenge, and introduces the debate on cultural relativism generally, which is a huge topic that cannot be tackled here, but is widely discussed elsewhere.[37] Without entering into that debate, suffice it to say that effective military training must fully accommodate and incorporate an understanding of cultural differences, including, of course, language (as will be discussed later). Although the basic legal principles remain the same, the manner of communicating these must be adapted to the particular circumstances.

Ultimately there is no simple answer to many of these questions. Training of military personnel concerning the treatment of children may in some cases simply be a waste of time and money, depending on the particular circumstances, and on how the training is carried out. Or indeed it may backfire.[38] It can be seen as a sort of temporary response—a 'band-aid' solution—to a complex situation.

It is certainly arguable that more attention and resources need to be devoted to prevention: first and foremost to preventing armed conflict, and also to preventing the involvement of children in armed conflict situations, as far as this is possible.[39] Those involved in human rights/IHL training of the military should ideally address the issue of prevention, as well as providing training on rules and conduct. That said, a number of those working in this field do endeavour to tackle both issues: ie they provide training and respond to humanitarian needs, while also exploring preventive strategies.[40]

However, the total prevention of armed conflict as such, (and accordingly the involvement of children), seems highly improbable, if not impossible. Among other things, some powerful vested interests thrive on the perpetuation of conflict (eg the arms industry, the traders in 'conflict diamonds' and certain other natural resources, etc), and violence and conflict seem to be, to some extent, intrinsic features of human societies.[41] Indeed, those in power in a number of countries base their economic survival on the continuation of armed conflict.[42]

In this context, the value of a possibly short-term, or 'band-aid', approach cannot be lightly dismissed. The ideal (and idealistic?) strategy may be to work for an end to armed conflict, and the exposure of children to armed conflict. But in the meantime—and it could be an interminable 'meantime'—there is, in conjunction with that strategy, room for, and indeed a need for, a more pragmatic approach.[43] So, there is a strong argument for a two-pronged strategy: a) making efforts to alleviate the suffering of those affected by armed conflict, through, *inter alia*, military training in accordance with existing law and policy, while b) also endeavouring to understand and address the root causes of conflict, and of the involvement of children.[44]

The latter, wider, issues are rightly the province of governments, inter-governmental organisations, NGOs and policy-makers generally. Those officers and others in national armed forces who are engaged in military training must necessarily keep a narrower focus, ideally while maintaining an awareness of the wider context.

Issues Excluded, Definitions and Outline

Before beginning to examine the relevant law and policy, below (Chapters Two to Six), it is necessary to state clearly what is and is not included in this book, and how certain key terms are defined.

a)   Issues Excluded

i   Training of Soldiers

As already stated, this book focuses on training of officers of national armed forces, and not on training of soldiers (see 'Definitions' below), despite the fact that soldiers generally are more likely to be 'on the ground' and actually faced with putting the relevant training into practice at that level. However, research on training of officers obviously does not preclude research on the training of soldiers, and indeed is directly relevant to and may inform a later study. Further, it is necessary to limit the scope of any research, and in this case it was felt that materials on the training of officers were likely to be more accessible, and perhaps more revealing, than those used in training soldiers. In any event, this book does repeatedly address the obligations of officers to train their subordinates, and ways in which this can most effectively be done. Also, (as expressed by an experienced officer and ICRC military trainer regarding the ICRC practice of training officers as opposed to soldiers),[45] training of officers has a 'multiplying effect'. Thus,

> [i]f one considers that a young officer will immediately command 30 men and soon a company of 100, and that a staff college graduate will command a battalion of some 600 men or an important staff branch, then it is obvious that this training can reach and influence people far beyond the individual officer concerned.[46]

ii   Training of Peace Support Personnel

This book also does not focus on training of peace support personnel as such. For obvious reasons, peace support forces consist generally of military personnel drawn from national armed forces of countries other than those involved in the particular conflict. Normally, in their countries of origin, they receive special pre-deployment training for this role, although in some countries (as in Australia) all members of the national armed forces receive training that prepares them, *inter alia*, for a peace support role.[47] In addition to their national training, training can be provided by organisations, such as the UN, for soldiers and officers who participate in their particular peace support missions. It goes without saying that it is advantageous to such missions if participating military personnel are already well-trained by their own national armed forces.[48] In that sense, although this book focuses on training in national armed forces and not on peace support personnel as such, it is nonetheless clearly relevant in the latter context.

iii   Training for Disturbances Not Constituting Armed Conflict

Further, this book will not set out the particular rules that apply to officers and soldiers in situations of internal disturbances and violence that clearly[49] fall below the level of armed conflict (eg riots), since: a) the relevant rules are not child-specific, and in any event summaries of these can be found elsewhere,[50] and b) basic principles set out in the text below express the main guidelines that are also relevant in such situations, eg the principle of proportionality, and, as regards children, the duty to treat them with special care.[51] In these situations,

> the primary role of the military is not to conduct hostilities against an organized armed opponent but to fulfil some of the functions normally carried out by the police in restoring and maintaining law and order. They must apply the constraints that guide police forces, particularly in relation to the use of force and firearms.[52]

iv   Training of Armed Opposition Groups

One category of combatant that has generally remained untouched by the proliferation of training programmes—and will also not be included here—is that of armed opposition groups, or non-governmental entities, despite the fact that such groups have frequently been responsible for some of the most flagrant violations of international law. Indeed, the armed opposition groups of today may be the governments of tomorrow, and vice versa. Why, then, have such groups not generally been the focus of training initiatives?[53] And why does the present research examine the training of officers of national armed forces, and exclude armed opposition groups? One reason is that national armed forces are more accessible, in general, than these groups—and the present research must necessarily be limited. Further, once again research on one population does not preclude the other—and in future other studies could be conducted on the training of armed opposition groups. It is possible that some such groups may provide better training for their fighters than some national armed forces. In any event, it is worth emphasising that, in fulfilling their dissemination obligations, governments could and should spread information on IHL not just to the military but to the population in general, thereby indirectly reaching armed opposition groups.

v   Training for Private Companies and the Police

Another category of combatant that this book cannot incorporate consists of those employed by private companies, such as Sandline International and Executive Outcomes, although again such companies have played a significant role in some recent conflicts.[54] Nor can this book examine police training, despite the fact that in some conflict situations the police are employed in a military role, and vice versa, as already mentioned.

vi   Peace Negotiations and Agreements

This book does not discuss the involvement of children—or those representing them—in peace negotiations and agreements. It is worth noting, however, that the UN, among others, is increasingly emphasising the importance of taking account, in such agreements and negotiations, of the needs and circumstances of children.[55]

vii   Regional Treaties and Policy

Finally, the international law and policy discussed in this text will include only law that is of universal application, and will not therefore look at regional treaties and policy. This is not to underestimate the importance of regional instruments, which can be very relevant to the subjects under discussion here.[56] However, the information presented below is intended as a summary of the main international principles pertinent to military training, and it is beyond the scope of this work to go into greater detail.

These, then, are the main issues excluded from the scope of this book. Before looking more closely at military training in national armed forces, it is useful to clarify the definitions of certain key terms as used in the text below, ie: 'child', 'officer' and 'armed conflict'.

b)   Definitions

i   Definition of 'Child'

How, then, is a 'child' defined in this book? Broadly, a child is understood here to be a person under 18, in accordance with Article 1 of the 1989 CRC: '... a child means every human being below the age of 18 years unless, under the law applicable to the child, majority is attained earlier'. Thus neither the beginning of childhood (ie from conception or from birth), nor its end, is rigidly defined in that treaty, but the guiding norm for the upper age limit is set at 18.[57]

In relation to military training, this loose definition does not present serious problems, since the relevant law certainly applies to children from birth. Further, it makes clear that persons over the age of 18 are not generally categorised as children in international law.

The upper age limit for childhood has in fact been a hotly contested issue in IHL, particularly as it relates to the use of child soldiers, and will be touched on below. Suffice it to say here that although the 1949 GCs and 1977 GPs tend to use an upper age limit of 15 for many of the protections to which children are entitled, the emerging norm is the age of 18 both for child civilians and child soldiers, (in accordance with, eg, the 2000 Optional Protocol to the Convention on the Rights of the Child on the Involvement of Children in Armed Conflict (hereafter 2000 Optional Protocol on Child Soldiers, discussed below)).[58]

Accordingly, for most military training purposes a child can be considered as any person from birth to the age of 15, although good practice, and recent national and international rules, encourage use of the upper limit of 18 years.

With some exceptions, no distinction will generally be made in this text between, eg, adolescents and younger children.[59] However, it is obvious that, depending on the age, abilities, cultural background etc of children, different considerations may come into play. In many cases common sense will dictate that certain rules apply more particularly to children within certain age categories, (and the law itself does sometimes specify precise age limits).

A number of writers have emphasised that some children in situations of armed conflict remain resilient, use great ingenuity in choosing survival strategies, and can be a source of stability and support for the wider community.[60] It is therefore counter-productive to view all children caught up in armed conflict as similar to each other, and as helpless victims. (Again, common sense should dictate that in some circumstances it is preferable to relate to them as 'competent survivors'.[61])

ii   Definition of 'Officer', 'Soldier', 'Military Personnel' and 'Combatant'

It is also necessary to clarify, in particular, the use in this text of the terms 'soldier' and 'officer'. The term 'officer' is used to describe commissioned officers only—and other personnel of national armies are generally described here as 'soldiers'.[62] (It is worth bearing in mind that those engaged in combat who are under 18 ('child soldiers', see below) are generally not officers. However, in some armed forces, perhaps particularly in armed opposition groups, they could be.)

Further, the term 'military personnel' is used here broadly to include all categories regardless of their role, while the term 'combatant' is limited to describing those engaged in a combat role.

iii   Definition of 'Armed Conflict'

The ICTY Appeals Chamber has ruled that:

> an armed conflict exists whenever there is a resort to armed force between States or protracted armed violence between governmental authorities and organized armed groups or between such groups within a State.[63]

One authority has observed, 'it is open to question whether all States have treated the threshold for armed conflict as being so low'. However, he emphasises the importance of the ICTY's support for this 'very expansive approach to the meaning of armed conflict'. [64]

In any event, this book will use the above broad definition of armed conflict.

c)   Outline

As stated at the start of this Chapter, this book aims to respond to the following questions: what are the obligations of officers of national armed forces in relation to children, either civilians or combatants, whom they or those under their command may encounter while participating in situations of armed conflict? How realistic and achievable are these obligations? How can compliance with them be encouraged, monitored, and/or enforced?

In order to respond to those questions, the text below will: 1) outline international law and policy relevant to the training of officers in national armed forces as regards the treatment of children at the outset, during and shortly after[65] situations of armed conflict, and consider training methodology (Part I); 2) examine existing military training programmes provided by 11 selected countries representing a range of different contexts and cultures, and by the ICRC (Part II);[66] and 3) summarise key points, and make recommendations regarding military training where it appears appropriate and necessary to do so (Part III).

The initial and most substantial section (Part I) below will, *inter alia*, set out the main pertinent legal obligations, and related 'good practice' policy.

Part I will start with a consideration of the nature of such obligations in Part I (A), which is further subdivided into: Part I(A)(1) (Chapters Two to Five), summarising the content of international law and practice regarding children that is pertinent to training, and encouraging compliance, of *officers*; and Part I(A)(2) (Chapter six), outlining international rules and principles that oblige *governments* and others to provide and monitor such training.

Part I(B) (Chapter Seven) will then consider the extent to which the obligations seem realistic and achievable, and the manner in which compliance can be encouraged—particularly through the training *methodology* used.

Endnotes

1 See Preface, above.

2 Convention (I) for the Amelioration of the Condition of the Wounded and Sick in Armed Forces in the Field, adopted 12 Aug 1949, entered into force 21 Oct 1950, 75 UNTS 31 (hereafter, 1949 GC I); Convention (II) for the Amelioration of the Condition of Wounded, Sick and Shipwrecked Members of Armed Forces at Sea, adopted 12 Aug 1949, entered into force 21 Oct 1950, 75 UNTS 85 (hereafter, 1949 GC II); Convention (III) Relative to the Treatment of Prisoners of War, adopted 12 Aug 1949, entered into force 21 Oct 1950, 75 U.N.T.S. 135 (hereafter, 1949 GC III); Convention (IV) Relative to the Protection of Civilian Persons in Time of War, adopted 12 Aug 1949, entered into force 21 Oct 1950, 75 UNTS 287 (hereafter, 1949 GC IV); Protocol Additional to the Geneva Conventions of 12 Aug 1949, and relating to the Protection of Victims of International Armed Conflicts (Protocol I), adopted 8 June 1977, entered into force 7 Dec 1978, 1125 UNTS 3 (hereafter, 1977 GP I); Protocol Additional to the Geneva Conventions of 12 Aug 1949, and relating to the Protection of Victims of Non-International Armed Conflicts (Protocol II), adopted 8 June 1977, entered into force 7 Dec 1978, 1125 UNTS 609 (hereafter, 1977 GP II).

3 There is some controversy as to the most appropriate term for describing the body of international law that regulates the actual conduct of hostilities once the use of force has started (ie the *'jus in bello'* (as opposed to the *'jus ad bellum'*: rules governing the process by which states decide whether or not to resort to the use of force)). Some writers prefer the term 'law of armed conflict', but in this book the term 'international humanitarian law' (IHL) will generally be used. The latter term seems particularly apt for discussion of the law regarding children in armed conflict, which has a largely humanitarian emphasis.

4 Indeed, it is estimated that modern armed conflicts particularly affect civilians. See eg, the often-quoted statistic that, 'in World War I about 5 per cent of those killed were civilians; in World War II about 48 per cent; and in some international armed conflicts the civilian casualties have reached 90 per cent, many of them children' (see eg, United Nations Children's Fund (hereafter UNICEF), UN Doc E/ICEF/1986/CRP2, 'Children in Situations of Armed Conflict', p 3). However, while this trend is generally recognised, statistics such as these may not be particularly accurate since they inevitably involve an element of guesswork.

5 Another UNICEF publication (E M Ressler, M, Everett, J M Tortorici and A Marcelino, *Children in War: A Guide to the Provision of Services* (New York, UNICEF, 1993), pp 66-67) categorises the causes of death of children in armed conflict as intentional, non-discriminatory, negligent, consequential or inadvertent.

6 See eg, D Pulkol, 'Proliferation of Small Arms and the Problem of Child Soldiers', in E Reyneke (ed) *Small Arms and Light Weapons in Africa: Illicit proliferation, circulation and trafficking* (Pretoria, ISS, 2000), pp 73-79. See also Report of the UN Conference on the Illicit Trade in Small Arms and Light Weapons in all its Aspects, UN Doc A/CONF192/ 15 (20 July 2001).

7　M Black, *Growing up Alone: Childhood under Siege* (London, UNICEF UK, 2001), p 2, (available at, http://www.unicef.org.uk). See also UNICEF, *The State of the World's Children 2001* (New York, UNICEF, 2001), p 36. However, most conflicts in history have profoundly affected children, even if this was not publicised as it is today.

8　IHL, as initially conceived, was intended to apply primarily to states, and later, to a limited extent, it was extended to non-governmental forces. (As regards the latter, see eg, Art 3 common to the 1949 GCs; 1977 GP II, and Arts 1(4) and 96 (3) of 1977 GP I). More recently, the jurisprudence of international tribunals, such as the International Tribunal for the Former Yugoslavia (hereafter ICTY) and the International Tribunal for Rwanda (hereafter ICTR), has increasingly incorporated non-governmental forces within the ambit of IHL. See eg, the ICTY Tadić case (*The Prosecutor v Dusko Tadić*, Case No IT-94-1-AR72, Appeals Chamber, 2 Oct 1995) which ruled, *inter alia*, that participants in non-international armed conflict can be liable for committing 'war crimes' under customary international law. See also Arts 8(2)(c) and 8(2)(e) of the Rome Statute of the International Criminal Court (UN Doc A/CONF183/9, 17 July 1998), (hereafter 1998 Statute of the ICC). The former lists as war crimes specific violations of Common Article 3 of the 1949 GCs; the latter adds 'other serious violations of the laws and customs applicable in armed conflicts not of an international character'.

9　Regarding Colombia, see Human Rights Watch (hereafter, HRW), *The 'Sixth Division': Military-Paramilitary Ties and US Policy in Colombia*, (New York, HRW, 2001); regarding Peru and the *rondas*, (paramilitary groups) see, HRW, 'Peru, Presumption of Guilt: Human Rights Violations and the Faceless Courts in Peru', 8:5(B) *HRW Reports* (1996). Regarding Serbia and Croatia, see eg, M Ignatieff, *The Warrior's Honor: Ethnic War and the Modern Conscience* (New York, Metropolitan Books, 1998), pp 131-132.

10　See eg, Coalition to Stop the Use of Child Soldiers (hereafter, CSC), *Child Soldiers Global Report* (London, CSC, 2001), p 324.

11　See eg, re Liberia, *ibid* p 235. Re Sierra Leone, see eg, A B Zack-Williams, 'Child Soldiers in the Civil War in Sierra Leone', 28:87 *Review of African Political Economy* (2001), pp 73-74.

12　Re Cambodia and Guatemala, see eg, CSC (2001), pp 108 and 183 respectively.

13　See eg, M Ignatieff, *Virtual War: Kosovo and Beyond* (New York, Metropolitan Books, 2000). Regarding the Kosovo conflict, he states: 'It was fought in VTC conference rooms … and all that a commander like Clark ever saw of the rush of battle was the gun camera footage e-mail every night … to his headquarters in Belgium' (p 111). He also comments that '[t]here is no guarantee that war directed at the nervous system of a society' (eg power stations) 'will be any less savage than war directed only at its troops' (p 170).

14　Such use could include, *inter alia*, the manipulation of biological and chemical weapons, the disruption of communication systems, and the enabling of small unmanned weapons systems to carry detailed information and detect threats directed against them. See eg, Ministry of Defence—UK, 'Nanotechnology: Its Impact on Defence and MOD' (London, Ministry of Defence, 2001), pp 1 and 5 (available at http://www.mod.uk, visited on 6 April 2001). See also eg, papers for San Remo International Institute of Humanitarian Law (hereafter San Remo Institute), *Seminar on International Humanitarian Law and Future Wars*, (San Remo, 24-27 Oct 2001).

15　See eg, Independent International Commission on Kosovo, *The Kosovo Report: Conflict, International Response, Lessons Learned* (Oxford, OUP 2000), p 93.

16　See eg, J Steele, 'US Gives Kosovo Monitoring Job to Mercenaries', *The Guardian* (31 Oct 1998). Re Sandline International, see generally—http://www.sandline.com/site/.

17 However, the categorisation of this conflict as an international armed conflict would be controversial (see post, Chapter Eight).

18 This issue is addressed, eg, in Crimes of War Project, 'A Defining Moment—International Law Since September 11', September 2002 Magazine, available at, http://www.crimesofwar.org/sept-mag/sept-home.html, visited on 1 March 2003.

19 See, http://www.hsph.harvard.edu/hpcr/ihl_research_meeting.htm, visited on 27 Jan 2003. The meeting was to explore four key topics: 1) the protection of civilians against hostilities; 2) the determination of civilian and combatant status; 3) the beginning and end of IHL application, and 4) legal mechanisms for implementing IHL. (These issues are touched on in Part I(A) below).

20 T R Gurr, M G Marshall and D Khosla, *Peace and Conflict 2001: A Global Survey of Armed Conflicts, Self Determination Movements, and Democracy* (University of Maryland, Center for International Development and Conflict Management, 2001), p 7, available at, http://www.bsos.umd.edu/cidcm/peace.htm, visited on 6 April 2001.

21 See eg, K J Gantzel, 'War in the Post World War II World: Some Empirical Trends and a Theoretical Approach', in D Turton (ed) *War and Ethnicity: Global Connections and Local Violence* (Rochester, University of Rochester Press, 1997), pp 125-126. See also, Col D Smith, 'Center for Defence Information Finds Wars on the Increase', 3:1 *Weekly Defence Monitor* (1999).

22 See M Kaldor, *New and Old Wars: Organized Violence in a Global Era* (Cambridge, Polity Press, 1999). According to Kaldor, new wars are 'a mixture of war, crime, and human rights violations' (p 11). They differ from 'old' wars particularly in their goals; their methods of warfare, and their financing within the 'new globalised war economy' (pp 6-9).

23 Customary law is defined in Art 38 of the Statute of the International Court of Justice (hereafter, ICJ) as 'evidence of a general practice accepted as law'. (This Statute is part of the Charter of the UN, 26 June 1945, 59 Stat 1031, TS 993, 3 Bevans 1153, entered into force 24 Oct 1945.) Thus, customary law is widely (although not universally) regarded as consisting of two main elements: the material facts as represented by the actual behaviour of states, and the subjective belief that such behaviour is required by law. See eg, R Higgins, *Problems and Process: International Law and How We Use it* (Oxford, Clarendon Press, 1994), p 19, and M N Shaw, *International Law* (Cambridge, CUP, 1999), p 58. The customary status of particular norms is important, not least because this generally renders them binding on all states, even states that are not party to treaties that articulate such norms. Further, as regards IHL, these norms promote standards of conduct that apply in both internal and international armed conflict.

24 Convention on the Rights of the Child, GA res 44/25, annex, 44 UN GAOR Sup (No 49) at 167, UN Doc A/44/49 (1989), entered into force 2 Sept 1990.

25 In theory, the law and policy of all ratifying states—191 at the time of writing—should be influenced by the provisions of the 1989 CRC. Only two states, the US and Somalia, had—at that time—not yet ratified the 1989 CRC (for the list of ratifications, see, http://www.unhchr.ch/pdf/report.pdf), although Somalia had recently signed it (see eg, http://www.un.org/ga/children/somaliaE.htm, visited on 15 July 2002). Nonetheless, despite its wide ratification, many of the States Parties have entered sweeping reservations to this treaty, which greatly undermine its impact. See eg, J Kuper, 'Reservations, Declarations and Objections to the 1989 Convention on the Rights of the Child', in J P Gardener (ed) *Human Rights as General Norms and a State's Right to Opt Out: Reservations and Objections to Human Rights Conventions* (London, BIICL, 1997), pp 104-119 (hereafter, (1997(a)).

26   See eg, the reports written by Graca Machel: G Machel, *The Impact of Armed Conflict on Children* (New York, UN, 1996) (UN Doc A/51/306 26 Aug 1996) (this examines various ways in which children are affected, including: as child soldiers; as refugees; as victims of sexual exploitation and violence, of landmines, and of sanctions); G Machel, 'The Impact of Armed Conflict on Children: A Critical Review of Progress Made and Obstacles Encountered in Increasing Protection for War-Affected Children', *International Conference on War-Affected Children*, (Winnipeg, Canada, Sept 2000), and G Machel, *The Impact of War on Children* (London, Hurst and Co, 2001).

27   See eg, S Detrick, (ed) *The United Nations Convention on the Rights of the Child: a guide to the 'Travaux préparatoires'*, (Dordrecht, Martinus Nijhoff, 1992), pp 502-517, and J Kuper, *International Law Concerning Child Civilians in Armed Conflict* (Oxford, Clarendon Press, 1997), pp 105-106 (hereafter, 1997(b)).

28   See n 26 above.

29   This is the Committee entrusted, under the 1989 CRC, with the task of monitoring and helping to implement this Convention (1989 CRC, Arts 43-45).

30   Appointment announced on 19 Aug 1997, effective on 1 Sept 1997, in accordance with General Assembly resolution 51/77 of Dec 1996 (UN Press release SG/A/647, 19 Aug 1997).

31   For the sake of convenience, the term 'peace support' will be used in this text to cover all these types of activity.

32   There were eight such peace support operations in 1991. This number increased to 18 by 1994 and at the time of writing was down to 15 (see, http://www.un.org/Depts/dpko/ dpko/pub/pdf/1.pdf, visited on 26 Oct 2001. For current information on the number of operations, see, http://www.un.org/Depts/dpko/dpko/cu_mission/body. htm).

33   U McCauley and C Ransquin, *Experiences of Training Members of Armed Forces on Child Rights and Child Protection, Before, During and After Conflict: Draft Lessons Learned Working Document* (Stockholm, Save the Children (hereafter SC) - Sweden (forthcoming—draft provided by the authors, 2001)), (hereafter 2001(a)), p 4. This document goes on to emphasise (*Id)* that: 'It is necessary for armed forces to understand all components of good governance including an observation of basic and fundamental human (child) rights. It is also important that they fully understand the real short and long term implications of human (child) rights abuses in order protect those rights out of conviction and not just because they are ordered to do so. Soldiers, not just trained on child rights and child protection but convinced of their importance can really make a difference to the quality of childhood for millions of children today and a quantum difference to their future.'

34   Keeva describes how, after the My Lai massacre in 1968, it became clear that some of the US soldiers involved did not know what was or was not allowed under the laws of armed conflict. Further, some of the US prisoners of war (hereafter POWs) 'found themselves vulnerable to accusations of war crimes by their Vietnamese captors', and had self-doubts which 'hurt' them, even if they had not done anything illegal (citing Col R Bridge). Apparently this was one of the reasons why training in IHL became a requirement for all US military personnel (S Keeva, 'Lawyers in the War Room', 77 *ABA Journal* (1991), p 55).

35   ICRC, 'ICRC Special Report: Stemming the Tide of Violence: ICRC Activities in Relation to the International Community's Prevention Strategies' (Geneva, ICRC, 1998), p 5. This report goes on to emphasise that '[s]preading knowledge of humanitarian law is, above all, the responsibility of States ...' (and see further below, Chapter Six, regarding state

responsibility). Nonetheless, one authority points out that certain rules, such as those prohibiting attacks on civilians, merely confirm what the soldier already instinctively knows or should know. Ignorance of the legal details of these rules should not therefore give rise to, or be an excuse for, breaches (F Hampson, 'Fighting by the Rules', 269 *IRRC* (1989), pp 111-24, (hereafter, Hampson (1989(a)).

36 See eg, comment by one authority on IHL that 'it is *prima facie* curious to find a structure of legal norms which is designed to regulate the conduct of a state of international relations which is in essence a descent into extra-legal violence.' H McCoubrey, 'Jurisprudential Aspects of the Modern Law of Armed Conflict', in M Meyer (ed) *Armed Conflict and the New Law* (London, BIICL, 1989), p 2. See also Ignatieff (1998), p 116; C Jochnick and R Normand, 'The Legitimation of Violence: A Critical History of the Laws of War', 35:1 *Harv Int'l LJ* (1994), pp 49-95 (hereafter 1994(a)) and C Jochnick and R Normand, 'The Legitimation of Violence: A Critical History of the Laws of War', 35:2 *Harv. Int'l L.J.* (1994), pp 387-416 (hereafter 1994(b)).

37 For texts on cultural relativism, see eg, T M Frank, 'Are Human Rights Universal?' 80:1 *Foreign Affairs* (2001), pp 191-204; B Ibhawoh, 'Cultural Relativism and Human Rights: Reconsidering the Africanist Discourse', 19:1 *Netherlands Int'l . Rev* (2001), pp 43-62. See also A An-Na'im, *Human Rights in Cross-Cultural Perspectives: A Quest for Consensus* (Philadelphia, University of Pennsylvania Press, 1992), and A An-Na'im, 'Human Rights in the Muslim World: Socio-Political Conditions and Scriptural Imperatives: a Preliminary Inquiry', 3 *Harv Hum Rts J.* (1990), pp 13-52.

38 For example, soldiers aware of IHL sanctions may more carefully conceal evidence of war crimes than those who are unaware of such sanctions. See eg, WCRWC, *Making the Choice for a Better Life: Promoting the Protection and Capacity of Kosovo's Youth* (New York, WCRWC, 2001), p 11. This describes corpses burned by combatants 'in attempts to destroy the identities of the victims and traces of the crimes', and '[o]thers removed from killing sites and disposed of elsewhere …. These acts, including the use of masks, serve to thwart attempts …' to obtain evidence for war crimes trials.

39 See eg, G Evans, 'Preventing Deadly Conflict: the Role of NGOs', *Lecture*, (London, LSE, 2 Feb 2001). See also recent report by the UN Secretary General, 'Prevention of Armed Conflict' UN Doc A/55/985-S/2001/574 (7 June 2001), and J Tyler and A Berry, *Time to Abolish War! A Youth Agenda for Peace and Justice* (Geneva, Hague Appeal for Peace, 2000), which sets out strategies specifically for involving young people themselves in campaigning for peace. Further, see D Mathews, *Fifty Stories of People Resolving Conflicts* (Oxford, Oxford Research Group, 2001—reprint 2002) regarding the peace-building work of individuals, NGOs, etc.

40 For example, the ICRC and its related organisations, although criticised for aspects of their policy (eg their rules about generally maintaining confidentiality, even in the presence of human rights abuses), do incorporate both approaches: they provide practical aid and training programmes, and also initiate reforms of international law and policy. Regarding debates within the ICRC on these issues, see eg, Ignatieff (1998), pp 156-159.

41 See eg, H Arendt, *On Violence* (New York, Harcourt Brace and Company, 1969); G Balandier, 'An Anthropology of Violence and War', 110 *International Social Science Journal* (1986), pp 499-511, and M Foucault, *Discipline and Punish: The Birth of the Prison* (Harmondsworth, Penguin Books, 1977). See also R D Kaplan, 'The Coming of Anarchy', *San Remo Seminar, Future Wars* (2001), p 18.

42 This has been the case to an extreme degree in, eg, Liberia and Sierra Leone. (See eg, D Keen, *The Economic Functions of Violence in Civil Wars* (Oxford, OUP, International Institute for Strategic Studies, Adelphi Paper no 329, 1998), and D Keen, 'Incentives

and Disincentives for Violence', in M Berdal and D Malone (eds) *Greed and Grievance: Economic Agendas in Civil Wars* (Boulder, Lynne Rienner Publishers, 2000), pp 19-41.

43 A similar point is made by Jochnick and Normand (1994(b)), p 416.

44 See also eg, I McConnan and S Uppard, *Children—Not Soldiers: Guidelines for Working with Child Soldiers and Children Associated with Fighting Forces* (London, SC, 2001), p 10, which both emphasises the importance of military (and other) training, and calls for the international community to address the root causes of conflict.

45 Lt Col D L Roberts, 'Training the Armed Forces to Respect International Humanitarian Law: The Perspective of the ICRC Delegate to the Armed and Security Forces of South Asia', 319 *IRRC* (1997), pp 433-446.

46 *Ibid*.

47 Australian army officer interviewed on 28 Nov 2001. As one interviewed UK officer pointed out (10 May 2001), this is to be expected in the Australian context, where the main role of the army (unlike that of the UK) has been in peace support operations.

48 See eg, The Challenges Project, 'Challenges of Peace Operations: Into the 21st Century: Concluding Report 1997-2002' (Stockholm, Elanders Gotab, 2002), available at, http: //www.peacechallenges.net/pdf/Concluding1.pdf, visited on 1 July 2002. This report emphasises that training, including legal training of military personnel, is primarily a national responsibility (paras 24, 60 and 67), and it calls for 'much more attention to be given to training and education' (para 70). A recent report on the massacre of Muslims in Srebrenica in 1995 highlighted the fact that the Dutch peacekeepers responsible for this 'safe area' at the time had 'inadequate' training as regards the 'peacekeeping aspect'. (See NIOD, *Srebrenica, a 'Safe Area': Reconstruction, Background, Consequences and Analyses of the Fall of a Safe Area* (Amsterdam, Boom Publishers, 2002), 'Epilogue').

49 Very often the categorisation of particular conflicts is unclear and disputed, however. In such cases, good practice is to apply the higher standard, as further discussed below (see particularly Chapter Two).

50 See eg, ICRC materials in Appendix Five below, and Lt Col D L Roberts, 'Internal Security Operations', *Lecture for Human Rights Course*, (San Remo Institute, June 2002).

51 Roberts draws attention to the particular vulnerability of children, eg a) in internal security operations, where soldiers instructed to aim rubber bullets at the legs of rioters may hit the heads of children, which are at exactly the same level (*ibid*, pp 16-17), and b) in unlawful assemblies, where soldiers should be equipped and trained to avoid attacks on stone-throwing children (*ibid*, pp 19-20).

52 *Ibid*, p 2.

53 There are some exceptions to this. For example, UNICEF and others have been involved in training armed opposition groups in Sudan (see eg, I Levine, 'Promoting Humanitarian Principles: the Southern Sudan Experience' (London, ODI Relief and Rehabilitation Network, 1997)), and the ICRC and others have conducted some training of the Liberation Tigers of Tamil Eelam (LTTE) in Sri Lanka (see Chapter Eight below). For further information on human rights and armed opposition groups see: ICHRP, *Ends and Means: Human Rights Approaches to Armed Groups* (Geneva, ICHRP, 2000), which refers, *inter alia*, to training of such groups, and to children (Summary of Findings, pp 10 and 11).

54 The training of combatants employed by private companies is certainly an issue that should be researched. Moreover, the existence of such companies raises many questions concerning the conduct of contemporary armed conflict, the extent to which state responsibility can be delegated, etc. (See eg, D Lilly, 'From Mercenaries to Private

Security Companies: Options for Future Policy Research' (London, International Alert, 1998)).

55 See eg, UN Doc S/RES/1379 (20 Nov 2001), Resolution on Children and Armed Conflict, (discussed in Chapter Six below), which calls for peace agreements to, *inter alia*, make provision for demobilisation, reintegration and rehabilitation of child soldiers, and the reunification of their families (para 8(e)). Also, see eg, 1989 CRC, Art 12, regarding the importance of including children in decisions affecting them, in accordance with their level of maturity and understanding.

56 In particular, the 1990 African Charter on the Rights and Welfare of the Child, (OAU Doc CAB/LEG/24.9/49 (1990) (hereafter 1990 African Charter), entered into force 29 Nov 1999) is of interest, in that it is a major regional 'child rights' treaty, and sets a higher standard for the protection of children in armed conflict than does the 1989 CRC. For example, it prohibits the direct participation in armed conflict of children under 18, and extends the legal protection of children to a wide range of conflicts, including 'internal armed conflicts, tension and strife' (Art 22). See eg, Kuper (1997(b)), pp 52-53.

57 For discussion of the debate, and compromise in the drafting of the 1989 CRC, regarding the definition of 'child', see eg, Kuper (1997(b)), pp 8-9, and Detrick (1992), pp 102-103 and 108-10.

58 UN Doc A/RES/54/263 (26 June 2000), Resolution on the Optional Protocols to the Convention on the Rights of the Child on the Involvement of Children in Armed Conflict, and on the Sale of Children, Child Prostitution and Child Pornography. Annex 1, Optional Protocol to the Convention on the Rights of the Child on the Involvement of Children in Armed Conflict.

59 Again, for the purposes of military training it is necessary to avoid excessive detail, and in any event to consistently aim for a high standard of treatment for all children.

60 See eg, J Boyden, 'Social Healing in War-Affected and Displaced Children' (Oxford, Refugee Studies Centre, University of Oxford, 2002), available at http://www.rsc.ox.ac.uk/casocialhealing.html, visited on 16 May 2002, pp 7-9, and 3.

61 *Ibid*, p 3.

62 There is no uniform international terminology for making these distinctions. For example, some publications may refer to 'officers, warrant officers, non-commissioned officers and soldiers', while others use different terminology, (eg, apparently in the US the distinction is generally made simply between 'officers' and 'enlisted men').

It was decided to focus here particularly on training relevant to commissioned officers, excluding officer cadets (those in training to become officers) and non-commissioned officers. This was for a number of reasons, including the fact that the level of training in many armed forces is very different for commissioned officers and for non-commissioned officers. However, armed forces themselves, of course, can and do make their own decisions as to the appropriate standard of training for these different categories of personnel.

63 *The Prosecutor v Dusko Tadić*, Case No IT-94-1-AR72, Appeals Chamber, 2 Oct 1995, para 70.

64 C Greenwood, 'The Development of International Humanitarian law by the International Criminal Tribunal for the Former Yugoslavia', 2 *Max Planck Yearbook of United Nations Law* (1998), p 115.

65 In some circumstances it is difficult to determine the duration of particular conflicts, since, eg, they may last many years, waxing and waning in intensity. Bearing that in mind, this book will nonetheless attempt to focus on the role of the military in the

immediate conflict period. However, effective military training should be in place at all times, including in times of peace, as is further discussed below. Among other things, disciplined armed forces that function with integrity and respect for IHL can themselves be a factor in preventing or reducing conflict.

66   In analysing existing training programmes (Part II—Chapters Eight and Nine) the object is generally to describe current practice and emphasise areas of good practice, since this project as a whole aims, among other things, to encourage collaboration and co-operation between the different countries and organisations involved in military training.

Part I

Law and Policy Relevant to the Training of Officers of National Armed Forces as Regards the Treatment of Children at the Outset, During, and Shortly After Situations of Armed Conflict

Part I(A)—Law and Policy

2

Part I(A)(1)—Law and Policy: Content of Rules Relevant to Officer Training— Parameters and Basic Principles

Introduction

This section of the book aims to strike a balance between two possible extremes. On the one hand, it must be sufficiently detailed to fulfil its primary aims: a) to provide a reference resource that can be used in the preparation of relevant training materials for officers at different levels, and b) to provide a source of guidance for officers on particular legal problems concerning the treatment of children. It is therefore too detailed to form, in itself, a training manual, and is not intended to be such.[1]

On the other hand, the rules presented in this section will not be analysed in great academic depth. This is because, firstly, this body of law is examined here only as it relates to military training. Officers of national armed forces do not generally require a comprehensive grasp of the finer points of international law concerning children, but rather a practical working knowledge of the main pertinent principles.[2] Secondly, thorough analyses of this body of law already exist[3] and there is no need to 're-invent the wheel'. That said, some of the material presented below is new, eg in relation to the jurisprudence of the ICTY and the ICTR (see Chapter Five).

Parameters of Discussion of Law and Policy

As regards the parameters of the discussion in this section, it is worth noting that the discussion generally includes both *IHL and human rights law*. These bodies of law do overlap to some extent[4] in that, eg, human rights law applies particularly in conflict situations that fall below the level of armed conflict, but that threshold can be difficult to determine.[5] Thus, military personnel may sometimes be deployed in situations where the categorisation of the conflict is vague or in dispute—eg the government of the country concerned categorises it as civil unrest or rioting (in which case human rights law would generally apply), while others in the international community categorise the particular conflict as a non-international armed conflict (largely the province of IHL). In order to ensure good practice, military personnel should therefore be aware that fundamental norms—based in both human rights law and IHL—continue to apply no matter how a particular conflict, or situation of civil unrest, is categorised, although different terminology might be used depending on the applicable body of law being referred to.[6]

That said, it is important to bear in mind that IHL and human rights law are primarily two separate bodies of law, with distinct applications, so that human rights law is normally intended to apply in times of peace, and IHL in times of armed conflict.[7]

In general, no major distinction is made in this book between *'international' and 'non-international' armed conflict*[8] as regards the relevant rules and principles outlined. This distinction is increasingly unpopular with international lawyers and others, and seen as artificial, since, *inter alia*, armed conflicts can fluctuate between these two categories (see the jurisprudence of the ICTY),[9] and in any event such distinctions are often controversial and unclear (as already mentioned).[10] Also, the rules regarding international armed conflict tend to be more detailed and set a higher standard than those concerning non-international armed conflict, and in relation to military training it seems advisable to train to the higher standard. For the purposes of such training therefore, the preferred approach here is to state rules as clearly as possible, incorporating the higher standard.[11]

The main focus and more detailed rules below are most relevant to training of *armed forces operating on land*, as opposed to naval or air forces. This is because children have been particularly caught up in conflicts on land (see eg Rwanda, Sierra Leone, Sri Lanka, Colombia, former Yugoslavia), where many of the most serious violations against them have been committed. Further, the majority of legal rules concerning the treatment of children in armed conflict are specific to conflicts on land, and most recent armed conflicts are, as already mentioned, internal armed conflicts, many of which take place without a major naval or air-force component. Nonetheless, the fundamental principles presented below, (and particularly in this Chapter) will apply to the training of *naval and air forces*, as well as those operating on land. Indeed, these basic rules, (as well as a few of the more detailed rules in Chapters Three and Four[12]) are very relevant to issues such as targeting in aerial and naval bombardment—and such bombardment remains a prominent feature of many of the major conflicts current (or in the recent past) at the time of writing. In any event, joint operations are becoming quite common in many armed forces.[13]

The material presented below is not directed toward any specific *level of officer*, as the principles outlined range in complexity from very simple to more complex, and could therefore be flexibly applied by different types of armed forces in different circumstances, as appropriate. However, as a guideline, the information here presented would normally be appropriate for training of senior officers with command and training responsibilities. Thus it could generally be used, in greater or lesser detail, for training the ranks of Captain to Major to Colonel.[14] This training would ideally be conducted during times of peace at army colleges, and could then be put into practice and assessed during field exercises. In addition, at least the basic principles could be conveyed to both officers and their troops as one component in mission-specific IHL refresher courses just before an army or unit embarks on operations, and where possible during the course of operations.

Finally, the rules outlined below should be communicated to both *conscripts and volunteers*, without distinction, as long as they are performing a similar role, and have similar responsibilities.[15]

Those, then, are the parameters of the discussion in this section (Chapters Two to Five, below) which largely summarises the content of rules relevant to the IHL and human rights law training of officers of national armed forces concerning children. Chapters Two (this Chapter) to Four will set out rules and principles relating to children as civilians and as combatants. Chapter Five will consider, *inter alia*, various international law mechanisms for encouraging compliance with these rules. The discussion will start by outlining some of the basic underlying norms.

As mentioned in the Foreword, key legal principles will be highlighted in the text and marked with*.

Basic Principles

a) International Humanitarian Law (IHL)[16]

To start with fundamental rules of IHL, it is worth noting initially that these rules do, of course, apply to children, although they do not specifically refer to them. Further, most if not all of the underlying principles of IHL are—at least in theory— so widely accepted that they are regarded as customary law.[17]

In introducing these IHL principles, one writer states:

> The purpose of armed conflict is to defeat the adverse party. The law of armed conflict only permits such actions as are imperative for this purpose and forbids acts that go beyond this and cause injury to persons or damage to property not essential to achieving this end. The law restricts both the means of waging war and the objects against which such means may be employed ....'[18]

* **Thus, belligerents are limited by IHL in their choice of methods or means of conducting armed conflict** (see eg 1977 GP I, Article 35(1) and 1907 Hague Convention IV Respecting the Laws and Customs of War on Land (hereafter 1907 Hague Convention IV),[19] Article 22**), and they are particularly prohibited from using such means and methods as will cause 'superfluous injury or unnecessary suffering' either to combatants or civilians** (see eg 1977 GP I, Article 35(2)). **Moreover, combatants should use only the minimum degree of force that is both necessary and lawful in order to achieve their mission, in accordance with,** *inter alia*, **the principles of military necessity and humanity.**[20] **These laws therefore aim to establish a framework for limiting certain methods of armed conflict, as well as for protecting those involved in or affected by armed conflict.**

> Fundamental rules in accordance with these principles are exemplified, eg, by the precept that civilians must, as far as possible, be protected in situations of armed

conflict. Thus, *inter alia*, according to the concept of distinction, combatants and civilians must be distinguished from each other, and only the former can legitimately be directly targeted (see eg 1977 GP I, Article 48 and Article 51(4)).

* **The challenge of complying with IHL often amounts, in essence, to finding the balance between military necessity and humanitarian considerations.**
    One writer argues that 'it is the relation between these two forces which determines the contents of the law of armed conflict at any given moment'.[21]

* **This difficult balancing act finds expression in the principle of proportionality, which was first set out in treaty form in 1977 GP I, and is generally accepted as a customary norm.**[22]
    For example, 1977 GP I (Article 51(5)(b)) expresses the proportionality principle in prohibiting indiscriminate attacks, defined as

    'an attack which may be expected to cause incidental loss of civilian life, injury to civilians, damage to civilian objects, or a combination thereof, which would be excessive in relation to the concrete and direct military advantage anticipated'.[23]

    The proportionality principle lies at the heart of military conduct, including conduct in relation to children, and putting it into practice is one of the most challenging tasks of the combatant of whatever rank. To instil an understanding of this principle must be one of the foundations of any military training that incorporates IHL. That said, there are of course certain IHL rules that are absolute and do not involve proportionality, eg the prohibitions against: direct targeting of civilians; the use of certain weapons, and the torture or other gratuitous ill-treatment of detainees and prisoners (whether military or civilian).

As a minimum, the basic IHL principles (particularly *unnecessary suffering, military necessity* and *proportionality*) should be conveyed to officers of all ranks, and by such officers to those under their command, in the course of their regular military training. These principles are to some extent vague and subjective, and, where possible, the training should acknowledge this problem while also seeking to clarify the principles, eg with reference to practical examples and case studies (see Chapter Seven). Once the gist of these principles is understood, they can provide a useful 'rule of thumb' in relation to, *inter alia*, the treatment of children. (Indeed, it is arguable that they should be observed with particular diligence when children are involved,[24] since children are entitled to special protection and care under international law.[25])

In short, a thorough training in the basic IHL rules would in itself provide a useful reference point for soldiers and officers in their dealings with children. For soldiers, it may suffice, as a minimum, to emphasise in such training that all protections articulated under IHL (for both civilians and combatants) apply equally to children.

b)   Human Rights Law[26]

As regards basic principles of human rights law relevant to military training concerning children, these can be found in all the main international human rights instruments, and in certain customary law norms. They include rules that apply to, eg, all 'persons', thus incorporating children, as well as rules that specifically refer to the entitlements of children. Not all human rights norms apply fully in times of armed conflict, but the fundamental norms, (particularly the prohibitions of arbitrary killing, enslavement, and torture and analogous ill-treatment), are non-derogable[27] and therefore apply in all circumstances.

i   Special Treatment of Children

* **A guiding human rights norm regarding children is that they are, as children, entitled to special treatment. The term 'special treatment' is meant here to have a positive construction, meaning the entitlement of children to additional assistance and protection.**[28]

This entitlement is expressed differently in the main international human rights legal instruments, but it is found in them all. Thus, eg, the International Covenant on Civil and Political Rights (hereafter 1966 ICCPR)[29] states that 'Every child shall have, without any discrimination … the right to such measures of protection as are required by his status as a minor, on the part of his family, society, and the State' (Article 24(1)). The Universal Declaration of Human Rights (hereafter, 1948 UDHR)[30] (Article 25(2)) and the International Covenant on Economic, Social and Cultural Rights (hereafter 1966 ICESCR)[31] (Article 10(3)) make similar provision, as do the main regional human rights instruments in Africa, Europe and the Americas.[32]

A number of these treaties also contain various general principles that apply to children, among others, and remain pertinent in situations of armed conflict. These include, eg, the right to family life (eg Article 23, 1966 ICCPR and Article 10 (1), 1966 ICESCR); to the enjoyment of health (eg Article 12, 1966 ICESCR), and to education (eg Article 13, 1966 ICESCR)).

* **The entire 1989 CRC can be seen as a detailed expression of the principle that children are entitled to special care and protection**.

It has been summarised as incorporating the four 'P's': the *protection* of children from neglect, exploitation and discrimination; the *prevention* of harm to children; the *provision* of assistance for their basic needs, and their *participation* (according to their individual capacity) in decisions on matters concerning them.[33] The latter 'participation' right for children was incorporated into the 1989 CRC as a relatively new and controversial concept in international law. Realistically, it is a right that may be particularly difficult to implement in many situations of armed conflict. However, efforts should be made to include children of sufficient competence in decisions affecting them, including in situations of armed conflict.[34]

Given, *inter alia,* the wide ratification of all the above treaties, and particularly the 1989 CRC, it is arguable that the special protection of children is now at least an emerging international customary norm. In any event, for ratifying states of relevant treaties it is a binding and non-derogable obligation that applies both in times of peace and armed conflict, and the training of officers should emphasise this principle.

ii   'Right to Life'

* **As regards general human rights law applicable to all persons, both adult and child, the 'right to life' is of primary importance, including in conflict situations. This right can be more accurately described as the right not to be arbitrarily deprived of life.**

Deprivation of life is clearly lawful (if not necessarily moral) in some situations, including both capital punishment and armed conflict. However, even in situations of armed conflict *arbitrary* deprivation of life is prohibited,[35] although this prohibition may be expressed differently in IHL (eg in terms of whether the deprivation of life is 'proportionate'). As mentioned above, human rights law and IHL overlap to some extent and there can be uncertainty as to the applicable law in particular circumstances. However, in conflict situations that may not be covered by IHL, human rights provisions continue to apply. This means, *inter alia,* that in all circumstances, including eg borderline situations of civil strife, the 'right to life' remains protected by law.

* **Thus, under the combined provisions of human rights law and IHL, all people, child or adult, are not to be arbitrarily deprived of life in any situation, including armed conflict, whether they are civilians or combatants.**

Again, this principle should be conveyed in military training.

Provisions articulating the 'right to life' are found in the 1948 UDHR (Article 3), the 1966 ICCPR (Article 6, and see its Optional Protocol aiming to abolish the death penalty[36]), and the 1989 CRC (Article 6), as well as, once more, in all the main regional human rights instruments.

The 1948 Convention on the Prevention and Punishment of the Crime of Genocide (hereafter 1948 Genocide Convention)[37] is relevant here, in that it prohibits genocide, as a particular form of killing or ill-treatment. Article II of this Convention defines genocide as including, *inter alia,* killing or harming members of a group, or 'forcibly transferring children of the group to another group' with the intention to destroy, in whole or in part, that group as such. This prohibition is restated in the Statute of the ICTY, the Statute of the ICTR, and the 1998 Statute of the ICC.

iii   Prohibition of Torture[38]

* **Another basic precept relevant to the treatment of children as well as adults in all situations including armed conflict, is the absolute human rights prohibition**

on torture and other cruel, inhuman or degrading treatment or punishment. This prohibition is also found in IHL.
Once more, it should form part of military training.

In human rights law, the prohibition is found, *inter alia,* in the 1966 ICCPR (Article 7); 1948 UDHR (Article 5); the 1984 Convention Against Torture (hereafter, 1984 CAT),[39] and all the major regional treaties.
Under IHL it is, of course, accepted that persons caught up in situations of armed conflict as combatants or civilians may inevitably suffer harm. However, they may not be harmed in a manner that amounts to torture, or other gratuitous or degrading treatment not strictly necessitated by the requirements of the conflict situation. As in human rights law, this applies particularly to detained or imprisoned persons. The IHL prohibition may be expressed differently from that found in human rights law, eg as a requirement to treat persons 'humanely' (as in 1949 GCs Common Article 3, and Article 27, 1949 GC IV).
Specifically as regards children, this principle is articulated in Article 37(a) of the 1989 CRC.[40]

In addition to those outlined above, there are other provisions of human rights law (such as due process rights, and the prohibition on slavery (relevant, eg, to forcible recruitment)) that are pertinent to military training regarding children. However, for the purposes of basic training it will suffice to emphasise the three principles above: 1) that children are entitled to special treatment, 2) that arbitrary deprivation of their lives is forbidden, and 3) that their torture and other inhumane treatment is prohibited.

In summary, officers and their subordinates should be trained, as a minimum, that these three fundamental human rights principles, and key IHL rules (such as military necessity, humanity and proportionality) outlined in this Chapter, represent underlying norms that should be known and observed by military personnel of whatever rank, in all conflict situations of whatever intensity. The general norms apply to both adults and children, and, in addition, children are entitled to special treatment under the applicable law.

Endnotes

1   Other summaries already exist that are complementary to, but not the same as, the material set out below. See eg, a summary of mainly IHL principles concerning children in armed conflict: ICRC, *Legal Protection of Children in Armed Conflict* (Geneva, ICRC, 2001). See also ICRC, *Children and War, Summary Table of IHL Provisions Specifically Applicable to Children* (Geneva, ICRC, 2001).

2   There are exceptions to this. While General Service Officers may not need in-depth knowledge of this area of law, some Specialist Officers may well require this. The latter could include officers involved in civil-military work, military police, medical personnel,

and legal officers. The text here will provide references to sources of more detailed information as necessary.

In any event, as Rogers points out (A P V Rogers, *Law on the Battlefield* (Manchester, Manchester University Press, 1995), pp 140–42): 'The law of war is becoming very complicated. One cannot really expect every soldier and officer to know every article and every nuance of the Geneva Conventions and Protocols … . It suffices if they understand the general principles of the law of war and then receive training or instructions specifically related to their mission.' Regarding the role of military lawyers in particular, see eg, Keeva (1991), pp 52–59.

3   See eg, G S Goodwin-Gill and I Cohn, *Child Soldiers: the Role of Children in Armed Conflict* (Oxford, OUP, 1994); Kuper (1997)(b), and J Kuper, 'Children and Armed Conflict: Some Issues of Law and Policy', in D Fottrell (ed) *Revisiting Children's Rights: 10 Years of the UN Convention on the Rights of the Child* (The Hague, Kluwer Law International, 2000), pp 101–113.

4   Indeed, some international treaties (see especially the 1989 CRC) incorporate both bodies of law.

5   The relationship between human rights and IHL is quite complex, and cannot be explored in depth here. Suffice it to say that fundamental human rights norms serve as a minimum standard, or safety net, applicable in all circumstances. Therefore, they cannot be derogated from in situations of conflict (as discussed in Chapter Six), such as borderline situations of civil strife, where the applicable legal regime is unclear. For further discussion see eg, F Hampson, 'Human Rights and Humanitarian Law in Internal Conflicts', in M Meyer (ed) *Armed Conflict and the New Law: Aspects of the 1977 Geneva Protocols and the 1981 Weapons Convention* (London, BIICL, 1989), pp 55–80 (hereafter, Hampson, 1989 (b)); F. Hampson, 'Using International Human Rights Machinery to Enforce the International Law of Armed Conflicts', 19:117 *Revue de Droit Militaire et de Droit de la Guerre* (1992), and T Meron, 'The Humanization of Humanitarian Law', 94:2 *AJIL* (2000) pp 239–278. Further, see ICRC website on the relationship between human rights law and IHL http://www.icrc.org/Web/eng/siteeng0.nsf/html/57JMBN!Open, visited on 1 July 2002). See also *The Prosecutor v Dragoljub Kunarac, Radomir Kovac, and Zoran Vukovic*, ICTY Case No IT–96–23–T and IT–96–23/1–T, Trial Chamber, 22 Feb 2001, para 467. Regarding relevant practice of the ICTY more generally, see Greenwood, (1998), pp 128–133.

6   See eg, ICJ, *Legality of the Threat or Use of Nuclear Weapons,* Advisory Opinion, ICJ Reports 1996, para 25, where the Court held that, in situations of armed conflict, the right to life must be determined in the framework of the law of armed conflict, although the human-rights-law right to life (as set out in Art 6 of the ICCPR) 'applies also in hostilities.'

7   See eg, *Banković and Others v Belgium and 16 Other Contracting States* (Application no 52207/99, 12 Dec 2001), regarding lack of jurisdiction of the European Court of Human Rights, under the European Convention on Human Rights (Convention for the Protection of Human Rights and Fundamental Freedoms, 213 U.N.T.S. 222, entered into force 3 Sept 1953, as amended) (hereafter ECHR), to hear an application concerning the NATO bombing of Belgrade. However, this case did not rule out the possibility that the ECHR could, in some circumstances, apply to situations of armed conflict.

8   *Note*: armed conflicts can also become 'internationalised' when other states become actively involved (eg through external logistic and/or technical support), even though the conflict is taking place within one state.

9   See eg, ICTY: *The Prosecutor v Dusko Tadíc,* No IT–94–1–A, Appeals Chamber, 15 July, 1999, paras 137, 141 and 145, and *The Prosecutor v Delalic et al (Celebici Case),* Appeals Chamber, Case No IT–96–21–A, 20 Feb, 2001, paras 10–26. See also comments of Judge Richard Goldstone (former Chief Prosecutor at the ICTY) on this 'ridiculous distinction', and that the ICTY 'narrowed the difference between international and non-international armed conflict. Why should innocent men, women and children have less protection in non-international war than in international?' (R Goldstone, 'A Rule of Law for the International Community: Is it Achievable?' *Lecture,* (London, LSE, 26 June 2001)).

10 Strictly speaking, the 1949 GCs and 1977 GP I generally apply to international armed conflict, and Art 3 of the 1949 GCs and 1977 GP II apply to non-international armed conflict, as their full titles indicate. Other treaties such as the 1989 CRC, the 1998 Statute of the ICC, the International Labour Office (hereafter ILO) Convention Concerning the Prohibition and Immediate Elimination of the Worst Forms of Child Labour (1999, No 182) (hereafter 1999 ILO Convention No 182) and the 2000 Optional Protocol on Child Soldiers, can apply in both international and non-international armed conflicts.

11 This approach is in accordance with the spirit of Art 41 of the 1989 CRC, which states that, where applicable, standards 'more conducive to the realization of the rights of the child' in other international instruments should prevail over 1989 CRC provisions. Further, this is the approach adopted by F de Mulinen, *(Handbook on the Law of War for Armed Forces* (Geneva, ICRC, 1989), p xvi), who states: 'armed forces cannot be taught and apply different ways of action and behaviour for international and non-international armed conflict ... . Thus, the Parties and armed forces involved in a non-international armed conflict have to follow in practice the more complete provisions on international armed conflict.'

12 Examples of more detailed rules relevant also to air and naval operations, are found eg in the 1949 GC IV prohibition on attacking aircraft employed for removing maternity cases (Art 22) (see Chapter Three below), and in recommendations to take account in attacks, (where realistic), of the possible particular vulnerability of child soldiers (see Chapter Four).

13 This applies particularly where specialist skills (eg medical or logistic) are transferable between the different branches of the military.

14 Military training of officers is generally undertaken at various levels. Some courses divide training on the basis of tactical, operational and strategic levels. The material outlined here is probably best suited for training at the operational level (usually Majors and Lt Cols), but it could also be relevant to the tactical, and to some extent, the strategic levels.

15 However, different training strategies and opportunities may apply to these two groups, as they enter military service through different routes.

16 Some of the basic IHL principles are increasingly difficult to apply in the changed context of current armed conflicts, and principles such as 'proportionality' and 'distinction' were on the agenda of the 2003 expert meeting organised by the Swiss government and others on IHL (as mentioned in Chapter One). And see eg, M N Schmitt, 'The Principle of Distinction in 20th Century Warfare', *San Remo Seminar, Future Wars* (2001), pp 24–44.

    As already stated, only a few of the main principles will be mentioned here. For fuller information on the pertinent law, see eg, A Roberts and R Guelff, *Documents on the Laws of War* (Oxford, OUP, 2000); L C Green, *The Contemporary Law of Armed Conflict* (Manchester, Manchester University Press, 2000), (re 'Basic rules', see, pp 123–25); D Fleck *et al* (eds) *The Handbook of Humanitarian Law in Armed Conflicts* (Oxford,

OUP, 2000); J Gardam (ed) *Humanitarian Law* (Aldershot, Dartmouth/Ashgate, 1999), and Rogers (1995) (re 'General Principles', see pp 1–26). See also military manuals of different countries, and model manuals such as that by de Mulinen (1987), and ICRC, *Fight it Right: Model Manual of the Law of Armed Conflict for Armed Forces* (ICRC, Geneva, 1999).

17   See eg, the *Nuclear Weapons Case* (above, n 6) para 79, stating that fundamental rules of IHL 'constitute intransgressible principles of international customary law'. And see n 23, Ch 1, above regarding customary law generally.

18   Green (2000), p 122. The object of armed conflict under IHL is therefore to defeat the adverse party, not to destroy it.

19   Hague Convention IV Respecting the Laws and Customs of War on Land, adopted 18 Oct 1907, entered into force, 26 Jan 1910, 3 Martens Nouveau Recueil (ser 3) 461, 187 Consol TS 227.

20   Roberts and Guelff (2000), p 10, (citing United States, Department of the Navy (jointly with Headquarters, US Marine Corps; and Department of Transportation, US Coast Guard), *The Commander's Handbook on the Law of Naval Operation,* NWP 1–14M, Norfolk, Virginia, October 1995, p 5–1), define these terms as follows: *military necessity*—'Only that degree and kind of force, not otherwise prohibited by the law of armed conflict, required for the partial or complete submission of the enemy with a minimum expenditure of time, life, and physical resources may be employed'; *humanity*—'The employment of any kind or degree of force not required for the purpose of the partial or complete submission of the enemy with a minimum expenditure of time, life, and physical resources, is prohibited'. Another key principle is that of *chivalry*—'Dishonorable (treacherous) means, dishonorable expedients, and dishonorable conduct during armed conflict are forbidden'. However, the latter term has become somewhat outmoded, although it still represents an ideal standard of military conduct.

21   Y Van Dongen, *The Protection of Civilian Populations in Time of Armed Conflict* (Amsterdam, Thesis Publishers, 1991), p 3. But see eg, Jochnick and Normand (1994(a)), pp 50–51, who argue that 'despite noble rhetoric to the contrary, the laws of war have been formulated deliberately to privilege military necessity at the cost of humanitarian values. … Through law, violence has been legitimated.' However, while acknowledging 'the difficulty of using law to humanize war' they 'do not condemn the effort itself'.

22   See eg, J G Gardam, *Non-Combatant Immunity as a Norm of International Humanitarian Law* (Dordrecht, Martinus Nijhoff, 1993), pp 147–154, and C Greenwood, 'Customary International Law and the First Geneva Protocol of 1977 in the Gulf Conflict', in P Rowe (ed) *The Gulf War 1990–91 in International Law and English Law* (London, Routledge, 1993) (hereafter 1993(a)), p 88.

23   See also Art 57(2) of 1977 GP I, articulating the proportionality principle in relation to precautions in attack. For practical examples of the proportionality principle, see eg, Rogers (1995), pp 14–17.

24   That said, military training must be flexible and adapt to the particular circumstances. For example, in situations where children are not the main focus of the training, it is important to concentrate on the other issues that may be seen to have greater priority. In such general training, the message (to quote one military lawyer) is not, eg: 'Do not abuse children', but 'Do not abuse *anyone*', including children. (Australian officer interviewed on 28 Nov 2000.) The term 'abuse' is used here to imply treatment that is unlawful in that it does not meet the criteria for being militarily appropriate in the

particular circumstances, since clearly the use of force (up to and including lethal force) is an inevitable part of the conduct of armed conflict.

25 As will be discussed, this entitlement is found eg in human rights law; certain IHL rules (such as Art 77(1) of 1977 GP I); implicitly and explicitly in 1989 CRC, and arguably in customary law. As regards customary law in this context, see Kuper (1997(b)), pp 123–127. Hampson argues, eg, that, in judging proportionality in relation to the use of weapons, a different calculation might have to be made if there are likely to be particularly severe consequences for one group of civilians, such as children (F Hampson, *Legal Protection Afforded to Children under International Humanitarian Law: Report for the Study on the Impact of Armed Conflict on Children* (Essex, University of Essex, 1996), pp 28–29). However, as one interviewed military lawyer rather bluntly put it, 'People don't join the army to protect children. They are trained to win a war.' (Australian officer involved in training, interviewed on 23 April 2001).

26 Where not otherwise stated, the information here regarding human rights law is drawn from Kuper (1997(b)), Chapter Two.

27 The issue of derogation (ie states being able to opt out of or limit particular human rights obligations) will be discussed below in Chapter Six, regarding the duties of governments.

28 For further discussion of the term 'special treatment' in relation to children, see eg Kuper (1997(b)), pp 10 and 14–18.

29 International Covenant on Civil and Political Rights, GA res 2200A (XXI), 21 UN GAOR Supp (No 16) at 52, UN Doc A/6316 (1966), 999 UNTS. 171, entered into force 23 March 1976.

30 Universal Declaration of Human Rights, GA res 217A (III), UN Doc A/810 at 71 (1948).

31 International Covenant on Economic, Social and Cultural Rights, GA res 2200A (XXI), 21 UN GAOR Supp. (No 16) at 49, UN Doc A/6316 (1966), 993 UNTS. 3, entered into force 3 Jan 1976.

32 As already mentioned, it is beyond the scope of this work to analyse the regional instruments. However, for brief discussion of these, see Kuper (1997(b)), Chapter Two.

33 See eg, G Van Bueren, *The International Law on the Rights of the Child* (The Hague, Kluwer Law International, 1998), p 15.

34 Boyden (referring to P Bracken and C Petty, (eds) *Rethinking the Trauma of War*, (London, SC and Free Association Books, 1998)) emphasises that treating children as 'passive victims' as opposed to 'competent survivors' has the effect 'that they are excluded from plans and decisions concerning them', with potentially negative personal and social consequences (Boyden, (2002), p 3).

35 The key word here is 'arbitrary'/unlawful deprivation of life. Thus, it is forbidden, eg, to deliberately target non-combatants, or to attack combatants who have laid down their arms.

36 Second Optional Protocol to the International Covenant on Civil and Political Rights, aiming at the abolition of the death penalty, GA res 44/128, annex, 44 UN GAOR Supp. (No 49) at 207, UN Doc A/44/49 (1989), entered into force 11 July 1991.

37 Convention on the Prevention and Punishment of the Crime of Genocide, 78 UNTS 277, entered into force 12 Jan 1951.

38 The prohibition of torture has been categorised, eg by the ICTY and the ICJ, as a customary norm. See eg, *Case concerning application of the convention on the prevention and punishment of the crime of genocide* (*Bosnia and Herzegovina v Yugoslavia* (*Serbia*

and Montenegro)), Request for the indication of provisional measures, ICJ Reports, 1993. In this ruling, the Court stated that 'Yugoslavia …, in breach of its obligations under general and customary law, has … tortured citizens of Bosnia and Herzegovina …' (para 1(2)(d)).

39 1984 Convention Against Torture and Other Cruel, Inhuman or Degrading Treatment or Punishment, GA res 39/46, (annex, 39 UN GAOR Supp (No 51) at 197, UN Doc A/39/51 (1984)), entered into force 26 June 1987.

40 Other particularly pertinent articles in this context include 1989 CRC Arts 6, 19, 34 and 38.

3

Part I(A)(1)—Law and Policy: Content of Rules Relevant to Officer Training Regarding Children—Child Civilians

Introduction

Having summarised, in Chapter Two, certain fundamental IHL and human rights provisions relevant to the training of officers of national armed forces as regards children (and others), more detailed measures will now be considered, starting with those concerning child civilians.

It is worth emphasising first that, under IHL, child civilians are entitled to protection: a) as members of the civilian population generally; b) as children, due to their particular vulnerability within the civilian population, and c) as child civilians in specific categories (eg enemy aliens) if they qualify as such. The information below will be presented under these three sub-headings.

Civilians Generally

* **As regards civilians generally, the fundamental principle in IHL is that civilians in the power of a party to the conflict are to be respected and protected in all circumstances, and treated humanely.**[1]

Under the 1949 GC IV (Article 27),[2] this concept entails wide-ranging obligations including, *inter alia*, respect for 'their persons, their honour, their family rights' and protection from acts or threats of violence, insults and public curiosity, as well as 'any attack on the honour' of women. (The term 'women' here includes 'girls' under the age of 18.)[3]

* **Measures should also be taken to minimise harm to civilians in or near the theatre of military operations.**

1977 GP I contains a number of civilian protection measures which are generally part of customary law but were not included in 1949 GC IV, and which are designed to safeguard civilians who are in the theatre of military operations.

These include the principle of distinction between combatants and civilians, and the prohibition on directly targeting both civilians (already mentioned)[4] and civilian objects. (In cases of doubt, schools and houses are specifically presumed to be civilian objects, under Article 52(3), 1977 GP I).

* **A concise guide to and summary of fundamental IHL rules regarding the treatment of civilians and other non-combatants is contained in Article 3 of the 1949 GCs (Common Article 3). This provides for humane treatment of 'persons taking no active part in the hostilities'. In relation to such persons, it prohibits 'at any time and in any place whatsoever ...: a) violence to life and person ..., b) taking of hostages ...,[5] c) outrages upon personal dignity ..., d) the passing of sentences and the carrying out of executions' without due process.**

Common Article 3 applies explicitly to situations where the conflict takes place in the territory of one State Party to the 1949 GCs (ie non-international armed conflicts), but it applies implicitly to all situations of armed conflict as a minimum standard.[6]

Certain provisions of Common Article 3 and 1949 GC IV are reaffirmed by Article 75(2) of 1977 GP I. The latter article absolutely forbids, in relation to all persons in the power of a party to the conflict, *inter alia*: a) violence to life, health or well-being; b) outrages upon personal dignity, including enforced prostitution and indecent assault, and ... e) threats to commit the foregoing acts.

At the least, officers of national armed forces should themselves know—and try to ensure that those under their command also know—the provisions of Common Article 3 of the 1949 GCs, and the fact that it applies to all those not actively engaged in combat, including children.

Child Civilians Generally

Turning now to consider provisions relating to child civilians generally, the key rules (in addition to those already cited regarding all civilians)—contained largely in 1949 GC IV, the 1977 GPs, and the 1989 CRC—can be quite simply stated, as follows:

* **children in armed conflict are entitled to special treatment and must be provided with the care and aid they require.** (*Main References* (hereafter *Refs.*): Article 77(1) of 1977 GP I, and, to a lesser extent, Article 4(3) of 1977 GP II, both incorporated within Article 38, 1989 CRC, and human rights provisions already outlined).

This principle underpins all others relating to child civilians, and, as far as possible, it should form the baseline against which military decisions regarding such children are taken.

It applies to children in all circumstances, including, eg, refugee or internally displaced children,[7] who are often particularly vulnerable. (Regarding such children, military personnel may be involved in eg camp management or border control near refugee or internally displaced persons camps.)

Further, the emphasis on providing 'the care and aid they require' takes into account the special needs of all especially vulnerable categories of children, such as very young children, girl children in many cases,[8] and children who are disabled.

Military personnel therefore need to be trained in their duty to ensure, as far as possible, proper protection of children, with particular awareness of those who may be especially vulnerable. This duty includes negative obligations to refrain from abusing children, as well as positive obligations to assist them, and to observe and report abuse perpetrated by others.[9]

* **children should not be ill-treated, and this includes, *inter alia*, a prohibition on indecent assault (ie any assault of a sexual nature, including the use of child prostitutes).**[10] (*Main Refs*: Article 77(1) of 1977 GP I; Article 4(3) of 1977 GP II; 1989 CRC, (eg Articles 6, 19, 34, 37(a) and 38(1) and (4)), and 2002 Optional Protocol to the Convention on the Rights of the Child on the Sale of Children, Child Prostitution and Child Pornography (hereafter 2002 Optional Protocol on the Sale of Children),[11] as well as human rights provisions already outlined)

    As regards sexual abuse, it is important to note the particular vulnerability of girls (although boys too may be subjected to this). In their training, officers should be made fully aware of the absolute prohibition on the abuse of children, including sexual abuse, and they should also sensitise those under their command to this issue.[12] The harm caused to children by sexual abuse is now exacerbated by the risk of HIV/AIDS infection, and indeed there is an explicit link between armed conflict and the spread of HIV/AIDS to children, among others.[13] The 2002 Optional Protocol on the Sale of Children strengthens the prohibition on sexual abuse of children, in requiring states to explicitly prohibit child prostitution etc (Article 1), and to punish those responsible (Article 3). This Protocol cites 'armed conflicts' as one of the 'contributing factors' in child sexual abuse (Preamble).

* **children, expectant mothers and maternity cases**[14] **should be granted priority in receiving relief consignments. Free passage of essential foods, clothing and tonics for them must also be granted, subject to certain security conditions.** (*Main Refs*: 1924 Declaration on the Rights of the Child and 1959 Declaration of the Rights of the Child[15] (Principle 2, and Principles 3 and 8 respectively); Article 23 of 1949 GC IV; Article 70(1) of 1977 GP I, and eg Articles 24, and 38(4) of 1989 CRC).[16]

* **zones should be established to protect child civilians (among others) from hostilities.** (*Main Refs*: Articles 14 and 15 1949 GC IV, and Articles 59 and 60 of 1977 GP I).

    1949 GC IV and 1977 GP I both contain a number of articles concerning the establishment of protective zones of different types in situations of armed conflict. Only one of these, 'hospital and safety zones' (Article 14, 1949 GC IV) makes a specific reference to children (under 15) as well as expectant mothers and mothers of children under 7. However, child civilians would be entitled to shelter in any of the other specified categories of zone.[17] It is important that officers in national armies are aware of the possibility of establishing such zones, (despite the obvious difficulties of doing so in some circumstances[18]). This would not apply to, eg, lower-ranking officers in highly-organised modern armies, where decisions on the creation of 'safety zones' would be made on a policy level, not by officers 'on the ground'.

* **children and maternity cases (among others) who are in besieged or encircled areas, should be allowed access to medical and religious facilities, and removed from those areas if possible.** (1949 GC IV, Article 17).

* **no party to the conflict may arrange for the evacuation of children, other than its own nationals, to a foreign country, unless this is essential for the health or safety of the children.**[19] **Where they can be found, parents or guardians must consent to such evacuation. In these situations, evacuated children must have an identification card, sent to the Central Tracing Agency of the ICRC.** (See Article 78 of 1977 GP I, which has largely superseded Article 24 of 1949 GC IV regarding evacuation). **Where children are removed temporarily to a safer area within the same country, parental or equivalent consent is again desirable, and they should be accompanied by a responsible person.** (See Article 4 (3)(e) 1977 GP II). **In evacuation or temporary removal, the views of the children themselves should be taken into account where possible.**[20] (See Article 12, 1989 CRC).

In some situations armies may have special units that deal with issues such as evacuation of the civilian population, and/or these issues may be the responsibility of NGOs, or inter-governmental organisations such as UNHCR. However, even in these circumstances officers and those under their command should be prepared for any eventuality, and be aware of the basic relevant principles, and, in particular, the importance of ensuring adequate identification of evacuated children, and of trying to maintain family (and community) unity (see also below).

* **children should be kept with their families and communities whenever possible**. (*Main Refs*: Articles. 27, 49 and 82 of 1949 GC IV; among others, Articles. 5, 7, 8, 16 of 1989 CRC; Article 23 of 1966 ICCPR and Article 10 of 1966 ICESCR).[21] **When separation of families does occur, children must be allowed to maintain family contact, eg through exchange of family news and other enquiries** (Articles 25 and 26, 1949 GC IV*).* **They should also be reunited with their families where possible** (Article 74, 1977 GP I; Article 4(3)(b), 1977 GP II, and Article 10, 1989 CRC).[22]

These provisions, among many others in international human rights law and IHL, acknowledge the pivotal role the family can play in child survival and development. According to one authority, '... a child living with his or her family in a war zone and repeatedly exposed to violence may in fact be far less susceptible to emotional or psychological distress than a child separated from his or her family and evacuated to a place of safety'.[23]

* **children should not be subject to the death penalty for offences related to the conflict which were committed when they were under 18** (Article 68, 1949 GC IV; Article 77(5), 1977 GP I, and Article 6(4), 1977 GP II).
Article 37(a) 1989 CRC has now extended this prohibition to forbid the death penalty for offences committed by children under 18 in any circumstances (as does the less widely-ratified 1966 ICCPR (Article 6(5)), **and it also forbids the imposition of a sentence of life imprisonment without possibility of release.**

Child Civilians in Specific Categories

The above two Sections have highlighted, respectively: key rules relevant to military training concerning the civilian population in general (including children), and pertinent rules specifically providing for children as a vulnerable group within the civilian population. This Section will now consider rules aiming to provide additional safeguards for children in several specific categories. These categories are:

a) children in occupied territory generally,[24]
b) children who are deprived of their liberty (detained or interned), including in occupied territory,
c) children who are orphaned or separated from their parents
d) children who are considered enemy aliens,[25]
e) expectant mothers, maternity cases and babies.

Basic relevant rules concerning children in these categories will be set out below, under the five headings.

a) Children in Occupied Territory Generally

* **For the purposes of military training, it is important to emphasise the underlying principle of international law regarding occupied territories, which is that it generally aims to preserve as far as possible the pre-conflict *status quo* (as regards, eg, public order and safety) until peace is restored. Thus, the provisions concerning children in occupied territories are largely designed to minimise disruption of their lives during the conflict, by facilitating continuity in crucial areas such as family life, schooling, and place of residence.**[26]
1949 GC IV contains a number of provisions specifically relating to children in occupied territory. 1977 GP I also contains relevant provisions, applicable to children whether or not in occupied territory.[27] The specific 1949 GC IV rules include, eg, provisions regarding the running of institutions 'devoted to the care and education of children'; forbidding changes in the 'personal status' of children (such as changing their nationality); providing for their health and nutrition, and ensuring that they and their parentage can be identified (Articles

50 and 136). Further, Article 51 of 1949 GC IV prohibits compulsory labour for those under 18 in occupied territory.[28]

b)   Children Deprived of Their Liberty

There are also a number of rules providing for children who are deprived of their liberty.[29] This Section will summarise the rules concerning *conditions of detention* that apply to child civilians who are interned or imprisoned (in connection with criminal proceedings),[30] including in occupied territory. (**Note:** Rules concerning *due process* for children involved in criminal proceedings will be summarised in the Chapter on 'Child Soldiers' below.)[31]

Many of the relevant provisions on conditions of detention for interned or imprisoned child civilians are found in the 1989 CRC, and in other treaties such as the 1966 ICCPR, as well as in 'soft law' such as the 1990 UN Rules for the Protection of Juveniles Deprived of their Liberty.[32] These provisions generally apply both in times of peace and in situations of armed conflict.

* **The 1989 CRC states that all 'institutions, services and facilities' responsible for children must conform with standards established by 'competent authorities', particularly as regards safety, health and adequate and appropriate staffing** (Article 3(3), and see also Article 24). **Further, children deprived of their liberty must be treated with humanity and respect, and in a way that takes into account the needs of people of their age. They are to be separated from adults unless this is not in their 'best interests',**[33] **and are generally entitled to maintain family contact through visits or correspondence** (1989 CRC, Article 37 (c)). **In keeping with their entitlement to be treated with humanity and respect, detained children are to be protected from ill-treatment.**

The 1989 CRC prohibits 'torture or other cruel, inhuman or degrading treatment or punishment' (Article 37 (a), as already mentioned), which covers, *inter alia*, the sexual abuse of captured children, to which girls are particularly vulnerable (and see also Articles 19 and 34).

Moreover, as mentioned above in Chapter Two, torture and analogous treatment are prohibited under customary law, and in other international treaties that are not quite as widely ratified as the 1989 CRC, such as the 1966 ICCPR and the 1984 CAT, which apply equally to adults and children.[34]

* **In addition to the largely human rights rules just outlined,**[35] **IHL—in 1949 GC IV—incorporates certain measures that explicitly regulate the treatment of children detained or interned in occupied territory** (see eg Articles 50 and 51 above). **These include the provision that 'proper regard' should 'be paid to the special treatment due to' children accused of offences** (Article 76). **There are also a number of specific IHL provisions—in 1949 GC IV and 1977 GP I—concerning conditions of detention for child internees and their relatives (eg regarding their support, accommodation, discipline, repatriation, health and educational needs, etc).**[36]

For most military training and reference purposes relating to children deprived of their liberty, a summary of the 1989 CRC provisions relevant to conditions of detention would suffice. However, as regards children deprived of their liberty in occupied territory, the pertinent IHL rules (immediately above) should, where possible, also be referred to.

c) Children who are Orphaned or Separated from their Parents

* **The fundamental rule is that orphaned or separated children are not to be left to fend for themselves, and must be treated with special care—including as regards providing for their identification, education and religion** (see eg, 1949 GC IV, Article 24 and, in occupied territory, Article 50).[37]

d) Children who are Considered Enemy Aliens

* **Children considered to be 'enemy aliens' are entitled to the same preferential treatment as children who are nationals of the state concerned** (1949 GC IV, Article 38 (5)), **eg as regards the provision of food and medical care.**[38]

e) Expectant mothers, maternity cases, and babies

* **Babies, expectant mothers, and maternity cases are entitled to special protection, being categorised among the 'wounded and sick' due to their particular physical vulnerability** (1977 GP I (Article 8(a)). See also 1966 ICESCR, Article 10(2)).[39]

1949 GC IV contains specific measures concerning *expectant mothers* (see above eg 1949 GC IV, Articles 14 (hospital and safety zones), 16 (particular protection and respect) and 23 (free passage of consignments)). 1949 GC IV also contains such measures regarding *maternity cases and nursing mothers*, prohibiting attacks on civilian hospitals caring for them (Article 18), and on land and sea convoys conveying them (Article 21). Aircraft exclusively employed for removing maternity cases may not be attacked, subject to agreement between the parties on flight details (Article 22). Further, maternity cases must be allowed access to consignments of essential items (Article 23), and provided with adequate medical treatment (Article 91). If internees, they must not be transferred if this would harm their health, unless their safety so requires (Article 127).

Note: The main international law rules concerning child civilians, as outlined in this Chapter, are incorporated into the 1989 CRC either specifically (eg by Article 37, regarding torture and deprivation of liberty), or more generally, (eg, under Article 38 (4): 'In accordance with their obligations under international humanitarian law to protect the civilian population in armed conflicts, States Parties shall take all feasible measures to ensure protection and care of children who are affected by armed conflict').

In summary, the rules regarding child civilians aim to provide certain protections for them as civilians generally, and also more specifically as child civilians, including within particular categories. Accordingly, military training should, as a minimum, emphasise that all IHL and human rights provisions relating to the protection of civilians generally apply equally to child civilians—and that there are, in addition, more detailed rules that apply to *child* civilians, which can and should be referred to as needed in the particular circumstances.

Endnotes

1   See eg, F Kalshoven and L Zegveld, *Constraints on the Waging of War: An Introduction to International Humanitarian Law* (Geneva, ICRC, 2001), pp 53 and 63–64, and Gardam (1993) generally.

2   *Note*: Under 1949 GC IV, Arts 14 to 26 apply to the entire population of states that are party to an armed conflict, but Arts 27 *et seq* apply only to 'protected persons' (ie persons in the power of a party to the conflict—including an Occupying Power—of which they are not nationals). Again, when aiming to apply the higher standard in training officers generally on the treatment of children, these distinctions need not be made.

3   Although 1949 GC IV does not explicitly address this issue, it is clear that this treaty, designed to protect civilians from the excesses of armed conflict, can be interpreted to incorporate the girl child under measures in defence of women. By analogy, the 1979 Convention on the Elimination of All Forms of Discrimination Against Women (GA res 34/180, 34 UN GAOR Supp (No 46) at 193, UN Doc A/34/46, adopted in 1979, entered into force 3 Sept, 1981) contains a number of provisions incorporating the girl child, eg, Art 10, regarding education. It thus includes 'girls' within the category of 'women'.

4   See Arts 48 and 51 of 1977 GP I, as mentioned above (Chapter Two). For more detailed information see eg, Gardam (1993).

5   The Commission on the Status of Women, in a recent UN Resolution, (UN Doc E/CN6/RES/46/1 'Release of women and children taken hostage, including those subsequently imprisoned, in armed conflicts' (Report on the forty-sixth session, 15 and 25 March 2002, p 18)), emphasised that violence directed against civilians contravenes IHL, and this included taking women and children as hostages. It called, *inter alia*, for an end to such hostage-taking and the release of all women and child hostages. See also UN Doc E/CN6/2002/4 (18 Dec 2001), containing a report of the Secretary General on the same issue.

6   See eg, J Pictet, (ed) *Commentary: IV Geneva Convention Relative to the Protection of Civilian Persons in Time of War*, (Geneva, ICRC, 1958), pp 36 and 38. See also ICTY: *The Prosecutor v Dusko Tadíc*, Case No IT–94–1–AR72, Appeals Chamber, 2 Oct 1995, para 102, reaffirming the judgment in the *Nicaragua* case (*Military and Paramilitary Activities in and against Nicaragua* (*Nicaragua v United States of America*) Merits, Judgment, ICJ Reports 1986, p 14) that Common Art 3 rules reflect 'elementary considerations of humanity', and, as such, these rules are applicable in both non-international and international armed conflict.

7   These two terms simply distinguish children who have had to flee from their homes either across the borders to another country (refugees), or within the borders of their own country (internally displaced persons). For the legal definition of a refugee, see Art 31 of the Convention relating to the Status of Refugees, (adopted on 28 July 1951, entered into

force 22 April 1954), 189 UNTS 150. There is no legal definition of an internally displaced person, but see UNHCR definition: 'persons who, as a result of persecution, armed conflict or violence, have been forced to abandon their home and leave their usual place of residence, and who remain within the borders of their own country'. (UNHCR, *The State of the World's Refugees 1997–1998: A Humanitarian Agenda* (Geneva UNHCR, 1997), p 99.)

8 It is estimated that women and girls constitute 80% of victims of armed conflict. (Machel (1996), pp 9 and 14).

9 The duty to report violations committed by others, especially by military personnel from the same armed force, can raise complex issues regarding eg, loyalty and intimidation, as mentioned further in Chapter Seven below.

10 The use of child prostitutes is not specifically prohibited in the 1949 GCs and 1977 GPs, but it is included within the general prohibition on indecent assault, and is prohibited, eg, under Art 34, 1989 CRC. This issue should, in any event, be discussed in military training, despite possible sensitivities in referring to it.

11 2002 Optional Protocol to the Convention on the Rights of the Child on the Sale of Children, Child Prostitution and Child Pornography. UN Doc A/RES/54/263 (2000). Entered into force, 18 Jan 2002 in accordance with its Art 14(1).

12 *Note:* eg, the jurisprudence of the ICTY, which has categorised rape as a war crime, and has also taken into account—in sentencing perpetrators—the youth of some of the rape victims. (See discussion below, Chapter Five). There have also been a number of reports criticising military personnel—including UN and other peace support personnel—for sexually abusing children, including child prostitutes. See eg, Kuper (1997(b)), pp 234–35; UNHCR and SC—UK, *Note for Implementing and Operational Partners on Sexual Violence and Exploitation: The Experience of Refugee Children in Guinea, Liberia and Sierra Leone* (London, SC—UK, 2002), and A Gillan, 'Sex Abuse Scandals Tarnish Work of Aid Agencies in Africa', *The Guardian* (20 April 2002).

13 See SC, *HIV and Conflict: A Double Emergency*, (London, SC, 2002). This report emphasises, *inter alia*, that '[i]n war, HIV/AIDS spreads rapidly as a result of sexual bartering, sexual violence, low awareness about HIV, and the breakdown of vital services in health and education', and that these factors particularly affect children (p 1).

14 'Maternity cases' would include women shortly before, during, or shortly after giving birth.

15 Geneva Declaration on the Rights of the Child, Records of the Fifth Assembly, Supplement no 23 League of Nations Official Journal (1924), and Declaration of the Rights of the Child, UN Doc A/1386(XIV), 20 Nov 1959.

16 See also Kuper (1997(b)), pp 86–87.

17 Such zones include neutralised zones (Art 15, 1949 GC IV) and non-defended localities and demilitarised zones (Arts 59 and 60 respectively of 1977 GP 1). In addition, there are other types of 'safety' zones that are established eg, by the UN Security Council, or by organisations such as UNICEF. See eg, Kuper (1997(b)), pp 80–83, and Hampson (1996), pp 58–63.

18 These include, *inter alia*, difficulties in deciding who controls these zones, and how, and in ensuring that the zones do not shelter combatants.

19 *Note*: children are the only category for whom evacuation out of country is envisaged. See further regarding evacuation: Hampson (1996), pp 65–67, and Kuper (1997(b)), pp 83–86 and 91.

20   *Note*: It is worth emphasising that the right of the child to express his or her views, under Art 12 of the 1989 CRC, does not mean that the child is entitled to make the final decision on any particular issue. Rather it means that such views should inform the decision-making process, as one of the key factors to be considered, and should be given increasing weight as the child matures.

21   The SC West Africa training materials emphasise that the most effective strategy to maintain family unity is to prevent family separation, and they suggest various practical measures that military personnel can undertake, including identifying, and taking appropriate action regarding: a) locations where separations are likely (such as border crossings), and b) categories of children most vulnerable to separation (such as disabled children). ECOWAS/CEDEAO and SC-Sweden (hereafter SC S) West Africa Regional Office, *Child Rights and Child Protection Before, During and After Conflict: Booklet for Senior Military Personnel* (Abidjan, ECOWAS, SC S West Africa Regional Office, 2001), p 74.

22   See further Kuper (1997(b)), pp 87–89. Hampson (1996), p 36, comments on the apparent tension in the rules between the concept of keeping families together, while also allowing for removal of children from areas of conflict.

23   J Boyden and S Gibbs, *Indicators and Perceptions of Psycho-social Vulnerability and Coping Mechanisms in Cambodia* (Geneva, UNRISD, 1997)—earlier draft cited in Hampson (1996), p 24. Nonetheless, in another context Boyden points out that the 'assumption that children's needs are best served within the context of the family' is a view that prevails 'despite a lack of qualitative information on child care or family circumstances and an unfamiliarity with children's own coping strategies during periods of political violence' (Boyden (2002), p 3).

24   Provisions concerning occupied territory, strictly speaking, apply only to international armed conflict. However, as regards military training these could be adapted to analogous situations in non-international armed conflicts if they reflect the higher standard.

25   Again, the concept of 'enemy alien' applies in international armed conflict, but could be extended to apply by analogy in non-international armed conflict. Indeed the ICTY has held that it is possible for persons to be considered 'protected persons' under IHL even if they have the same nationality as the opposing party, but do not owe allegiance to the state and do not receive its diplomatic protection (*The Prosecutor v Dusko Tadíc*, Case No IT–94–1–A, Appeals Chamber, 15 July 1999, paras 167–169).

26   See eg, Hampson (1996), p 29. For example, as regards education, the Occupying Power has an obligation to ensure the education of children, and may not indoctrinate them. However, if, eg, schools are used for subversive activities, the Occupying Power may have the right to temporarily close them.

27   For example, see Art 78, 1977 GP I, regarding evacuation, as mentioned above.

28   For more detailed discussion of these provisions, see Kuper (1997(b)), pp 90–94. Again, in some situations responsibility for children in occupied territory would be assumed by special, possibly civilian, units linked to the army, or by other specialised agencies. The legal regime becomes more complex in relation to prolonged belligerent occupation (see eg, the Israeli/Palestinian situation), where, in some circumstances, human rights law can become as relevant as, or even more relevant than, IHL.

29   In 1989, the Secretary General of the UN appointed a Special Rapporteur on the application of international standards concerning the human rights of detained juveniles. See UN Doc E/CN4/Sub2/1989/58 (1 Sept 1989), resolution 1989/31 of the Sub-Commission on Prevention of Discrimination and Protection of Minorities, appointing

M C Bautista to this post. See also her two initial reports, both entitled 'Application of International Standards Concerning the Human Rights of Detained Juveniles', prepared pursuant to UN Sub-Commission Resolution 1990/21, UN Doc E/CN4/Sub2/1991/24 (2 July 1991) and Resolution 1991/16, UN Doc E/CN4/Sub2/1992/20 (3 June 1992).

30 These principles apply whether the deprivation of liberty is before, during or after trial.

31 Normally the civil authorities would conduct criminal proceedings concerning child civilians, although—perhaps especially in occupied territories—this role could be undertaken by the military. However, military personnel are generally more likely to be involved in criminal proceedings involving child soldiers, hence the relevant due process provisions are summarised under that heading (Chapter Four below).

32 The focus here is on the main pertinent treaty provisions, and 'soft law' (see Chapter Five) will not be described in this Chapter. However, such law is worth referring to for more detailed guidance on good practice. For military training purposes, it will generally suffice in this context to cite treaty provisions from the 1989 CRC only. (Thus all the relevant specific provisions of, eg, the 1966 ICCPR will not be referred to here, although again it is worth noting that the 1966 ICCPR, and other human rights treaties, contain a number of pertinent provisions regarding conditions of detention).

33 Art 10 (2)(b) of the 1966 ICCPR contains similar provisions regarding the separation of children from adults. However, it is worth bearing in mind that some detained children may wish to be accommodated with trusted adults, and account should be taken of their views, in accordance with Art 12 of the 1989 CRC.

34 Again, protection from torture is a non-derogable right in these treaties (see Chapter Six), and has been categorised as a customary norm (see n 38, Ch 2 above).

35 Although the 1989 CRC incorporates both human rights and IHL principles, the rules regarding conditions of detention are derived primarily from human rights law.

36 In relation to internees, 1949 GC IV provides that the Detaining Power must support those dependent on internees if they have no other source of support (Art 81); family members should generally be accommodated together (Art 82 and see also 1977 GP I, (below)), and the accommodation, and nutritional, educational and recreational requirements of child internees must be provided for (Arts 85, 89 and 94). Moreover, disciplinary punishments must be appropriate to, *inter alia*, the age of the internee (Art 119). The release, repatriation, or return should be arranged of, among others, internees who are children, pregnant women, or those with young children (Art 132). 1977 GP I contains additional relevant provisions, including that there should be separate accommodation for children detained or interned for reasons related to the conflict, unless they are housed with family members (Arts 75(5) and 77(4)). It also specifies that the cases of pregnant women and mothers of dependent infants, who are arrested, detained or interned due to the armed conflict, must be considered with utmost priority (Art 76).

37 See eg, Kuper (1997(b)), p 94.

38 See eg, *Ibid*, pp 94–95. And see n 25 above, regarding concept of 'enemy alien' in non-international armed conflict.

39 See eg, *Ibid*, p 95.

4

Part 1(A)(1)—Law and Policy: Content of Rules Relevant to Officer Training Regarding Children—Child Soldiers[1]

Introduction

Having considered in Chapter Three the main international law principles pertinent to military training as regards child civilians, it is now relevant to look at those provisions concerning child soldiers. Child soldiers are discussed below in two categories: a) child soldiers as combatants; and b) captured child soldiers.

Large numbers of child soldiers—estimated in 2001 at over 300,000 under 18s at any one time[2]—participate in armed conflicts worldwide, although in most cases such participation is contrary to, and explicitly prohibited by, both national and international law.

As regards child soldiers within national armed forces, such soldiers are generally those aged 15–17, since it remains lawful (although in contravention of the current higher standard) to incorporate this age-group in national armed forces, depending on the applicable legal regime in the particular country (see discussion below). However, some national armed forces may in fact unlawfully use child soldiers under the age of 15, as do many armed opposition groups.

It is commonly assumed that child soldiers (and to a lesser extent adult soldiers) are predominantly male, but in fact there are many girls who become 'soldiers' and who fulfil a multiplicity of roles in some armed forces, and particularly in armed opposition groups.[3] This has implications for the training of officers of national armed forces. For example, it requires that: a) officers and soldiers should be sensitised to avoid gratuitous discrimination against girls in all areas of military life, from recruitment to demobilisation; b) the particular health needs of girl soldiers generally, including those who are captured and detained, should be provided for, and c) rules regarding sexual conduct should be reiterated. As regards the latter, sexual abuse of child soldiers (which can include males as well as females) is apparently widespread in some armed forces,[4] although it is legally prohibited.[5]

It is also sometimes assumed that child soldiers can quite easily be identified as such—an impression fuelled by media images of very small children carrying large weapons. However, in reality it can be difficult to determine whether someone is or is not a 'child' soldier. Among other things, a child under 18, or even 15, can look considerably older, and in many situations of armed conflict there is no opportunity to ascertain age. Moreover, birth registration is incomplete or non-existent in some countries.[6]

* That said, **certain basic rules continue to apply to child soldiers, male and female, (a) as combatants, and (b) when captured, as they apply to all children and indeed to everyone. These include,** *inter alia*, **the prohibitions on arbitrary deprivation of life, and on torture and other ill-treatment, as differently articulated in both IHL and human rights law (see above, Chapter Two).**[7]

As regards the more detailed IHL and human rights rules (below), many of these apply equally to military personnel whether adult or child (ie under 18), whether combatants or prisoners. However, there are additional measures that apply specifically to child soldiers, particularly when captured. Again, the relevant rules are to be found in the 1949 GCs; 1977 GP I or II if they apply,[8] the 1989 CRC and related international treaties. These rules will now be considered.

Child Soldiers As Combatants

The discussion of child soldiers as combatants falls under three headings: i) general rules regarding eg child recruitment and participation; ii) child soldiers within the officers' own armed forces, and iii) child soldiers in opposing armed forces.

a)   *Rules Regarding Child Soldiers As Combatants Generally*

The fundamental IHL rules concerning child soldiers include the following:
* **children under 15 should never participate in armed conflict**[9] (Article 77(2), 1977 GP I; Article 4(3), 1977 GP II, and Article 38(2), 1989 CRC). **This standard is now being steadily raised to the age of 18** (see below).[10]
    It is worth noting that, under the wording of Article 38(2), 1989 CRC,[11] states are obliged to take 'feasible measures' to prevent direct participation of all children under 15 in their jurisdiction, thus including those in non-government forces as well as those in their own armed forces.

* **when, in contravention of the law, children under 15 (although for many countries the norm is, or is becoming, 18** (see below)**) do participate in hostilities and are then captured, they are entitled, as children, to special treatment.** (Article 77(3), 1977 GP I, and Article 4(3)(d), 1977 GP II).

* **children under 15 should never be recruited as combatants, and this includes voluntary recruitment** (Article 77(2), 1977 GP I; Article 4(3)(c), 1977 GP II, and

Article 38(3), 1989 CRC). **Voluntary recruitment of those over 15 is permitted, subject to national legislation** (see below).

* **when recruiting among persons between the ages of 15 and 18, priority should be given to those who are oldest** (Article 77(2), 1977 GP I and Article 38(3), 1989 CRC).[12]

* (as with child civilians), **no-one should be subject to the death penalty for offences related to the conflict which were committed when they were under 18** (Article 68, 1949 GC IV; Article 77(5), 1977 GP I, and Article 6(4), 1977 GP II). **Article 37(a) of 1989 CRC has now extended this prohibition to forbid the death penalty for offences committed in any circumstances by persons under 18** (as does Article 6(5) of the 1966 ICCPR), **and it also forbids the imposition of a sentence of life imprisonment without possibility of release.**

The rules regarding child soldiers above were originally set out in the 1977 GPs, and (as regards the death penalty) in 1949 GC IV. They were then reaffirmed and further elaborated in the 1989 CRC either specifically (eg Articles 37(a), and 38(2) and (3)), or in general terms under the wording of Article 38(1).[13]

When drafting Article 38 of the 1989 CRC, many of those involved in the Working Group wished to raise existing standards to prohibit anyone under the age of 18 from participating in armed conflict. However, this could not be agreed, and the drafting of the pertinent provisions (Article 38 (2) and (3)), proved to be among the most contentious in the whole Convention, as already mentioned (in Chapter One above). That controversy continued for many years, but agreement on the 2000 Optional Protocol on Child Soldiers—which strengthens the prohibition on use of child soldiers within ratifying states—was finally reached in 2000, after six years of negotiations.[14]

* **Among other things, the 2000 Optional Protocol on Child Soldiers establishes 18 as the minimum age for conscription by, and direct participation in hostilities with, government forces of ratifying states** (Articles 1 and 2).[15] **As regards the voluntary recruitment of those under 18, it requires governments to raise the minimum age beyond the current minimum of 15, and to make a binding declaration stating the minimum age they will respect** (Article 3 (1) and (2)). **Countries must ensure safeguards are in place for the proper regulation of voluntary recruitment** (Article 3(3)). **In relation to non-governmental forces, this Optional Protocol goes further and prohibits any recruitment or use in hostilities of children under 18, requiring states to criminalise such practices** (Article 4).

* **Prior to this, the 1998 Statute of the ICC did specifically make it a war crime to conscript or enlist children under 15 into armed forces, or to use them to participate actively in hostilities** (Article 8(2)(b)(xxvi) and Article 8(2)(e)(vii)).

This prohibition applies to both international and non-international conflict, but, in setting the applicable age at 15, falls short of criminalising the involvement of those under 18.

* **Moreover, the 1999 ILO Convention No 182, concerning the prohibition and elimination of the worst forms of child labour,**[16] **included a prohibition on 'all forms of slavery or practices similar to slavery, such as … forced or compulsory labour, including forced or compulsory recruitment of children for use in armed conflict'** (Article 3(a)). **Under this Convention, children are defined as those under 18** (Article 2).

    It therefore incorporates a ban on *forced* recruitment of children under 18, although it fails to comprehensively ban either participation in combat of under-18 year olds, or their voluntary recruitment.

To summarise, as regards developments since the 1989 CRC: the 1998 Statute of the ICC makes participation in armed conflict of children under 15 a war crime; the 1999 ILO Convention No. 182 prohibits forced recruitment of children under 18, and the 2000 Optional Protocol on Child Soldiers, *inter alia*, establishes 18 as a minimum age for conscription and direct participation in armed conflict. It therefore seems that a shift is underway towards a comprehensive ban on the participation in armed conflict of child soldiers under the age of 18, although this has not yet been achieved.

b)   Child Soldiers in Own Armed Forces

* **Officers of national armed forces could encounter child soldiers either in their own or in opposing forces. If in their own forces, child soldiers (ie generally those aged 15–17, as already mentioned) should, in accordance with good practice and the higher standard in current IHL** (see above), **only be in training as voluntary recruits, and should not be directly engaged in combat. If a particular army does in fact use child soldiers under the age of 18 in combat, they should, like any other soldier, be trained to observe at least the fundamental IHL and human rights rules** (as summarised in Chapter Two).[17]

    These fundamental rules of course include the concept that IHL and human rights principles apply equally to children, and indeed encourage the special protection of children. However, it may be unrealistic to expect child soldiers to treat young people who appear to be their age or older as 'children'.

* **On the training process—as opposed to the content of the training—it is important to mention here the practice in some armed forces of 'initiation ceremonies' ('hazing' of recruits etc). On occasion these can include, eg, beating, bullying, sexual abuse, and general humiliation of recruits under 18.**[18] **Such practices constitute inhuman and degrading treatment, and—as regards recruits who are under 18—they are strictly illegal under Articles 34 and 37(a) of 1989**

CRC, as well as under other international law such as Article 7 of the 1966 ICCPR, and the 1984 CAT.

Officers should clearly not engage in such practices, and should ensure as far as possible that those under their command also refrain from participating in these activities.[19]

* **Regarding recruitment—as mentioned above, international law increasingly discourages conscription, and prohibits forcible recruitment, of those under 18.**

Although, strictly speaking, neither conscription nor deployment of children aged 15 to 17 is illegal (except in those countries that have ratified treaties such as the 2000 Optional Protocol on Child Soldiers), such activities could be in breach of, *inter alia,* the prohibition on employing children in work harmful to their health or dangerous to life (Article 10(3), 1966 ICESCR), and of various articles in the 1989 CRC. The latter include Article 3 (duty to take account of the best interests of the child), Article 19 (protection of children in care of others), and Article 24 (right of child to enjoyment of health).

In situations such as refugee and 'internally displaced person' camps, children can be particularly vulnerable to forcible recruitment. Officers of national armies and those under their command should be trained both to refrain from such recruitment themselves, and to observe and report to the appropriate authorities if others (eg armed opposition groups) are forcibly recruiting under 18s in these situations.[20]

c) Child Soldiers in Opposing Armed Forces

Officers of national armed forces may also find themselves or their troops confronting child soldiers in opposing forces. In this situation, again the fundamental IHL rules apply. It is unrealistic to expect a soldier or officer in a combat situation to behave differently towards a child soldier who may be threatening his or her life than s/he would behave towards an adult. A guiding principle here is, again, the proportionality principle. Certainly a soldier or officer whose life is in imminent danger is entitled and indeed trained to take necessary measures in self-defence—using minimum force—whether his or her opponent is an adult or a child. Moreover, the purpose of military operations is generally to defeat the opposing armed forces, and this means that, depending on the circumstances, combatants confronted by child soldiers may need to prioritise their mission, and will therefore not necessarily be limited to acting solely in self-defence.[21]

However, when realistically possible, the presence of child soldiers in an opposing armed force should arguably affect, eg, the assessment of proportionality in decisions regarding tactics and strategy, so that a particularly stringent test should be applied to the balance between humanitarian considerations and military necessity. Thus, eg, Ugandan troops fighting the Lord's Resistance Army (LRA) in Northern Uganda, have apparently refrained on some occasions from attacking LRA troops when they realised that those in the front line were children (knowing, too, that the LRA is notorious for the forcible conscription of children).[22]

* In short, **officers and soldiers confronting child soldiers in an opposing force can act in self-defence (using minimum force), and in furtherance of the military mission. However, the presence of opposing child soldiers should, wherever possible, be taken into account in decisions eg regarding proportionality.**

Captured Child Soldiers—Minimum Standards Applicable to All Detained Children[23]

International rules concerning child soldiers in combat pose some challenging dilemmas for military training and practice, as outlined above. Different challenges arise once child soldiers are captured, and deprived of their liberty.

For reasons already mentioned, the present research does not generally make a distinction between rules relating to international and to non-international armed conflict. That approach will largely be followed here as regards captured child combatants, since they are, as children, entitled to special treatment in custody, and many rules regarding the treatment of children deprived of their liberty apply in times of peace and in conflict, and whatever the category of conflict.[24]

However, some mention must be made of the legal distinction between international and non-international armed conflict in this context, since the relevant law, strictly applied, only grants POW status to captured combatants in international armed conflict.[25]

The discussion below will therefore look at the fundamental rules applicable to all children deprived of their liberty, including child soldiers in situations of armed conflict. A separate Appendix (Appendix One) will contain the rules applicable to captured child soldiers in 1) non-international, and 2) international armed conflicts (including eg rules regarding repatriation and internment of child POWs). These latter rules are summarised in the Appendix as they contain more detail than would be necessary for most military training, or even reference, purposes. Thus, unless such detail is specifically required, it would generally suffice to rely on the information set out below regarding all detained children.

It is important to bear in mind here the statement in Article 41 of the 1989 CRC, encouraging the application of higher standards 'more conducive to the realization of the rights of the child'. Thus, where a number of legal provisions are relevant, as with captured child combatants, the higher standard should prevail.

For the purposes of this book, it will suffice to summarise the main treaty law provisions, but again those involved in military training who would like further guidance on good practice may wish in addition to refer to pertinent 'soft law'.[26] Most of the general rules are derived from human rights law (this Section, below), while the more specific rules regarding the treatment of children in either non-international or international armed conflict (Appendix One) are largely based on IHL.

a)   *Captured Child Soldiers—and Conditions of Detention*

The rules regarding conditions of detention are summarised above, in Chapter Three, regarding child civilians deprived of their liberty. These rules apply equally to child soldiers.

b)   *Captured Child Soldiers and Due Process*[27]

Officers of national armed forces may need to be aware of the main due process rules regarding captured child soldiers, since they may be called upon to conduct pertinent disciplinary proceedings. It is less likely, although not impossible, that military authorities may have to conduct criminal proceedings against child civilians, especially in occupied territory, as mentioned in Chapter Three above. In either case, the basic due process provisions set out below would apply.

'Children' in this context would generally include those who committed offences while under-age, but who are, at the time of trial, over 18, as well as those who are still under age at the time of trial.[28]

Realistically, however, it must be acknowledged that the relevant legal standards are unlikely to be met in most situations of armed conflict. Nonetheless, efforts should be made to comply with the law as fully as possible in the circumstances.

Disciplinary proceedings may range from reprimands for fairly minor offences to formal court hearings. When court proceedings are involved, military personnel may be subject to military courts, which often operate quite differently from their civilian counterparts[29] As regards children there is a strong argument for applying, in any such hearings, the due process principles applicable to them in civilian courts. Indeed, there is an equally strong argument, where possible, for actually conducting proceedings against them in civilian (rather than military) courts,[30] or through other less formal channels (in accordance eg with Article 43(3)(b) of 1989 CRC),[31] and also for demobilising them as soon as possible.[32]

In any event, very young children are not normally subject to criminal proceedings, as states generally incorporate in their domestic law the notion of a minimum age of criminal responsibility, and are unlikely to proceed against child soldiers below that age.[33] That said, this minimum age varies considerably from country to country.[34]

The fundamental applicable due process standards, then, are as follows:

* **The 1989 CRC stresses that arrest, detention and imprisonment of children should be a last resort, and for the shortest appropriate period of time** (Article 37(b)). **However, this provision must be differently interpreted as regards child soldiers, since they are usually detained by opposing forces simply due to the fact that they are captured combatants, and they can be detained until, eg, cessation of hostilities, without having to be charged with a particular offence.**

In this context, 1989 CRC, Article 37(b) can therefore be interpreted as encouraging attempts to minimise the impact of arrest, detention and imprisonment, eg by repatriation, or detention in civilian facilities or in a neutral country (see Appendix One).

* **When they are charged with an offence, however, the due process provisions below apply fully to captured child soldiers.**

* **Under the 1989 CRC, the aim of the juvenile justice system is to deal with children in a proportionate manner** (1989 CRC, Article 40(4)), **and to treat them with regard to their sense of dignity and worth, reinforcing their respect for the rights of others, and taking into account their age and the desirability of promoting their reintegration into society** (Article 40(1), 1989 CRC, and see Article 14(4), 1966 ICCPR). **The aim is constructive rather than punitive. A speedy legal procedure is recommended** (1989 CRC, Article 40(2)(iii), and see 1966 ICCPR, Article 10(2)(b)).

* **As indicated by a number of the rules already discussed,**[35] **special care must be taken when questioning children—including captured child soldiers.**
   In particular, children should not be compelled to testify or confess guilt (1989 CRC, Article 40(2)(b)(iv), and see 1966 ICCPR, Article 14(3)). Further, they must not be subjected to inhuman or degrading treatment, but must again be handled with respect, taking into account the needs of a person of their age (1989 CRC Article 37 (c)). This would apply whether they are being questioned for routine information, or because they are suspected or accused of infringing the law.

* **As with adults, children should not be accused of committing an offence if the act or omission in question was not prohibited by law at the time it was committed** (1989 CRC, Article 40(2)(a) and 1966 ICCPR, (Article 15(1)), **and they are also presumed innocent until proved guilty** (1989 CRC, Article 40(2)(b)(i) and 1966 ICCPR, Article 14(2)). **They must be promptly informed of the charges against them in such a way that they understand these** (see 1989 CRC, Article 40 (2)(vi) and 1966 ICCPR, Article 14(3)(a)).[36] **Their parents must be notified 'if appropriate'** (1989 CRC, Article 40 (2)(b)(ii)), **and the child should be consulted as to his/her views on this, where possible** (Article 12, 1989 CRC).

* **As regards the hearing itself, the child is entitled to a fair hearing before a competent body, with legal or other assistance, in the presence of his or her parents or guardians where appropriate** (1989 CRC, Article 40(2)(b)(iii)). **The child is also entitled to privacy** (1989 CRC, Article 40(2)(b)(vii) and see Article 14(1), 1966 ICCPR) **and to the assistance of an interpreter if necessary** (1989 CRC, Article 40(2)(b)(vi) and see Article 14(3)(f), 1966 ICCPR). **It is essential that the hearing be conducted in such a way that the child fully understands the proceedings.**
   In addition to these procedural safeguards, the child can benefit from other more detailed rules contained in the 1966 ICCPR and not reiterated in the 1989 CRC,[37] such as the rule against double jeopardy (Article 14(7) 1966 ICCPR), and

that adequate time and facilities must be allowed for the preparation of the case (Article 14(3)(b) 1966 ICCPR).

* **Regarding punishment, as already mentioned, the death penalty is forbidden for children who were aged under 18 at the time of the commission of the offence** (Article 68, 1949 GC IV; Article 77(5), 1977 GP I; Article 6(4), 1977 GP II, and Article 37(a), 1989 CRC), **as is a life sentence without possibility of release** (1989 CRC, Article 37(a)). **The prohibition against torture and analogous treatment also applies** (Article 37(a), 1989 CRC; Article 7, 1966 ICCPR, and 1984 CAT [38]).

The latter prohibition incorporates a ban on the use of corporal punishment, (and indeed there is an explicit IHL prohibition against corporal punishment of POWs, in 1949 GC III (Article 87)).[39]

* **In cases where child soldiers have clearly been forcibly conscripted and/or compelled to commit violations, the fact of such compulsion should be taken into account both as regards the decision to proceed to trial and in mitigation of punishment.**

However, this is a complex issue as the extent of the coercion may be hard to determine, and victims and their families may feel aggrieved if they see child perpetrators of violations treated leniently.[40]

Note: As indicated earlier in this Chapter, the related two Sections containing more detailed rules on captured child soldiers in non-international and in international armed conflict are set out in a separate Appendix (Appendix One).

In summary, it is clear that there are many legal rules relevant to the treatment of child soldiers by officers of national armed forces, whether the child soldiers are encountered within their own forces or in opposing forces, (both in combat and when captured and detained). These rules incorporate guidance on, *inter alia*, the recruitment and participation of children in situations of armed conflict, as well as guidance on due process procedures for captured child soldiers. Again, a number of the pertinent rules are, on paper, quite straightforward, but may be difficult to apply in practice. Competent military training must endeavour to bridge this gap.

Endnotes

1   Graca Machel (see n 26, Ch 1 above) apparently prefers not to use the term 'child sol-dier', on the basis that 'a true soldier has a sense of right and wrong as well as a sense of honour. The 12 year old who has been trained for only three weeks, the child who was taught to shoot not at targets but at live persons, is not a soldier.' (T A El-Haj, 'The Impact of Armed Conflict on Children', 122 *Childright* (1995), p 12). This is a very valid point. Nonetheless in this book the term 'child soldier' is preferred, since it is currently widely used, although perhaps with variations in meaning. The Cape Town Principles and Best Practices (1997) define child soldiers as 'any person under 18 years of age who

is part of any kind of regular or irregular armed force or armed group in any capacity … other than purely as family members.' These principles emphasise that the term not only refers to a child who is carrying or has carried arms, but includes eg cooks, porters, messengers and girls recruited for sex (Cape Town Principles and Best Practice on the Prevention of Recruitment of Children into the Armed Forces, and Demobilization and Social Reintegration of Child Soldiers in Africa (Cape Town, 30 April 1997), p 1).

2   See CSC (2001), p 1. For further statistical information on numbers of child soldiers in particular countries; a description of the role and experiences of such children; an over-view of the impact of armed conflict on them, and other information relating to child soldiers generally, see *ibid*. See also UNICEF statistics in the Introduction to Chapter One, above.

3   See eg, McConnan and Uppard (2001), pp 106–114, and R Brett, 'Girl Soldiers: Challenging the Assumptions', 6 *Child Soldiers Newsletter* (2002), pp 7–10.

4   See eg, L. Alfredson, 'Sexual Exploitation of Child Soldiers', 2 *Child Soldiers Newsletter* (2001), p 7.

5   For example, in both IHL and general human rights law sexual abuse is prohibited as a form of 'inhumane treatment', and there are also other child-specific prohibitions (eg in 1989 CRC (Arts 19 and 34), as already mentioned). The 2002 Optional Protocol on the Sale of Children explicitly reinforces the prohibition on sexual abuse (see above, Chapter Three).

6   See eg, CSC (2001), p 21.

7   It is worth bearing in mind again that the human rights provisions are most pertinent in situations not covered by IHL, such as low-level internal conflicts.

8   As mentioned above, most current armed conflicts are non-international armed conflicts, and therefore the 1949 GCs would not strictly apply, apart from customary principles articulated in them, and Common Art 3. Similarly, the 1977 GPs do not apply unless they have been ratified by the parties to the conflict, and, in the case of GP II, the conflict meets the criteria concerning the requisite level of organisation and intensity, etc. How-ever, in aiming to incorporate a high standard in military training regarding children, 1949 GC and 1977 GP principles can be referred to, whether or not they strictly apply.

9   Again, in aiming for simplicity and the higher standard, for the purposes of military training it should be emphasised that this prohibition includes both direct and indirect participation. (The legal rules on this point are complex in that eg 1977 GP 1 (Art 77(2)(c)) and the 1989 CRC (Art 38(2)) prohibit 'direct' participation, while eg the 1977 GP II (Art 4(3)(c)) prohibits any participation).

10 As mentioned above (n 56, Ch 1 above), the 1990 African Charter already sets a higher standard for ratifying states regarding children in armed conflict, eg in prohibiting participation in armed conflict of any child, defined as those under 18 (Art 22).

11 States 'shall take all feasible measures to ensure that persons who have not attained the age of 15 years do not take a direct part in hostilities'. The wording of Art 77(2) 1977 GP I is very similar, and the analogous Art 4(3)(c) of 1977 GP II also applies to all children in the jurisdiction.

12 1977 GP II, relating to non-international armed conflict, does not contain an analogous provision, but again adherence to the higher standard in 1977 GP I and the 1989 CRC is to be preferred.

13 Under Art 38(1): 'States Parties undertake to respect and to ensure respect for rules of international humanitarian law applicable to them in armed conflicts which are relevant to the child'.

14 It was adopted on 25 May 2000, and came into force on 12 Feb 2002, having received the requisite 10 ratifications (see its Art 10) by 12 Nov 2001. (See, http://www.unhchr.ch/pdf/report.pdf for the up-dated number of ratifications).

15 Parties to the Protocol must take 'feasible' measures to avoid direct participation (Art 1), but must ensure no compulsory recruitment of those aged under 18 (Art 2).

16 See also ILO Convention No 138 Concerning the Minimum Age for Admission to Employment (June 1973), 1015 UNTS 297 (1976). Both of these ILO conventions (No 138 and No 182) are considered fundamental, and fall within the scope of the 1998 ILO Declaration on Fundamental Principles and Rights at Work, which has established a follow-up mechanism binding on all States by virtue of their membership of the ILO.

17 As outlined in Chapter Two, fundamental IHL rules oblige combatants generally to act in accordance with the principles of military necessity and humanity, and to comply with certain customary norms, including those regarding distinction and proportionality. Fundamental human rights rules include the principle that children are entitled to special treatment, the right not to be arbitrarily deprived of life and the prohibition on torture.

18 See CSC (2001): eg, Overview, p 25; Sierra Leone, pp 323–325, and the UK, p 421. There have also been reports of bullying of young recruits in the Russian army (BBC Monitoring Service, 'Bullying, Albeit Less, Remains a Problem in the Russian Army: Excerpts from Report by Russia TV on 30th June', (30 June 1998)). See also Resolution 1166 (1998) of the Council of Europe Parliamentary Assembly (available at http://stars.coe.fr/ta/ta98/eres1166.htm, visited on 16 Nov 2001), and Alfredson (2001), p 7.

19 In any event, ill-treatment of military personnel in training can be counter-productive, resulting in brutalised troops unwilling or unable to comply with IHL and human rights rules (see Chapter Six).

20 In recent conflicts in Rwanda, the Great Lakes and Sierra Leone regions, some camps were built close to borders and children were snatched for recruitment and other purposes. On the problem of recruitment from refugee camps, see R. Brett, 'Recruiting Child Soldiers: The Link between Displacement and Recruitment', 1:122 *Refugees* (2001), p 19, available on the UNHCR website, http://www.unhcr.ch. See also CSC, 'Displacement and Child Soldiering', 4 *Child Soldiers Newsletter* (2002), pp 6–8.

21 As one interviewed officer said, 'Soldiers need to be aware of children, but the military is not an NGO .... Their first priority is the military mission, including self-survival'. (Australian officer interviewed on 23 April 2001).

22 E-mail 14 Aug 2001, from Save the Children staff member involved in military training in Uganda, and see Chapter Eight (regarding Uganda) below. Moreover, McConnan and Uppard (2001), p 41, note that 'professional armed forces ... find it hard to open fire on young children, as was the case in Vietnam and N Ireland' (although clearly there are exceptions to this).

23 The basic rules will be briefly outlined here, as more detailed information regarding detained children generally can be found elsewhere (see eg, Van Bueren (1998), Chapters Seven and Eight).

24 The 1989 CRC, in any event, arguably applies in its entirety in all situations, including situations of armed conflict, as it contains no derogation clause (see eg, I Cohn, 'The Convention on the Rights of the Child: What it Means for Children in War', 3:1 *Int'l J Refugee L* (1991) pp 100–111). The 1984 CAT similarly applies (see Art 2(2)). Further, as mentioned above, certain fundamental rules—regarding special treatment of children, the 'right to life', protection from torture, etc—are also non-derogable and continue to

apply. See also eg, Kuper (1997(b)), pp 21–24 and Chapter Six below, regarding derogation.

25   It is certainly arguable that, in relation to detained child soldiers, the level of protection
conferred by POW status or conferred by the 1989 CRC (whichever sets the higher
standard), should be applicable in all situations of armed conflict, due to the child's
entitlement under international law to special protection.

26   The relevant rules are found mainly in the 1989 CRC, although some can be found in
other international treaties (such as the 1966 ICCPR), and certain 'soft law' instruments such as the UN Rules for the Protection of Juveniles Deprived of their Liberty
(already mentioned in Chapter Three)), and the 1985 UN Standard Minimum Rules for
the Administration of Juvenile Justice (also known as the 'Beijing Rules'). The latter two
are not, strictly speaking, binding. However, they provide a guide to 'good practice', and
various principles particularly in the Beijing Rules are incorporated in the 1989 CRC,
or elaborate existing norms, and as such are binding. Some relevant rules are also contained in the 1955 Standard Minimum Rules for the Treatment of Prisoners, which apply
to prisoners generally.

27   Reference is made in this section to provisions of the 1966 ICCPR, since this treaty
contains many relevant rules concerning due process. However, to avoid excessive detail,
other pertinent rules (eg in the UDHR, Arts 9, 10 and 11) are not cited in the text here.

28   This is in accordance with eg IHL provisions prohibiting the imposition of the death
penalty, which rely on the age at which the offence was committed (see eg, 1977 GP 1,
Art 77(5), already mentioned).

29   However, in some countries no distinction is apparently made. Sweden, eg, has no
system of military courts but tries all combatants before civilian courts. (Swedish officer
interviewed on 31 May 2001).

30   In international armed conflict, 1949 GC III (Art 82) subjects POWs, in effect, to the
military law of the detaining power. The extent to which juveniles could be dealt with
by civil, as opposed to military courts, would be determined by that law. Additional
legislation may therefore be required to facilitate the use of civilian courts, as proposed
in the text here. In any event, the Fundamental Guarantees set out in 1977 GP I (Art 75)
and 1977 GP II (Arts 4,5 and 6) would apply (eg providing for humane treatment, and
specifically prohibiting violence to life, outrages on personal dignity, etc).

31   See eg, debate in Sierra Leone regarding the appropriate forum for hearings regarding
violations committed by child soldiers in that conflict (CSC (2001), p 326). Here, the
Prosecutor (D Crane) stated in 2002 that the recently established Special Court for Sierra
Leone did 'not intend to prosecute children, but rather people who forced children to
commit crimes during the country's war' (see, http://www.irinnews.org (Nov 2002))
See also debates in Rwanda (eg, SC S, 'Rwanda: "Children of Genocide" Released from
Prison', 2/01:2 *Children of War* (2001)). Indeed, in Sept 2000 the UN Committee on
the Rights of the Child hosted a discussion day on state violence against children, and
expressed concern at the application of military law to those under 18. It urged States
Parties to review, *inter alia,* criminal legislation applying to armed forces, to ensure it
appropriately reflects 1989 CRC, Arts 37 and 40 (CRC/C/100 (14 Nov 2000), Report on the
Twenty-Fifth Session, para 688, point 7).

32   Even when they are detained during investigation for war crimes, UNICEF argues that
the demobilisation of child soldiers 'should be immediate, and not be conditional on
what they have done' (Black (2001), p 29). See also McConnan and Uppard (2001), pp 7–8.
However, this view is contested (see eg, debates in Sierra Leone and Rwanda).

33 For example, in Rwanda, where 1,200 children were detained in prison in connection with the genocide, 'UNICEF initially requested the release of all children under the age of 14—the legal age of criminal responsibility—and their relocation to a re-education centre, and subsequently supported the rehabilitation of those aged between 14 and 18' (Black (2001), pp 27–29, referring to V Torres, *The protection and best interest of children in conflict with the law in Rwanda*, (UNICEF, Rwanda, 1995)).

34 See eg, UN Doc E/CN4/Sub2/1991/24, (2 July 1991), (Bautista Report on Detained Juveniles—n 29, Ch 3), p 11, regarding the minimum age for criminal responsibility in various countries.

35 See, *inter alia*, 1989 CRC Arts 37(a) and (c); 40(1) and (2)(b)(iv), and 1966 ICCPR Arts 7 and 14(3).

36 With children, the requirement regarding understanding must be taken particularly seriously, and may entail more than translation into the appropriate language (eg the use of simple concepts and examples by way of explanation).

37 See also Art 41 of the 1989 CRC, mentioned above, specifying that the higher standard should prevail.

38 *Note*: Art 14 of the 1984 CAT provides that persons subjected to torture or analogous treatment attributable to a public official shall be entitled to redress and compensation.

39 See eg, General Comment 20 (para 5) of the Human Rights Committee, stating that 'the prohibition' (against torture, under Art 7 of the 1966 ICCPR) 'must extend to corporal punishment, including excessive chastisement ordered as punishment for a crime or as an educational or disciplinary measure.' Human Rights Committee, General Comment 20, Art 7 (Forty-fourth session, 1992), Compilation of General Comments and General Recommendations Adopted by Human Rights Treaty Bodies, UN Doc HRI/GEN/1/Rev5 (26 April 2001).

40 Again, see eg, debates in Sierra Leone and Rwanda, (above, n 31).

5

Part I(A)(1)—Law and Policy: Content of General Rules Relevant to Officer Training Regarding Children— Landmines, Culpability/Command Responsibility, and Selected War Crimes Trials (1998-2001)

Introduction

Having summarised, above, provisions relevant to the training of officers of national armed forces regarding child civilians and child soldiers, it is appropriate now to consider some other pertinent legal issues. These are provisions regarding: a) the use of certain weapons; b) culpability and command responsibility, and c) relevant aspects of selected ICTY and ICTR[1] war crimes trials.

These three issues do not specifically focus on children, and may seem to have little in common with each other. However, they are linked by the fact that they should form part of general IHL and human rights training for officers, and, in addition, they all contain elements that are important as regards military training on children. Thus, eg, basic general training should emphasise the prohibition on the use of landmines, and training on children should emphasise the particular danger that such weapons pose to children.

Landmines

IHL contains various prohibitions on the use of weapons that cause 'superfluous injury' or 'unnecessary suffering' (see eg 1977 GP I, Article 35(2)[2]), as already mentioned. It also incorporates specific bans on, or measures to restrict the use of, particular weapons, such as incendiary weapons and mines (see eg the 1980 UN Convention on Prohibitions or Restrictions on the Use of Certain Conventional

Weapons Which May be Deemed to be Excessively Injurious or to Have Indiscriminate Effects,[3] (hereafter the 1980 Weapons Convention)).

In general, the body of law regarding use of particular weapons places the
responsibility for enforcing and observing these limitations on states that are party
to the relevant treaties. However, officers of national armed forces also need to be
broadly aware of the content of this body of law, and it should be included within
their basic IHL training.[4] Specifically as regards military training concerning
children, there is one category of weapon that merits separate attention, due to its
disproportionate impact on them. This is the category of landmines.

Unexploded ordnance poses a similar danger to children, and officers of national
armies should also be aware of the need to dispose effectively of this.[5]

Despite the fact that landmines are still being used in some conflicts, there is
growing international support for a fairly comprehensive ban on these weapons,
as expressed in the 1997 Convention on the Prohibition of the Use, Stockpiling,
Production and Transfer of Anti-Personnel Mines and on their Destruction[6] (the
'Ottawa Convention'—discussed below). However, it seems that alternative weapons
are being designed to circumvent the ban.[7] In any event, military training regarding
the use of such weapons remains necessary, since they are so indiscriminately
lethal, and so pervasive, and, further, it is likely to take many decades to clear
existing minefields.

Studies such as the 'Machel Reports'[8] set out the reasons for the particular
impact of landmines on children. These reports first put this issue in context,
explaining, *inter alia*, that:

> children in at least 68 countries live amid the contamination of more than 110
> million landmines;[9]

and that

> [l]landmines have been employed in most conflicts since the Second World War,
> and particularly in internal conflicts. Afghanistan, Angola[10] and Cambodia alone
> have a combined total of at least 28 million landmines, as well as 85 per cent of the
> world's landmine casualties … African children live on the continent most plagued
> by landmines …, but all countries are affected to some extent.[11]

According to another source, '[o]ver 90% of all landmine victims are civilians, half
of whom are children', and '[o]f the estimated 26,000 civilians killed or maimed
every year by landmines, 8,000 to 10,000 are children.'[12]

The Machel reports also elaborate on the reasons why landmines pose a
particular danger for children. These include the fact that:

> children are naturally curious and likely to pick up strange objects they come across.
> … Children are also more vulnerable to the danger of landmines than adults because
> they may not recognize or be able to read warning signs. Even if they are aware
> of mines, small children may be less able than adults to spot them …. The risk to
> children is further compounded by the way in which mines and unexploded ordnance
> become a part of daily life. Children may become so familiar with mines that they

forget they are lethal weapons. ... The victims of mines and unexploded ordnance tend to be concentrated among the poorest sectors of society, where people face danger every day when cultivating their fields, herding their animals, or searching for firewood. In many cultures, these are the very tasks carried out by children. ... Child soldiers are particularly vulnerable, as they are often the personnel used to explore known minefields.

Further

[a] mine explosion is likely to cause greater damage to the body of a child than to that of an adult. Anti-personnel mines are designed not to kill, but to maim, yet even the smallest mine explosion can be lethal for a child. ... For the children who survive, the medical problems related to amputation are often severe, as the limb of a growing child grows faster than the surrounding tissue and requires repeated amputation. As they grow, children also need new prostheses regularly.[13]

In training officers of national armies regarding landmines, a summary of information such as the above should be included in order to emphasise the threat they pose particularly to children, and to further encourage avoidance of their use, even by countries that are not party to the 1997 Ottawa Convention.

As regards the relevant international treaty law, provisions that are particularly pertinent to the protection from landmines of (among others) child civilians and child soldiers include the following:

* **The 1980 Weapons Convention, Protocol II** (Articles 3(2), 3(3) and 3(4)) **prohibits the use of mines, booby traps, and 'other devices', that is indiscriminate or directed against civilians.**[14] **It also explicitly prohibits,** *inter alia,* **booby traps associated with 'children's toys or other portable objects or products especially designed for the feeding, health, hygiene, clothing or education of children'** (Article 6(1)(b)(v)).

* **This Protocol was amended** (Amended Protocol II, adopted in May 1996[15]) **to encompass both international and non-international armed conflict,**[16] **and to explicitly prohibit indiscriminate use of landmines in sites used for civilian purposes, such as places of worship and schools** (Articles 3(7) and (8)(a)). **The amended Protocol also provides for all feasible measures to protect civilians** (Article 3 (10)), **and for an 'effective advance warning' as to the placement of mines, booby-traps and other devices that might affect the civilian population** (Article 3(11)).

* **The 1989 CRC as a whole aims to ensure,** *inter alia,* **the prevention of harm to children. It is therefore obvious that the use of landmines in relation to children—including actions such as employing child soldiers to explore minefields, or using mines in areas frequented by child civilians—is completely contrary to the spirit and specific provisions of the 1989 CRC** (eg Articles 4, 6, 24, 37 and 38).[17]

In addition, landmine use affecting children breaches child-protection provisions in general human rights law, such as Article 24 of the 1966 ICCPR.

* **The 1997 Ottawa Convention makes no specific mention of children, but it is now the guiding international standard on anti-personnel landmines. It prohibits their use in all circumstances** (Article 1(1)) **and requires,** *inter alia*, **that stockpiles in ratifying countries be destroyed within four years of the treaty's entry into force** (Article 4) **and that mines already in the ground be destroyed within 10 years** (Article 5(1)).

In the context of child-focussed training for officers of national armies, it is important to remember that, even if the Ottawa Convention succeeds in its long-term aim of banning the use of anti-personnel landmines, there still remains the formidable task of trying to ensure the protection of children and others from the effects of the millions of landmines that are already in place.[18] Officers and those under their command therefore have a role to play both in refraining from use of these prohibited weapons, and in facilitating the provision of information to children and others about the dangers of landmines, and ways of avoiding harm.[19]

Culpability and Command Responsibility

In addition to the rules outlined above concerning landmines, another general set of principles that is of particular relevance for training officers regarding the treatment of children are those concerning culpability and command responsibility.[20] This topic should normally be included in basic IHL training for officers,[21] and child-specific training should emphasise further that the personal liability of officers extends to violations against children that are committed by themselves and/or those under their command.

Although it is a truism that in situations of armed conflict both IHL and human rights law are generally 'honoured more in the breach than in the observance', there is, internationally, increasing pressure to challenge the impunity of those (including soldiers and officers) who are responsible for such breaches of international law, whether affecting combatants or civilians, adult or child.[22]

It is reasonable to assume that awareness of their possible liability for violations should contribute towards greater compliance with the law. Indeed this is the most likely scenario. However, as mentioned earlier, awareness of possible liability might also, in some situations, contribute to greater efforts by officers and others to conceal violations and thus evade culpability.

The law regarding culpability and command responsibility is not child-specific, and therefore will not be summarised in detail here.[23] The following section briefly outlines some of the key relevant *treaty* provisions. Selected *case law* on this issue is examined in the final section of this Chapter, below. In addition it is worth noting that there are applicable *customary law* principles: eg, a 1998 ICTY case confirmed that it is a norm of customary law that military commanders may be held criminally responsible for the unlawful conduct of their subordinates.[24]

Pertinent treaty provisions include:

* provisions regarding 'grave breaches' set out in the 1949 GCs[25] (as elaborated by 1977 GP I), such as Article 146 of 1949 GC IV, which obliges states to enact legislation 'necessary to provide effective penal sanctions for persons committing, or ordering to be committed, any of the grave breaches' defined in Article 147 of 1949 GC IV (and see below, Chapter Six, regarding state responsibilities). **Jurisdiction is universal so that, eg, under Article 146 of 1949 GC IV, a ratifying state must search for those suspected of committing 'grave breaches' and 'bring such persons, regardless of their nationality, before its own courts,' or extradite them to another state for trial.**

The 'grave breaches' cited in Article 147 include acts committed against protected persons and property such as 'wilful killing, torture or inhuman treatment … unlawful deportation or transfer or unlawful confinement …' as well as, *inter alia*, forced conscription into hostile armed forces, deprivation of due process, taking hostages, or wanton destruction of property.

Similar rules regarding grave breaches are contained in the other three 1949 GCs (1949 GC I, Articles 49 and 50; 1949 GC II, Articles 50 and 51; 1949 GC III, Articles 129 and 130).

1977 GP I expands the 1949 GC definition of grave breaches, eg by incorporating wilful violations of 1977 GP I, including direct or indiscriminate attacks on civilians (Article 85).

1977 GP I also obliges States to repress grave breaches resulting from a failure to act (Article 86(1)).

* provisions in 1977 GP I, which define armed forces as those that are 'under a command responsible … for the conduct of its subordinates …', and that are subject to an internal disciplinary system which, *inter alia*, enforces compliance with IHL (Article 43(1)). 1977 GP I confirms that superiors bear 'penal or disciplinary responsibility' for a breach of the 1949 GCs or 1977 GP I committed by a subordinate, if they knew or should have known of the breach and failed to take all feasible measures to prevent it (Article 86(2)). Further, it regulates the 'Duty of Commanders', including their duty to prevent, suppress and report breaches (Article 87(1)), and, according to their level of responsibility, to ensure that those under their command are aware of their obligations under the 1949 GCs and 1977 GP I (Article 87(2)).[26]

Commanders must also, where appropriate, initiate disciplinary or penal actions against those committing breaches (Article 87(3)).

* provisions in the Statute of the ICTY (which applies - regarding a conflict categorised as partly international and partly non-international[27]—to a range of offences, including genocide (defined to specifically include reference to children)).[28] This Statute states, concerning individual criminal responsibility, that '[a] person who planned, instigated, ordered, or otherwise aided and abetted in the planning, preparation or execution of a crime referred to in Articles 2 to 5' of the Statute 'shall be individually responsible for the crime' (Article 7(1)).

Such a person will not escape criminal responsibility or lessen punishment due to their official position, including as head of state (Article 7(2)).

Similarly, a superior will be liable for the acts of their subordinate if they knew or should have known of the commission of such acts, and failed to take appropriate measures to prevent or punish this (Article 7(3)).

Nor would an accused person be relieved of criminal responsibility on the grounds that they were following orders, but this may mitigate punishment (Article 7(4)).

* **provisions in the Statute of the ICTR (which applies—regarding a non-international armed conflict—to a range of offences again including genocide).**[29] **The Statute of this tribunal, too, provides for individual criminal responsibility of officers and others** (Article 6)**, in the same terms as Article 7 of the Statute of the ICTY** (above)**.**

Note: Both the ICTY and the ICTR are limited to addressing issues arising from specific conflicts (in the former Yugoslavia and in Rwanda), but nevertheless their jurisprudence gives an indication as to how international criminal law may in future be applied, eg in the ICC.

* **provisions in the 1998 Statute of the ICC (which covers a wide range of offences, including a number of violations specifically referring, or relevant, to children (eg trafficking of children; using soldiers under the age of 15, and sexual violence)[30]). Again, this Statute provides for individual criminal responsibility if a person,** *inter alia*, **commits a crime; orders, solicits or induces the commission of a crime; facilitates or in any other way contributes to the commission or attempted commission of a crime, or directly incites others to commit genocide** (Article 25(3)).

The ICC has jurisdiction only over persons who were over 18 at the time of the alleged commission of a crime (Article 26). A child soldier who committed a violation as defined by this Statute could not therefore be tried by the ICC.

Official capacity is irrelevant, so that the Statute applies equally, eg, to a head of state, and immunities attached to official capacity will not bar the exercise of the jurisdiction of the ICC (Article 28). Military commanders, or persons acting as such, can be held criminally responsible for violations committed by forces under their 'effective command and control, or effective authority and control'. In order to be held responsible, the commander must or should have known of the commission of the crimes in question, and failed to take appropriate measures to prevent, investigate or punish them (Article 28(a)). In similar circumstances, superiors are criminally responsible for crimes committed by subordinates under their effective authority and control (Article 28(b)).

A person will be criminally responsible for a crime committed under orders from a government or a superior, whether civilian or military, unless the person was under a legal obligation to respect the order, the person did not know that the order was unlawful, and the order was not manifestly unlawful (Article 33).

Specifically as regards children, the 1998 Statute of the ICC articulates various procedural measures to protect children who participate in its proceedings. These include, *inter alia,* provision for employment by the Prosecutor of legal experts on violence against children (Article 42(9)), and for the selection of judges with similar expertise (Article 36(8)(b)); provision that the Prosecutor must, in investigating and prosecuting crimes, take into account the age and gender of victims and witnesses and the nature of the crime, including whether it involves violence against children (Article 54(1)(b)), and that the ICC must take into account those same factors in protecting the safety and well-being of victims and witnesses (Article 68(1)). Further, the ICC can conduct *in camera* proceedings that involve children (Article 68(2)).[31]

The 1998 Statute of the ICC came into force on 1 July 2002,[32] and, at the time of writing, the court was not yet operational. In a statement made on 7 May 2002, Olara Otunnu (UN SRSG/CAC) said that when the ICC was functioning, he intended to work to ensure that those responsible for recruiting child soldiers would be among the first to be indicted.[33]

* *Note*: It is significant that, under their Rules of Procedure and Evidence, the ICTY, the ICTR and the ICC all make special provision for child witnesses, thereby clearly anticipating, and even encouraging, evidence from children.

The rules of the ICTY and the ICTR allow for child witnesses who do 'not understand the nature of a solemn declaration' to 'testify without that formality' if the Tribunal thinks 'that the child is sufficiently mature to be able to report the facts of which the child had knowledge, and understands the duty to tell the truth'. However, 'a judgment ... cannot be based on such testimony alone.' (Rule 90(B) of the ICTY, and Rule 90(C) of the ICTR). As an exception to Rule 90(C), the ICTR rules further state that 'no corroboration of the victim's testimony' is required in cases of sexual assault (Rule 96(i)).

Under the rules of the ICC, the 'Victims and Witnesses Unit' must 'give due regard to the particular needs of children ...'. In order to facilitate their participation and protection as witnesses, the Unit may assign, with parental or other agreement, 'a child-support person to assist a child through all stages of the proceedings' (Rule 17(3)). The staff of the Unit may also include, among others, persons with expertise on children, and particularly on traumatised children (Rule 19(f)). There are additional pertinent rules,[34] including that, in making directions or orders, the ICC must take account of the needs of all victims and witnesses, specifically including children (Rule 86).

In short, the main point to emphasise in child-focused military training as regards command responsibility and culpability is simply this: that officers and those under their command or control are, in general, fully liable for violations they commit, and this includes violations against children. Indeed, recent statutes and rules of major international tribunals make specific provision for prosecuting violations committed against children. (Again, culpability for such violations should arguably be enforced with particular diligence, due to the vulnerability of children and their corresponding entitlement to special treatment (eg 1977 GP I, Article 77 (1); 1977 GP II, Article 4(3), and the 1989 CRC, as already discussed)).

Under the treaty provisions outlined in this Section, above, and related provisions, legal cases have been taken to national military courts and international tribunals. By way of example, the Section below will consider some of the pertinent international cases, primarily in the ICTY but also in the ICTR.

International Tribunals

'War crimes' tribunals have increasingly emphasised the fact that those in command—up to the highest levels of government—are responsible for violations committed by themselves and/or their subordinates.[35] Following this trend, recent judgments of both the ICTY and the ICTR have indicated a growing awareness of the impact of armed conflict on children, and the fact that military personnel, including officers, are liable for offences committed against children, among others.[36] This section will therefore briefly discuss a few cases of the ICTY and the ICTR that were current at the time of writing, and that indicate the approach taken by these two tribunals to the culpability of officers—and those in an analogous position of power—for violations against children.

This section will not discuss earlier war crimes tribunals, although they, too, on occasion took particular note of crimes affecting children.[37] Nor will this section deal with pertinent cases heard by national courts (eg as regards Somalia and Vietnam, among others),[38] or by international tribunals regarding command responsibility as such, (since there are other writings on this,[39] and the focus here is specifically on responsibility for violations against children).

In the cases below the facts and the law are separately described. Each of those categories is then further analysed in terms of reference made to child soldiers and/ or child civilians, and any other salient features of the particular case.

Cases such as these can be usefully summarised in IHL training of officers and soldiers, to exemplify the approach being taken by international tribunals regarding violations committed against children, among others.

Cases—ICTY

i   The Prosecutor v Tihomir Blaskic[40]

Case concerning the responsibility of a commander.

Facts: This case concerned attacks committed by mainly Croatian forces against the Muslim population in the municipalities of Vitez, Busovaca, Kiseljak and Zenica in the Lasva Valley in central Bosnia between 1 May 1992 and 31 January 1994.

Reference to Child Soldiers
In this case there are no direct references to child soldiers, but mention is repeatedly made of the perception of young males as potential soldiers. For example, in describing an attack (16 April 1993) on areas of Vitez, it was stated that 'Muslims were arrested, segregated on the basis of their age and sex and the men of fighting age driven to detention areas or to the battle front lines' (eg paragraph 499). There are a number of other references to arrest and confinement of 'men of fighting age', and to violations committed against them, including their being 'taken to the front lines and made to dig trenches' (eg paragraphs 567, 570, 573, 599). (No definition is provided of 'fighting age', but it seems from the trial transcript that the selection was generally made on the basis of appearance, and, on that basis, many males under 18 (and probably some under 15) were likely to have been selected.)

Reference to Child Civilians
The facts of this case contain numerous references to child civilians being killed (often with extreme brutality, eg by being burned alive),[41] arrested and detained (eg paragraphs 351, 365, 409, 413, 416, 507); to their dwellings being destroyed (eg paragraphs 418, 546), and to their being used as human shields (eg paragraphs 549, 714) which 'inflicted considerable mental suffering upon' them (paragraph 716). Reference is made to the fact that 'men, women and children were attacked without distinction' (paragraph 507) and civilians killed 'regardless of age or gender' (paragraph 750).

Law: The legal element of this judgment contains no specific mention of the law relating to either child soldiers or child civilians. However, the fact that children, among others, were indiscriminately targeted was taken into consideration as an '*aggravating circumstance*'. Thus, for example, the tribunal stated:

> The status of the victims may be taken into account as an aggravating circumstance. Judgments have indicated that the victims were civilians and/or women. This Trial Chamber notes that in this case many crimes targeted the general civilian population and within that population the women and children. These acts constitute an aggravating circumstance (paragraph 786, and see also paragraph 783).

This judgment also makes a number of references to *command responsibility*, citing, *inter alia*, Articles 43(1), 86(2) and 87 of 1977 GP I (paragraphs 327 and 329).[42] Reference is made specifically to command responsibility in relation to women and children:

> General Blaskic admitted to the Trial Chamber that he knew that civilians were being detained at Dubravica primary school. These included *inter alia* the women and children who had been placed around General Blaskic's command post for two weeks. Nonetheless he announced that he had not made any effort to investigate the circumstances under which people were detained ...' (paragraph 732). 'The Trial Chamber accordingly concludes that General Blaskic did know of the circumstances and conditions under which the Muslims were detained in the facilities mentioned

above. In any case, General Blaskic did not perform his duties with the necessary reasonable diligence. As a commander holding the rank of Colonel, he was in a position to exercise effective control over his troops in a relatively confined territory' (paragraph 733).

Sentence: General Blaskic was sentenced to 45 years.

ii   The Prosecutor v Zoran Kupreskic, Mirjan Kupreskic, Vlatko Kupreskic, Drago Josipovic, Dragan Papic, Vladimir Santic, also known as Vlado[43]

Facts: This case concerned a Croatian attack on the Muslim population of Ahmici, a small village in central Bosnia, on 16 April 1993.

Reference to Child Soldiers
There is no explicit reference to child soldiers, but there are indications that young people may have been involved in the conflict, in that eg '... even small Croatian children had camouflage uniforms, made for them by the mothers' (paragraph 48); an 'intervention squad' was formed, 'composed of selected young men ...' (p 47, n 137), and 'the Croats saw signs of ... Muslim militancy .... The young men would shoot at anything ...' (paragraph 139, and n 145, p 139).

Reference to Child Civilians
In this case there are detailed descriptions of attacks on civilians, including children, involving, eg, killing of children of all ages; killing of their families (often witnessed by the children); forcible evictions of families from their homes, and the destruction of their homes (paragraphs 34, 37, 214, 217, 219 – 226). One witness described the ethnic cleansing of the village of Strane, in which 'not a single Muslim man, woman or child had remained ...' (paragraph 93). Another witness spoke of hearing one of the accused, 'Vlado', saying before the attack of 6 April 1993 that 'no men from 12 to 70 years of age should be left alive ...' (paragraph 167). That attack was described as 'a one-sided offensive by heavily-armed HVO' (Croatian Defence Council) 'soldiers or paramilitaries against unarmed civilian men, women and children' (paragraph 200). Mention was also made of witnesses finding 'burnt bodies', including of children (paragraphs 185 and 188), and of the use of 'fragmentation bullets' against civilians, including children (paragraph 239).[44]

Law: As regards the law in this case, there is again no specific mention of the law relating to either child soldiers or child civilians. However, there is reference to *military training*—eg in defence of the HVO, it was argued that 'the HVO soldiers received instruction on the laws of war' (paragraph 128), including a seminar organised by the ICRC (p 44, n 129)!

In the course of its Legal Findings, the Tribunal did emphasise the violations committed against children, and once more seemed to view these as constituting *aggravating circumstances*. The Tribunal stated, eg, that:

'[o]n 16 April 1993, in a matter of few hours, some 116 inhabitants, including women and children, of Ahmici, a small village in central Bosnia, were killed and about 24 were wounded; 169 houses and two mosques were destroyed. The victims were Muslim civilians. The Trial Chamber is satisfied ... that this was not a combat operation. Rather, it was a well-planned and well-organised killing of civilian members of an ethnic group, the Muslims, by the military of another ethnic group, the Croats ...' (paragraph 749). 'The attack was carried out in an indescribably cruel manner, sparing not even the lives of women and small children. The many bodies of civilians found in the village after the attack, specially those of very young children, the wholesale destruction of Muslim—and only of Muslim—houses and even the destruction of the livestock of the Muslim families, do not match the picture the Defence tried to paint, which was that of a military battle between two armies' (paragraph 762). '... Above all the intentional killing of children, at least one of which was only three months old, cannot be reconciled with the view that this was an action demanded and guided by strategic or tactical necessities ...' (paragraph 762).

Sentence: The Trial Chamber sentenced the accused as follows: Zoran Kupreskic—ten years imprisonment; Mirjan Kupreskic—eight years imprisonment; Vlatko Kupreskic—six years imprisonment; Drago Josipovic—15 years imprisonment; Dragan Papic—acquitted, Vladimir Santic—25 years.

The above sentences were later either overturned or reduced by the Appeals Chamber,[45] although the pertinent facts as outlined above were not in issue. The Appeals Chamber based its sentencing decisions on various grounds, including certain procedural challenges, and the fact that in some instances it was unsafe to rely on identification evidence given by a single witness. The amended sentences were: Zoran Kupreskic, Mirjan Kupreskic, and Vlatko Kupreskic—convictions reversed, released immediately; Drago Josipovic—12 years imprisonment; Dragan Papic—acquitted, Vladimir Santic—18 years.

iii   The Prosecutor v Dragoljub Kunarac, Radomir Kovac, and Zoran Vukovic ('The rape camp case')[46]

Facts: This case concerned the Serbian occupation of the city and municipality of Foca, during the armed conflict between the Bosnian Serbs and the Bosnian Muslims, from early 1992 to mid-1993. The accused, all Serbs, were charged with violations of the laws and customs of war and with crimes against humanity committed against Bosnian Muslims, including torture, rape, enslavement and outrages upon personal dignity. Issues of command responsibility were raised particularly as regards one of the accused, Kunarac.

Reference to Child Soldiers
There is no explicit reference to child soldiers.

Reference to Child Civilians
This case contains a large number of references to violations committed against child civilians, not least because many of those raped and otherwise abused[47] by the

accused were under the age of 18. The witnesses in this trial included rape victims aged between 15 and 17 at the time of the offences (see eg Evidence, Section III (B) 2: (a)(i) re witness FWS-87, paragraphs 53-75; (e)(i) re witness FWS–50, paragraphs 235-244; (f)(i) re witness FWS–191, paragraphs 254-272; (g)(i) re witness FWS–186, paragraphs 284-293); h(i) re witness FWS–190, paragraphs 297-305; (l)(i) re witness FWS–175, paragraphs 368-376). Most of these witnesses were raped repeatedly, by numerous soldiers, over a period of months (see eg paragraphs 37, 63, 73, 81, 117, 174).

Evidence was also taken from certain protected witnesses regarding physical abuse and rape, but the ages of these witnesses are not mentioned in the evidence (see eg paragraph 28), and it is possible that they included some who were under 18 at the time. In addition, in the evidence it emerged that one of the girls who was raped, subsequently sold to Montenegrin soldiers and still missing at the time of trial, was only 12 at the time of these events (see eg paragraphs 42, 63 and 75). Throughout the evidence, reference is made to the victims of the rapes as 'girls', or 'women and girls', thereby repeatedly emphasising their youth (see eg paragraphs 28, 35, 36, 37, 39, 40, 41, 56, 63, 67, 68, 81, 83, 174, 178, etc)

Further, during attacks on various localities, the evidence describes child civilians as among those 'brutalised, beaten and sometimes even killed' (paragraph 24, regarding an attack on a village where none of those attacked had weapons, 'and a lot of children were among this group of people'). Mention is also made of conditions in some of the places of detention, where, in addition to the fear and actuality of rape, there were 'no hygiene facilities and even less food', so that '[d]etainees, in particular children, were affected by this regime' (paragraph 30).[48]

Law: The ICTY made legal history in this case by handing down the first convictions of rape and enslavement as crimes against humanity.[49]

In discussing the Applicable Law (Section IV) the Judgment referred directly to *children, and the law relating to them*. For example, it described the enslavement charges as relating 'solely to the treatment of women and children … and [their] forced or compulsory labour or service …' (paragraph 516); it referred to provisions of 1977 GP II and 1949 GC IV, concerning 'minimum protections to be extended to civilians, in particular women and children, to whom special protection is consistently granted' (paragraph 528, and see paragraphs 529 and 531), and it cited the 1989 CRC as specifically forbidding 'trafficking in children' (paragraph 536).

In its Findings (Section V), the Tribunal described its approach to the evidence of witnesses who were minors at the time (paragraph 565), emphasising that their difficulties in recalling events in detail did not generally discredit their evidence. Throughout this section, again, many of those involved in the case are described as 'girls' (eg paragraphs 739, 740, 747, 749-755, 759, etc).

In relation to Sentencing (Section VI), the Tribunal took into account, as *aggravating circumstances*: '(t)he youthful age of certain of the victims of the offences committed by Dragoljub Kunarac' (paragraph 864, specifying their ages); the 'very young age of AB (about twelve years) …' as regards the accused Kovac (paragraph 874), and 'the youthful age of FWS–50—about fifteen and a half years

...' as regards the accused Vukovic (paragraph 879, which also describes as 'an aggravation' that 'his offences were committed against a particularly vulnerable and defenceless girl ...').

The ICTY Press Release on this Judgment contained the full text of its summary, as read out by the presiding Judge at the hearing.[50] In sentencing the accused, the Judge's summary emphasised the *strong views of the Tribunal regarding the treatment of children*, eg describing Kovac's treatment of '12-year-old AB, a helpless little child for whom you showed absolutely no compassion' as '[p]articularly appalling and deplorable' (p 8).[51]

The Judge's summary also dealt with the issue of *responsibility*, pointing out that in the ICTY cases it was 'generally desirable to prosecute and try those in the higher echelons of power'. However, although the three accused were not 'political or military masterminds ...', the ICTY would 'not accept low rank or a subordinate function as an escape from criminal prosecution' (p 3). As regards Kunarac, the Judge stated that he was '... somebody whom your men undisputedly are said to have held in high esteem. By this natural authority you could easily have put an end to the women's suffering. Your active participation ... is therefore even more repugnant' (p 6).

Sentence: Dragoljub Kunarac was sentenced to 28 years imprisonment, Radomir Kovac, to 20 years imprisonment and Zoran Vukovic, to 12 years imprisonment.[52]

The three cases described above indicate that the ICTY took account, as regards both fact and law, of the particular seriousness of offences committed against children. It is not necessary to labour this point further here, but it is worth noting that there have been other ICTY cases that categorise violations against children as 'aggravating circumstances', and/or generally address the issue of military conduct towards children.[53]

The ICTR, too, has heard some cases concerning violations of international law committed against children, among others, and one such case is briefly discussed below. Although this particular case concerns the acts of a political figure—and not a military commander—it again illustrates the approach taken by an international tribunal to: a) violations committed against children, and b) responsibility of superiors for acts of their subordinates, whether civil or military—and the case explicitly links the latter two categories.

Cases—ICTR

The Prosecutor v Jean-Paul Akayesu[54]

Facts: This case concerned the responsibility of Akayesu, the former mayor of Taba commune in Rwanda, for the killing of, and other acts of violence towards, members of the Tutsi community by Hutu Interahamwe (militia) in 1994. These acts included ordering, instigating, aiding and abetting murder, torture and acts of sexual violence, amounting to, *inter alia*, crimes against humanity and genocide.

In respect of these acts, Akayesu was, among other things, found individually responsible for genocide and crimes against humanity (Judgment, Verdict).

Reference to Child Soldiers

Many children did participate in the Rwandan massacres in 1994 as members of the Interahamwe.[55] The Akayesu case does not directly address this issue, but indirect reference is made in repeatedly describing as 'young' an Interahamwe fighter who was killed by the people of the Taba commune, after he had killed a Tutsi teacher (see eg paragraphs 211, 215, 326, 331, 336, 359, 360, 673(i)).

Reference to Child Civilians

There are numerous references in this case to child civilians as victims of all forms of violence, including rape and genocide.

In describing the Historical Context of the Events in Rwanda in 1994, eg, the Judgment states that 'the killing of Tutsi which henceforth spared neither women nor children continued up to 18 July 1994 ...' (paragraph 111).[56] A number of witnesses gave evidence of the massive scale of the death and injury of children, among others, in Rwanda during this period. In addition to evidence of victims of the attacks, (eg Witness JJ (paragraph 422), and Witness OO (paragraph 426)), evidence was given by eg, Dr Zachariah, of Médecins Sans Frontiers, who described how, 'on the way to the border ... he had crossed streams and rivers in which the mutilated corpses of men, women and children floated by at an estimated rate of five bodies every minute' (paragraph 159).[57] Akayesu himself confirmed that the killing started on 19 April 1994 in his region, when 'the Interahamwe had killed a good number of people, who had sought refuge ..., including elderly people, women and children' (paragraph 355).

The Judgment emphasised that 'even newborn babies were not spared. Even pregnant women, including those of Hutu origin, were killed on the grounds that the foetuses in their wombs were fathered by Tutsi men' (paragraph 121).[58] Further, 'the Tutsi were killed solely on account of having been born Tutsi' (paragraph 124).

The Judgment also found that during the events of 1994 'Tutsi girls and women were subjected to sexual violence, beaten and killed ... in the commune of Taba ...' (paragraph 449). In its Findings, the Tribunal repeatedly referred to 'the rape of girls and women ...'—again, as in the *Kunarac* case, using the term 'girl' to emphasise the youth of the victims (eg paragraphs 391, 403, 416, 403, 421, 422, 429, 430, 433, 444, 445, 452, 692, 694, 696, 697 and 731). Details were given of various specific incidents, including '... the testimony of Witness J, a Tutsi woman, who stated that her six year-old daughter had been raped by three Interahamwe when they came to kill her father' (paragraph 416), and the evidence of Witness JJ, who testified '... that the Interahamwe took young girls and women from their site of refuge ... into a forest in the area and raped them. Witness JJ testified that ... she could not count the total number of times she was raped ...' (paragraph 421), and of 'hearing the cries of young girls around her, girls as young as twelve or thirteen years old' (paragraph 422).[59]

Law: In considering the question of *'Genocide* in Rwanda?', and assessing the massacres' 'scale, their systematic nature and their atrociousness', the ICTR judgment stressed that:

> these people had the intention of completely wiping out the Tutsi from Rwanda so that—as they said on certain occasions—their children, later on, would not know what a Tutsi looked like, unless they referred to history books (paragraph 118).

It concluded that

> ... genocide was, indeed, committed in Rwanda in 1994 against the Tutsi as a group' (paragraph 126). In support of that conclusion, the Tribunal found, *inter alia*, that 'the majority of the Tutsi victims were non-combatants, including thousands of women and children, even foetuses' (paragraph 128).[60]

This case also addressed the issue of the *responsibility* of Akayesu, as a government official, for the acts of his subordinates. It specifically made the analogy between someone in his position and a military commander, thereby making it absolutely clear that military commanders would have been held accountable in similar circumstances. For example, in analysing the law relating to charges under Article 4 of the ICTR Statute (violations of 1977 GP II and of Common Article 3 of the 1949 GCs), the Tribunal stated:

> The four Geneva Conventions—as well as the two Additional Protocols ... were adopted primarily to protect the victims as well as potential victims of armed conflicts .... The category of persons to be held accountable in this respect then, would in most cases be limited to commanders, combatants and other members of the armed forces. Due to the overall protective and humanitarian purpose of these international legal instruments, however, the delimitation of this category of persons bound by the provisions in Common Article 3 and Additional Protocol II should not be too restricted. The duties and responsibilities of the Geneva Conventions and the Additional Protocols, hence, will normally apply only to individuals of all ranks belonging to the armed forces under the military command of either of the belligerent parties, or to individuals who were legitimately mandated and expected, as public officials or agents or persons otherwise holding public authority or *de facto* representing the Government, to support or fulfil the war efforts. The objective of this approach, thus, would be to apply the provisions of the Statute in a fashion which corresponds best with the underlying protective purpose of the Conventions and the Protocols, (paragraphs 630–631) ... [I]t is clear from the above that the laws of war must apply equally to civilians as to combatants in the conventional sense' (paragraph 634).

Sentence: Akayesu was sentenced to life imprisonment.[61]

This case demonstrates that the ICTR, like the ICTY, took into account violations committed against children, both in terms of the facts and the applicable law.

That said, all four cases outlined in this section—as well as others that have been heard by the ICTY and the ICTR—indicate that in some circumstances military personnel and others in positions of power commit violations in vast numbers and with scant regard for any limiting factors. However, they also indicate an increasing resolve on the part of some international actors to address the issue of impunity for such violations. As mentioned above, these cases can therefore be cited as examples, and discussed in military training, as an indication that international courts do take account of violations committed against children, and of command responsibility for such violations.

In summary, this Chapter touches on a number of key issues—concerning land-mines, command responsibility and culpability, and war crimes trials—that should be incorporated in general IHL military training. In the context of military training concerning children, the particular relevance of these three issues should be high-lighted to emphasise, *inter alia*: a) the particular impact of landmines on children; b) that rules on command responsibility and culpability incorporate and sometimes specifically apply to the treatment of children, and c) that war crimes trials increas-ingly take a serious view of violations committed against children.

Endnotes

1   See UN Doc S/RES/808 (22 Feb 1993), Resolution on the Establishment of an Interna-tional Tribunal for the former Yugoslavia, and UN Doc S/RES/955 (8 Nov 1994), Resolu-tion on the establishment of an International Tribunal for Rwanda and Adoption of the Statute of the Tribunal.

2   Similar prohibitions can also be found in various other IHL instruments, starting with the 1868 St Petersburg Declaration Renouncing the Use, in Time of War, of Explosive Projectiles Under 400 Grammes Weight, 18 Martens Nouveau Recueil (ser 1) 474, 138 Consol TS 297, entered into force 29 Nov/11 Dec 1868.

3   Convention on Prohibitions or Restrictions on the Use of Certain Conventional Weapons Which may be Deemed to be Excessively Injurious or to have Indiscriminate Effects, and Protocols, UN Doc A/Conf.95/15, Annex I (1980), entered into force 2 Dec, 1983.

4   See eg, de Mulinen (1987), pp 924–930, and 936–938.

5   For example, a recent report on young people in Kosovo reported that one of their major fears concerned landmines and unexploded ordnance (WCRWC (2001), p 2). This fear was well founded, as there were apparently millions of such weapons in Kosovo. For example, between 1 June 1999 and 20 Sept 2000, of the 516 people killed or injured by these weapons, 199 were between the ages of 10 and 19 (*Ibid*, p 39).

6   Convention on the Prohibition of the Use, Stockpiling, Production and Transfer of Anti-Personnel Mines and on their Destruction, Ottawa, Sept 1997, 36 ILM (1997) 1507–19. By 31 Dec 2002, 130 States had ratified this treaty.

There remain some loopholes in this ban. For example, the 'Ottawa Convention' does not deal with anti-tank mines as such, and therefore only covers anti-tank mines that detonate in the same way as anti-personnel mines (Roberts and Guelff (2000), p 647).

7   See eg, S Wright, 'A Worse Fate Still to Come?' 3 *Landmine Action Campaign* (2001), pp 4–5.

8   See Ch 1, n 26.

9   Machel (1996), para 111, citing statistics from the UN Dept of Humanitarian Affairs.

10   This report stated that of the 70,000 largely landmine-related amputees in Angola, 8,000 were children. *Ibid*, para 112.

11   *Ibid*, quoting from J Williams, *The Protection of Children Against Landmines and Unexploded Ordnance* (Washington DC, Vietnam Veterans of America Foundation, 1996), p 1.

12   See ECOWAS/CEDEAO and SC S West Africa Regional Office, (2001), p 39.

13   Machel (1996), paras 113–118. See also the second 'Machel Report' (Machel (2000)) emphasising that 'Children's right to adequate nutrition and living standards is compromised when fields, pastures, factories and workplaces cannot be used' due to the placement of mines (p 26).

14   *Note*: the prohibitions in the 1980 Weapons Convention did not originally extend to non-international armed conflict, or to the manufacture or transfer of the specified weapons, and therefore further treaties were enacted to address those issues (see text).

15   Protocol on Prohibitions or Restrictions on the Use of Mines, Booby-Traps and Other Devices, as amended (Protocol II to the 1980 Weapons Convention, as amended on 3 May 1996), GA res 51/89, adopted 8 Jan 1997.

16   It does not extend to internal disturbances and tensions (eg riots, isolated acts of violence) (Art 2).

17   This Convention also specifically provides for measures to promote physical and psychological recovery and reintegration for child victims of, *inter alia*, armed conflict (Art 39), which directly applies to victims of land mines.

18   See eg, L Zecchini, 'Afghanistan's Mine Menace', *Guardian Weekly* (25–31 Oct 2001), regarding the 'tens of millions of mines' in Afghanistan, largely left by Soviet forces in 1989, and including '"butterfly" mines, or mines hidden in dolls or pens, which were particularly tempting for children'.

19   This role can take the form of presentations by military personnel themselves, or such personnel can encourage and facilitate the work of others with experience of mine-awareness programmes, such as UNICEF, SC and the ICRC. See references to mine-awareness work of SC in Machel (1996) para 122, and of UNICEF in Machel (2000), p 27. The ICRC conducts mine awareness programmes in many countries, some of which have a specific focus on children (see ICRC, *Special Report: Mine Action* (Geneva, ICRC, 1999), pp 36 and 40).

20   For recent articles on this issue generally, see eg, E Greppi, 'The Evolution of Criminal Responsibility under International Law', 81:835 *IRRC* (1999), pp 531–553, and G. Dufour, 'La défense d'ordres supérieurs existe-t-elle vraiment?' 82:840 *IRRC* (2000), pp 969–992. See also eg, A Mitchell, 'Failure to Halt, Prevent or Punish: The Doctrine of Command Responsibility for War Crimes', 22:3 *Sydney L Rev* (2000), pp 382–410. This article, *inter alia*, discusses the distinction between 'superior orders' and 'command responsibility', and proposes adoption of a more precise formulation of the doctrine of command responsibility.

21   For a useful summary of IHL regarding 'criminal responsibility' of military personnel, including as regards superior orders, see Rogers (1996), pp 130–148. He points out, *inter alia*, that '[l]iability is clear if the commander commits a war crime himself or orders the

commission of a war crime, but very often his responsibility will be less sharply defined because he will be remote from the scene of the crime or from those who have committed it.' (*Ibid*, (1996), p 130). See also C Greenwood, ('Command and the Laws of Armed Conflict' (Camberley, SCSI, Occasional Paper no 4, 1993), (hereafter (1993(b)), p 1), who states that the laws of armed conflict 'are of the greatest importance to the commander. If he orders his troops to take action contrary to the Geneva Conventions or any of the other laws of armed conflict … he exposes them to the risk of reprisals by the enemy and makes himself liable to trial as a war criminal.'

22 See eg, M Griffin, 'Ending the Impunity of Perprtrators of Human Rights Atrocities: A Major Challenge for International Law in the 21st Century', 838 *IRRC* (2000), pp 369–389; M Lattimer and P Sands, *Justice for Crimes Against Humanity* (Oxford, O.U.P, 2001), and S R Ratner and J S Abrams, *Accountability for Human Rights Atrocities in International Law* (Oxford, OUP, 2001). The efforts that were made by the US to avoid possible ICC trials of US citizens also rather perversely attest to this new climate of accountability. See eg, I Traynor, 'East Europeans Torn on the Rack by International Court Row', *The Guardian*, (17 Aug 2002), and UN Doc S/RES/1422 (12 July 2002), on UN Peacekeeping.

23 Again, despite the fact that many of these provisions are not child-specific, they clearly apply to offences committed against children, among others.

24 See Judgment in the '*Celebici Case*' (*The Prosecutor v Delalic et al* ('*Celebici*'), Case No IT-96-21-T, Trial Chamber, 16 November 1998), paras 338–343.

25 These were preceded, eg, by the 'Charter of the International Military Tribunal' (Agreement for the Prosecution and Punishment of the Major War Criminals of the European Axis (London Agreement), 8 Aug, 1945, 58 Stat 1544, EAS No 472, 82 UNTS 280) which explicitly provided for individual responsibility for crimes against peace, war crimes and crimes against humanity (Art 6).

26 Rogers (1996), p 142 emphasises that Art 87(2) of 1977 GP I makes it clear 'that the responsibility for instructing others in the law of war is not limited to those who are involved in running formal courses'.

27 See eg, Roberts and Guelff (2000), pp 566–567.

28 The ICTY has jurisdiction over persons committing grave breaches of the 1949 GCs (Art 2), violations of the laws or customs of war (Art 3), genocide (Art 4) and/or crimes against humanity (Art 5). The definition of genocide specifically includes the forcible transfer to another group of children of a group targeted for intentional destruction (Art 4(2)(e)).

29 The ICTR has jurisdiction over genocide (Art 2, defined as above, n 28), crimes against humanity (Art 3), and violations of 1977 GP II (Art 4) and Common Art 3 of the 1949 GCs. As pointed out in Roberts and Guelff (2000), p 617, '[t]he major innovation in the ICTR Statute was the express extension of international criminality to such violations'.

30 The offences covered in the ICC Statute include genocide (Art 6); crimes against humanity (Art 7); war crimes (Art 8) (the latter two offences defined more broadly than in the equivalent articles in the ICTY and ICTR Statutes), and, at a future stage, the crime of aggression (Art 5(1)(d) and (2)). Arts 6, 7 and parts of 8 apply to both international and internal armed conflicts. The child-specific provisions include the definition of genocide (Art 6(e) as defined in the ICTY Statute); the categorisation of trafficking in children as enslavement, a crime against humanity (Art 7(2)(c)), and the prohibition on the use of soldiers under the age of 15 (Arts 8(2)(b)(xxvi) and 8(2)(e)(vii)). Other crimes particularly pertinent to children include rape, sexual slavery and other forms of sexual violence (Arts 7(1)(g), 8(2)(b)(xxii) and 8(2)(e)(vi)), and intentional attacks against buildings dedicated to education (Arts 8(2)(b)(ix) and 8(2)(e)(iv)). (As regards child-specific provisions in

the 1998 Statute of the ICC generally, see CICC, *The International Criminal Court and Child Victims of Genocide, War Crimes and Crimes Against Humanity* (New York, CICC, 2001)).

31 Provision is also made for a Victims and Witnesses Unit to provide protective measures and other assistance for victims and witnesses at risk on account of their testimony (Art 43(6)).

32 For the dates and status of ratifications, see, http:www.un.org/law/icc. See also eg, AI USA, 'The Rome Statute Enters into Force—A Major Step Towards Ending Impunity for the Worst Crimes', *AI USA Press Release* (30 June 2002) (available at, http:www.amnesty— usa.org/, visited on 1 July 2002), and http://www.iccnow.org/ (visited on 30 Aug 2002) for updated information on the ICC.

33 CRIN (Child Rights Information Network) report, 'Special Session Update No 2', (8 May 2002).

34 Other ICC rules particularly relevant to children, and not summarised in the text here, include: Rule 75(1) (regarding statements by a child witness that might incriminate their parent); Rule 88 (provision for measures to facilitate the testimony of traumatised victims or witnesses, including children); Rule 89(3) (providing that someone acting on behalf of a child victim may apply to participate on their behalf); and Rule 112(4) (providing that, in order to reduce subsequent traumatisation, the Prosecutor may use audio or video recording to question, *inter alia*, a child).

35 See eg, ICTY: *The Prosecutor v Radislav Krstic*, Case No IT-98-33-T, Trial Chamber, 2 Aug 2001, in which General Krstic was found guilty of genocide and sentenced to 46 years of imprisonment. See also, ICTY: *The Prosecutor v Dusko Sikirica et al.*, Case No IT–95–8, Trial Chamber, 13 Nov 2001, in which one of the accused, Sikirica, was sentenced to 15 years of imprisonment for, among other things, murder. Sikirica's crimes were aggravated by his role as Commander of Security within the camp (para 138). See also ICTY: *The Prosecutor v Milosevic et al 'Kosovo'*, Second amended indictment, Case No IT-99-37-PT, 29 Oct 2001; *The Prosecutor v Milosevic "Croatia"*, Initial indictment, Case No IT–50–I, 8 Oct 2001, and *The Prosecutor v Milosevic "Bosnia and Herzegovina"*, Initial indictment, Case No IT–51–I, 22 Nov 2001, in which the former President of the Federal Republic of Yugoslavia, Milosevic, was charged, *inter alia*, with genocide, crimes against humanity, grave breaches of the 1949 GCs, and violations of the laws or customs of war.

36 Also of interest in this context is the Women's International Tribunal on Japanese Military Sexual Slavery, a 'peoples' tribunal' held in 2000. This tribunal heard evidence of the use of 'comfort women', including young girls, by the Japanese army in WW II. It found, *inter alia*, that the 'comfort stations' constituted crimes against humanity under the law then applicable. See C Chinkin, 'Women's International Tribunal on Japanese Military Sexual Slavery', 95:2 *AJIL* (2001), pp 335–341.

37 See eg, re the Nuremberg Tribunal, Kuper (1997(b)), p 155.

38 Regarding Somalia, see eg, *Elvin Kyle Brown v Her Majesty the Queen*, Court Martial Appeal Court of Canada, Judgment, 6 Jan 1995, (CMAC 372) concerning the killing of a 16-year-old Somali youth by Canadian peacekeepers in 1993. Regarding Vietnam, see eg, Court-Martial of William J Calley, Jr. Among other things, Calley was charged with killing 'one oriental human being, approximately two years of age' (*United States v Calley*, US Court of Military Appeals (1973) 22 USCMA 534, 48 CMR 19).

39 See eg, Greenwood (1993(b)); Rogers (1995) and I Bantekas, 'The Interests of States versus the Doctrine of Superior Responsibility', 838 *IRRC* (2000), pp 391–402.

40 *The Prosecutor v Tihomir Blaskic* , Case No IT–95–14–T, Trial Chamber, 3 March 2000.

41 See eg, para 416, 'other bodies were found in the houses so badly charred they could not be identified and in positions suggesting that they had been burned alive. The victims included many women and children. The British UNPROFOR battalion reported that: "[o]f the 89 bodies which have been recovered from the village, most are those of elderly people, women, children and infants". An ECMM observer said he had seen the bodies of children who from their position, seemed to have died in agony in the flames ....'

42 For discussion of command responsibility specifically in relation to the *Blaskic* case, see M. Feria-Tinta, 'Commanders on Trial: The Blaskic Case and the Doctrine of Command Responsibility Under International Law', XLVII:3 *Netherlands Int'l L. Rev.* (2000), pp 293–322.

43 *The Prosecutor v Zoran Kupreskic, Mirjan Kupreskic, Vlatko Kupreskic, Drago Josipovic, Dragan Papic, Vladimir Santic, also known as 'Vlado'*, Case No IT–95–16–T, Trial Chamber, 14 Jan 2000.

44 This para stated, *inter alia*: '... they appeared to be using fragmentation bullets. Witness T described how the bullets prevented her from helping her two and a half year old child Maida, who had been shot and was apparently injured, with blood running down her face: "... from the shooting I couldn't help her, because bullets were falling all around her, and the bullets—the earth would be—shot up into the air when the bullet touched it. There were bullets all around and bullets going into the tree trunks" ' (para 239).

45 *The Prosecutor v Zoran Kupreskic, Mirjan Kupreskic, Vlatko Kupreskic, Drago Josipovic, Dragan Papic, Vladimir Santic, also known as 'Vlado'*, Case No IT–95–16–A, Appeals Chamber, 23 Oct 2001.

46 *The Prosecutor v Dragoljub Kunarac, Radomir Kovac and Zoran Vukovic*, Case No IT–96–23–T and IT–96–23/1-T, Trial Chamber, 22 Feb 2001.

47 In addition to general ill-treatment, such as beatings and inadequate food and shelter, the abuse included eg being threatened with murder, locked up without any contact with the outside world (para 68), and being made, at gun point, to dance naked on a table (para 71).

48 This para (30) describes conditions in Partizan Sports Hall, where one witness described the rape of the woman next to her 'in full view of the other detainees and her ten-year old son ...'.

49 J Mertus, 'Judgment of Trial Chamber II in the Kunarac, Kovac and Vukovic Case', *ASIL Insights* (March 2001), and A Osborn, 'Mass Rape Ruled a War Crime: Hague Tribunal Finds Serbs Guilty of Systematic Enslavement and Torture of Bosnian Muslim Women', *The Guardian* (23 Feb 2001).

50 See, http://www.un.org/icty/pressreal/p566-e.htm, visited on 12 March 2001.

51 Vukovic, too, was criticised for raping Witness FWS–50, who 'was 15 years old at the time, which you knew ...' (p 9).

52 The three defendants in this case appealed against their convictions and sentences, but their appeals were dismissed. ICTY Appeals Chamber: *Prosecutor v Kunarac, et al.* Case No IT–96–23 and IT–96–23/1–A (12 June 2002).

53 As regards findings of 'aggravating circumstances', see eg, *The Prosecutor v Anto Furundzija*, Case No IT-95-17/1-T, Trial Chamber, 10 Dec 1998, para 283 (confirmed in Case No IT–95–17/1–A, 21 July 2000, Judgment of the Appeals Chamber); *The Prosecutor v Dusko Tadíc*, Case No IT–94–1–T, Trial Chamber, 14 July 1997, Sentencing Judgment, para 56, and *The Prosecutor v Delalic et al.* (*'Celebici'*), Case No IT–96–21–T, Trial Chamber, 16 Nov 1998, para 1268. More generally, see eg, *The Prosecutor v Dario Kordic*

and *Mario Cerkez*, Case No IT–95–14/2–T, Trial Chamber, 26 Feb 2001, paras 718, 744, 754, 755.

54 *The Prosecutor v Jean-Paul Akayesu*, Case No ICTR–96–4–T, Trial Chamber, 2 Sept 1998.

55 See eg, CSC (2001), p 315.

56 This section also mentions the role of the media in anti-Tutsi propaganda. It cites one politician, involved in such propaganda, who encouraged participants at a meeting in 1992 'to avoid the error of earlier massacres during which some Tutsi, particularly children, were spared' (para 100).

57 He also witnessed 'on 22 April 1994, the aftermath of the massacre of the family of a moderate Hutu … by the Presidential Guard, and, on the same day, the killings of children in the Hotel Pascal in Butare and the executions of tens of Tutsi patients and nurses in Butare Hospital, including a Hutu nurse who was pregnant by a Tutsi man and whose child would therefore be Tutsi' (para 159). S Cox, a cameraman and photographer, also saw evidence of massacres of 'mostly Tutsi' (para 161). L Hilson, a journalist, described the situation in Kigali central hospital as '"absolutely terrible", wounded men, women and children of all ages were packed into the wards, and hospital gutters were "running red with blood"' (para 160).

58 In this context, Akayesu apparently cited a proverb indicating that normally it was considered taboo to attack a pregnant woman, but that in exceptional circumstances, such as those prevailing at the time, the taboo could be ignored (para 121). One pregnant Tutsi witness who appealed to Akayesu for help stated that 'he replied that … "when rats are killed you don't spare rats that are still in the form of fetus"'. She later miscarried after being beaten (para 428). See also C McGreal, 'Rwandan guilty of genocide', *The Guardian* (3 Sept 1998).

59 Witness JJ also 'testified to the humiliation she felt as a mother, by the public nudity and being raped in the presence of children by young men' (para 423). See also eg, paras 428 and 430 (the rape of girls in the presence of their mother).

60 One witness referred to the comment made by a Rwandan Armed Forces soldier to those 'persecuting' her and her children, that '… you are killing children, although children know nothing: they have never done politics' (para 128).

61 *The Prosecutor v Jean-Paul Akayesu*, Case No ICTR–96–4–T, Trial Chamber, Sentence, 2 Oct 1998. This judgment was confirmed by the Appeals Chamber (1 June 2001).

6

Part I(A)(2)—Law and Policy: Obligations of Governments—Treaty Law, 'Soft Law', and the Committee on the Rights of the Child

Introduction

Part I(A)(1) above has outlined the content of international law relevant to the training of *officers*, and various implementation mechanisms. It aimed to answer the questions: a) what are the rules and standards of conduct, specifically regarding the treatment of children, that are pertinent to the training of officers of national armed forces? and b) what are the main legal mechanisms (which should also be referred to in training) for encouraging compliance?

Part I(A)(2) below will outline the body of law and policy that places on *governments* the obligation to ensure that their armed forces receive this training. It aims to answer the question: what are the obligations of states to provide pertinent IHL and human rights training for their military personnel—in particular, for officers of their national armed forces? This part of the book is therefore of particular relevance to those involved in government and the formulation of policy.

The starting point here is that states are obliged to comply with customary international law regarding armed conflict, and with pertinent IHL and international human rights treaties that they have ratified. Many states do, of course, frequently and catastrophically fail to fulfil these obligations, as already mentioned. Nonetheless, limited compliance is sometimes achieved—and it is essential to achieving (and, ideally, increasing) such compliance that states disseminate and provide training in the applicable law for their military personnel who bear ultimate responsibility for the conduct of armed conflict.[1]

Indeed, compliance with the relevant obligations can have other significant advantages. For example, adherence to IHL rules, even if it may prolong the conflict, may, in the words of one authority, 'help to attain other objects. The conflict is being fought in order to achieve peace. That may be easier if there is little of the bitterness usually produced by atrocities'.[2]

Moreover, it is arguable that the duty of states to provide IHL training for their armed forces is itself a customary law principle, (eg in accordance with 1907 Hague Convention IV (see below), widely considered as customary).[3]

The discussion below will first consider pertinent IHL treaty provisions regarding state obligations, before outlining those in human rights law. It will then briefly examine 'soft law' provisions, and the role of the Committee on the Rights of the Child.

Treaty Law[4]

a)   IHL

The dissemination and military training obligations placed on states, as set out in IHL and related law, do not specifically focus on children (other than those in the 1989 CRC), and therefore once more only some of the main relevant provisions will be briefly summarised below.[5]

Starting with the earlier IHL treaties—under *1907 Hague Convention IV*, (Article 1), ratifying states 'shall issue instructions to their armed land forces which shall be in conformity with the Regulations' annexed to it. Under the widely-ratified *1949 GCs* (Article 1), ratifying states 'undertake to respect and to ensure respect' for these treaties 'in all circumstances'—thereby implying a dissemination and training obligation. (Indeed, the duty to 'respect and ensure respect' could be interpreted, in relation to military training, to mean an obligation to ensure adequate training of a country's own armed forces, and, where possible, to assist or encourage the training of armed forces belonging to other countries.[6]) The 1949 GCs also contain specific articles regarding the duty of states (with the assistance of organisations such as the ICRC) to widely disseminate, and provide training (to military personnel among others) on, their provisions (as in 1949 GC IV, Article 144).[7]

The relevant measures in *1977 GP I* are analogous to those of the 1949 GCs in: a) providing that states undertake to 'respect and ensure respect' for this treaty (Article 1), and b) containing specific Articles regarding the duty of states, (in conjunction with the ICRC and others), to disseminate, and train their armed forces (among others) on, its contents (see eg, Articles 81, 82 and 83). However, 1977 GP I goes further than 1949 GC IV in various respects, including in that it expressly provides, 'also in peacetime', for collaboration between ratifying states and the ICRC (and related organisations) in training 'qualified personnel' on the 1949 GCs and 1977 GP I (Article 6). Moreover, Article 82 of 1977 GP I makes provision for legal advisers to guide military commanders on, *inter alia*, training.[8]

As regards other important IHL treaties that articulate state obligations concerning military training:[9] the *1977 GP II* provisions are brief, stating only that 'This Protocol shall be disseminated as widely as possible' (Article 19), and the *1980 Weapons Convention* also obliges states to disseminate, and train the military on, its provisions (Article 6).

Looking now at child-specific state obligations pertinent to military training, the *1989 CRC* provides, *inter alia,* that ratifying states 'shall respect and ensure the rights set forth in this Convention' to all children in their jurisdiction, without discrimination (Article 2); that they 'shall undertake all … measures, for the implementation of the rights recognized in this Convention' (Article 4); and that they should 'make the principles and provisions of the Convention widely known … to adults and children alike' (Article 42). These provisions make clear the duty of states to disseminate and train on the contents of the 1989 CRC, including all the IHL provisions relevant to the protection of children, which are incorporated into Article 38.[10] The *2000 Optional Protocol on Child Soldiers*, too, obliges ratifying states to train military personnel on its provisions (see particularly Articles 6, 7,and 8).[11]

The above brief summary indicates that ratifying states have a wide range of treaty obligations to provide IHL and relevant human rights training for their military personnel, including such training specifically regarding children.

b)   *International Human Rights Law*

States involved in armed conflict are also obliged—under both treaty and customary law—to comply with basic international human rights norms (see Chapter Two regarding, in particular, the entitlement of children to special treatment; the 'right to life' and the prohibition on torture). As already mentioned (Chapter Two), these norms apply particularly in situations that fall below the level of an 'armed conflict', or where the categorisation of a conflict is unclear or disputed. Once more, it is essential, in working towards compliance, that states fulfil their duty to ensure dissemination of, and training in, the relevant human rights law for their military personnel.

This duty is set out, explicitly or implicitly, in, *inter alia*: the *1948 Genocide Convention* (Article V)[12] and the *1966 ICCPR* (Article 2, which, again, calls for states to 'respect and ensure' the ICCPR rights to persons within their jurisdiction).[13] The *1984 CAT* (Article 10(1)) expressly provides that ratifying states must ensure:

> that education and information regarding the prohibition against torture are fully included in the training of law enforcement personnel, civil or military … and other persons who may be involved in the custody, interrogation or treatment of any individual subjected to any form of arrest, detention or imprisonment.[14]

See also the dissemination obligations set out in the *1989 CRC* (as above, regarding IHL)—which combines both human rights law and IHL in one treaty.

Derogation
In the words of one authority, human rights derogations 'allow suspension or breach of certain obligations in circumstances of war or public emergency'.[15] However, derogation is only allowed 'to the extent strictly required by the exigencies of the situation' (as stated, eg, in 1966 ICCPR, Article 4(1)). Further, a number of

provisions of human rights law (such as the 'right to life') remain non-derogable in all circumstances.

As regards children in armed conflict, the issue of derogation from human rights law has been analysed elsewhere.[16] Suffice it to say here that the key human rights principles relevant to such children are non-derogable and therefore continue to apply at all times. Thus, under human rights law, in situations of conflict states are obliged to ensure, *inter alia,* that children remain entitled to special treatment, and to protection from arbitrary deprivation of life, from enslavement and from torture and other gratuitous ill-treatment.

Further, it is arguable that, since the 1989 CRC does not contain a derogation clause, it continues to apply as a whole to children in times of conflict as well as peace, and therefore as far as possible children remain entitled to all its provisions in all circumstances.[17]

The influential Human Rights Committee, established under the 1966 ICCPR, has recently issued a 'General Comment' (No 29) on its Article 4, regarding derogation.[18] Although General Comment No 29 applies specifically to the ICCPR, it sheds light on the nature of derogation more generally. It emphasises that derogation measures 'must be of an exceptional and temporary nature …', and that:

> two fundamental conditions must be met: the situation must amount to a public emergency which threatens the life of the nation, and the State party must have officially proclaimed a state of emergency' (paragraph 2).

It also states that:

> (d)uring armed conflict, whether international or non-international, rules of international humanitarian law become applicable and help, in addition to the provisions … of the Covenant, to prevent the abuse of a State's emergency powers …' (paragraph 3).

This General Comment further requires that every derogation be 'proportional' (paragraph 4), and reiterates that no derogation is allowed from certain articles, eg concerning the 'right to life' and prohibition of torture (paragraph 7).[19] Moreover, no derogation 'may be inconsistent with the State party's other obligations under international law, particularly the rules of international humanitarian law' (paragraph 9).

Thus the right to derogate from human rights provisions remains strictly circumscribed, and arguably does not apply to the key measures applicable to children, even in situations of conflict. States therefore cannot escape their obligations to children under international human rights law, and must ensure that their military and other relevant personnel are trained accordingly.

'Soft' Law

As outlined above, states are obliged, under IHL and human rights treaty rules, to encourage compliance with these rules through, *inter alia*, the provision of training on the relevant law (including that concerning children) for officers and others in their national armed forces.

In addition, particularly in recent years, various resolutions and reports of international organisations, most notably the UN, have emphasised the destructive impact of armed conflict on children (and the subsequent potentially destabilising effect of these children on society generally), and have, *inter alia,* encouraged states to provide child-specific military training as one strategy to ameliorate this. Many of these initiatives fall into the category of 'soft law', described by one authority as instruments that, while 'not *per se* legally binding, ... may well have a number of legally relevant effects ...'.[20] It is arguable that some of the pertinent UN resolutions can be considered binding in international law. These include, particularly, UN Security Council resolutions,[21] and, possibly, UN General Assembly resolutions that are unanimously adopted.[22]

A number of the pertinent documents have resulted from the Security Council's now annual debate on children in armed conflict, held on 20 November, International Children's Day. On that occasion in 2001 the Security Council was addressed, for the first time in its history, by a former child soldier (from Sierra Leone).[23]

States therefore need to be broadly aware of these developments, including those regarding military training. Indeed, states may be under increasing pressure to take account of these developments, since some of the more recent UN resolutions[24] propose taking action against states that ignore their duties to children in armed conflict, and they set out specific enforcement measures for this purpose.

a) Impact of Armed Conflict on Children

UN resolutions and reports that refer to children in armed conflict generally mention the hardships faced by such children, thereby drawing attention to this issue, its effect on society, and the need for the proposed action. This is the backdrop against which pressure is mounting for states to provide improved military training.

A few examples of UN documents referring to the impact on children of armed conflict are: a) the report of the UN Secretary-General, considered during the Special Session of the General Assembly on Children, held in May 2002;[25] b) UN Security Council resolution S/RES/ 1397(2001), (which, *inter alia,* recognises 'the harmful and widespread impact of armed conflict on children and the long-term consequences this has for durable peace, security and development,' (preamble), and expresses 'its determination to give the fullest attention to ... the protection of children in armed conflict ...' (paragraph 1), before going on to propose a number of measures to enhance such protection (discussed further below));[26] c) other UN resolutions that focus on specific countries, such as UN General Assembly resolution A/56/281 regarding Sierra Leone,[27] and d) various reports by Olara Otunnu, including his Annual General Reports.[28] Otunnu's 2000 report on 'Protection of children affected by armed conflict' notes the significant number of Security Council debates, resolutions, etc since October 1999 that address 'the protection of war-affected children' and the hardships they face.[29]

Further, a 1998 UN General Assembly Resolution[30] proclaims 2001–2010 as the 'International Decade for a Culture of Peace and Non-Violence for the Children of the World'. Among other things, it acknowledges 'that enormous harm and suffering are caused to children through different forms of violence at every level of society throughout the world' (Preamble).

b)   Special Treatment of Children in Armed Conflict

As well as referring to the impact of armed conflict on children, many of the pertinent international reports and resolutions call for states and others to provide special care for such children, thus emphasising this basic underlying principle, relevant to military training as already discussed. For example, UN Security Council resolution S/RES/1296 (2000) urges parties to conflicts to 'make special arrangements to meet the protection and assistance requirements of women, children and other vulnerable groups …' (paragraph 10).[31]

c)   Training of Military Personnel

Of particular relevance here is the fact that—in addition to referring to the impact of armed conflict on children and their need for special consideration (above)—the UN has also, in various General Assembly resolutions and other initiatives, specifically emphasised the responsibility of states to provide military training concerning children, as one approach to addressing this issue. Thus, eg, a 1997 General Assembly resolution[32] recommends, *inter alia*, that States Parties to the 1989 CRC promote dissemination and awareness of standards on the rights of the child, including 'training activities', as a means of ensuring protection of children in armed conflict (paragraph 18); asks the UN Secretary General, as well as states and international organisations, to consider methods of organising regional training programmes for military personnel regarding the protection of children and women in armed conflict (paragraph 33), and invites governments to integrate instruction into their military programmes on responsibilities to civilians, particularly women and children (paragraph 34). Subsequent General Assembly resolutions on the rights of the child also incorporate similar statements regarding military training.[33]

Other UN documents stress the need for states to comply with IHL rules regarding children. They thereby indirectly encourage military training concerning children, although they do not explicitly refer to training as such.[34]

Further, in his 2000 report on 'Protection of children affected by armed conflict',[35] Otunnu calls for an 'era of application', in which the international community must begin to 'redirect its energies from the juridical task of developing standards to the political project of ensuring their application and respect on the ground' (paragraph 11). It is clear that military training in the applicable law is a key component in ensuring such respect.[36]

The ICRC, too, has issued a number of 'Plans of Action' referring to children in armed conflict, including their 'Plan of Action for the years 2000–2003',[37] annexed to Resolution 1 of the 27th International Conference of the Red Cross and Red Crescent. Such resolutions carry weight since they are adopted by 'states comprising virtually the entire international community'.[38] The 2000–2003 Plan of Action deals with various issues relating to children in armed conflict, and calls for, *inter alia*, the integration by states of their relevant IHL obligations into military training (Final Goal 1.4).

In addition to those of the UN and the ICRC, there have been other recent international initiatives that, among other things, explicitly urge states to train military personnel regarding the treatment of children. These include, eg, the International Conference on War-Affected Children, held in Canada in September 2000.[39]

Moreover, certain reports and resolutions of the UN and others refer to the need to provide, *inter alia*, training for peace support personnel regarding the treatment of children,[40] and some regional initiatives have also encouraged military training regarding children.[41] In 2003 specific 'Child Rights and Child Protection' training materials for UN peace support personnel were in the process of being finalised.[42] These peace support and regional developments are, again, beyond the scope of the present work, but they do indicate the increasing importance placed on training regarding this body of law.

d) Related Issues

As is evident from the above, there have been a great many recent (at the time of writing) 'soft law' initiatives, either directly or indirectly encouraging states to train their military personnel as regards the treatment of children in situations of armed conflict. In addition to these, there have been other UN initiatives that are more broadly relevant to this issue. Some of these rather lengthy documents will be briefly summarised below.

Certain of the pertinent UN documents refer to the appointment of 'Child Protection Advisors',[43] specialist advisors attached to peace support operations. Again—while not focussing here on such operations—these appointments are a measure of the attention being paid by the UN, including the Security Council, to the protection of children in situations of armed conflict. The role of these advisers incorporates, among other things, ensuring that guidance is provided on the law regarding children, and monitoring observance of this law by military personnel.

Another growing trend is evidenced in various UN resolutions and reports that propose concrete action to enforce international law regarding children in armed conflict, as part of the new 'era of application' (mentioned above).[44] For example, a July 2000 report of the Secretary General[45] calls for, *inter alia*, '[m]easures to encourage compliance with obligations and commitments' (p 6), including the following: that member states should 'make any … assistance for State or non-State parties to armed conflict contingent on compliance with international standards that protect children in armed conflict' (recommendation 6), and that they:

> consider … measures to discourage corporate actors within their jurisdiction from engaging in commercial activities with parties to armed conflict which engage in

systematic violations of international standards that protect children in times of armed conflict' (recommendation 7).[46]

This report also recommends that the Security Council 'should demand that parties involved in armed conflict not commit egregious crimes against children, or face the possibility of targeted sanctions if they fail to comply' (recommendation 9).

A more recent UN resolution along similar lines is UN S/RES/1379 (2001), in which the Security Council, *inter alia,* calls for states to end impunity and 'prosecute those responsible for genocide, war crimes and crimes against humanity and other egregious crimes perpetrated against children', and, where feasible, to exclude such crimes 'from amnesty provisions and relevant legislation, and ensure that post-conflict truth-and reconciliation processes address serious abuses involving children' (paragraph 9(a)). This resolution also calls for the Secretary General to provide 'a list of parties to armed conflicts that recruit or use children in violation of the international obligations applicable to them' in situations which create a threat to international peace and security (paragraph 16). On 16 December 2002, the Secretary General submitted a report to the Security Council, in which he listed parties to conflicts that were on the Security Council's agenda and that were continuing to recruit and use child soldiers.[47]

The UN initiatives cited immediately above thus address certain wider issues concerning armed conflict, some of which (eg taking steps to end impunity, and withholding assistance from armed forces that commit violations) may have direct implications as regards military training, while others (eg imposing restraints on the international corporate sector) are not directly relevant to such training. However, as regards the latter category, it is important to repeat in this context that the duty of states to monitor and enforce law and policy regarding children in armed conflict extends much further than simply providing relevant training to their armed forces—and that ultimately all efforts to encourage compliance with international law regarding such children are inter-related.

Committee on the Rights of the Child

In addition to their obligations under international treaty law and the demands of 'soft law' (above), states are under growing pressure from the Committee on the Rights of the Child to limit the impact of armed conflict on children, including through the provision of appropriate military training. Although the performance of this Committee has been uneven, and obviously depends to quite a large extent on the strengths and weaknesses of its individual members, it has, in recent years, become more questioning and assertive. It has the potential to become more effective in future due in part to the fact that, at the time of writing, the Committee had recently been expanded from 10 to 18 members.[48]

One development as regards the Committee's role in military training is the guidance that the Committee has prepared for states submitting their initial reports under the 2000 Optional Protocol on Child Soldiers (summarised in Chapter Four above).[49] Under this Protocol (Article 8(1)), states must, within two years after its entry into force in that country, submit a comprehensive report on the measures they have undertaken to implement the Protocol. Thereafter, states must provide further information on implementation of the Protocol when they submit their periodic reports under the 1989 CRC (Article 44(1)).[50] As regards military training, the Guidelines specify that the country reports must be accompanied by '[c]opies of … administrative and other relevant instructions to the armed forces, both of a civil and military character …' (Introduction), and must indicate measures taken to disseminate the Protocol in the relevant languages 'to all children and adults, notably those responsible for military recruitment …' (Article 6, paragraphs 1 and 2). More generally, the Guidelines call, *inter alia*, for states to provide information on the extent to which their school curricula incorporate human rights and humanitarian principles (including materials on children) (Article 3(5)). States are also asked to report on measures taken to raise awareness of the Protocol amongst armed opposition groups (Article 4) and to provide training to 'peacekeeping personnel' (Article 6, paragraphs 1 and 2).

Further, in its annual 'General Discussion' days, the Committee has shown particular concern regarding children in armed conflict. Its first such discussion, in 1992, focussed on 'Children in Armed Conflict', and ultimately resulted, among other things, in the initial Machel report, and the appointment of Olara Otunnu (see Chapter One above). During that discussion, the Special Rapporteur on the Sale of Children called for military curricula 'to include international humanitarian law, and particularly child-related issues …'.[51] More recently, in 2000, the Committee held a day of discussion on 'State Violence against Children'.[52] Its subsequent report, under the heading 'Awareness-Raising, Sensitization and Training', encouraged states, among others, to give 'priority to raising awareness about the problem of violence against children' (paragraph 14), and to 'ensure training in child rights for all relevant professional groups including … police and security forces …' (paragraph 16).

Moreover, in its Concluding Observations on country reports, the Committee has made specific recommendations regarding military training to a number of countries, including some of those that will be examined in Chapters Eight and Nine below.[53] The Committee's Concluding Observations generally start by highlighting positive aspects in the reports, before discussing areas of concern, and making recommendations.

It is relevant to note here that the Committee can—either on its own initiative or at the request of a state—involve appropriate agencies (eg UNICEF) in providing 'technical advice or assistance' (under Article 45(b) of 1989 CRC) to facilitate state compliance with any of its recommendations, including as regards child-specific military training.

To exemplify the approach taken by the Committee in monitoring country reports, certain of its Concluding Observations relevant to military training are summarised below, in chronological order, regarding a number of the countries to be discussed in Chapters Eight and Nine.

For example, concerning the initial report of *Colombia* (1995),[54] the Committee suggested that '… a new attitude … should be developed, particularly as regards the police and military, in order to enhance respect for all children', and that '… training programmes should be strengthened … and the rights of the child should be included in … the training curriculum' (paragraph 22). In its Conclud- ing Observations on Colombia's second periodic report (2000),[55] the Committee observed that measures to promote awareness of the 1989 CRC generally needed to be strengthened (paragraph 28), and encouraged Colombia to continue undertak- ing systematic training on the 1989 CRC 'for all professional groups working for and with children …' (paragraph 31).

The Committee's Concluding Observations on *Sri Lanka's* initial report (1995)[56] referred to the concern of the Committee at 'the large number of children affected by the armed conflict …' and expressed regret that this report did not 'give compre- hensive information on the effect of armed conflict on children, their involvement in the armed forces and the way the authorities handle child soldiers prisoners of war' (paragraph 24). In this context, it recommended that Sri Lanka submit additional information to the Committee within two years about these issues (paragraph 44). It also recommended, *inter alia*, that Sri Lanka provide training for 'professional groups, including … the military' regarding the provisions of the 1989 CRC (paragraph 32).[57]

As regards the initial report of *Australia* (1997),[58] the Concluding Observations did not refer directly to military matters, but did recommend the creation of a federal body to implement the 1989 CRC generally, and monitor its implementation (paragraph 24).

The Committee's Concluding Observations on *Uganda* (1997)[59] acknowledged Uganda's difficulties in implementing the 1989 CRC, due, *inter alia*, to the armed conflict in the north (paragraph 6). It expressed concern 'that the training on chil- dren's rights provided to all professional groups, including members of the police and security forces and … army officials … is insufficient and unsystematic' (para- graph 11), and that IHL rules 'applicable to children in armed conflict are being violated' in Northern Uganda 'in contradiction to the provisions of Article 38 of the Convention' (paragraph 19). The Committee went on to express concern about the abduction, killings and torture of children in this armed conflict, and the involve- ment of child soldiers (paragraph 19).

Concerning *South Africa* (2000),[60] the Committee, *inter alia*, welcomed human rights training prepared for the police (although no mention was made of the military) (paragraph 6). It expressed concern that 'professional groups', among others, 'are generally not sufficiently aware of the Convention and the rights-based approach enshrined therein', and recommended that greater efforts be made in this regard (paragraph 16).

On *Sierra Leone* (2000),[61] the Committee recognised the difficulties in that country resulting from 'many years of armed conflict' (paragraph 5). While accepting that progress had been made in disseminating the 1989 CRC, it expressed concern at the lack of implementation on a practical level, recommending the provision of 'training on its provisions for professionals …' and others 'to develop a culture of … respect for human rights' (paragraph 21). It also expressed concern at 'the massive participation of children in armed forces' in Sierra Leone, noting that there was no minimum age in national legislation for voluntary recruitment (paragraph 26). The Committee devoted a later section (paragraphs 70–75) to 'Armed Conflict', referring to forcible recruitment of 'children as young as five', and the effects of the armed conflict on children in Sierra Leone, before going on to make a number of recommendations.[62]

Regarding *Israel* (2002),[63] the Committee cited, among other difficulties impeding the implementation of the CRC, 'the disproportionate use of force by the Israeli Defence Forces' (paragraph 4), and it commented on the deterioration of Palestinian child health and access to education 'as a result of the measures imposed by the Israeli Defence Forces' (paragraphs 43 and 51). The Committee specifically called for Israel 'and other non-State actors' to comply with 'rules of engagement for military and others using and/or targeting children in the armed conflict' (paragraph 58).

In respect of the *UK* (2002),[64] the Committee expressed concern that 'about one third of the annual intake of recruits into the armed forces are below the age of 18 years, that the armed services target young people, and that those recruited are required to serve for a minimum period of four years raising [*sic*] to six years in the case of very young recruits.' The Committee was also concerned at 'widespread allegations that young recruits have been the victims of bullying'; that some 'children below the age of 18 years take direct part in hostilities overseas', and about the 'negative impact of the conflict situation in Northern Ireland on children ...' (paragraph 51). It accordingly made a number of recommendations to address these issues (paragraph 52).

Thus, the above information indicates that the Committee on the Rights of the Child is one avenue through which military training on children has been monitored to some extent. Such training may be more rigorously monitored in future, given the expanded membership and role of the Committee (under the 2000 Optional Protocol on Child Soldiers).

In summary, taken together, international treaty law, 'Soft Law', and the initiatives and recommendations of the Committee on the Rights of the Child—as outlined in this Chapter—variously articulate the obligation of states to provide military training regarding children, as one essential component of their duty to 'respect and ensure respect' for the pertinent law

Endnotes

1   As indicated in Chapters Two to Five above, states must ensure that the officers in their national armed forces receive training on, *inter alia*: a) the law relating to military conduct, including the law regarding children, and b) on their duty, as officers, to ensure adequate training of their subordinates on these matters.

2   Hampson (1989), p 119. (However, as noted in the Introduction (Chapter One) by no means all conflicts are fought in order to achieve peace!) Hampson points out that it is

also in the interests of military necessity, and 'vital to the efficient conduct of operations, that the armed forces should remain disciplined', in accordance with IHL, *ibid,* p 20.

3   Regarding the customary law status of 1907 Hague Convention IV, see eg, T Meron, 'War Crimes in Yugoslavia and the Development of International Law', 88 *AJIL* (1994) pp 78, 80. The customary law norms include Art 1 of this Convention (mentioned in the text below), obliging states to provide military training for their armed forces, in conformity with its provisions.

4   Many of the measures outlined below oblige governments to disseminate the provisions of the relevant law to the population as a whole, not specifically to military personnel. In that way, the relevant law could be disseminated to non-governmental armed forces, as already mentioned (Chapter One).

5   For general information on state obligations regarding dissemination and training, see eg, F de Mulinen, 'The Law of War and the Armed Forces' 202 *IRRC* (1978), pp 18–43 (1995 updated version available at http://www.icrc.org); Hampson (1989), pp 112–113; D Klenner, 'Training in International Humanitarian Law', 82:839 *IRRC* (2000), pp 653–661, and U Palwankar, 'Measures Available to States for Fulfilling their Obligations to Ensure Respect for International Humanitarian Law', 298 *IRRC* (1994), pp 9–25.

6   Hampson ((1989(a), p 121) points out that costs (eg of training) can also be reduced through cooperation between states.

7   Art 144, 1949 GC IV provides, *inter alia,* that this Convention should be included in 'programmes of military and … civil instruction'. The 1949 GCs also set out rules to ensure their dissemination to eg, POWs (Art 41, 1949 GC III), and those in charge of places of internment (Art 99, GC IV).

    In addition, the 1949 GCs allow for the involvement of the ICRC and/or another 'impartial humanitarian body' in eg offering 'services to the parties to the conflict' (Common Art 3), and carrying out certain 'humanitarian activities' (Art 9, 1949 GC I, GC II, and GC III, and Art 10, 1949 GC IV). This can be interpreted to include a role for such bodies in training and dissemination of IHL, and states should facilitate this. Specifically as regards military training activities of the ICRC, see eg, D Klenner, 'Does International Humanitarian Law Still Stand a Chance? Reflections on Instruction and Training for the Military and Armed Groups and on the Role of the International Red Cross (ICRC), on the Occasion of the 50th Anniversary of the Four Geneva Conventions in August 1999' (Geneva, ICRC, 1999), available at, http://www.icrc.org, pp 3–5.

8   It is good practice for armed forces to employ such advisers, whether or not their governments are party to 1977 GP I. See also, Keeva (1991) pp 52–59.

9   There are also international 'soft law' documents regarding IHL training and dissemination. See eg, the 1978 ICRC, 'Fundamental Rules of Humanitarian Law Applicable in Armed Conflict'—a summary of IHL aimed to facilitate its dissemination (206 *IRRC* (1978), pp 247–249); and the 1999 Bulletin on the Observance by United Nations Forces of International Humanitarian Law, which sets out the fundamental principles and rules of IHL applicable to the UN armed forces (Secretary-General's Bulletin, UN Doc ST/SGB/1999/13, 6 Aug 1999). However, the latter mainly relates to peace support operations, which are, as already mentioned, beyond the scope of this research.

10 Further, under the reporting mechanism of the 1989 CRC, (whereby ratifying states must report regularly to the Committee on the Rights of the Child), states should widely disseminate their country reports (Art 44 (6)), and this would of course include any information in these reports on military training.

11 Art 6 specifies that states must take 'all necessary measures' to ensure implementation and enforcement of the Protocol, and that they undertake to disseminate it widely to both adults and children. Art 7 provides for states for cooperate with each other in implementing the Protocol. Art 8 sets out the mechanism for regular reports to the Committee on the Rights of the Child.

12 *Note*: The 1948 Genocide Convention can be considered both as part of IHL and of human rights law. By Art V, states undertake to enact the necessary legislation to give effect to this Convention, and also to provide penalties for persons guilty of genocide and related acts.

13 1966 ICCPR, Art 2(1). States must also take the necessary legislative and other steps to give effect to ICCPR rights (Art 2(2)), and must ensure effective enforceable remedies for their violation, determined by a competent authority (Art 2(3)). Similar provisions are contained in some of the regional treaties (eg African [Banjul] Charter on Human and Peoples' Rights, adopted 27 June 1981, OAU Doc CAB/LEG/67/3 rev 5, 21 ILM 58 (1982), entered into force 21 Oct 1986, Art 1), although these will not be discussed here.

14 Art 10(2) specifies that the prohibition against torture etc shall be included in rules issued on the duties of the listed categories of persons.

15 R Higgins 'Derogations Under Human Rights Treaties' 48:281 *BYIL* (1976-7), p 281. See also eg, J Oraá, *Human Rights in States of Emergency in International Law* (Oxford, Clarendon Press, 1992).

16 See eg, Kuper (1997(b)), pp 21-24.

17 See eg, Cohn (1991).

18 'General Comment No 29, States of Emergency (Art 4)', UN Doc CCPR/C/21/Rev1/Add11 (31 Aug 2001), Note 5. This General Comment replaced General Comment No 5 (1981).

19 General Comment No 29 also sets out other rights that remain non-derogable, even though they are not specified in Art 4(2) of the ICCPR. See eg, para 13.

20 N Rodley, 'Soft Law, Tough Standards', 43:7.3 *Interights Bulletin* (1993), pp 43-44. He describes the legal effects of these instruments as including: that they may reflect an actual rule of law; they may help to elaborate the scope of established legal rules, or they may reflect an emerging rule of general international law.

21 Art 25 of the UN Charter imposes a duty on UN member states to 'accept and carry out the decisions of the Security Council …', and this clearly includes its resolutions.

22 See eg, R Higgins, *The Development of International Law Through the Political Organs of the United Nations* (London, OUP for the Royal Institute of International Affairs, 1963), pp 4–5, and Rodley (1993), p 43.

23 Fourteen year-old Alhaji Babah Sawaneh was 10 years old when rebels from the Revolutionary United Front abducted him. He was trained to shoot and he participated in attacks during which people were killed, houses burnt and properties destroyed. He was released by UN peacekeepers in January 2000, two years after his abduction (Former Sierra Leoneon Child Soldier Appeals for Action, UN Doc Press release SC/7219, 20 Nov 2001, pp 14–15).

24 See eg, UN Doc S/RES/1379 (20 Nov 2001), on Children and Armed Conflict, discussed further below.

25 UN Doc A/S–27/3 (4 May 2001), We the Children: End-decade review of the follow-up to the World Summit for Children, Report of the Secretary-General. See also the outcome document of the Special Session, UN Doc A/S–27/19/Rev1 (10 May 2002), 'A World Fit for Children', paras 20–32.

26 UN Doc S/RES/1379 (20 Nov 2001). This is one of a number of UN resolutions and reports that emphasise the long-term impact on society of 'war-affected children'. See also eg, UN Docs A/53/482 (1998), para 11; S/RES/1261 (25 Aug 1999), Resolution on Children and Armed Conflict, and S/RES/1265 (17 Sept 1999), Resolution on the Protection of Civilians in Armed Conflict.

27 See particularly eg, Section II(C) and Section III(E) of this resolution.

28 See eg, Otunnu's Second Annual Report to the General Assembly on the Protection of Children Affected by Armed Conflict, UN Doc A/54/430 (1 Oct 1999). See also his First Annual Report, UN Doc A/53/482 (12 Oct 1998) and his Third Annual Report, UN Doc A/55/442 (3 Oct 2000) (cited in text), both entitled 'Protection of children affected by armed conflict', both at Section II.

29 This report (UN Doc A/55/442, 3 Oct 2000) states: 'Since October 1999, some 37 debates, 7 resolutions, and 6 presidential statements have contained references and provisions on the protection of war-affected children ...' (para 20). See also eg, UN Docs S/PRST/1998/18 (29 June 1998), Statement of the Security Council on Children and Armed Conflicts; S/RES/1265 (1999), (preamble); UN Doc S/RES/1296 (19 Apr 2000), Resolution on the Protection of Civilians in Armed Conflict (preamble); UN Doc S/2002/1300 (26 Nov 2002), Report of the Secretary-General to the Security Council on the Protection of Civilians in Armed Conflict (paras 31 and 36), and UN Doc S/2002/1299, 26 Nov 2002, Report of the Secretary General on Children and Armed Conflict (discussed below).

30 UN Doc A/RES/53/25 (19 Nov 1998), Resolution on the International Decade for a Culture of Peace and Non-Violence for the Children of the World (2001–2010).

31 See also eg, UN Docs A/53/482 (1998) (para 6) and S/RES/1265 (1999) (preamble and para 13), and ICRC, 'Plan of Action for the Years 2000–2003, 27th International Conference of the Red Cross and Red Crescent', 836 *IRRC* (1999) 880–895, Final Goal 1.1 (this Section, below).

32 UN Doc A/RES/51/77 (20 Feb 1997), on the Rights of the Child.

33 See eg, UN Doc A/RES/52/107 (13 Feb 1998), on the Rights of the Child (Section IV, para 16). See also UN Docs A/RES/53/128 (23 Feb 1999): A/RES/54/149 (25 Feb 2000) and A/RES/55/79 (22 Feb 2001), Resolutions on the Rights of the Child.

34 See eg, UN Doc S/RES/1379 (20 Nov 2001), Resolution on Children and Armed Conflict. Para 8(a) lists the main international treaties relating to children in armed conflict. See also 'A World Fit for Children' (2002), para 43.

35 UN Doc A/55/442 (3 Oct 2000), mentioned above.

36 In this context, Otunnu has also obtained various 'commitments' regarding children (eg to avoid the use of child soldiers) from parties to conflicts. See eg, UN Doc E/CN4/2001/76, Rights of the Child, Additional Report of the Special Representative of the Secretary-General for Children and Armed Conflict, paras 29–31; Report of the Secretary-General, UN Doc A/56/342–S/2001/852 (7 Sept 2001), Children and Armed Conflict, paras 11–14, and UN Doc E/CN4/2000/71 (9 Feb 2000) Rights of the Child, Additional Report of the Special Representative of the Secretary-General for Children and Armed Conflict, paras 22–35; 36–43; 60–71; and 72–83.

37 See: IRRC (1999), pp 880–895. See also, ICRC 'Plan of action concerning children in armed conflict', endorsed by the Council of Delegates (Geneva, ICRC, 1995).

38 See T Meron, *Human Rights in Internal Strife: Their International Protection* (Cambridge, Grotius, 1987), p 109.

39 For information about this conference, see http://www.waraffectedchildren.gc.ca/. For example, under the heading of 'Prevention', the experts attending that meeting recommended that governments 'train military forces in child rights, placing emphasis on the specific needs of women and girls …' (p 47). This detailed recommendation required, eg, that the training be conducted by 'military officers conscious of these issues' in a manner reflecting the language, culture etc of the trainees, involving organisations with relevant knowledge, and implemented 'on a long term basis and updated regularly'. The experts also recommended that 'bilateral military assistance should include training on international human rights and humanitarian law' which emphasises children's rights *(ibid)*.

40 Indeed, the UN Secretary General has issued a Bulletin (already mentioned, n 9 above), on 'Observance by United Nations Forces of International Humanitarian Law', which contains a useful summary of basic IHL norms, including as regards children, and which explicitly articulates the duty of UN peace-support personnel to comply with the applicable law.

41 See eg, Accra Declaration on War-Affected Children in West Africa, adopted by West African Ministerial Conference on War-Affected Children, Accra, Ghana, 27–28 April 2000, para 7 of the Preamble and para 8. In his Third Report, Otunnu describes steps taken by a number of regional organisations to address issues concerning children affected by armed conflict (UN Doc A/55/442 (2000), paras 26 to 35).

42 U McCauley, *Training Manual for UN Peacekeepers' Regarding Children*, (forthcoming—draft provided by the author, 2002).

43 See eg, UN Docs S/RES/1260 (20 Aug 1999), Resolution on the situation in Sierra Leone (para 6); S/RES/1279 (30 Nov 1999), Resolution on the situation concerning the Democratic Republic of the Congo (para 4); S/RES/1314 (2000), (para 12), and S/RES/1379 (2001), (para 2)).

44 See eg, UN Doc E/CN.4/2002/85 (7 Feb 2002), Rights of the Child, Additional Report of the Special Representative of the Secretary-General for Children and Armed Conflict, Olara Otunnu, paras 9–13.

45 UN Doc A/55/163–S/2000/712 (19 July 2000), Children and Armed Conflict.

46 In addition, it recommends that the Security Council 'continue to investigate the linkages between illicit trade and the conduct of war; to sanction States, and to encourage Member States … to take measures against corporate actors, individuals and entities involved in illicit trafficking in natural resources and small arms that may further fuel conflicts where victims are largely children and women' (recommendation 8).

47 UN Doc S/2002/1299 (2002). Five countries were specified in this context: Afghanistan, Burundi, the DRC, Liberia and Somalia. The report also highlighted other conflicts, not on the Security Council's agenda, where child soldiers were used. These countries included Colombia, Myanmar, Nepal, the Philippines, Sudan, Northern Uganda and Sri Lanka (para 41–47). See also related report published by the CSC (CSC, *Child Soldiers 1379 Report* (London, CSC, 2002), hereafter, CSC (2002)).

48 This followed an amendment to Art 43(2) of the 1989 CRC, adopted by the Conference of the States Parties on 12 Dec 1995 and approved by the General Assembly (UN Doc A/RES/50/155 (28 Feb 1996)). See also eg, UN Press Release, 'Committee on the Rights of the Child holds Discussion with State Parties', 29 Jan 2003.

49 UN Doc CRC/OP/AC/1 (12 Oct 2001), 'Guidelines regarding initial reports of States Parties to the Optional Protocol to the Convention on the Rights of the Child on the involvement of children in armed conflict'.

50 States Parties to the Optional Protocol who are not party to the 1989 CRC must submit a report every five years, after the initial report. *Ibid* Introduction.

51 UN Doc CRC/C/SR.39 (12 Oct 1992), Summary Record of the 39th meeting, General Discussion on Children in Armed Conflict, para 8. The Special Rapporteur also mentioned that 'all existing entities, governmental, non-governmental and intergovernmental, should incorporate child-related issues into their mandates, particularly where those mandates concerned armed conflicts' (para 9).

52 UN Doc CRC/C/100 (14 Nov 2000), Report on the twenty-fifth session, Thematic Discussion Day on Violence against Children, paras 666–688.

53 Reference to armed conflict, military training, and/or relevant dissemination was also made by the Committee in relation to various countries not specifically discussed in this Chapter. See, eg, the Committee's List of Questions to Myanmar, where it asked for further information on 'training programmes on the rights of the child for ... military personnel' (UN Doc CRC/C/Q/Mya1 (19 June 1996), List of Issues to be taken up in connection with the considerations of the initial report of Myanmar, para 7); and its Concluding Observations on the Russian Federation, expressing concern at 'the lack of respect for the rights of children in areas of ongoing armed conflict ...', and calling for the state to ensure the protection of children and other civilians (UN Doc CRC/C/15/Add110 (10 Nov 1999), Concluding Observations of the Committee on the Rights of the Child: Russian Federation, paras 56 and 57). See also the Concluding Observations on India, (UN Doc CRC/C/15/Add 115 (23 Feb 2000), eg paras 16, 19, 24, 25, 63 and 64).

54 UN Doc CRC/C/15/Add30 (15 Feb 1995), Concluding Observations of the Committee on the Rights of the Child: Colombia.

55 UN Doc CRC/C/15/Add137 (16 Oct 2000), Concluding Observations of the Committee on the Rights of the Child: Colombia.

56 UN Doc CRC/C/15/Add40 (21 June 1995), Concluding Observations of the Committee on the Rights of the Child: Sri Lanka.

57 Sri Lanka's Second Periodic Report was submitted in 2002, (UN Doc CRC/C/70/Add17, 19 Nov 2002), and was scheduled to be discussed by the Committee after the completion of this research.

58 UN Doc CRC/C/15/Add79 (10 Oct 1997), Concluding Observations of the Committee on the Rights of the Child: Australia.

59 UN Doc CRC/C/15/Add80 (21 Oct 1997), Concluding Observations of the Committee on the Rights of the Child: Uganda.

60 UN Doc CRC/C/15/Add122 (28 Jan 2000), Concluding Observations of the Committee on the Rights of the Child: South Africa.

61 UN Doc CRC/C/15/Add116 (24 Feb 2000), Concluding Observations of the Committee on the Rights of the Child: Sierra Leone.

62 The Committee also specifically requested that sexual abuse in the context of the armed conflict should be among the issues discussed by the Sierra Leone truth and reconciliation commission (para 88).

63 UN Doc CRC/C/15/Add195 (9 Oct 2002), Concluding Observations of the Committee on the Rights of the Child: Israel.

64 UN Doc CRC/C/15/Add188 (9 Oct 2002), Concluding Observations of the Committee on the Rights of the Child: United Kingdom of Great Britain and Northern Ireland.

Part I

Law and Policy Relevant to the Training of Officers of National Armed Forces as Regards the Treatment of Children at the Outset, During, and Shortly After Situations of Armed Conflict

Part I(B)—Impact of Law and Policy

7

Part I(B)—Impact of Law and Policy: Methodology

Introduction

The previous sections of this book, Chapters Two to Six above, have largely addressed the following questions:

1) what training and/or reference information regarding children should be available to officers of national armed forces (ie the content of law and policy);

2) who is responsible for providing such training or ensuring that it is provided (ie officers/superiors to their subordinates, and governments to all military personnel); and

3) what are the key available international mechanisms for enforcing or encouraging compliance (eg war crimes trials; UN initiatives; pressure and guidance from the Committee on the Rights of the Child, etc).

Before concluding Part I of this book,[1] it is, in particular, necessary to address the following questions, to be examined in this Chapter: how realistic or achievable are the legal obligations, and international policy, relating to military training concerning children? That is: how likely is it that the pertinent body of law and policy can or will (even partially) be complied with, and achieve its aim of providing greater protection for children in situations of armed conflict? And, what can be done to make effective compliance more likely?

These questions can be addressed at different levels. However, as regards the primary question, it is arguable that it is both realistic and achievable to at least *provide* basic instruction on law and policy regarding children to all officers (and soldiers) of national armed forces.[2] Such training could be, as mentioned eg in Chapters Two and Three above, simply the bare minimum: to the effect that all IHL and human rights provisions regarding combatants and civilians generally also include and apply to children.[3] This simple rule should, where possible, be refined to state that: a) it is good practice to observe the relevant provisions with particular diligence as regards children, due to their international law entitlement to special treatment, and b) there are more detailed rules specifically concerning children—as civilians and as combatants—which should be referred to as and when the particular circumstances so require.

However, a more complex challenge is to examine the impact that military training regarding children may actually have. It is one thing to provide training, quite another for it to achieve its aim of minimising the damage inflicted on children in situations of armed conflict.

Certainly, if one looks at world events is it easy to conclude that the relevant body of law and policy has, and has had, little impact. As stated repeatedly in this book and elsewhere, children in vast numbers are physically and emotionally harmed in situations of armed conflict—often as a result of unlawful acts of combatants—and arguably this is increasingly the case (see Chapter One above).

Even when and if appropriate training is provided, full and global compliance—especially in extreme circumstances such as armed conflict—is an impossibility. The law on military training regarding children, like most law, can only ever have a limited impact. In any event, different parties to conflicts can have different perceptions of events. There are often clear cases of violations, but there are also some circumstances where one party may consider legitimate an action (including one resulting in many child casualties) that an opposing party considers a violation, and vice versa.[4] There is sometimes no 'objective' truth, and hence no way of assessing the extent to which the law has or has not been complied with.

Further, when considering whether the law on military training regarding children is realistic and achievable, additional factors come into play. Law and related policy are, in themselves, only one piece of a complex jigsaw puzzle composed of additional key elements such as international politics and finance, media pressure, etc. All of these factors can make it more or less likely that the law is adhered to in a given situation.

Moreover, the impact of this body of law depends on compliance at the level of government as well as, eg, at the level of the armed forces as a whole, and/or the individual officer or soldier. It is also closely related to the issue of enforcement and monitoring, already discussed.

In any event, the fact that full compliance may be impossible to achieve—or at least impossible to assess—does not negate the effort to improve compliance, and to strengthen the impact of the relevant law. Progress can be achieved, even if perfection cannot.

These wider factors will not be further discussed here. For the purposes of the present research, it is enough simply to locate, within this broader socio-political perspective, questions about the impact of law and policy regarding military training on children, before focussing on one of the questions highlighted above: what can be done to improve the effectiveness of military training—specifically the training of officers of national armed forces regarding children?

The following section will therefore briefly consider the question of how such training is provided: ie it will examine training methodology. This is obviously a crucial element in any analysis of the effectiveness of military training. Even the most pertinent and accurate training can be worthless if not conveyed and monitored in an appropriate manner. That said, it is beyond the scope of this research to discuss training methodology—as such—in depth, and in any event much has already been written on how people learn, and on teaching techniques generally, including some literature on military training.[5]

The Section below will thus only summarise some key methodological points concerning: 1) military training in general—and particularly the training of officers—on IHL and related law and policy, and 2) military training specifically on the treatment of children. A separate discussion will also highlight certain central issues regarding civil-military co-operation, since a significant number of military training programmes relating to the treatment of children are run by NGOs and other international organisations such as UNICEF and the ICRC. The latter discussion is likely to be too detailed for most military training or even reference purposes, and accordingly can be found in Appendix Two.

The information in Sections (1) and (2) below should be most useful for, eg, NGOs becoming involved in military training, or less experienced military trainers, since experienced military and other trainers are likely to be very familiar with the concepts discussed. It should also be of interest to those with an academic or more general concern regarding military training about children.

Background

It is perhaps useful (if rather elementary) to start with a working definition of learning, since 'the learning process is fundamental to training'.[6] One 'Toolkit' of training techniques defines learning as '... a relatively permanent change in behaviour that occurs as a result of practice or experience'.[7]

Also by way of background, it is worth summarising selected research findings on how to maximise the effectiveness of learning. These findings include research on 'information processing' to the effect that:

–   Working memory can only store five to nine bits of information at any one time:
–   A person must retrieve information from long-term memory and transfer it to working memory before s/he can incorporate it into his/her responses to stimuli;
–   'Organized structures of stereotypic knowledge' which researchers call 'schemas,' permit people to retrieve information from longer-term memory into working memory.[8]

Other research on how adults learn most effectively shows that training tends to be more successful when:
–   participants have been involved in defining, or refining, their own learning objectives;
–   the content is focussed on real problems faced by the participants;
–   training is undertaken in a varied and participatory environment ...'[9]

The 'Toolkit' of training techniques states that the average adult attention span is about 45 minutes (which means there should be a change of activity after that period). It also recommends that the maximum lecture or presentation time, without a break, should be 20 minutes.[10] Obviously these guidelines refer to optimal conditions, and would not necessarily apply to training in, or in preparation for, situations of armed conflict.

The trainer must also ensure that the process encourages trainees to use as many of their senses as possible, to maximise their potential for learning. Research in the field of educational psychology apparently shows that people remember the largest amount of information when they both say it and 'do' it (ie act on it in some way), and they remember the smallest amount when they only read it.[11]

Further,

'[t]raining methods can be classified in three modes: *Presentation* in which emphasis is placed on the trainer showing or telling the participants facts, new skills or responses; *Interaction* in which trainer and participants (or participants without the trainer's immediate intervention) examine and discuss facts, skills or attitudes, work co-operatively or competitively and learn from each other; *Search* in which the learner seeks new knowledge, skill or understanding …'.[12]

1   Training Methodology for Military Personnel: General

Turning now to general IHL/human rights training methodology for military personnel, particularly officers of national armed forces, a number of issues are emphasised by various writers on this subject (some of whom are themselves officers). Certain of these issues concern the conduct of combat itself. Without attempting a comprehensive overview of relevant factors, various central points are outlined below which relate to military training in general but obviously apply equally to such training specifically concerning children.

Note: For ease of reference, key phrases will be italicised. Further, the text below generally refers to training in IHL, but this term here incorporates training in fundamental human rights principles.

a)   Basic Considerations

In situations of armed conflict, the *military mission is the central task* of officers and their subordinates. This can lead to tension between the requirements of the mission, and the requirements of international and national law. For example, one writer states:

[m]en trained to do battle and ready if need be to lay down their lives in the accomplishment of their duty do not wish to be encumbered with regulations which to their minds are just fanciful theories propounded by jurists who have no idea of the military realities. At best, even though soldiers might perhaps be inclined

to observe certain elementary humanitarian principles, they are not sure their adversaries will do likewise and they consequently yield to the urge to consider themselves free of any such obligation.'[13]

Law and related policy can thus be perceived as both irrelevant and as an obstacle to the achievement of the central task.[14]

However, one officer involved in military training writes: '[t]his apprehension can and of course must be overcome by *good, well thought out and well presented training*, by trainers who are experienced in operations and are therefore credible and, above all, who believe in their subject'[15] (emphasis added).

Also, officers and their subordinates, particularly those engaged in combat, clearly have to *operate in extreme circumstances*. While they are trained precisely for this, such circumstances can profoundly affect their judgment generally, as well as their ability to recall and act on their training. Thus, '[t]he capacity of the human mind to process complex information in situations of extreme adversity, such as those on the battlefield, is quite limited.'[16] One officer has written,

> '... there are not too many professions that require you as a matter of duty to be prepared to lay down your life .... There may be fear, fatigue, frustration, anger, hunger and stress, which in turn may prompt a desire for revenge or retribution. We must accept these as part and parcel of the military life, but we can certainly try to control them as best we can. It is this vital element of control that must be emphasized ...'.[17]

Further, the *style of IHL (and other) training* is, in itself, an essential element in its effectiveness. The aim of IHL training for military personnel is, at least in part, to inculcate principles concerning, eg, proportionality and humanity, and military training itself should therefore be conducted in a disciplined and humane manner. Military personnel who are brutally treated and humiliated in the training process may well be more likely to inflict such treatment on others encountered in the course of their work, regardless of any theoretical IHL training that they have received.

There is also the issue of *motivation*—ie what is the incentive for military personnel to operate in accordance with IHL and related rules? In addition to 'professional pride', the ICRC argues that the 'learning incentive' for fighting ethically—in accordance with IHL—is that 'such rules have a direct bearing on the success of military operations and the survival of both the individual combatant and his unit'.[18]

One writer points out that a key motivating factor is 'the individual soldier's conscience. That needs to be an informed conscience rather than a product of unthinking prejudice', and it:

> needs to be reinforced in three ways: He must know that the same standards are shared by his commanding officers and those responsible for the conduct of the conflict. He must be used to confronting moral dilemmas in practice ... [through] training exercises .... Finally, the soldier must know that a breach of the rules will entail punishment.[19]

As regards punishment, another writer states: 'legalists are right to insist that law can and does influence battlefield behaviour in important ways,' including through 'threats of punishment *ex post*' (ie after the event). However, he sees such threats as having less impact in encouraging ethical behaviour than 'legal norms structuring day-to-day operation of combat forces' that 'achieve their effect *ex ante*' (ie before violations can be committed).[20]

There can also be other motivating factors to behave in accordance with IHL, such as the power of the media. One writer notes that, since the Korean War 'an aggressive and sceptical news media has emerged, willing to question the use of military force, capable of projecting the consequences of this force into millions of living rooms …'.[21] (This can be particularly true of conflicts that adversely affect large numbers of children.[22]) Public reaction to the consequences of military action (and particularly perceived IHL violations) can then impact on officers and soldiers—eg, in influencing political decisions on the course of the conflict, and in leading to prosecutions for war crimes.

b)   Training Challenges

Thus, a major challenge in military training is to *balance the demands of military effectiveness with the demands of 'ethics'*, in accordance with IHL. One writer argues—perhaps somewhat idealistically—for:

> creating a personal identity based upon the virtues of chivalry and martial honour, virtues seen by officers as constitutive of good soldiering. Faced with a hard case, officers are more likely to do the right thing if they ask themselves: 'What is required of honourable soldiers, here and now?' rather than 'What does international law require?' … The appeal is as much to their professional pride as to universalistic ideas.[23]

Or, as another writer states '… no substitute exists for discretion and good judgment by individuals.'[24]

Other challenges facing military training on IHL include problems such as: a) the vagueness of IHL concepts like 'proportionality' and 'unnecessary suffering,' as discussed in Chapter Two above.[25] This obviously poses difficulties for training, and is one reason to opt for military training that, where possible, emphasises reliance on individual judgment based on general principles, rather than 'black-letter' law;[26] b) the fact that in some circumstances combatants include 'people who are virtually excluded from society—often young people without jobs, education or future prospects—and who are caught up in a spiral of violence', and who then 'find it difficult to respect a degree of dignity in others which they do not accord themselves'.[27] Similarly, as already mentioned, child soldiers who do not regard themselves as 'children' may not be inclined to grant others of their age-group the special treatment to which children are theoretically entitled under international law; and c) another obstacle to effective training is the transfer and rotation of key trained staff, particularly when IHL training is primarily dependent on the personalities of individual trainers, rather than being incorporated into on-going curricula.[28] These three factors, among others, clearly present challenges to military training, and should be taken into account in training preparation and planning.

c) *Training Approach Generally*

According to one authority, the emphasis in military training is increasingly on *'preventive law,'* in order that training serves to 'provide input beforehand so that the unit can find solutions to problems and accomplish its mission within legal constraints.'[29] The ICRC emphasises that various 'common problems which may appear in conflict situations' (eg the fact that IHL is 'virtually unknown in many parts of the world') must 'be addressed well ahead of time, ie before war breaks out or, where a war has already been fought, before any further conflicts erupts ...'.[30] This reinforces the importance of pre-deployment training.[31] Such training also provides an opportunity for evaluation, since:

> it is important to understand attitudes of military prior to training. Pre-deployment training of some forces provides us with a rich opportunity to try to capture what may or may not affect the impact of training and what it means to individuals and military units that are trained.[32]

The point is repeatedly made in the literature that *'legalistic' military training is, in itself, inadequate*—ie the role of 'black letter' law is limited. 'Training is most effective if soldiers learn to make use of their own judgment, and certain "default rules", rather than simply learn the law in an abstract or theoretical sense.'[33] One writer summarises key principles based on 'the new learning' (from social-historical analyses of combat), including that 'military effectiveness depends greatly on ground-level ingenuity and improvisation by field officers and combat groups ...'.[34] However,

> (t)he proper mix of rules and standards depends on many factors. In particular, they include the degree of situational judgment required by soldiers assigned to various tasks and the level of education or motivation the soldiers possess .... Where loyalties to the state are weak, public order is insecure, and soldiers are poorly educated or unmotivated, strict, bright-line rules remain essential.[35]

d) *Timing*

Further, an experienced UK officer commented in the course of this research that *timing of training* 'will have an impact on the methodology used'. He accepted that IHL should be part of normal training, and an annual

> study day on the subject may be unavoidable even if one knows that not much of it will sink in (one hopes at least the core principles) because the soldiers will see it as an academic subject rather than something of immediate and necessary application. On the other hand, once soldiers have been warned for an operational deployment, the

legal aspects of that deployment suddenly become important, relevant and, therefore, interesting and the more formal approach may well have greater impact, especially when coupled with discussion of likely scenarios and ... rules of engagement.[36]

Officers must also be trained to be aware of the different tasks that they need to perform, depending on, eg, *whether the armed conflict has not yet started, or whether it is during or after the conflict*. Thus, eg, before conflict, the key tasks would include: providing training on legal standards and codes of conduct; disseminating information on rules of engagement and on sanctions for violations of legal standards. During the conflict, such tasks include: integrating rules of engagement into the planning of military operations, monitoring application of standards in the theatre of operations, and stopping and sanctioning violations.[37]

e)   Flexibility of Style, Content, and Context

Moreover, in teaching IHL and related law and policy it is one of the tasks of the officer to ensure the *appropriate level of training* for their subordinates.[38] Depending on rank and circumstances, complexity will vary. For example, only certain officers, such as military lawyers, would generally need to be familiar with, or refer to, the detailed rules concerning the treatment of children as outlined above, in Chapters Three and Four.

One authority emphasises that,

> [a]s a general rule, the higher the level the greater should be the range of knowledge of the law of war. Though problems are more complex, they are not so urgent, and the commander has more time and, especially, a staff at his disposal, to work out solutions. However, even at the level of units comprising a staff, the teaching of the law of war should not be too concerned with minute details. Apart from fundamental or current matters, the problem mainly consists in knowing where to search and find answers and solutions to the questions raised. If a particular question cannot be answered ... one should know to what superior or parallel level or service one should apply. Needless to say, at commander-in-chief and government level all problems related to the law of war should be solved.[39]

Given the different military populations that require training, and the diverse circumstances in which and for which they are trained, it is also clearly *essential to prioritise*. Accordingly,

> [a] selection has to be made, which means that priorities must be established, with regard to the subjects as well as to the persons to be taught. There will inevitably be, on the one hand, matters of primary and of secondary importance, and on the other, there will be some persons who should receive instruction before others ...[40]

It is therefore necessary in military training to *bear in mind the whole range of possible differences in personnel*, not only in role and rank, but also in, eg, level of education, motivation, culture, and commitment to the particular cause at issue in that conflict.[41] Differences in language are also crucial, and these must be taken into account both in terms of ensuring that the training language or dialect itself is spoken and understood by those to whom it is addressed, and in ascertaining the appropriate level of complexity.

As regards *cultural differences*, military training on IHL will generally be more effective when efforts are made to take account of these. One approach to this issue is, where appropriate, to incorporate traditional values into such training by linking these values to IHL rules. The ICRC is exploring this approach:

> Most societies have traditional codes of conduct which serve to protect women, children and the elderly in time of war, prohibit certain types of warfare, or establish mechanisms for the settlement of differences. Where such codes of conduct are widely accepted, they can be related to the universal rules of humanitarian law and help to strengthen its impact.[42]

Similarly, training must not only take account of differences between those being trained, but it must also be *context-specific*: ie adapted to the particular circumstances.[43] Such training aims to ensure that, as far as possible, military personnel can apply in practice, in that situation, the rules they may have learned in theory. This again illustrates the importance of practical, on-going, training, where knowledge and skills are tested in realistic scenarios.

One report on military training lists a number of factors that might dictate what should be incorporated into the content of a training session. These include:

> *the group to be trained*: their level of formal education, their rank and responsibility within the armed force; *the mandate*: peacekeeping or enforcing, regular or irregular armed force in internal or international conflict; *the duration of the training*: time available to do training and what the priority issues are for the time available; *local relevant issues* for the force or group being trained, and the *training environment and resources* available to the trainer.[44]

f)   Training Techniques and Course Outlines

Bearing in mind the more general points outlined above, specific training techniques and course outlines are proposed by various writers.

As regards *course outlines*, one experienced military trainer writes:

> The leaders must exert some imagination to conceive of exercises and a suitable scenario.
>
> The outline of teaching with general needs in mind will be as follows:
>
> Lectures, regulations, booklets and if possible films, may serve to give an introductory lesson to the company. For privates the main part of the work will be done during individual or squad combat exercises; for non-commissioned officers and officers it will be done during practical training sessions.
>
> For majors and upwards there will be a few lectures but mainly seminars at which more complex problems may be discussed. At these levels, practical training will take place during tactical and special exercises, at commander-in-chief level during strategic exercises. For the ranks from major to colonel there will be individual work as

well as staff work, above them it will be mainly be staff work. At division and higher levels, relations with the civilian authorities and the population will also be dealt with, while at commander-in-chief level a large part of the work will be devoted to international problems.[45]

A suggested model for a basic training session, which could be adapted depending on circumstances, is:

- An introductory exercise which draws out participants' own ideas/understanding relating to the topic;
- A relevant participatory activity (eg, simulation, case study, role play, discussion topic) … which would form the main body of the training session;
- General reflection and discussion on the exercise …;
- Analysis of the basic principles/model/concepts involved or development of a conceptual framework (a short presentation, handouts, overheads, video);
- Experimentation or practice (either during or after the workshop) of the concepts, skills, and attitudes developed within the training sessions;
- Review, feedback and evaluation.[46]

Regarding specific *training techniques*, one experienced officer[47] describes the training spectrum as including

> class room lectures and activities (such as interactive CD's, distance education, and role playing), seminars and conferences, field training, tactical exercises without troops, command post exercises, and exercises in the field.

In this context it is suggested that, especially for lower ranks, '[r]epeated exercises are essential',[48] so that behaviour in accordance with IHL becomes 'as automatic to every soldier as is his use of weapons'.[49] As another writer puts it '… when the shooting starts, soldiers follow those principles that repetitive or potent experiences have etched into their minds …', and '… the most consistent prescription for improving decision-making under stress remains training, training and more training.'[50] One recommended technique is 'a single schema [that] would organise the rules and give soldiers a realistic chance of retrieving them from memory during a stressful moment'[51] (similar to the concept of 'default rules' mentioned above).

Another authority argues that:

> when establishing teaching concepts it is important to avoid pictures which may be interpreted in a manner contrary to what was intended. Simplification by the use of pictures is sometimes dangerous.[52]

He also advises against '… expensive training methods [that] can be used on a large scale only in a few countries.'[53]

The ICRC has used some innovative techniques for communicating the message of IHL to military personnel, among others. They have, eg, made a CD, a documentary film and a book featuring a group of famous African musicians, 'appealing for more humanity in time of war,' and addressed particularly to children, especially child soldiers.[54]

g)   Evaluation

A key aspect of military training is the need to find some way of *evaluating its impact*. This is a challenging task. As one officer involved in ICRC training writes,

> Results are very difficult to quantify. One can boast of the number of students who have passed through our hands or enumerate the courses held (in our region 1,500 students and some 25 courses since June 1995). The true results will be seen only on the ground, in some far-flung corner of the region. If only 10% of what we teach is remembered, if a soldier as a reflex action or a senior officer as a function of his rank and command thinks, no matter how briefly, of the law and applies it, then our work will have been worthwhile.[55]

One NGO argues, in the light of its military training experience, that '[m]onitoring and evaluation [must] be incorporated at the beginning of the programme.'[56] Nonetheless, this NGO, too, emphasises the difficulties inherent in attempting 'impact measurement', and comments that few child-specific military training programmes have, in the past, 'incorporated a strategy on impact measurement, and mechanisms for monitoring and evaluating, in their planning phases'.[57] This would probably be an accurate statement regarding many, if not most, military training programmes on IHL in general.

The 'Toolkit' of training techniques describes various methods for evaluating the impact of training. These are:

– 'reaction evaluation'—which measures the reaction of the participants to the whole, or a section, of the training, through the use of 'feedback' during the session, and a 'reaction questionnaire' at the end of the event;[58]
– 'learning evaluation'—which 'measures changes in the participants' skills, knowledge, attitudes and practice, by comparing pre-training standards with post-training results.' Suggested methods for monitoring achievement of the training objectives include: practical tests; written tests; case study exercises, and problem solving exercises;[59]
– 'performance evaluation'—'which measures the change in the participants job performance over a period of time that can be attributed to the training by comparing the participant's performance before and after their attendance at a training event.' Here, 'the real test is if they can put the learning into practice "on the job"';[60]
– 'impact evaluation'—which 'is long-term evaluation and usually outside the remit of the facilitator. It will normally be carried out by training officers or departments when the organisation needs to know how effective its overall approach to training is.'[61]

In short, this Section ((1) above) has summarised some of the methodological issues that should be seriously considered in undertaking training of officers of national armed forces on their obligations under international law generally, including those concerning children. Section (2), below, will now outline certain issues more specifically pertaining to military training as regards the treatment of children.

2   Training Methodology For Military Personnel: On Children

Military training concerning the treatment of children requires consideration of various additional methodological problems. The most obvious of these is, perhaps, the fact that training regarding children can be perceived by military personnel as a rather minor, 'soft', sub-heading within the already marginal subject of IHL and international law generally (as mentioned in Section (1) above). However, this perception can vary widely, depending on the context. Military personnel deployed in situations where they encounter significant numbers of child soldiers or child civilians may welcome training on how to deal with this situation.[62]

The discussion below will highlight selected key issues pertaining to military training on children, again—as in Section (1) above—without attempting a comprehensive overview. Since much of this training is conducted by NGOs, the approaches discussed below come largely from NGO sources. This style of working may therefore be more applicable to training conducted primarily by NGOs or other non-military bodies, rather than by the military. That said, the NGO and military approaches can inform each other—they do not need to be mutually exclusive.

First, however, it is worth reiterating that, although the impact of military training specifically concerning children may be limited, this does not detract from the obligation to provide such training.[63] As Save the Children comment, such training 'is not something "good" on the part of the force', but rather a legal obligation that should be supported by the state,[64] (as is evident from Chapter Six above). In any event, once again the assumption underlying military training (although perhaps questioned by the cynical) is that a limited impact remains a goal worth aspiring to.

What, then, are some of the methodological issues to bear in mind as regards military training concerning children?

Many of the factors identified in the Section (1) above regarding military training in general are of course also relevant to such training on children. Thus, eg, *child-focussed military training must be both 'practical and participatory'*, in order to be effective.[65] Among other things, this means that case studies of military scenarios involving children should be used in training. Such case studies can be incorporated as one element in general IHL training—eg to illustrate key concepts such as 'the appropriate use of deadly force', and 'using necessary force to accomplish a mission.'[66] In that way, consideration of issues involving children can be included in the IHL syllabus without necessarily dealing with 'children' as a separate topic (and see ICRC materials described in Chapter Nine).

Further, in aiming to sensitise military personnel concerning children, it may be useful for the training to include exercises that focus on the trainees' own *family roles* eg as parents or siblings of children. It has also been suggested that

> *[u]sing soldiers own childhood experience in the training* is very valuable and so is *hearing from children* themselves (if children's participation can be done in a safe and child friendly environment and in a meaningful way).[67] (emphasis added).

However, the demanding reality of military life means that child-centred and labour-intensive[68] approaches such as the latter are unlikely to find a place in the busy training schedules of most national armed forces, or to be seen as a priority.

An additional factor to bear in mind regarding military training on children is, again, that of *cultural differences*. Indeed, some of the most profound differences between cultures are manifested in their treatment of, and attitude towards, children.[69] For example, one writer points out that, in training on humanitarian principles in the Sudan, 'there were differences of perception between those conducting the training, and the soldiers being trained, regarding such fundamental matters as the concept of a right, and definition of a child.'[70]

This writer also recounts, *inter alia,* as regards methodology, that in the Sudan training it was on occasion effective to hold workshops for a group of *participants that included both combatants* (in this case from an armed opposition group) *and civilians*. In particular, it was important to discuss, in the presence of both military commanders and parents, the commitment made by the military to avoid child recruitment.[71]

Again, as with military training generally, training on children's issues should be *context-specific*. Thus, it should:

> combine a mixture of existing materials with their [trainers] own specific knowledge of the context and the specific resources available to them. There is always a need to focus on specific issues relevant to the context, and most of the existing materials are or should be adapted locally.[72]

The *choice of methodologies* for such training will again be influenced by factors such as rank and command responsibilities of those being trained and their level of education; the allocated time; the learning environment; the context of deployment if known, etc.[73] Once more, *pre-deployment training* is advised, and here it can provide opportunities to evaluate the impact of training specifically on changing attitudes towards children.[74]

A particular training problem concerns *child soldiers*. One aspect of this problem is that, in the words of one writer,

> child soldiers have no vocational identity as professional soldiers and no corresponding sense of warrior's honour. Much less is manifestly wrongful to a child than to an adult. Children's moral sensibility develops gradually over time. Also, children cannot anticipate the full range of consequences likely to follow their acts. What is reasonably foreseeable to an adult soldier will often not be foreseeable to a child soldier ...[75]

This rather sweeping generalisation may well be accurate, although with some exceptions. It clearly has implications both in training child soldiers themselves (if the particular national armed forces use soldiers under the age of 18), and in training adult soldiers on how to respond to children encountered in opposing forces. As regards the latter, questions to be addressed include: how are such child soldiers likely to conduct themselves in combat—and indeed is it possible to predict this?[76] Should allowance be made for the fact that the opposing force consists partly—or largely—of child soldiers? Or that, eg, they are lightly armed? There is no simple answer to these questions, but guiding principles can be found in basic norms such as proportionality and military necessity (see Chapters Two and Four above). In any event, these difficult questions should be discussed in the context of training for specific conflicts.

Finally, a major challenge for military training concerning children, (as with such training generally), is its *evaluation*. For example, in their training work in West Africa, Save the Children decided that, given the size of their training project and the difficulty of evaluating abstract concepts such as changes in behaviour of military personnel,

> more restricted monitoring criteria had to be established. And for the time being the evaluation process will primarily be carried out at national level. Initially the impact measurements will focus around the inclusion of children in training and on military curricula. But wider measurements of what could be described as changing attitudes or displays of genuine political will should also be included in early attempts to monitor progress.[77]

They stress that 'impact measurement' of the training must focus on both: a) changes of behaviour and attitude at the personal and unit level, and b) changes of policy at the institutional level.[78] In this context, they suggest various ways in which training can be evaluated, using both quantitative data (eg numbers of personnel trained, number of training sessions held, number of violations reported and type of persons reporting violations (military, civilians, children), and geographic coverage), and qualitative data (eg changes in codes of conduct and rules and regulations; the creation of child protection structures within the military hierarchy; reduced incidences of violations committed against children, and readiness to report such violations). They argue that children themselves should be involved in 'measuring visible and direct changes they see for themselves and their communities', and that partner agencies should be included in the evaluation process.[79]

Thus, this Section (2) has highlighted some of the specific methodological issues that arise as regards military training concerning children. As already mentioned, Appendix Two briefly outlines certain other, more detailed, issues relating to civil-military cooperation in this context, based largely on the experience of Save the Children in West Africa.

In summary, it is evident from the material presented in this Chapter that there are numerous complex methodological considerations that have to be taken into account in any IHL military training, including training concerning the treatment of children. Accordingly, even if such training is brief, it should be planned with considerable attention to the appropriate training methodologies.

To sum up some of the key points already mentioned: military training in general, including that concerning children, must inevitably operate within the limitations imposed by, *inter alia*, the nature and goal of the military mission and the inherent extreme nature of situations of armed conflict. The aim is to find a balance between military effectiveness and 'ethics', in accordance with the requirements of international law (and compliance with international law can arguably enhance military effectiveness). Clear, well-presented, varied training, delivered in an appropriate manner for the particular personnel and circumstances, can motivate military personnel towards improved compliance with legal norms. However, 'legalistic' training is generally not recommended (except, of course, for military lawyers). Rather, military training, including as regards children, should broadly aim to incorporate methodologies that emphasise the development of judgment and changes in attitudes. Further, the impact of all training programmes should, as far as possible, be consistently evaluated.

Endnotes

1   As outlined in Chapter One above, this text is divided into three substantive parts: **Part I(A) and (B)**, which examines and summarises the content and implementation of international law and policy relevant to the training of officers in national armed forces as regards the treatment of children at the outset, during, and shortly after situations of armed conflict; **Part II**, which outlines existing training programmes provided by a range of different countries and the ICRC; and **Part III**, which summarises key points and emphasises certain recommendations that have emerged from this research.

2   It is possible, at least in theory, to monitor the actual provision of relevant training—and indeed the Committee on the Rights of the Child may increasingly perform this role (see above, Chapter Six). However, while it may be relatively easy to monitor the quantitative aspect of military training, the qualitative aspect presents a far greater challenge, as is discussed below.

3   Apparently, this is, broadly, the practice in the US armed forces (see Chapter Nine below).

4   At the time of writing, this was precisely the case as regards, eg, the on-going conflict in Israel/Palestine. See eg, J Freedland, 'Parallel Universes', *Guardian Weekly* (25 April–1 May 2002). See also, A Klarsfeld, 'Ne refusez pas à l'Etat juif la légitime défense', *Le Monde* (18 April 2002), and E Said, 'Thinking Ahead: After Survival, what Happens? Edward Said offers Thoughts in a Time of Tragedy', *Al-Ahram Weekly* (4–10 April 2002), available at http://www.ahram.org.eg/weekly/ 2002/580/op2.htm, visited on 13 April 2002. It should be noted, however, that even in that conflict, leaders on both sides have occasionally expressed regret over the deaths of children caused by their forces.

5   See eg, CMA, *CMA Training Skills Pack* (London, CMA, 1995); de Mulinen (1995); P Firkin *et al.*, *Training Skills and Methodologies* (UK, Contolearn, 1999); M S Martins, 'Rules of Engagement for Land Forces: A Matter of Training, Not Lawyering', 143 *Military L Rev* (1994), pp 3–160; M Osiel, 'Obeying Orders: Atrocity, Military Discipline, and the Law of War', 86:5 *California L Rev* (1998), pp 939–1129; M Osiel, *Obeying Orders: Atrocity, Military Discipline and the Law of War* (N.J., Transaction Publishers, 1999); T Pickles, *Toolkit for Trainers* (Brighton, Pavilion, 1995); Roberts (1997); R J Steinberg, (ed) *Human Abilities: An Information Processing Approach*, (New York, Freeman, 1985). See also G H Aldrich, 'Compliance with the Law: Problems and Prospects', in H Fox and M A Meyer (eds) *Effecting Compliance* (London, BIICL, 1993), pp 3–13 and Hampson (1989(b)), p 118.

6   SC and UNHCR, 'Action for the Rights of Children [hereafter ARC]: Facilitator's Toolkit', CD-Rom (Geneva, UNHCR, Aug 2001), p 3.

7   *Ibid*, p 4. The vagueness of the term 'relatively permanent' is problematic. For military training purposes the learning should, at the very least, be sustained throughout each particular mission. The *Joint Training Manual for the Armed Forces of the United States* (1 June 1996) (CJCSM 3500.03) uses a similar definition of 'lessons learned', as, *inter alia*, 'a changed behavior based upon previous experiences which contributed to mission accomplishment' (GL–9).

8   Martins (1994) pp 74–75, citing: E B Hunt 'Human Abilities: An Information Processing Approach,' in R.J. Steinberg (ed), (1985), pp 63–100; G A Miller, 'The Magical Number Seven, Plus or Minus Two: Some Limits on Our Capacity for Processing Information', 63 *Psychol Rev* (1956), pp 81–97, and C S Bos and S Vaughn, *Strategies for Teaching Students with Learning and Behaviour Problems* (Needham Heights, MA, Allyn & Bacon, 1991), p 56.

9   ARC Toolkit (2001), p 3.

10 *Ibid*, p 25.

11 *Ibid*, p 16. The research indicates that people remember: '10% of what we read; 20% of what we hear; 30% of what we see; 50% of what we see and hear together; 80% of what we say; 90% of what we say while we do it.'

12 See McCauley (draft, 2002) Section Eight.

13 de Mulinen (1995), p 2.

14 See eg, Roberts (1997), p 1, and Osiel, (1998), p 1021. The perception of law as a hindrance is not helped by comments from international lawyers such as that apparently made by Jean Pictet, ICRC representative during the drafting of the 1977 GPs: 'If we cannot outlaw war, we will make it too complex for the commander to fight!' Osiel (1998), p 993 (comment attributed to Pictet by Waldemar A Solf).

15 Roberts (1997), p 2. See also *ibid*, pp 3 and 6. Unsurprisingly, Save the Children, (McCauley and Ransquin (2001 (a)), p 21) have found that 'in general, military to military training is more sustainable and can be more technical, since it is based on a mutual understanding of the working environment'.

16 Osiel (1998), p 959. See also Martins (1994), p 75.

17 Roberts (1997), p 4.

18 ICRC (1998(a)), p 5. See also Osiel (1998), p 1027, who refers to research indicating that 'ethical behavior and technical competence are highly correlated …' among US officers (US Army War College, *Study on Military Professionalism* 13 (30 June 1970)). de Mulinen ((1995), p 8) argues that 'only men convinced of the need and credibility of the law of war will wish to do and know how to do what is required to ensure its respect.'

19 Hampson (1989(b)), pp 115–116.

20 Osiel (1998), p 1022. In this context, it is worth emphasising once more that officers and soldiers should be trained that they have a duty to report violations, including those against children, that are committed by, among others, their colleagues. They may of course find it difficult to do so, and feel disloyal and/or intimidated. Training should nonetheless address this issue without simplifying it, and emphasise the importance of such reporting.

21 Martins (1994), p 35. See also, T Allen and J. Seaton, (eds) *The Media of Conflict: War Reporting and Representations of Ethnic Violence* (London, Zed Books, 1999).

22 See eg, Kuper (1997(b)), pp 192–193.

23 Osiel (1998), p 955. See also *ibid* p 1045, '… any persuasive account of what makes men willing to fight ethically must be compatible with a more general account of what makes them willing to fight at all'.

24 Martins (1994), p 89. Keeva (1991), p 54, quotes a high-ranking US army lawyer, Hays Parks (and see Chapter Nine below), as follows: '[a] commander will ask the JAG' (Judge Advocate General's office) '… can I do it? Is it legal? and the JAG will say, yes, you can. But any good commander … will ask, is this the way we *want* to fight a war? … It underlines the fact that few legal decisions are made in a vacuum. They are often fraught with political and moral considerations.'

25 See also eg, Osiel (1998), p 987.

26 The term 'black-letter law' refers to strict application of the letter of the law as written, eg, in treaties, as opposed to law as it is applied or interpreted. Another (US) term for this would be 'bright-line law'.

27 ICRC (1998(a)), p 4.

28 See eg, McCauley and Ransquin (2001(a)), p 7.

29 Martins (1994), p 108 makes this point with particular reference to the role of military lawyers.

30 ICRC (1998), p 4.

31 Further, it reinforces the need to provide adequate training for national armed forces generally. Among other things, where no additional peace support training is provided, good basic training in itself can provide a form of pre-deployment training for the later involvement of armed forces in peace support missions (as mentioned in Chapter One, above).

32 McCauley and Ransquin (2001(a)), p 28.

33 Martins (1994), p 83. He argues for 'internalized principles rather than external, written texts …'. Under this model, 'leaders would assist soldiers in acquiring the judgment necessary to apply the default principles across a wide variety of situations.' See also Osiel (1998), p 1092, who states that 'standards are more effective than bright-line rules in promoting dialogue and deliberation among those whose conduct they govern.'

34 Osiel (1998), p 1026. Moreover, once trained to use their own judgment 'the soldier who faces a situation will first ask himself: Is this order lawful? If so, I must obey. If not, I cannot obey without facing liability. If I suspect that the order is illegal, my proper course depends on how much time is available for deliberation.' If there is not time to deliberate, the soldier must obey the order immediately. However, if there is time, the soldier must seek guidance from fellow soldiers or request clarification from a superior (*Ibid*, p 1095).

35 *Ibid*, p 1082.

36 E-mail of 14 Nov 2002.

37 ECOWAS/CEDEAO and Save the Children Sweden, West Africa Regional Office, *Child Rights and Child Protection Before, During and After Conflict: Training Manual for Military Personnel* (Abidjan, Dec 2000), pp 27-28.

38 de Mulinen (1995), pp 8–9, argues that 'there can never be only one correct method, but there are principles valid in general for every type of teaching. The methods used to teach the privates … will be quite different from those suitable to levels and specialists confronted by problems demanding consideration and study. It is important to avoid teaching systems which are too complicated.' See also *ibid*, p 10. And see Roberts (1997), p 3: 'A soldier can understand why he has to learn the basic principles of camouflage and concealment or how to use his weapon correctly. The law, difficult as it might at first

appear, must be presented in an equally meaningful, credible and digestible way. As one of the principles of war is "simplicity of action", the law of war has also to be simple and straightforward.'

39 de Mulinen (1995), p 6. See also *ibid*, p 7, for a table of training priorities for different ranks. Martins, ((1994), p 96), states, regarding the teaching of rules of engagement, that '... the assumptions of the legislative model ... are more tenable as applied to brigade commanders than to individual soldiers, and the greater volume and complexity of guidance from authorities above brigade makes the legislative approach more defensible at that level.'

40 de Mulinen (1995), p 2.

41 However, de Mulinen ((1995), p 3) argues that 'to spread knowledge of the law of war throughout the world in general, among civilians as much as among members of armed forces, considerable efforts must be made to adapt teaching methods and means to the special circumstances reigning in different regions of the world .... For the armed forces, the situation is quite different. There is less need, if at all, to adapt instruction to the various regions, because armed forces by their very nature resemble each other to such an extent ... that they are in many respects practically identical ...'.

42 ICRC (1998(a)), p 10. This was one of the techniques used by UNICEF and others in providing IHL training in the Sudan (Levine (1997), pp 18–20).

43 For example, McCauley and Ransquin (2001(a), p 6) found that 'preparation for engagement and training must be based on situation analysis in relation to both needs of the armed force to be trained ...' and local factors.

44 See *ibid*, p 18.

45 de Mulinen (1995), p 10.

46 McCauley and Ransquin (2001(a)), p 17.

47 E-mail of 17 Sept 2002 from Australian officer involved in training.

48 de Mulinen (1995), p 10.

49 *Ibid*, pp 5–6.

50 Martins (1994), p 6 and p 76. He also writes (p 91) 'Experience is the best trainer.'

51 *Ibid*, p 84. Martins also emphasises here that one cannot expect a soldier 'under stress' 'to consult, interpret and deconflict a body of rules and orders that leaders stack on him for the first time during the current operation.' An example of a 'schema' would be the word METT-T—used in training US junior officers to remember five key concepts: mission, enemy, terrain, troops and time. *Ibid*, p 73.

52 de Mulinen (1995), p 10. He elaborates that '[f]or example, an illustration of the prohibition of a particular action against a specific object might give the impression that any other hostile act against that same object is lawful.'

53 *Id*.

54 The ICRC has also produced a video featuring a demobilised Liberian child soldier recounting his experiences. Further, it has worked with Circus Ethiopia, a non-profit organisation, eg hosting a half-day session on IHL for officers and soldiers in the Ethiopian Defence Forces, followed by a special Circus show. ICRC (1998(a)), pp 7 and 9, and 17–18.

55 Roberts (1997), p 8. One experienced Australian army officer, interviewed on 28 Nov 2000, described his evaluation technique as follows: about a month after the training, he meets again with the same group and asks them to discuss incidents during that period, their reactions etc. They discuss this, and meet a few weeks later. On each occasion he

takes the opportunity to review the rules. This officer stressed his preference for 'the human element' as opposed to, eg, questionnaires.

56 McCauley and Ransquin (2001(a)), p 6.

57 *Ibid*, p 23.

58 ARC Toolkit (2001), p 65. This also points out that '[t]he main difficulty in reaction evaluation is to devise a way of accessing useful information without frustrating the participants because of its length.'

59 *Ibid*, p 66. The Toolkit also emphasises here that participants should know the results of the monitoring so that they can measure their progress.

One constructive use of 'learning evaluation' is found in many armed forces: ie the requirement that military personnel demonstrate their knowledge of IHL, in exams that are a pre-requisite for promotion to higher ranks.

60 Performance evaluation 'can only be conducted several weeks or even longer after the training—and then repeated several months later to check for further changes over time ...'. It is a key test of the impact of military training, but, for obvious reasons already mentioned, extremely difficult to conduct as regards armed conflict.

61 *Ibid*. The Toolkit notes that this is: 'A comparison of the productivity, effectiveness or performance of all or part of the organisation or particular parts of its work. These are then compared after a *programme* (not just one workshop or course) of training and development. The effect or the impact is then assessed to find out if there is a difference being brought about by the training.'

62 This was borne out by a small survey, by the author, of officers from a wide range of countries who were attending an IHL training course at the San Remo Institute in 2001. See Appendix Three.

63 Indeed, this is the case regarding all IHL military training, as already mentioned. And see U McCauley and C Ransquin, *Putting Children on the Military Agenda in West Africa: Documentation of the Process to Date* (Stockholm, Save the Children Sweden (forthcoming—draft provided by the authors), 2001(b)), p 20.

64 McCauley and Ransquin (2001(a)), p 8.

65 *Ibid*, p 19.

66 Martins ((1994), pp 137–139) outlines two case studies—for use in general IHL training—on these concepts and involving children. They are based on real incidents that occurred in Somalia in 1993, one involving a Somali boy who was shot by US peacekeepers and fatally wounded, and the other involving a Somali boy who was chased by the peacekeepers but not fired at, (both instances of actions described by Martins as being in accordance with IHL principles).

67 McCauley and Ransquin (2001(a)), p 19. See also McCauley and Ransquin (2001(b)), pp 12 and 23, describing the process of involving children with first-hand experience of armed conflict in one of their military training projects. This report emphasises the 'powerful ability' of the children 'if well supervised ... and cared for, to express their views on how war affects them and how they view the role of the military', and the strong emotional impact this has on the military personnel involved. Nonetheless, 'few of the participating soldiers were initially open to the idea of child participation and a number remained sceptical at the end.' Further, 'token participation [of children] does not serve any purpose'.

68 This approach is labour-intensive not only in locating suitable child participants and gaining their co-operation, but in ensuring their well-being throughout the training process.

69 See eg, P Alston, (ed) *The Best Interests of the Child: Reconciling Culture and Human Rights*, (Oxford, OUP, 1994).

70 Levine (1997), p 20. He states *(ibid)* 'Childhood in southern Sudan usually ends, in community perception, with the initiation of boys to manhood and with puberty in girls. At this point, both boys and girls take on the privileges and responsibilities of adulthood.' Further, he elaborates that 'manhood' was, in previous times, considered to start between about 16 and 18, but with the absence of so many adult men (largely due to the armed conflict) the age of initiation had fallen sometimes to 12 or 13. Clearly this would have implications as regards, eg training on 'child' soldiers.

71 *Ibid,* p 18.

72 McCauley and Ransquin (2001(a)), p 17.

73 *Ibid,* pp 19–20.

74 McCauley and Ransquin *(ibid,* pp 14 and 28) suggest, rather ambitiously, the pre-deployment use of a form designed to gather relevant bio data on soldiers (eg their age, education, perceptions of children, etc), which would, among other things, measure attitudes towards children both on and off duty. After deployment, there could be a 'follow-up'—including interviews with sample groups—to try and assess the impact the training had in practice.

75 Osiel (1998), pp 975–976. Indeed, these characteristics of many child soldiers are among the reasons for opposing their use in armed conflict.

76 In fact, depending on the circumstances and the armed forces involved, child soldiers may be—or be perceived to be—more lethal than their adult counterparts (see, eg, comments in San Remo Chart (Appendix Three)).

77 McCauley and Ransquin (2001(b)), p 21. The authors emphasise, *inter alia*, that one means by which armed forces can show a commitment to training concerning children is 'through financial, technical or material allocation of resources'. McCauley and Ransquin (2001(a)), p 7.

78 McCauley and Ransquin (2001(a)), p 23.

79 *Ibid,* pp 24–26.

Part II

Practice: Training for Officers of National Armed Forces on the Treatment of Children—Country Studies and the ICRC

8

Part II—Introduction and Country Studies (Category A)

Introduction

Part I of this book, in the above Chapters, has examined law and policy relevant to the training of officers of national armed forces on the treatment of children in situations of armed conflict. It has outlined both the content of the pertinent law and policy, and ways in which its effective implementation can be encouraged. The following section, Part II (Chapters Eight and Nine), will briefly describe the practice of 11 different countries as regards the training they provided for officers of their armed forces, largely in the years 2001–2002. Separate information will also be given at the end of Chapter Nine on relevant training initiatives of the ICRC.

The aim of Part II is to move from a primarily theoretical analysis of the relevant law and policy, and their implementation, (Part I), to an examination of how these obligations are in fact put into practice 'on the ground'.[1] Do the selected countries actually provide training on children for officers in their national armed forces? If so, how do they tackle this task? Are there any examples of 'good practice' in the selected countries that could provide a useful model for other countries to adapt, as required?

a)   Selection of Countries

The 11 countries were chosen[2] using the criteria that they would include: in **Category (A)**, countries selected primarily on the basis that they were currently or recently involved in armed conflict 'at home' (within their own jurisdiction), and that they represented different regions, with experience of different types of armed conflict (ie Bosnia and Herzegovina, Colombia, Israel, Uganda, Sierra Leone, South Africa, Sri Lanka); and in **Category (B)**, countries selected primarily on the basis that they were or had recently been substantially involved in peace support or other military activities 'abroad', and/or in training of armed forces other than (and of course including) their own—once more, bearing in mind geographic representation (ie Australia, South Africa (again), Sweden, the United Kingdom, and the United States).

In both cases (Category (A) and (B)), it was felt that the practice of the selected countries could illustrate the dilemmas posed by, and the solutions (if any) found to, the obligation to provide national military training concerning children in armed conflict. The Category (B) countries were included as it seemed relevant to consider countries where the recent experience of armed conflict was considerable, and yet more indirect than that of the countries in Category (A). As regards specific training on children, there appeared to be only one of the five countries in Category (B) that provided this (ie Sweden, largely through Save the Children (as discussed above, and see below)).

Some of the countries falling into Category (A) were previously and/or at the time of writing also involved in peace support activities (eg Bosnia and Herzegovina, South Africa and Sri Lanka), although—with the possible exception of South Africa—those activities were less significant in recent history than their experience of armed conflict 'at home'.[3] In any event, the 'Background Notes' on each country mention the categories of conflict (eg international armed conflict), and types of military activity (including peace support operations), engaged in by that particular country.

The countries selected in Category (A) come largely—although not entirely—from 'the south', and those in Category (B) largely from 'the north'. However, no value judgement is implied by this selection.[4] (Indeed, it is worth noting that the countries that contribute most personnel to UN peace support operations have generally been countries 'in the south', and not those 'in the north'.[5])

Africa is slightly over-represented in Category (A), for the simple reason that this continent has experienced a large number of conflicts in recent years,[6] with a significant involvement of children, and also because, at the time of writing, some innovative military training initiatives were underway on that continent (eg in West Africa, as already mentioned). By way of contrast, one of the countries in 'the north'—the US—went on record in the context of this research (see below) stating that it provided no specific military training on the treatment of children.

That said, countries that are relatively affluent and stable, such as most of those in Category (B), clearly have greater resources to devote to military training.[7] Again, this is not a value judgement but a reality that must be taken into account, and perhaps a reason why such countries can and should—and often do—offer assistance to other countries through, *inter alia,* the provision of military training.

b)   Parameters

As far as possible, the information set out below concerning the 11 selected countries is purely descriptive, as the object of this research is not to apportion criticism or praise. As already mentioned, there are, in any event, many factors that contribute to the standard of military training in particular countries—including their relative affluence or poverty, and the extent to which the society has been stable or destabilised by, *inter alia*, armed conflict. Nonetheless, elements of good practice will be highlighted where it appears useful to do so, with the aim of disseminating training information that could be applicable in other contexts or countries.

The 11 country summaries are inevitably impressionistic, given the available research resources and time limitations. With the exception of Uganda (see below),[8] it was not possible to visit the 11 countries, observe training, interview officers, interview children involved, etc. Uganda was chosen as the exception, since it was essential that at least one of the 11 selected countries—and one that offered military training specifically on children—was visited as part of this research in order to include a 'field-based' perspective of such training. The Save the Children Denmark training in Uganda seemed ideal for this purpose, as the continuing conflict in Northern Uganda was, in 2002, affecting large numbers of children (both as civilians and as soldiers) and had done so for many years; the Save the Children Denmark training was designed specifically for officers of the Ugandan army, and it was scheduled to be conducted at a suitable stage in the research process (although in fact this did not happen as planned—see Uganda country report, below).

In general, therefore, the nature of the country research is neither anthropological nor 'field-based', and is drawn from information provided largely by 'official' governmental and/or military sources, as well as by organisations such as NGOs, the ICRC, or UNICEF, or by a combination of these. Clearly some of these sources may, to a greater or lesser extent, have provided information that was influenced by their own political or other agenda. However, it is generally beyond the scope of this research to attempt an independent assessment of information provided, again with the exception of Uganda. It is therefore important to emphasise that, although the visit to Uganda highlighted some problems in their pertinent military training, it is likely that visits to many of the other selected countries would also have revealed problems.

Since information on the 11 countries came from many sources, most wishing to remain confidential, the summaries below do not, with a few exceptions, name individual informants.[9] The summaries nonetheless indicate any organisations involved (not individuals), and fully cite published materials.

In gathering the information, reliance had to be placed on certain key contacts in the selected countries, as well as visits to organisations that serve as a central focal point for relevant materials and expertise. In the latter context, the author met with staff of the ICRC,[10] the Committee on the Rights of the Child,[11] the San Remo Institute[12] and the office of Olara Otunnu.[13]

Difficulties were sometimes encountered in locating appropriate contacts in particular countries, and in obtaining the required information. For example, all 11 selected countries were asked for information on any proceedings taken against officers in their national armed forces for violations committed against children. Where such information was provided it is mentioned in the country study, but most countries did not supply this. Further, the military establishment in some of the selected countries that were, at the time of writing, involved in armed conflict, clearly (and understandably) had other priorities—and in some cases appeared reluctant to provide the information requested. On occasion it therefore proved impossible to obtain much information. There are accordingly some gaps in the information gathered, and the information provided regarding one or two of the 11 countries is minimal.

It is also important to note that the situation regarding national military train-ing is frequently in a state of flux. For example, some countries that previously had little or no general IHL military training were, by 2002, apparently providing this (eg Colombia and Sri Lanka) and the opposite also applied (eg possibly Uganda). Also, as awareness has grown of problems affecting children in armed conflict (reflected in, *inter alia*, UN and other initiatives, outlined in Chapter Six above), this awareness seemed in some countries to be increasingly expressed in military training.[14]

Further, within most armed forces there is wide variation in the levels of mili-tary training provided, according to staff rank and function. As stated in Chapter One of this book, the focus here is generally on training for the ranks of Captain to Major to Colonel. However, different armed forces provide different training to the various levels of command, and therefore, in examining the information provided, it was not always possible to compare 'like with like'.

Within those constraints, the information gathered is as accurate as possible, and some useful and interesting information has emerged (as discussed below), which gives an indication of practice in diverse countries and regions at the time of writing. The findings are summarised at the end of Chapter Nine.

As regards the information provided in Chapters Eight and Nine on each of the 11 countries, this consists of: the key treaties the country had ratified, signed, etc., and an outline of training provided in that country, including both general IHL and child-specific training. Appendix Three contains a more detailed chart, or check-list, indicating, by country, the training provided in the selected countries on key principles concerning children, (principles outlined in Chapters Three and Four). When insufficient information has been obtained concerning a particular country, the chart is omitted.

Further, Appendix Four contains brief notes setting out relevant background information on each country. These 'Background Notes' generally mention the con-flicts involving the particular country (in the post WW II period only) and broadly categorise these (eg as international or non-international armed conflict), and they also contain basic information on the involvement of children (eg their role in the national armed forces). The 'Background Notes' are placed in an Appendix as they do not focus on military training as such, and in any event contain information that readers may already know, and/or can find in other sources. However, they do place the military training information in a general historical and cultural context, and some readers may find them of interest.

Notes:

1) The information on both general and child-specific training set out below is presented without any critical comment, despite the fact that a few of the 11 selected countries have been severely criticised for the treatment of children by their armed forces. The aim here is simply to provide, as far as possible, an overview of practice in the relevant countries and not, as already mentioned, to apportion criticism or praise.

2) All 11 countries discussed below have sent military representatives for training in IHL and/or human rights law to the San Remo Institute. However, this does not necessarily mean that IHL and/or human rights training are generally provided for the armed forces in those countries.

3) In the country summaries below, the term 'law of armed conflict' (LOAC) is used, rather than IHL, where the country in question used that term in the information provided.

4) Most of the country summaries were finalised between September and November 2002, and were largely up-to-date to that period (referred to in the text as 'the time of writing').

Country Studies—Category (A): Countries Currently or Recently Involved in Armed Conflict

a)   Bosnia and Herzegovina (hereafter BiH)

i   Relevant Treaties Signed, Ratified, etc.

– the 1949 GCs (became a party on 31 December 1992 –succession of States[15])
– the 1977 GPs (became a party on 31 December 1992 –succession of States)
– the 1989 CRC (became a party on 1 September 1993 –succession of States)
– the 1997 Ottawa Convention (ratified on 8 September 1998)
– the 1998 Statute of the ICC (ratified on 11 April 2002)
– the 1999 ILO Convention 182 (ratified on 5 October 2001)
– the 2000 Optional Protocol on Child Soldiers (signed on 7 September 2000)

ii   Background Notes—See Appendix Four

iii   Training of Officers of the Armed Forces of BiH—General

In 2001, the ICRC provided training courses in IHL to the armed forces of BiH, as well as providing publications and audio-visual equipment. The ICRC also organised the translation into BiH's three national languages of two books on IHL.[16] Moreover, in February 2001, the ICRC helped organise a five-day IHL 'training of trainers' workshop for officers of the armed forces of the Republika Srpska and of the Federation of BiH.[17]

A Lieutenant Colonel in the armed forces of the Federation of BiH,[18] (who was also a Liaison Officer for SFOR[19]), provided further information on IHL training in that particular branch of the Bosnian armed forces, in a letter dated 1 March 2002, which stated:

> We started with this training three years ago by sending some people abroad for training. A few of us (contrary to the large numbers of those who attend trainings and later do not implement it) have realised the importance of this issue and

in cooperation with the ICRC ... we made a plan how to implement this in the regular training procedure at all levels in the Army of the Federation. First of all we organised a course for instructors who will be giving the lectures on the subject. We continued the work by preparing a CD-ROM, lectures and practical exercises on the subject and later also video material. After receiving a huge help from ICRC Sarajevo we started with the training. All the officers, the low-rank officers and the privates, attend courses and exercises on the subject. They receive literature and leaflets regularly and also exchange their experiences. In other words, everything necessary is done in order for them to understand the importance of this issue.

Later we received modern equipment, computers and LCD projectors, which accompanied by very good quality literature are providing a good basis of knowledge on the subject. For the last three years I have been giving two-day lectures to every class at the Command staff training.

My plans for the future are to extend the lectures' duration to one week per class and to build a training field for the practical part of the course.

A British officer working in BiH further stated, in October 2002, that a training review was underway at that time, and that 'it is anticipated that SFOR may be asked to help with initial training which will then be built in to their [Bosnian] training directives.'[20]

iv   Training of Officers of the Armed Forces of BiH—Regarding Children

The letter from the Lieutenant Colonel cited above stated that military training regarding children in BiH would be dealt with in the 'civil sphere', by humanitarian organisations. He had no information on this and it did not prove possible to obtain such information from other sources, except to ascertain that no relevant training was, at the time of writing, conducted by UNICEF[21] or by Save the Children.[22]

Accordingly, it seemed likely that, if indeed any child-specific training was available to the Bosnian armed forces, this would only have been the material contained in general IHL training, probably provided by the ICRC (and see Chapter Nine below, regarding ICRC training materials).

Summary: The information above indicates that some IHL training was being provided in BiH, largely by the ICRC and, to some extent, by others (such as the Lieutenant Colonel cited). It is, however, unclear whether any child-specific training was provided.

b)   Colombia

i   Relevant Treaties Signed, Ratified, etc.

– the 1949 GCs (ratified on 8 November 1961)
– the 1977 GPs (1977 GP I acceded on 1 September 1993, GP II acceded on 14 August 1995)
– the 1989 CRC (ratified on 28 January 1991)

- the 1997 Ottawa Convention (ratified on 6 September 2000)
- the 1998 Statute of the ICC (ratified on 5 August 2002)[23]
- the 2000 Optional Protocol on Child Soldiers (signed on 6 September 2000)

At the time of writing, Colombia had not ratified the 1999 ILO Convention 182.

ii   Background Notes — See Appendix Four

iii   Training of Officers of the Colombian Armed Forces (CAF)— General

Note: Since the information below was compiled, there has been a change of government in Colombia, with the election of Alvaro Uribe on 27 May 2002. However, it has not proved possible to obtain further research information regarding military training and policy under the new government.

The Colombian army had apparently been implicated in human rights violations and breaches of IHL in the course of the protracted armed conflict in Colombia (see 'Background Notes'). However, according to the official information provided, it appears that, since the late 1990s, efforts were being made to remedy this situation.[24] Such efforts included measures to improve military training in IHL and human rights law,[25] and to strengthen military accountability through various judicial and other mechanisms. (The CAF was also being considerably expanded.[26]) Indeed, the research information provided on Colombian military training (and summarised below) was notable in placing the issue of military training squarely in a context of military discipline and accountability.

Accordingly, in a letter to the author in 2001,[27] the Colombian Ambassador to the UK stated that the Colombian government:

> has included a scheme to modernise the Armed Forces within a framework of strict human rights observance and constant training in this area. Over 100,000 members of the Armed Forces have received such training, which has contributed to a substantial fall in the levels of reported human rights abuses committed by law enforcement agents.[28] The Colombian Government is, however, aware that much remains to be done and is working on it.
>
> A Military Criminal Justice Corps and a new Military Criminal Code were introduced with a view to guaranteeing transparency in the actions of the military and their observance of these principles.
>
> Under the extraordinary powers granted by the Colombian Congress, the Colombian Government issued 11 decrees that constitute the core of this new legislation for the Armed Forces. These decrees regulate the military and police services, their disciplinary regime, career structure, health system and set up a statute for professional soldiers.
>
> As a specific measure to promote human rights observance, Law 548 of 1999 established that no minor under 18 may be recruited into the Armed Forces and

penalises such recruitment. [29] Similarly, this law set up mechanisms to protect women in armed conflict and victim support programmes among other types of programme.

In addition, on 12 August 1999 the Colombian President promulgated a special policy to promote and guarantee Human Rights and International Humanitarian Law, entrusting its implementation to the Vice-President of Colombia .... He is responsible for co-ordinating the multiple efforts of States agencies to uphold fundamental rights.

The Vice-President heads a human rights promotion strategy to raise public awareness of the significance of these rights and International Humanitarian Law. One of the instruments to monitor progress in this regard is the 'Human Rights Observatory' ....

Further information on these initiatives is contained in two official publications for the year 2000, the 'Annual Human Rights and International Humanitarian Law Report 2000' ('Annual HR and IHL Report 2000'), and the 'Policy on Human Rights and International Humanitarian Law Progress Report: March 2000' ('Policy Report 2000').[30] These publications refer, *inter alia*, to: a) *improved IHL and human rights training for the armed forces*, consisting of a new educational model that is incorporated into the curricula of military academies, and that 'is aimed at ensuring that humanitarian principles, internalised by military ... personnel, translate into specific conducts in such a way that respect for human rights becomes part of the soldier's ... permanent attitude'.[31] The Annual HR and IHL Report 2000 asserts that 97,000 members of the police and armed forces:

> have received training in the last five years, most of them in combat zones .... Each member of the ... Armed Forces in Colombia receives on average ninety hours a year of training in Human Rights and [IHL] during his or her general training, which lasts for four years in the case of an officer, two years in the case of an enlisted person, and 1.42 years for executive personnel.[32]

Further, military personnel were apparently given additional training on these subjects during promotion, and at other key stages in their careers.[33] Training assistance had been provided by the US; by the Raoul Wallenberg Institute in Sweden; by Canada; by the San Remo Institute, and—on an on-going basis—by the ICRC;[34] b) *information on state action in response to violations of international law by the armed forces*, stressing, *inter alia*, that accusations of such violations were followed up 'both in the internal judicial system and in the Inter-American system ...'.[35] Various initiatives in this context included, eg, the 1999 Forced Disappeared Persons Bill;[36] a 1999 Penal Code;[37] and a new military criminal justice system 'responsible for investigating and punishing criminal behaviors by Security Force members in active service ...':[38] c) *information indicating that 'The People's view of their Police and Armed Forces' is generally positive* (although it must be borne in mind that this information is contained in an official Ministry of Defence report),[39] and d) *summaries of many cases under investigation concerning human rights and IHL violations*. In most of the cases cited, the perpetrators were members of the guerrilla or paramilitary forces. However, one case, described in some detail, concerns an incident near the town of Pueblo Rico in 2000, when Colombian soldiers killed a group of children (see below), apparently as a result of 'human error'.[40]

iv   Training of Officers of the CAF—Regarding Children

The above information indicates that the CAF did, at the time of writing, receive training in IHL and human rights law generally, and operated in a climate where many mechanisms seemed to be in place to monitor and enforce compliance with legal norms. That said, one contact working for the 'Defence for the Colombian People'[41] stated that the Colombian Ministry of Defence had informed her:

> that they didn't give any special treatment to children. In certain cases, they hand them over to the 'Colombian Institute for Familial Well-being'. They also told me that the information concerning military training is confidential. Courses in human rights are optional.[42]

Indeed, aside from the new legislation penalising recruitment into the armed forces of those under 18 (as above), no additional information concerning Colombian military training specifically regarding children was unearthed in the course of this research, with one exception. The exception was a conference, apparently held under the auspices of the Colombian navy in June 2000, on 'Rights of Minors'.[43] Save the Children Colombia was, at the time of writing, not involved in military training.[44]

However, the description of the CAF killing, in 2000, of the children in Pueblo Rico seems to indicate that the deaths of civilian children at army hands was not taken lightly (although that event was apparently particularly well-publicised). In that incident, six children were killed and four others injured. The soldiers apparently mistook the group of children for guerrillas, when in fact they were simply on a school trip. It was accepted by the Public Prosecutor's office that the soldiers had not intended to harm civilians, and indeed that they had been profoundly distressed by the event.[45] Nonetheless, investigations were continuing, and the Minister of Defence was reported as saying that he would:

> be watching personally to see that these investigations are brought to a successful conclusion, and you can rest assured that if it should turn out that any members of the Armed Forces were to blame, they will be duly penalised.[46]

Summary: It appears that the CAF were, at the time of writing, provided with widespread basic training on IHL, with the assistance of the ICRC. Further, there had been a number of legislative and other initiatives to encourage CAF compliance with IHL and human rights law, including legislation to prohibit recruitment of those aged under 18 into the CAF. Nonetheless, it seemed that there was, as yet, little child-specific training provided to CAF personnel, despite the fact that, among other things, child soldiers were still being used by other armed forces within Colombia.

c)   *Israel*[47]

i   Relevant Treaties Signed, Ratified, etc.

–   the 1949 GCs (ratified on 6 July 1951)
–   the 1989 CRC (ratified on 3 October 1991)

At the time of writing, Israel had not ratified the 1977 GPs, the 1997 Ottawa Convention, the 1998 Statute of the ICC,[48] the 1999 ILO Convention 182 or the 2000 Optional Protocol on Child Soldiers.

ii   Background Notes—See Appendix Four

iii   Training of Officers of the Israeli Defence Forces (IDF)—General

The ICRC was involved to some extent in IDF military training, having apparently, among other things, carried out IHL dissemination sessions, on a quarterly basis, for Israeli Civil Administration cadets in 2001. Also, the ICRC stated that in 2001 'dialogue was maintained' with IDF soldiers 'in the field' regarding, *inter alia*, the role of the ICRC.[49]

As regards general IHL training in the IDF, according to information provided by a Corporal in the IDF Public Relations Branch:[50]

> The IDF training program concerning the international humanitarian law has developed significantly in the last decade. The Military Law School, under the Military Advocate General, is in charge of teaching and training IDF officers on the different issues of international humanitarian law. This training has become an integral part of the officers' training, and especially of the operational officers' training.
>
> There are several stages of training junior and senior officers in the area of international humanitarian law.
>
> The first stage of the training takes place in the Officers' school. During the first part of the officers' course, the cadets participate in an international law workshop combined with learning and exercising of the opening fire regulations. This workshop is instructed by officers of the military law school.
>
> Further, in the company and battalion commanders' courses, the officers participate in a revision seminar dedicated to humanitarian law. It includes a chapter about the commanders' responsibility on their subordinates' behavior.
>
> In addition, in the curriculum of the College for Tactical Command (academic studies within a military framework taken before becoming a company commander) there is a course of 14 hours in which the international humanitarian law is instructed in a more profound way.
>
> Except for those constant frameworks of instruction, there are many lectures on international humanitarian law given to numerous IDF units in the navy, airforce, and the army. The lecturers are officers from the Military Advocate General's

Assistant for International Law's office and legal advisers of the Navy, the Judea and Samaria Division and the Gaza Division.

The IDF also has an 'Ethical Code' comprising, *inter alia*, certain 'Basic Values', which are: 1) Defence of the State, its Citizens and its Residents ..., 2) Love of the Homeland and Loyalty to the Country ..., and 3) Human Dignity.[51] This Code also sets out other values, including: 'Human Life',[52] and 'Purity of Arms'.[53]

There is, in addition, a separate 'Pocket Guide' for IDF soldiers serving in the Occupied Territories, which starts by encouraging soldiers to carry out their duties 'without causing needless harm to the civilian population'. It sets out a few key principles, eg obliging IDF soldiers to allow medicine and other basic necessities into Palestinian villages, and to prevent Israeli civilians from harming Palestinian civilians and their property. It also explicitly forbids the beating, abusing, degrading or 'punishing' of Palestinians by the IDF.[54]

iv   Training of Officers of the IDF—Regarding Children

As regards IDF training specifically on children, the IDF Public Relations Branch letter (above)[55] went on to state:

> IDF soldiers and officers are instructed to act properly towards children and to refrain from maltreatment of children as much as possible, and also to avoid causing harm to children who are not involved in military activity in the West Bank and in the Gaza Strip.
>
> Unfortunately, in many cases they are to be found in areas of combat.
>
> According to IDF regulations, every complaint or report about children maltreatment must be investigated. Disciplinary, command or criminal measures may be employed against the offenders. Those measures will be taken according to the severity of the incident.
>
> Unfortunately, we do not have exact numbers of children maltreatment complaints. We know of several incidents, which are in different stages of fact examination or investigation. Soldiers who have behaved not according to the legal and moral norms are punished severely.

The 'Pocket Guide' for IDF soldiers serving in the Occupied Territories (mentioned above) contains an explicit reference to children in connection with the use of rubber bullets, stating: 'It is forbidden to fire "rubber bullets" at children'.

Summary: The information presented above regarding the IDF came from official sources, and, despite repeated attempts, it did not prove possible in the available time to obtain reliable information from other sources on IDF training regarding children. According to the official sources therefore, the IDF does provide its personnel with IHL training, including some basic training regarding the treatment of children.

d)   Sierra Leone

i   Relevant Treaties Signed, Ratified, etc.

- the 1949 GCs (ratified on 10 June 1965)
- the 1977 GPs (acceded on 21 October 1986)
- the 1989 CRC (ratified on 18 June 1990)
- the 1997 Ottawa Convention (ratified on 25 April 2001)
- the 1998 Statute of the ICC (ratified on 15 September 2000)
- the 2000 Optional Protocol on Child Soldiers (ratified on 16 May 2002)

At the time of writing, Sierra Leone had not ratified the 1999 ILO Convention 182.

ii   Background Notes—See Appendix Four

iii   Training of Officers of the Republic of Sierra Leone Armed Forces (RSLAF)—General

After the cessation of hostilities in 2000/2001, a 'new army' was created in Sierra Leone, and was 'being trained by the IMATT team ... a team of trainers—mostly British army, but also including Australian, Canadian, American'.[56] According to another source, more than 8,000 Sierra Leonean soldiers were taught the basic rules of behaviour in combat under a 'British short-term training programme' (presumably IMATT).[57]

In addition, in 2001 the ICRC conducted training seminars for the RSLAF, UNAMSIL officers, RUF commanders, and the Civil Defence Force.[58] In total, the ICRC training apparently reached more than 8,500 soldiers and officers.[59]

Further information on military training in Sierra Leone came, in 2002, from a British Lieutenant Colonel acting as an adviser (on training and civil-military relations) to the RSLAF:[60]

> ICRC have already been involved in ... LOAC ... training, with the treatment of children being subsumed into this subject. The initial intention of the ICRC was to train the trainers, but they have also got involved in supplying teaching materials and arranging training for two officers in San Remo .... ICRC has also conducted a seminar at which all the senior officers in the Army were present.
> *Training Materials.* Our training materials have all been provided by the ICRC, or are locally reproduced copies. The aspiration is to eventually replace these with our own materials—however, the ICRC material is regarded as excellent (and culturally sensitive enough) to make this a very low priority.
> *Training Providers and Training Methods.* Training has been provided by ICRC and Caritas,[61] by legal officers, and increasingly by those in the chain of command as a part of routine training. Individual Training Directives (training objectives) are in the process of being produced; LOAC is one of the first six training objectives ... which come into effect 01 Jan 03. This will require all RSLAF soldiers and officers to

receive LOAC training every year, with this training being monitored and reported as a measure of military effectiveness of the units.' [The training should] 'take between 1-4 hours (depending upon the educational and literacy level of the participants) each year. This does not sound very much but it should be remembered that the initial training has already been received (and will in future be incorporated into all initial recruit training); also, trainees will be tested and re-trained if they fail to achieve a satisfactory standard. The teaching will involve role-playing and lectures. The tests will be knowledge based and conducted verbally (to overcome the illiteracy problem). Responsibility for this training lies firmly with the chain of command.' [The LOAC training will probably be] 'delivered by regimental officers, along with fitness and weapon handling.

Perceived Importance of the Training. … I have been struck by the importance given to it [the training] by senior Sierra Leonean officers. Personnel from "westernised" armies tend to take LOAC training for granted and pay lip service only to much of it. This is perhaps understandable, because the principles are thoroughly integrated into the cultural milieu …. Our soldiers still do wrong, of course, but there is never any doubt that they should know the difference between right and wrong …. In Sierra Leone … the appropriate behaviour has to be learned in a different way. To illustrate this last point, all the senior Sierra Leonean officers with whom I have discussed the subject believe inadequate time is being given to LOAC training and that we will be forced to increase it after the first year.

iv   Training of Officers of the RSLAF—Regarding Children

According to the UNICEF Child Protection Officer in Sierra Leone:[62]

On issues of children, we have been using the modules developed by Save the Children—Sweden with ECOWAS. A senior civil servant in the Ministry of Defence [a Sierra Leonean [63]] has also been attending all the regional training programmes run by Save the Children in conjunction with the ECOWAS countries. He is our main focal point. As the IMATT team were carrying out the training (batches of 1000), UNICEF in conjunction with some social workers from various NGOs were carrying out training on child protection issues. [64] There was one training for the foot soldiers and a longer training for the officers—again using the Save the Children Sweden manuals. In all we have trained about 7000.

The Ministry of Defence civil servant and one social worker also apparently:

carry out follow ups on the training and how the solders, once deployed, are using what they learned. … From the IMATT side, the collaboration is to ensure that we have training time with the new recruits, provide facilities, develop timetable etc.[65]

Further, '[i]n collaboration with the Ministry of Defence, UNICEF supported the development of a child protection unit within the force HQ of the new army.' [66]

As regards methodology, the UNICEF Child Protection Officer also commented that, within the framework of the Save the Children Sweden/ECOWAS modules (summarised in the Sierra Leone Chart, Appendix Three):

on the ground the level of education of the soldiers is very low, training has to be carried out in local languages, so we usually do small groups (30 or less) and it is all interactive. In certain cases we could use flip charts but not in general. For the officers it was different, we developed power point presentations, overheads, handouts etc. [67]

In addition, the Save the Children Sweden Regional Advisor on Children in Armed Conflict and Displacement commented that: 'SC-Sweden's partnerships with all its NGOs in the ECOWAS region take as their starting point in terms of training materials the manuals' (the Save the Children Sweden/ECOWAS manuals). However, apparently 'variations are introduced by the partners in term of their target audience (rank and peacekeeper/ national military) and this is definitely the case in Sierra Leone.' Further, the variations do not 'exist currently as additional written training materials. [They are] rather delivered from the trainers' own experience ….'. [68]

Summary: At the time of writing, it appeared that Sierra Leone was, in the aftermath of its protracted armed conflict, providing training in IHL to members of its armed forces, including specific training on children, largely based on the Save the Children Sweden/ECOWAS West Africa materials. It seems that in this context, where so many children had been caught up in conflict, the need for some child-focussed military training was being recognised.

e)   South Africa

i   Relevant Treaties Signed, Ratified, etc.

– the 1949 GCs (acceded on 31 March 1952)
– the 1977 GPs (acceded on 21 November 1995)
– the 1989 CRC (ratified on 16 June 1995)
– the 1997 Ottawa Convention (ratified on 26 June 1998)
– the 1998 Statute of the ICC (ratified on 27 November 2000)
– the 1999 ILO Convention 182 (ratified on 7 June 2000)
– the 2000 Optional Protocol on Child Soldiers (signed on 8 February 2002)

ii   Background Notes—See Appendix Four

iii   Training of Officers of the South African National Defence Force (SANDF)—General

According to one authority,[69] SANDF 'has embraced the necessity to teach IHL, and co-operates closely with the regional office of the ICRC' in providing this. SANDF also sent selected members of its staff to the San Remo Institute for IHL training (and see San Remo Chart, Appendix Three, for comments from SANDF personnel). Aside from that, this source commented that:

there is no generic training whatsoever for officers on the treatment of children.[70] What we have is a civic education programme, which was introduced post-1994, aimed at all ranks and levels of training, for the purpose of inculcating the necessary values and norms of defence in a democracy.

This programme included information on gender issues, cultural diversity, democratic concepts and practices, military professionalism, civilian control etc.[71]

In SANDF, all combatants started initially with the same basic training, but special training was additionally provided for those sent on peace support operations.[72]

iv   Training of Officers of the SANDF—Regarding Children

As indicated above, SANDF therefore did—in conjunction with the ICRC—offer some IHL training to its officers, but its 'civic education programme' contained 'nothing focussing on how the military should interact with and treat children'.[73]

Similarly, training for the Senior Command and the Staff Duties course at the South African Army College, including their peace support operations module, apparently had 'no focus on children—not surprising, perhaps, as the entire course focuses on the operational level of war (and peacekeeping).' There was also

> no mission-specific training on children for our contingents that deployed to DRC [Democratic Republic of the Congo], Ethiopia/Eritrea and Burundi .... However, these were staff officers and specialists such as air cargo handling teams who were not expected to have much to do with local people. In the case of Burundi, it's basically a V.I.P. protection team. Training on children will obviously become more salient when SANDF assumes more 'conventional' peacekeeping roles.[74]

However, a Lieutenant Colonel in the South African Ministry of Defence confirmed that children *were* in fact specifically mentioned in the SANDF training material as 'part of Lecture IV of the Law of Armed Conflict (LOAC) module' based on 1949 GC IV.[75] This lecture did refer to various key issues affecting children in armed conflict, such as: child welfare; relief supplies; zones, and family contact (see South Africa Chart, Appendix Three). Apart from that, the Lieutenant Colonel stated that:

> In all other respects children are treated in accordance with the rules laid down for the protection of civilian persons. As far as child soldiers are concerned, as best be ascertained, if they voluntarily give up their arms they will be treated as civilian persons. If however they act as belligerents they will be treated in accordance with the Rules of Conduct and Engagement (ROCE) in force at the time. However, there is no training material on this subject.

Save the Children South Africa had apparently considered providing military training to SANDF, as conducted by Save the Children in other regions of Africa. However, at the time of writing, it was felt that such training 'would require resources that we do not have.'[76]

Summary: It appears that SANDF personnel did, with ICRC assistance, receive some IHL training. In addition, there was apparently specific basic training on child civilians (see Appendix Three)—although it was not clear if this training was offered to all SANDF personnel, or only those of certain ranks. Training was not provided as regards child soldiers.

f)   Sri Lanka

i   Relevant Treaties Signed, Ratified, etc.

- the 1949 GCs (ratified on 28 February 1959)
- the 1989 CRC (ratified on 12 July 1991)
- the 1999 ILO Convention 182 (ratified on 1 March 2001)
- the 2000 Optional Protocol on Child Soldiers (ratified on 8 September 2000)

At the time of writing, Sri Lanka had not signed the 1977 GPs, the 1997 Ottawa Convention or the 1998 Statute of the ICC.

ii   Background Notes—See Appendix Four

iii   Training of Officers of the Sri Lankan Army (SLA))—General

With the help of the ICRC, the SLA formally launched an IHL training programme in 2001. In total, the ICRC estimated that 10,000 military personnel benefited from this initiative.[77] By the end of 2001, the Sri Lankan Sunday Observer newspaper wrote that '24,044 servicemen including 898 officers' were trained during the year on IHL and human rights law 'with a view to minimizing the human rights violations by servicemen.' This article also stated that:

> According to research conducted by the Army, only 125 servicemen were trained on humanitarian law from 1997 to 2000. But, 98% of the sample group have stated that is was very important to learn ... IHL.[78]

An article written in 1997 by an ICRC military delegate in South Asia stated that the 'post of a permanent ICRC delegate to the armed and security forces in South Asia was established in June 1995' and thus was a relatively recent development in a vast region covering India, Pakistan, Sri Lanka and Afghanistan.[79] The article described aspects of the ICRC approach to military training in general as well as in the specific region, including their 'two-strand' strategy of 'offering courses at military academies and staff colleges' in addition to offering courses for instructors (junior and warrant officers) who could then give instruction to the lower ranking personnel.[80] The ICRC has also provided some training for the LTTE.[81]

Another ICRC military training delegate in the region confirmed, in December 2001, that the ICRC syllabus for the training of officers was 'sometimes taught by the ICRC and, increasingly at lower levels, by SLA instructors trained by the ICRC'. However, there was, at that time, no specific SLA training on children.[82]

The following summary gives an overview of the level of IHL training in the SLA at the time of writing: 1) as regards the *ICRC syllabus*, mentioned above, the course outline for officer cadets included: a lecture on IHL[83]; a lecture on Behaviour in Action,[84] and a lecture on Conduct of Operations.[85] The ICRC course outline for Junior Command courses began with a lecture on Commanders Responsibility,[86] followed by a lecture on Conduct of Operations (as above); 2) as regards the *IHL training provided by the SLA itself*, materials sent in 2002 by an officer in the SLA Directorate of Humanitarian Laws[87] indicated various initiatives (apparently recent), outlined in: a) an interesting document listing 'Steps Taken by Army to Minimize IHL/HR Violations', and expressing the intention to minimise human rights violations committed by the SLA;[88] b) a document summarising the 'Outcome of Field Research on IHL/HR—SL Army', which concluded that '[g]enerally it is clear that 40% of troops have no knowledge of IHL. Therefore, it becomes important that regular IHL/HR training should take place in order to prevent ... violations ...'; c) a document entitled 'Rules of War' to be signed and adhered to by all SLA Officers and Soldiers, summarising 11 key principles;[89] d) various course summaries, including outlines of: two three-day 'Refresher/Advanced' courses for 'Officer Instructors', (one on Human Rights Law and another on IHL) (2001); a five-day Human Rights Law 'Instructor Course for Officers' (2001); and two five-day courses for Senior Commanding Officers, (one on IHL and one on Human Rights Law) (2002), and e) sample questions from the 'IHL/HR Law Advanced Course for Officer Instructors', (incorporating eg an assignment on human rights violations by the SLA, and steps taken to prevent these).

iii   Training of Officers of the SLA—Regarding Children

An ICRC delegate to Sri Lanka confirmed in December 2001 that, in general 'there are no training materials re: treatment of children' in the SLA, and that '(t)hey are often spoken of in the same breath as women and included in "vulnerable groups" particularly in relation to arrest and detention'.[90]

However, later that month this delegate sent information concerning a UNICEF-backed 'proposal to conduct just the sort of IHL training which the Sri Lanka army does not do just now in respect of children.' It was thought that the training might start sometime in 2002, and would focus specifically on the treatment of captured child combatants while in military custody (see below).[91]

Further, the information on IHL training of the SLA, received from the SLA officer in 2002 (mentioned above), indicated that progress was being made in integrating some materials on children, as follows: a) attention was being given to the proposed UNICEF 'Training of Sri Lankan Security Forces in the Protection of Captured Child Combatants while in Military Custody'. The Introduction to this proposal referred to the fact that '(m)any children under the age of 18 years join the LTTE, and some of these are captured . .' by the SLA. It stated that '(h)aving suffered one form of abuse of their rights (recruitment) they then find themselves in a new vulnerable situation where further abuses may take place'. The aim of the UNICEF-backed training was therefore to train 'senior and mid-ranking Officers' of the SLA in 'proper ways' of handling captured child combatants, and to develop guidelines for this purpose; and b) two of the course outlines mentioned above contained modules on children: one on 'Problems of Children in War Areas of Armed Conflict' (Instructor Course for Officers on Human Rights Law, 2001), and one on 'Women and Child Rights in Conflict' (Training Programme on Human Rights Law for Senior Commanding Officers, 2002). However, without access to the materials used in those two courses it was clearly not possible to assess their content.

Summary: It appears that the SLA was, as of about 2001, offering widespread basic IHL training to its personnel, with the assistance of the ICRC. An interesting initiative was the concept of requiring SLA combatants to sign and adhere to a document summarising basic IHL 'Rules of War'. In addition, some training regarding children seemed to be underway, or about to be initiated, although at the time of writing this was apparently limited either to a specific aspect (captured child soldiers) or to a few training courses. Further, the available information indicated that training on children was not included in IHL courses (only in human rights courses). Therefore attention may not have been paid to issues such as the training of SLA personnel regarding conduct in combat towards children in opposing forces (the LTTE).[92]

g)   Uganda

i   Relevant Treaties Signed, Ratified, etc.

– the 1949 GCs (acceded on 18 May 1964)
– the 1977 GPs (acceded on 13 March 1991)
– the 1989 CRC (ratified on 17 August 1990)
– the 1997 Ottawa Convention (ratified on 25 February 1999)
– the 1998 Statute of the ICC (ratified on 14 June 2002)
– the 1999 ILO Convention 182 (ratified on 21 June 2001)
– the 2000 Optional Protocol on Child Soldiers (acceded on 6 May 2002)

ii   Background Notes—See Appendix Four

Note: Since the author visited Uganda for the purpose of observing military training on children, as already mentioned, the factual information under each heading below will be presented first, followed by the author's brief observations.

The reasons for selecting Uganda as the one country to visit for observation of military training regarding children have already been outlined in the Introduction to this Chapter, above. However, the author was not ultimately able to observe such training, as the session scheduled for September 2002 was postponed at the last moment due, among other things, to an escalation of conflict in the region.[93] Nonetheless, the visit was fruitful and informative, as the author was still able to go to the conflict zone around Gulu in Northern Uganda[94] (where the training was scheduled to take place), and interview Ugandan People's Defence Forces (UPDF) personnel in the region, as well as some former child soldiers who had been abducted by the Lord's Resistance Army (LRA) and later escaped. (In any event, as regards observing military training on children, the author was able to both observe and conduct such training for officers attending the San Remo Institute (see Chapter Nine below)).

The postponed training did apparently finally take place in December 2002, involving about 150 officers and ten facilitators. It was a two-week general human rights training workshop, with four days devoted to issues concerning children.[95]

iii   Training of Officers of the Ugandan People's Defence Forces (UPDF)—General

It proved difficult to ascertain the level of general IHL training in the UPDF. One of the interviewed UPDF officers involved in the training concerning children (discussed below) stated that 'All [UPDF] soldiers must learn something about the laws of armed conflict—at least the basics. The higher ranks learn more. The UPDF has worked with the ICRC on dissemination.'[96] However, a Save the Children Denmark staff member, also involved in training, commented that the impression in their training sessions was that UPDF soldiers seemed to have little basic IHL training. This staff member pointed out that the ICRC had apparently withdrawn from an active role in training the UPDF after six of their delegates were killed in April 2001, in a region of the Democratic Republic of the Congo then under the control of the UPDF.[97] Nonetheless, in 2001 the ICRC apparently launched a three-month radio and poster campaign in Uganda on the basic rules of IHL.[98]

In addition, some UPDF officers had participated in peacekeeping courses in Sweden, including seven officers who were also trained on 'child rights'.[99] Further, in 2002 the Ugandan Human Rights Commission was apparently engaged in preparing a human rights training manual for the UPDF.[100]

Observations: It seemed somewhat ironic that, in the one country visited by the author specifically to observe military training, it proved difficult to ascertain the level of general IHL training. That said, perhaps this difficulty can be attributed precisely to the fact of being physically present in the country, in the sense that the reality 'on the ground' is bound to be more complex than the reality 'on paper'. However, it could also be partly due to the time constraints of the stay in Uganda, and the fact that a planned visit to a military training establishment in Jinja proved impossible to organise during that period.

In any event, it is again important to stress that the intention here is not to criticise UPDF training, but to indicate some practical difficulties that only become evident during a research visit, and that can be encountered in military training in many countries, particularly when resources are limited and there is an on-going armed conflict.

iv   Training of Officers of the UPDF—Regarding Children

The section below will summarise: a) information on UPDF training concerning children (the focus here is on the UPDF 'Fourth Division', since they were apparently the 'state fighting force');[101] b) relevant information from the author's visit to the region in September 2002, and c) observations. Since the situation in Northern Uganda is extremely complex, the information below can only highlight a few of the main issues arising.

a)   UPDF Training Concerning Children

According to the Save the Children Denmark 'Briefing Pack',[102] the decision to conduct child-specific training in Northern Uganda was prompted by a number of factors, including: 1) the obvious fact that so many children were involved in the conflict, and that 'the LRA consists 90% of children who are abducted', and 2) 'concerns of alleged abuse' by the UPDF 'of returning formerly abducted children—needs and welfare not met, no system of monitoring, prolonged stay in barracks' etc.[103]

The 'Briefing Pack' also outlined a number of child-specific training sessions provided for the UPDF by Save the Children: 1) sensitisation of senior UPDF officers—60 officers (May 1999); 2) training of child rights trainers in Gulu—15 trainers (June 1999), and c) training of the core team of the UPDF Child Protection Unit on psychological support and child rights (July 2000).[104]

A later 'Project Progress Report' by Save the Children Denmark regarding the period January to June 2002 pointed out that the security situation (following the start of 'Operation Iron Fist' (see 'Background Notes')) 'slowed down the implementation of project activities within the Fourth Division', and that 'most of the trained UPDF personnel have been relocated and have been engaged in the Operation Iron Fist'.[105] This report also expressed other concerns about the implementation and evaluation of the child-specific training within the UPDF (such as inadequate linkages between the Fourth Division and the Ministry of Defence regarding observance of child rights, and insufficient focus on prevention of child abduction and recruitment), and outlined strategies to address some of these.[106]

As well as offering child-specific training, Save the Children Denmark had, in conjunction with the UPDF, established some Child Protection Units, eg in the UPDF Gulu barracks. These 'units' were established as a focal point within the barracks to receive and temporarily house children who were formerly abducted by the LRA, and who had escaped, been captured in combat, or 'rescued' by the UPDF. According to the Save the Children Denmark 'Briefing Pack', since this initiative started (in about November 1999), '5,500 children have passed through the CPU [Child Protection Unit]'.[107]

In addition to the above Save the Children initiatives, the Ugandan Human Rights Commission apparently intended to incorporate, in the human rights training manual being prepared for the UPDF (mentioned above), information specifically concerning the treatment of children.[108]

b)   Pertinent information from visit to region—September 2002.

In a meeting in Gulu on *23 September 2002* (attended by a UPDF Brigadier and other UPDF personnel; a Save the Children Denmark representative; a representative from the Ugandan Human Rights Commission, and the author), the UPDF Brigadier who had made the decision to postpone the scheduled child-specific training gave his reasons for doing so, including the following: 1) the conflict in the region was too intense at that time for him to allow 20 to 25 officers to meet for five days in a comfortable hotel,[109] and 2) soldiers in the region were 'in a state of deprivation' and that the army was 'overstretched financially'. They needed concrete resources, eg vehicles, not training on rights; 3) the Brigadier felt that Save the Children should put more resources into provision for the families of UPDF soldiers, rather than focussing on abducted children, stating that the former 'are civilian victims as well'; 4) he emphasised that the 'ultimate solution is to stop the insurgency', and 5) he was concerned that it was difficult to assess the impact of the scheduled training, and questioned whether indeed such training had an impact that continued beyond the conclusion of the workshop.

A different perspective on the Save the Children/UPDF child-specific training was provided on the following day (*24 September 2002*) by a Lieutenant Colonel in the UPDF who had been involved as a trainer on their previous courses. He made a number of key points, highlighting some of the dilemmas and realities as he saw them. This officer first commented on the huge numbers of abducted children in the LRA, stating that 'the cheapest biological weapon is children'. He then described the efforts of the UPDF to adapt to this 'new phenomenon', in which armed children were in the opposing force, the LRA, and yet the local population expected the UPDF to rescue such children from the LRA. The UPDF had to evolve a new strategy—use of absolute minimum force. They would not, eg, use a 'scorched earth' policy—and 'that is one reason why it has taken so long to quash the rebellion. You cannot speak of victory when you have killed 100 or 200 children.' On occasion the UPDF had refrained from attacking when children were in the LRA front line.[110]

This officer further commented that if a UPDF soldier confronted a child soldier with a gun, the child was a legitimate target if he did not drop his gun. However, the UPDF have found that they could:

> demoralise children by applying sufficient fire so that they see it is good to surrender. The message has spread in the community and within the LRA that the UPDF will not harm those who surrender. However, the problem with surrendering *en masse* is intimidation by LRA commanders (who may then retaliate against the children's families). So, the children prefer to be captured in battle—that way their families will be safe.

This officer stated that 8000 UPDF soldiers had received some training on the treatment of children in recent years,[111] and that before any battle with the LRA there was always a briefing, including orders on trying to rescue children, and to use minimum force. He emphasised the need for continuous training, as soldiers 'rotate'.

As regards sexual abuse of children by the UPDF, this officer stated that military personnel involved in such abuse 'would be surrendered to a court of law'. Sex with minors (under 18) and rape are both prohibited in Ugandan law, where they are, in theory, capital offences, although in practice there is usually an alternative 'heavy sentence'.

Finally, this officer made the interesting point that he felt child-specific training for the UPDF was useful not least in that 'soldiers have their own children, and become better parents for their own children after the training.'

Following this meeting, on *25 September 2002* the author interviewed (in the presence of their 'social worker') three recently escaped former LRA child soldiers about their treatment by the UPDF. The intention, in interviewing them, was to have an impression of their experience of how the UPDF actually dealt with children in practice. Obviously this was a tiny sample and cannot be considered representative'. Nonetheless, the statements of these three child soldiers, who were aged between about 13 to 15, were informative.

They were being housed by an NGO, the Gulu Child Support Organisation,[112] one of the NGOs that receive and then reintegrate into the community such child soldiers, as well as many 'child mothers' abducted by the LRA and used as 'wives'.

All three had passed through the Gulu Child Protection Unit in the UPDF barracks, *en route* to the Gulu Child Support Organisation (two for periods of two weeks, and one for five days), and all complained of their treatment at the hands of the UPDF while in the Child Protection Unit. Their complaints included being beaten ('beating is common, almost routine in the main barracks'); harshly interrogated ('the problem is that they probe you so much it is hard to be consistent', and 'the UPDF is more interested in information-gathering than in helping us'), and being put under pressure to join the UPDF ('they are trying to lure you to become a member of the UPDF'). They also complained of inadequate food while in UPDF hands (which was particularly resented as their perception was that food was available, but not shared).

Finally, on *29 September 2002*, the author was able to observe a video made of the July 2000 'Training of Child Rights Trainers' workshop. The workshop consisted of about 20 persons, including two women, and not all of the participants were officers (although Save the Children had requested officers only). The video provided a graphic illustration of the challenges faced in providing child-specific training in this context, not least the problems encountered in encouraging trust and communication between the participants themselves.[113] Highlights of the video included a discussion of the definition of 'child'; a debate about the differences between a 'rights-based' and a 'needs-based' approach to children, and a session on international law. Apparently the latter subject is often difficult, partly due to lack of basic IHL training, and also due to the perception that international 'treaties are "up there", not here with us in Gulu'.[114] There was also a session on communication with children, and the differences between an interview, and interrogation.[115] In addition, the training included a visit by the UPDF personnel to the Gulu Child Support Organisation, during which they heard the moving and harrowing testimony of a young woman who had been abducted by the LRA.[116]

c)   Observations

The saga of the 2001/2002 Save the Children/UPDF child-specific military training in Uganda—and its last-minute cancellation—clearly highlighted the difficulties encountered in trying to conduct rather long and ambitious workshops of this nature in areas of on-going armed conflict. It also illuminated some problems in civil-military cooperation regarding: 1) communication, co-ordination, and an understanding of the hierarchy within the different branches of the armed forces,[117] as well as between the armed forces and the NGOs involved in training; and 2) the challenges faced in trying to ensure that there is a 'trickle down' of information from those who attend training workshops (ie passing on of information by the trainees to their colleagues and subordinates), and that there is adequate monitoring and evaluation of the training process as a whole. Further, it illustrated some dilemmas faced by NGOs regarding their role in such situations—eg do they respond to immediate needs that they see as a priority (such as establishing and maintaining the Child Protection Unit)? Or that others see as a priority (eg providing material resources for the families of the UPDF, as the Brigadier requested)? Do they try to take a longer-term and more strategic approach (eg providing military training, or even encouraging a negotiated settlement to the conflict, and putting resources into that)?

In addition, it was discouraging to observe that the former LRA child soldiers in the Gulu Child Support Organisation had little positive to say about their experience of the UPDF in the Child Protection Unit. This could be due, in part, to the acknowledged fact that child-specific training had not recently been held in the region, and in any event there had been transfer of trained staff.

Finally, there are dilemmas inherent in incorporating workshop encounters between military personnel and children who have been caught up in a particular conflict in which the military are still engaged. On the one hand, if conducted properly, such encounters could sensitise military personnel and greatly enhance the effectiveness of training on child rights and child protection in a military context (eg by encouraging different considerations to be weighed in the balance regarding proportionality, as has apparently happened in Uganda on occasion). On the other hand, military personnel may, eg, find such encounters inappropriate or even counter-productive. These issues should be openly discussed in well-conducted training.

Summary: The information gathered regarding Uganda indicates that both IHL and child-focussed military training were provided at certain times to certain personnel, although apparently not on a consistent basis. It also highlights some of the complex issues involved in trying to provide child-specific training in situations of on-going conflict. As mentioned, these include problems with trying to provide regular, effective training (including the challenge posed by forward planning, given the unstable situation), and problems with civil-military cooperation. The Ugandan country study also highlights the many dilemmas involved in conducting an armed conflict against an army of forced recruits, many of them still children, and some strategies that have been evolved in response to this (see eg interview of 24 September 2002). It again underlines the rather obvious point that the reality 'on the ground' is more challenging than would be apparent 'on paper'.

In summary, it is clear from the above that the selected countries currently or recently involved in armed conflict 'at home' (Category A) had developed a range of different strategies as regards both provision of military IHL training in general, and provision of such training specifically concerning children. The strategies of these countries will be summarised and compared with those of countries in Category (B) at the end of Chapter Nine below.

Endnotes

1   Part II is therefore intended to both supplement and illustrate Part I with practical examples of current practice. The core of this book nonetheless remains the summary of relevant law and policy and mechanisms for encouraging their implementation, as set out in Part I(A) and (B).

2   The selection was made after consultation with members of the Advisory Committee for the research on which this book is based (see Acknowledgements, above). Useful guidance was also given by members of the UN Committee on the Rights of the Child, in a meeting with the author on 23 May 2001.

The intention originally was to study about 40 countries, but it quickly became apparent that this was not feasible within the available time and resources. Unfortunately this meant that a number of countries whose military training practice might have been of particular interest (eg India and Russia) had to be omitted.

3   To some extent, this is a subjective judgement.

4   In fact, some commentators argue that certain countries in Category (B) bear responsibility for destabilising other countries, including some of those in Category (A), eg through colonialism and/or neo-colonialism—although others would dispute this view. It is beyond the scope of this work to discuss such issues here, but see eg, F Fanon, *The Wretched of the Earth* (London, Penguin, 1963); E Galeano, *Open Veins of Latin America: Five Centuries of the Pillage of a Continent* (New York, Monthly Review Press, 1973), and M Davis, *Late Victorian Holocausts: El Nino Famines and the Making of the Third World* (London, Verso, 2001).

5   See http://www.un.org/Depts/dpko/dpko/contributors/December2002Summary.pdf, on p 4. The nine countries contributing most substantially were all 'developing countries', with Australia—the country contributing most from Category (B)—in tenth place.

6   See eg, A Gnaedinger, 'Security Challenges for Humanitarian Action' 841 *IRRC* (2001), pp 171–182. In fact, the ICRC carries out 40% of its activities in Africa (*ibid*). See also the John Hopkins University website, at http://www.sais-jhu.edu/CMtoolkit/index.php?name=gro-regional, visited on 12 Dec 2002.

7   See eg, J Borger, 'Mideast War Game "Fixed to Ensure US Victory"', *Guardian Weekly* (29 Aug–4 Sept 2002), which describes 'the biggest war game in United States military history, staged [in Aug 2002] at a cost of \$250m with 13,000 troops …'.

8   In 2000, the Research Assistant on this project at that time also attended an early SC military training session, held in the Ivory Coast, for ECOWAS countries. However, the

object of that visit was to have some idea of the approach being taken, and to make initial contacts, and detailed observations of the training process itself were not made.

9   Given the role and rank of some of the informants contacted in the course of this research, the desire for confidentiality was understandable—and a decision was made to generally adopt a 'blanket' policy of anonymity, since any misunderstandings regarding identification of sources could possibly have had serious consequences for the informants. However, if readers require any information on a particular source, a request can be made to the author.

10   15–16 Jan 2001, and 24–25 May 2001.

11   23 May 2001.

12   14–18 Oct 2001, and 10–14 June 2002.

13   4 Jan 2000, and 31 May–1 June 2001.

14   Thus, even during the course of this research project, both the UK and Australia, eg, indicated that their military training programmes were being adjusted to pay more attention to law and policy affecting children.

15   With a Declaration of Succession, a newly independent state declares itself to be bound by a treaty which was applicable to its territory prior to independence.

16   These were: *Respect for international humanitarian law, a handbook for parliamentarians*, and *IHL: Answers to your questions*. ICRC, *ICRC Annual Report 2001* (Geneva, ICRC, 2002(a)), p 261.

17   ICRC news, 'Bosnia-Herzegovina: Former adversaries attend training course' (ICRC, 22 Feb 2001).

18   It did not prove possible to obtain specific information regarding military training in the Republika Srpska (Serbian Republic) branch of the armed forces of of BiH (see BiH 'Background Notes', Appendix Four).

19   SFOR was the NATO-led Stabilisation Force (again, see Appendix Four).

20   E-mail of 28 Oct 2002.

21   E-mail of 27 Nov 2002.

22   E-mail of 19 Jan 2003.

23   In a Declaration however, Colombia rejected the jurisdiction of the ICC over war crimes committed 'by Colombian nationals or on Colombian territory' (Art 8 of the 1998 Statute of the ICC) for a period of 7 years (Art 124, *ibid*). See, http://untreaty.un.org /ENGLISH/ bible/englishinternetbible/partI/ChapterXVIII/treaty10.asp, visited on 15 Sept 2002.

24   As mentioned in the Introduction to this Chapter, the present research cannot verify or assess the actual impact 'on the ground' of relevant initiatives in the 11 selected countries (with the limited exception of Uganda).

25   All but one of the military academies in Colombia had included IHL in their curricula by the end of 2001 (ICRC (2002(a)), p 228), and the ICRC held seminars in six army and navy schools in order to also include IHL in practical instruction (*id*).

26   See Republic of Colombia, Ministry of National Defense [*sic*], *Annual Human Rights and International Humanitarian Law Report 2000* (hereafter Annual HR and IHL Report 2000) (Colombia, Jan 2001), p 13. This states that 'by the end of 2001 there will be three times as many professional soldiers as there were at the start of the present government in 1998' and 'air mobility capability will have doubled …'.

27   Letter from V G Ricardo, Ambassador, Colombian Embassy in UK, dated 22 Aug 2001.

28   See eg, The Office of the Vicepresident [*sic*] of Colombia, *Policy on Human Rights and International Humanitarian Law Progress Report: March 2000* (hereafter Policy Report 2000), (Bogota, 2000), p 25, which states: '… the number of complaints against the Military Forces for human rights violations went down from 2,000 in 1996, to 463 in 1997, to 319 in 1998, to only 40 in 1999 … a very significant 98 per cent.' See also Chapter VII on 'Complaints and Proceedings against Members of the Police and the Armed Forces in Human Rights and [IHL] Cases', Annual HR and IHL Report 2000, pp 96–99. Both the latter Report (pp 103–117) and the Policy Report 2000 (pp 57–65) contain information on specific cases of IHL or human rights violations committed by, among others, members of the armed forces.

29   The Annual HR and IHL Report 2000, p 6, states that, in 1999, all persons under 18 who 'had joined the ranks of their own free will' were released from the armed forces and the police, and that this resulted in the release of 'more than a thousand minors'.

30   Both publications already cited, (see n 26 and 28 above).

31   Policy Report 2000, p 16. See also Annual HR and IHL Report 2000, p 32.

32   Annual HR and IHL Report 2000, p 41.

33   *Ibid,* p 42.

34   *Ibid,* pp 44–45. A chart provided by the Colombian Embassy on specific human rights and IHL courses for the Colombian military in 2000 indicated that IHL training of the army was almost entirely conducted by the ICRC in the form of one or (occasionally) two day courses, while the navy tended to provide its own training. See also, ICRC (2002(a)), p 228. The ICRC had apparently been involved in Colombia since 1980, and ICRC activities in 2002 included 'Regular contacts and dissemination sessions on the ICRC mandate and IHL … carried out in the field for some 2,300 military officers at division, brigade and battalion level …' (ICRC, 'Colombia: ICRC operations in 2002' (9 Sept 2002)).

35   See eg, Annual HR and IHL Report 2000, p 45.

36   This Bill characterised forced disappearance as a crime, and extended responsibility for this crime to, *inter alia,* public servants, including the armed forces. Policy Report 2000 (pp 33–34).

37   This Code, *inter alia,* incorporated into Colombian criminal law 'a number of conducts that constitute breaches of [IHL]', including eg homicide, bodily harm, torture and sexual abuse of persons protected by IHL. The purpose of characterising breaches of IHL as criminal was 'to ensure that more severe sanctions are imposed for attacks against persons and property protected by [IHL] …' (*Ibid,* pp 34–35).

38   Annual HR and IHL Report 2000, p 51. The new justice system provided, *inter alia,* for separation of prosecutors and judges from the line of command (*Ibid,* pp 53–54).

39   Annual HR and IHL Report 2000, pp 100–102. This states that the Colombian armed forces were, 'along with the Church … looked on most favourably of all private and public institutions by the vast majority of' Colombians (according to a recent Gallup poll).

40   Annual HR and IHL Report 2000, pp 171–177.

41   This is apparently part of the Delegation on the Rights of Childhood, Adolescence and Women, under the auspices of the official human rights ombudsman.

42   E-mail of 30 April 2002. This information seems to contradict the official position already summarised regarding training in human rights law.

43   This conference was mentioned in the chart provided by the Colombian Embassy (above, n 34). No additional details were supplied regarding this conference.

44   E-mail from SC Colombia representative, 6 June 2002.

45 It was reported that, on discovering that they had killed school children and not guerril-las, the soldiers 'felt nothing but pain and despair, and burst into tears and began sobbing' (*El Tiempo*, 17 Aug 2000, cited in Annual HR and IHL Report 2000, p 173. See also *El Tiempo*, 19 April 2002 (http://eltiempo.terra.com.co/) and *El Pais*, 19 April 2002, (available at http://elpais-cali.terra.com.co/HOY/NAL/A220N6.html, visited on 8 May 2002)).

46 Annual HR and IHL Report 2000, p 177.

47 *Note*: The case studies presented here will not include a separate study on Palestine. This is partly because only 11 countries could be studied, and it was necessary to cover different geographical regions. It was also because the present research focuses on training of officers of national armed forces, and Palestine was, at the time of writing, not generally recognised as a separate nation state—although its status was disputed. It was an 'authority' with special rights in international law. It was said (UN Doc below) that the goal of the Oslo peace process was to establish an independent Palestinian state; relations between more than 100 states and the Palestinian Authority were similar to inter-state relations, and the Palestinian Authority had observer status in many international organisations. As stated in UN Doc E/CN4/2001/121 (16 March 2001) 'Question of the violation of human rights in the occupied Arab territories, including Palestine', para 37: '[t]he Palestinian question is, therefore, seen by many as a colonial issue and the recognition of Palestinian statehood as the last step in the decolonization process initiated by the General Assembly in its resolution 1514 (XV)'.

48 Israel had signed the 1998 Statute of the ICC, but later announced that it would not ratify it (see, http://www.iccnow.org/html/country.html#I, visited on 19 Aug 2002). Israel also signed, on 5 Aug 2001, an agreement with the US, protecting US nationals from transfer, extradition or surrender to the ICC (see, http://www.iccnow.org/html/country.html#I, visited on 19 Aug 2002).

49 ICRC (2002(a)), p 331.

50 Letter of 19 March 2002.

51 This states, regarding 'Human Dignity': 'Every human being is of value regardless of his or her origin, religion, nationality, gender, status or position' (IDF website, http://www.idf.il/english/doctrine/doctrine.stm, visited on 2 Aug 2002).

52 This states regarding 'Human Life': 'The IDF servicemen and woman will act in a judicious and safe manner in all they do, out of recognition of the supreme value of human life …'.

53 As regards 'Purity of Arms': 'The IDF servicemen and women will use their weapons and force only for the purpose of their mission, only to the necessary extent and will maintain their humanity even during combat. IDF soldiers will not use their weapons and force to harm human beings who are not combatants or prisoners of war, and will do all in their power to avoid causing harm to their lives, bodies, dignity and property.' (IDF website, http://www.idf.il/english/doctrine/doctrine.stm, visited on 2 Aug 2002).

54 See 'English Translation of Pocket Guide for soldiers serving in the occupied territories', on website: http://www.btselem.org/english/special/soldiersbooklet/index.asp, visited on 19 Aug 2002.

55 Letter of 19 March 2002.

56 E-mail from Child Protection Officer, UNICEF Sierra Leone, 10 Nov 2001. IMATT (the International Military Advisory Training Team)—was part of the UK government's programme of assistance to restore stability in post-conflict Sierra Leone.

57 ICRC, 'Sierra Leone: Promoting International Humanitarian Law', 2:7 *ICRC News* (2002).

58 For information on these bodies see Sierra Leone 'Background Notes', Appendix Four.
59 ICRC (2002(a)), p 114.
60 E-mail of 10 Sept 2002.
61 Caritas Makeni is the local NGO partner of CAFOD (the English and Welsh Catholic Fund for Overseas Development). CAFOD is one of the 154 Catholic organisations of Caritas Internationalis working on relief, development and social service (see http://www.caritas.org).
62 UNICEF e-mail, 10 Nov 2001.
63 'The British are providing technical support to the Ministry of Defence only. They are not in positions of authority.' UNICEF Child Protection Officer e-mail, 22 Nov 2001.
64 According to the Child Protection Officer (*Id*): 'The training by IMATT consists of 1. Military training for the new army, 2. technical support in the areas of logistics, administration, engineering, etc. During the military training which takes place at two camps, there are some sessions on human rights, international humanitarian law, child rights etc. When this training started the contact person at the Ministry of Defence contacted UNICEF to explain that he has been trained as part of an ECOWAS training programme to teach soldiers about issues pertaining to child rights, child soldiers etc. He asked our assistance in incorporating this into the training of the new military. UNICEF contacted the British training team who stated that this was not a problem and a schedule was drawn up. UNICEF mobilised 10 trainers from among the child protection agencies it works with. UNICEF carried out a trainers of trainers programme with them in order for them to facilitate the training of the new recruits. This was done in collaboration with the Ministry of Defence. We started this training before the final modules were available from SC/ECOWAS. Each trainer was an experienced social worker so we were able to adapt and develop our own training programme .... We carried out the training of over 6,000 recruits before the modules came in.'
65 *Id.*
66 *Id.* And see below regarding the Ugandan army Child Protection Units.
67 *Id.*
68 E-mail of 28 Feb 2002.
69 E-mail from staff member in the South African Institute of Security Studies (ISS), 25 Jan 2002.
70 However, according to a SANDF officer, reference to children is apparently included in their general IHL training (as mentioned in the text below).
71 ISS e-mail, 25 Jan 2002.
72 Interview with South African Major General, 18 Dec 2000. His view was that, in peace support training, the main difference (from conventional training) is that 'there is no enemy .... The job of the soldier is to mediate.'
73 ISS e-mail, 25 Jan 2002. The writer concluded that military training on children 'wasn't a priority' when the civic education programme was drafted.
74 *Id.*
75 Letter of 5 April 2001. The letter also indicated that SANDF was interested in the SC S West Africa/ECOMOG training, but SC South Africa was not offering such training at the time (see text).
76 E-mail from SC South Africa, 30 Aug 2002. Also e-mails from SC S (7 May 2001), and SC South Africa (26 Feb 2002).

77 ICRC (2002(a)), p 193. Some members of the SLA, including senior officers (male and female), were also provided with a sex education programme by an organisation (Institute for Development of Community Strengths) cooperating with officials in the armed forces. The goal was to 'reduce or control the spread of STDs/HIV/AIDS among the army soldiers'. Report available at, http://www.unaids.org/ bestpractice/digest/files/ sexforsoldiers.html, visited on 25 Feb 2002.

78 R Kangaraarachchi, 'Army training on Humanitarian Law, a success' *Sunday Observer* (9 Dec 2001).

79 Roberts (1997), p 5.

80 Training was apparently given at three main levels, and covered the three services (army, navy and air force), as well as paramilitary. It incorporated 'junior ranks … young officers … and senior officers and staff officers'. *Ibid,* pp 6–7.

81 Regarding the LTTE, see Sri Lanka 'Background Notes', Appendix Four. An example provided to the author of a five-day ICRC training for the LTTE included modules on, *inter alia,* the 1949 GCs, IHL principles, human rights law, and command responsibility. (E-mail from former ICRC delegate, 2 March 2002.)

82 E-mail of 6 Dec 2001.

83 The lecture included modules on the nature of IHL; its main principles (limitation, proportionality, humanity, military necessity); protective zones, and victims of armed conflict.

84 This included an introduction emphasising the duty to operate within IHL, and the commander's responsibility.

85 This incorporated a list of prohibited actions, such as attacking civilians.

86 This, *inter alia,* dealt with liability, and stressed the need to respect IHL.

87 Attachments to e-mail of 7 Jan 2002.

88 The list of 'steps taken' included: training had been carried out at field level; officers had been trained as instructors of IHL; refresher courses had been conducted for trained officer instructors; IHL was included in all courses at training establishments; human rights training had 'for the first time' been integrated into the training of instructors; an IHL training video was produced; arrangements made for soldiers to pledge adherence to IHL (see below); an IHL training manual for officers was being developed; IHL questions were included in officers' promotion exams, and handbooks, posters etc. were distributed to the troops.

89 These included: 'I will fight only enemy combatants and attack only military objectives; I will not kill, torture or abuse prisoners of war; I will treat all civilians humanely; I understand that disobeying these rules is a crime …'.

90 E-mail of 6 Dec 2001.

91 Letter of 18 Dec 2001.

92 However, such training may no longer be necessary since, at the time of writing, it seemed that a ceasefire was in place (see 'Background Notes').

93 The practical difficulties encountered in organising week-long military training sessions on children, especially during an on-going armed conflict, were illustrated by the Ugandan experience. Thus, eg a SC Denmark (hereafter SC D)/UPDF training session had initially been scheduled for Nov 2001. However, this was rescheduled—due to lack of funding—until a session was finally confirmed for the end of June 2002. On this occasion the training was again postponed a few days beforehand, as the LRA was apparently in Gulu, the venue for the training, and officers could not be spared for the training. Despite

this, the Sept 2002 training was scheduled to take place—once more—in Gulu, and was again cancelled at the last moment, and for similar reasons.

94 See Uganda 'Background Notes', Appendix Four.

95 Telephone interview with SC D staff member, 4 Dec 2002.

96 Meeting with UPDF Lt Col, 24 Sept 2002.

97 SC D staff member interviewed, 23 and 29 Sept 2002. See also ICRC (2002(a)), p 124.

98 *Ibid*, p 125. However, this campaign could have taken place prior to the April attack on the ICRC delegates.

99 See SC D, 'Briefing Pack: Strengthening the Child Protection Unit, UPDF Fourth Division Gulu' (Copenhagen, SC D, Jan 2001), p 7.

100 Interview with SC D staff, 29 Sept 2002.

101 SC D, 'Project Progress Report: Mainstreaming Child Rights into the Uganda People's Defence Forces (UPDF)' (Copenhagen, SC D, Jan–June 2002).

102 SC D (Jan 2001).

103 *Ibid*, p 1.

104 *Ibid*, pp 2–4. This document summarised the outcome of these training sessions, including 'increased awareness of the military on child rights and protection issues within the Fourth Division', and 'improved welfare … of the returning formerly abducted children' within the Child Protection Unit (*ibid*, p 6). See also report on UPDF training in ICRC (2002(a)), p 125.

105 SC D (Jan–June 2002), p 1 and see also p 11.

106 *Ibid*, pp 6–7 and p 10.

107 SC D (Jan 2001), p 1.

108 Interview with SC D staff, 29 Sept 2002. See also above, regarding the Dec 2002 human rights training of the UPDF.

109 The Brigadier stated that his conscience would not allow this, and 'What about the soldier in the trenches? Has he eaten?'.

110 As already mentioned in Chapter Four above.

111 According to this officer, 'every induction training of new recruits includes child protection', although this occurs mainly in the Fourth Division where there is most experience of encountering child soldiers.

112 At the date of the visit, the Gulu Child Support Organisation was housing about 130 formerly abducted children of both sexes, and a number of babies. A later visit on the same day to the Gulu Child Protection Unit in the Fourth Division Barracks found the unit then housing about 60 former LRA abductees, mainly children but including some adults.

113 The training included a number of 'ice-breaking' games for this purpose!

114 Discussion with SC D staff, 29 Sept 2002.

115 The participants felt that sometimes the UPDF needed to obtain information concerning the conflict from the former LRA members. However, the trainers emphasised that there was a need to decide the purpose of any interview session, and to adapt techniques accordingly—ie to interrogate for specific information only, or to interview more generally.

116 The workshop participants also participated in a football game with some of the young ex-LRA members, an event that was apparently very popular.

117 The Sept 2002 UPDF child-specific training was authorised by those in command in Gulu, but this decision was over-ridden at the last moment by the Brigadier, shortly after his arrival in the region.

9

Part II—Country Studies (Category B) and the ICRC

Introduction

The Introduction to Chapter Eight, above, has outlined the reasons for examining training in countries such as those in Category (B)—ie countries with considerable current or recent experience of armed conflict 'abroad' (not within their own jurisdiction); and/or that were or had recently been substantially involved in training of armed forces other than their own, and/or in peace support activities. The selection of these countries proved difficult, and in some ways the final choice regarding Categories (A) and (B) was unsatisfactory, as already mentioned (particularly in seeming to fall broadly into a 'north/south' divide). Nonetheless, the military training practice of the selected countries is revealing.

Country Studies: Category (B)—Countries Substantially Involved in Armed Conflict 'Abroad', and/or in Training, and/or in Peace Support Operations

a) Australia

i   Relevant Treaties Signed, Ratified, etc.

- the 1949 GCs (ratified on 14 October 1958)
- the 1977 GPs (ratified on 21 June 1991)
- the 1989 CRC (ratified on 17 December 1990)
- the 1997 Ottawa Convention (ratified on 14 January 1999)
- the 1998 Statute of the ICC (ratified on 2 July 2002)
- the 2000 Optional Protocol on Child Soldiers (signed on 21 October 2002)

Australia had, at the time of writing, not ratified the 1999 ILO Convention 182.

ii   Background Notes—See Appendix Four

iii   Training of Officers of the Australian Defence Force (ADF)—
          General

At the time of writing, officers of the ADF apparently received comprehensive
military training, including in IHL. According to a letter (November 2001) from the
ADF 'Director-General Defence Education and Training Policy',[1] the ADF:

> trains its officers progressively throughout their careers. Operations Law modules,
> including the Law of Armed Conflict and International Humanitarian Law, are
> covered within the three Services. The treatment of children in conflict is covered,
> in these modules, in 'civilians in conflict'.

It appeared that the training made no mention of child soldiers (see below).

By way of example of the general IHL training provided in 2002 by the ADF, the
above letter (November 2001) enclosed documents on: a) the *Initial Officer Training—All Services*—at the Australian Defence Force Academy. This included, in
their Military Law Exam, questions on all basic aspects of the LOAC;[2] b) the *Learning Outcomes' chart for Mid-Ranking Officers—All Services*—at the Australian
Command and Staff College. This included modules assessing, *inter alia*, the students' ability to 'identify where operations will be affected by legal considerations,
identify and source legal advice and incorporate legal advice and considerations in
the operational plan'; c) the *course outline for Senior Officers—All Services*—on
Legal Studies, for the College of Defence and Strategic Studies. This described a
two day course which aimed to, *inter alia*, 'provide an overview of the development
of International Law and International Humanitarian Law', including familiarising
participants with the principles of and recent developments in IHL, and with the
role of the UN; d) the *course outline for Specialist Officers—All Services—Legal
Officers Levels 1–3*, on Operations Law and LOAC subjects. This was a five day
course containing modules on LOAC issues, including modules for exercises,[3]
and e) the *Army All Corps Officer Training Continuum Audit* for Junior to Senior
Officers. Again, under the heading 'Military Justice', this contained modules on
'Individual Military Skills', which include the sub-headings 'Apply Military Law', and
'Comply with Operations Law'.

iv   Training of Officers of the ADF – Regarding Children

As already indicated above, in 2001 children were considered within the ADF
general IHL training modules as part of the topic 'civilians in conflict'. There was
apparently no training on child soldiers as such. Interestingly, a separate message
to the author in 2001 from an officer in the ADF, contacted in relation to this
research, stated, 'Your letter asking for info made people look closely at what we are
doing to train officers on the issue of child soldiers, so you have already achieved a
key objective …'.[4]

The ADF 'Director-General Defence Education and Training Policy' also stated in his November 2001 letter that:

> The complex issue of children in conflict is one that ADF takes seriously. To date there have been no charges laid for crimes against children in an operational environment within the ADF.

The Australian Red Cross distributed information on IHL which included specific, rather basic, materials on 'Women and War', and 'Children and War', and did, among other things, mention child soldiers. However, it was unclear to what extent this information was incorporated within military training. According to one source, it seemed unlikely that it was in fact included.[5] The Chart in Appendix Three therefore refers to the Red Cross material in italics, to highlight this uncertainty.

Summary: It appears that the ADF provided varying levels of IHL training tailored for the different officer ranks in its armed forces. However, training on children seemed limited to issues involving child civilians, as part of the general training on civilians, and therefore did not specifically address the issue of child soldiers.

b)   South Africa

Note: South Africa is included here as one of the countries in this category, Category (B)—particularly as regards its involvement in peace support activities in Africa. Since it is also included in Category (A), the relevant information regarding South Africa can be found above, in Chapter Eight, and in the Chart in Appendix Three.

c)   Sweden

i   Relevant Treaties Signed, Ratified, etc.

- the 1949 GCs (ratified on 28 December 1953)
- the 1977 GPs (ratified on 31 August 1979)
- the 1989 CRC (ratified on 29 June 1990)
- the 1977 Ottawa Convention (ratified on 30 November 1998)
- the 1998 Statute of the ICC (ratified on 28 June 2001)
- the 1999 ILO Convention 182 (ratified on 13 June 2001)
- the 2000 Optional Protocol on Child Soldiers (signed on 8 June 2000)

ii   Background Notes—See Appendix Four

iii   Training of Officers of Swedish National Armed Forces—General

All Swedish officers apparently received training on general rules of IHL and international human rights law. The Swedish National Defence College, eg, conducted a course on these issues for officers (Captains and Majors) selected to become Majors and Lieutenant Colonels.[6] The course consisted of a minimum of 60 hours of training.[7]

According to a Swedish officer involved in training:[8]

> The aim with the IHL training is to give the students as commanders and staff members an increased knowledge and understanding of the importance of IHL during peace, conflict and war .... This training is mainly conducted in class-rooms with lectures, seminars and exercises often together with civilian representatives.[9]

This IHL training also addressed issues particularly relevant to participation in UN and NATO peace support operations.[10]

iv   Training of Officers of Swedish National Armed Forces— Regarding Children

As regards training concerning children, the Swedish armed forces apparently worked closely with Save the Children Sweden, which provided experts and conducted training courses at the National Defence College, and advised during exercises.

An example of the work of Save the Children Sweden in this context was the training provided in 2001/2002 to Swedish military personnel regarding their participation in peace support operations. Although the present research does not focus on such operations, it is the main context within which the Swedish armed forces generally operate, and therefore a good example of their approach to training on children. At the time of writing, the Save the Children Sweden training was being evaluated, with a view to revising it and possibly handing it over to the Sweden Armed Forces International Centre (SWEDINT) in future.[11] This training was only being provided to officers, but that was also being reconsidered as Save the Children Sweden had found that, contrary to their expectations, there had been 'no trickle down' effect to lower ranks.[12]

According to the outline of the 2001/2002 Save the Children Sweden training session mentioned above, it lasted for between one and three hours 'as an integral part in the general PKF preparatory training before the mission'.[13]

The training started with an introduction stressing, *inter alia*, that in some instances over 50 per cent of the civilian population were children, and therefore awareness of international law regarding children was fundamental. The training accordingly included an overview of the contents of the 1989 CRC. Its introduction also emphasised the need to understand the impact of armed conflict on children, and the important role played by officers and soldiers in preventing and reporting violations, and in generally protecting children.[14] The training methodology 'comprises lectures involving a dialogue between the trainer and the participants. Each section is illustrated by case studies from the current mission area and actual events'.[15]

The outline of this training session can be found in Appendix Five as an example of a useful short session that could be adapted for use by other countries, and for contexts other than peace support operations.

Summary: The Swedish armed forces apparently provided comprehensive IHL training for their officers, with a particular emphasis on peace support operations (their core area of activity). In addition, Sweden was unusual in providing child-specific training to officers generally, although changes were envisaged as to how (eg by SWEDINT, not Save the Children Sweden) and to whom (soldiers as well as officers) this training would in future be provided.

d)   United Kingdom

i   Relevant Treaties Signed, Ratified, etc.

- the 1949 GCs (ratified on 23 September 1957)
- the 1977 GPs (ratified on 28 January 1998)
- the 1989 CRC (ratified on 16 December 1991)
- the 1997 Ottawa Convention (ratified on 31 July 1998)
- the 1998 Statute of the ICC (ratified on 4 October 2001)
- the 1999 ILO Convention 182 (ratified on 22 March 2000)
- the 2000 Optional Protocol on Child Soldiers (signed on 7 September 2000)

ii   Background Notes—See Appendix Four

iii   Training of Officers of the UK Armed Forces—General

The UK armed forces provided training in three ways: a) training the trainers;[16] b) training the officers,[17] and c) training the soldiers.[18] In addition, legal problems were sometimes incorporated into exercises, and mission-specific training was carried out before any operational deployment.

A letter (January 2002) to the author from an officer in the UK army headquarters, Army Legal Services,[19] stated:

> UK officers receive formal training in LOAC throughout their careers. This training is delivered during career courses at central schools and is exercised in practice on field exercises. The academic training can be summarised as follows: Officer Cadets at the Royal Military Academy Sandhurst receive two hours of lectures which cover the status of individuals; rules of combat; the wounded; sick; medical personnel; chaplains; prisoners of war and the protection of civilians. Captains attending the Junior Staff Course receive a one hour lecture on LOAC. This lecture revises the principles of LOAC and goes on to relate them to an operational scenario being considered by the Course. Majors attending Staff College receive a day of lectures on international law relating to armed conflicts.
>
> .... The main legal reference work available to officers is the Manual of Military Law Part 3.[20] This publication is expected to be replaced by a new LOAC manual that is being written for the use of all three services. A useful *aide-memoire* that is widely distributed throughout the Army is the 'Soldier's Guide to the Law of Armed Conflict'. [21]

... In addition to the training referred to above commanders deployed on operations will also have two additional aids. The first is a deployed legal adviser; and the second is civil-affairs officers inside the headquarters. Although the civil-affairs officers are non-lawyers they are responsible for ensuring that the needs of vulnerable people are addressed and they tend to liase closely with the headquarters' legal adviser.

In a subsequent letter in 2002,[22] this officer also provided 'a copy of a typical and recent presentation given by legal officers. Such presentations are tailored to particular audiences and are continually evolving and being updated.' In addition, he enclosed a transcript of the current LOAC training video.

As regards the legal officer's presentation, this started by emphasising that LOAC 'is not designed to impede operations' but to ensure that violence is used to defeat the enemy, and is not to cause unnecessary suffering. It then set out the purpose of LOAC,[23] before discussing fundamental LOAC issues (such as the sources of international law; basic principles;[24] distinction between military objectives and non-military objectives;[25] prohibitions;[26] targeting considerations,[27] and compliance[28]).

The transcript of the LOAC training video illustrated and again summarised certain very basic principles such as the protection of civilians and other non-combatants.

Further, the publication 'A Soldier's Guide to the Law of Armed Conflict'—referred to in the officer's first letter (January 2002) above as 'widely distributed throughout the Army'—covered in somewhat more detail the key LOAC principles, as set out in its Table of Contents.[29]

iv   Training of Officers of the UK Armed Forces—Regarding Children

As regards training concerning children for personnel in the UK armed forces, the Army Legal Services' initial letter (January 2002) stated,

> There is no specific module within the [LOAC] training for children—they are only referred to indirectly by virtue of being within the wider category of civilians .... I am not aware of any child related disciplinary action being taken against soldiers occurring in an on-duty or operational context. There is therefore no specific training in the UK army on the law of armed conflict which relates exclusively to children. This is because they are subsumed within the wider category of 'civilians'. Nevertheless within the category of care for civilians emphasis is given to the special needs of children as regards their welfare, the need for safety zones, evacuation, free passage of relief supplies, and family news. Chapter Eight of the 'Soldier's Guide to the Law of Armed Conflict' sets out these requirements in a brief but easily comprehended fashion' (see UK Chart in Appendix Three).

In his subsequent letter (April 2002), this officer went on to draw attention to the mention of 'women and children as having special protection' in both the enclosed training presentation and the video transcript. He then acknowledged that:

[t]hese references are not extensive, but in the provision of such training there are a number of important messages that need to be addressed and we are continually striving to strike the appropriate balance.

He noted plans to update the video so that it would include areas of LOAC that 'have developed since its production' (the implication here was that this could include more information on, among other things, children).[30]

In response to queries regarding training on child soldiers, this officer stated, in the same letter (April 2002),

> ... of course the specific provisions relating to such are at Article 77(3) and (4) of AP I [1977 GP I] ... With regard to our own provision of Law of Armed Conflict training to Officers ... we do not necessarily provide any particular training to commanders or potential commanders on such specific provisions. Again, whilst acknowledging the importance of such provisions, the number of other messages that need to be addressed in any training course requires that we adopt a different approach to specific issues. Any commander on an operation has on his staff an ALS [Army Legal Services] officer with experience in operational law and the law of armed conflict and it is his responsibility to provide the commander with advice on such specific issues. Additionally, it is routine for commanders to receive an operations specific legal brief before deployment. If it were considered likely that our soldiers would encounter child soldiers then Article 77 would be briefed.[31]

Summary: The UK armed forces appeared to provide IHL training for their personnel of all ranks, but with little specific mention of children, other than certain of the key provisions relating to child civilians. No general training was provided on child soldiers, although 'operations specific' guidance was apparently given when necessary.

e)   United States

i   Relevant Treaties Signed, Ratified, etc.

–   the 1949 GCs (ratified on 2 August 1955)
–   the 1989 CRC (signed on 16 February 1995)
–   the 1999 ILO Convention 182 (ratified on 2 December 1999)
–   the 2000 Optional Protocol on Child Soldiers (ratified on 23 Dec 2002)

At the time of writing, the US had not signed or ratified the 1977 GP's or the 1997 Ottawa Convention. The US had signed the 1998 Statute of the ICC (31 December 2000), but later notified the UN that it did not intend to ratify (6 May 2002).[32]

ii   Background Notes—See Appendix Four

iii   Training of Officers of the US Armed Forces—General

The information on general IHL training of the US armed forces outlined below is drawn from a presentation by Colonel Hays Parks, one of the senior lawyers in the office of the Judge Advocate General of the US Armed Forces.[33] (Apparently due to time constraints, lesson plans for officers could not be provided for the purposes of this research.[34])

According to this presentation, in the US 'renewed emphasis was placed on law of war[35] training, with mixed initial results' after the much-publicised 1968 My Lai massacre in Vietnam.[36] The revised training incorporated principles that were intended to apply throughout the different branches of the US armed forces: '1) Mandatory training for all …; 2) Simplicity of principles; 3) "Marrying" of law of war obligations to military effectiveness …; 4) A positive approach'.[37] As regards the 'positive approach', Hays Parks contrasted this with earlier instruction in which 'the law of war was taught as a list of negatives' that was often:

> perceived as placing unwarranted limits on the military commander's ability to fight and win. In the mid-1970s, the approach was reversed to emphasize the consistency between the law of war (and, today, human rights law) and the efficient, disciplined use of military force.[38]

In 1977, this officer was involved in preparing a list of nine basic law of war rules, later incorporated into the training of the US armed forces. These rules stated, *inter alia*, that soldiers: fight only enemy combatants; do not harm enemies who surrender; do not kill or torture prisoners; collect and care for the wounded; destroy no more than their mission requires; treat civilians humanely; and try to prevent, and to report to their superiors, violations of the law of war.[39]

'Law of war' training in the US armed forces was apparently tailored to the individual, 'commensurate with his or her duties and responsibilities'.[40] By way of example, training of the US Navy 'established formal levels of individual training. Level One is the minimum level of understanding for all members . . ; Level Two is the minimum level of understanding for members whose military speciality … involves participation in combat operations,' or whose rank etc requires additional training; and 'Level Three is the minimum level of understanding for naval personnel whose military job . . . involves participation in the direction of combat operations.'[41]

As regards 'law of war' training provided to 'judge advocates (uniformed attorneys)' in the US armed forces, this included a basic course of 39 hours classroom instruction, plus some other activities. A more advanced training then offered 69 hours of 'core instruction', among other options. Apparently, 'emphasis is on training [judge advocates] to be effective law of war trainers'.[42]

The US armed forces maintained four permanent Combat Training Centres, offering 'hands-on, realistic' training for various combat and peace operations, which could include eg role-players acting as civilians in exercises.[43]

This officer's presentation also emphasised throughout that successful training depends to a large extent on both the cultural context, and the commitment of the higher echelons of the military.[44] It concluded by emphasising that: 1) law of war training is a continuous process; 2) it is only likely to be successful if part of an overall, comprehensive programme, and 3) what works in the US may not work elsewhere.

iv   Training of Officers of the US Armed Forces—Regarding Children

As regards training in the US armed forces concerning children, an e-mail of 27 February 2002 from Colonel Hays Parks[45] to the author stated that:

> [t]o the best of my knowledge, no military training materials or courses discuss children as such. Children are civilians, entitled to protection from intentional attack, so long as they do not take an active part in hostilities. 'Child soldiers' are at risk during such time as they take an active part in hostilities, as are adult civilians. If captured, they would be segregated from adult prisoners, civilian internees, or detainees for their protection.

In a later communication (14 March 2002), he added that:

> I can say that having served as a Marine Corps infantry officer in Vietnam in 1968–1969, where children often were used by the Viet Cong for military purposes, that the U.S. armed forces have a long tradition of respecting children as civilians so long as they are not taking an active part in hostilities.

Nonetheless, in his presentation outlined above, Hays Parks noted that, on occasion, members of the US armed forces had committed violations (that were 'very, very wrong') including against civilians (some of whom were, of course, children) eg in Vietnam.[46]

Summary: Post-Vietnam, the US apparently began to carry out comprehensive 'law of war' training of its military personnel, according to their particular rank and role. As regards children, it seemed that no specific training was provided, but rather reliance was placed on general rules, such as those regarding the protection of civilians, and those regarding conduct in armed conflict (eg the principle of distinction).

The ICRC and the San Remo Institute

In addition to summarising information regarding military training on children in 11 selected countries (Part II, Chapters Eight and Nine above), this section of Chapter Nine will go on to consider the training conducted on this issue under the auspices of the ICRC. The reasons for singling out the ICRC in this context include the fact that it is a unique organisation with an official treaty-based role in relation to IHL, which includes conducting military training almost worldwide.

Indeed, as is evident from the country-specific information above, the ICRC provides at least basic IHL training in most of the 11 countries described. Further, as already mentioned, all 11 of the selected countries send representatives to the

San Remo Institute. This Institute is supported by the ICRC, and provides IHL and human rights training for military personnel of all nationalities.[47]

The San Remo Institute offers many courses, including an international military course on the law of armed conflict: a course for military doctors; a course on human rights and the armed and security forces; a course for training programme managers; a course for planners and executors of air operations, and a course for planners and executors of naval operations.[48]

This Institute has begun to include, in some of these courses, training sessions on military conduct in relation to children, one such session being offered as part of an Advanced Course for Officers in 2001, and another in June 2002, as part of the Human Rights Course.[49] During the 2001 course, the author circulated a questionnaire and interviewed all of the 23 participants, (who came from a wide range of countries), on, *inter alia*, their views as to whether, in their personal opinions, it was 'necessary or useful to focus any training on specific groups such as women or children'. Their very interesting and varied responses are outlined in Appendix Three. To sum up, it was clear that, in the main: a) officers from countries where (women and) children were particularly affected by armed conflict did feel that specific training on this phenomenon was necessary; b) some officers from countries that did not have such direct experience felt that child-focussed training would be necessary only in relation to specific operations where children were likely to be encountered; c) others felt that child-focussed training was not required, as the protection of children was already a cultural norm, and/or included in general IHL training. A few of the officers also commented on the fact that child soldiers could be particularly unpredictable and dangerous opponents.

As regards other ICRC initiatives relating to military training on children, in 1998 the ICRC published a manual entitled '*To Serve and Protect*', outlining human rights law and IHL relevant to professional law enforcement practices.[50] This manual contains one chapter devoted to 'The Special Position of Children in Society'.[51] It opens with an Introduction reiterating the need of children for special care and protection, and then summarises information on the 1989 CRC; the administration of juvenile justice;[52] arrest of juveniles;[53] the use of force and firearms against juveniles,[54] and the treatment of children in situations of armed conflict.[55]

However, for the purposes of this book it is more significant that in June 2002 the ICRC published a new and comprehensive Teaching File on 'The Law of Armed Conflict', primarily for the use of ICRC delegates in conducting military training. This File covers all aspects of basic IHL training, presented in both written materials and slides, and a number of the modules in the Teaching File include separate information on children (and women)[56] within the context of the general topic being discussed. In this way, information on the treatment of children is incorporated into the various relevant topics without the need for a separate training session specifically on children. Given the wide international reach of the ICRC, the new Teaching File could have a significant impact in incorporating some military training on children across a broad spectrum of situations and countries.

The information regarding children that is contained in the different sections of the ICRC Teaching File is set out below in Appendix Five.[57] However, to summarise, this information consists of: a) an *Introduction*, that begins by stressing the need for members of armed forces to be 'well acquainted' with their legal obligations as regards child protection and welfare; b) a section in the lessons on the *conduct of operations*, which defines 'children' as meaning those under 18, and sets out basic principles regarding the treatment of child civilians (eg the entitlement to special treatment), and child soldiers (eg as members of opposing forces;[58] and provisions regarding the prohibition on direct participation of those under 15, and regarding the treatment of children on capture); c) a section in the lesson on *internal conflicts*, which reiterates 1977 GP II provisions regarding the need of children for 'care and aid'; family reunification; removal from conflict zones, and the prohibition on recruitment or use of those aged under 15; d) a section in the lesson on *internal security operations in connection with internal disturbances*, (where the main international legal instruments pertain to human rights law), which deals with, *inter alia*, use of firearms against children, and rules for their arrest and detention.

In short, the ICRC has played a vital role in military training across a wide range of countries and situations. New courses at the San Remo Institute and, in particular, the new Teaching File with its increased emphasis on children, may in future have an impact on military conduct towards children in (at least some) situations of armed conflict.

In summary, the information set out in Part II above indicates that, at the time of writing, all 11 selected countries did provide some IHL training for their armed forces. For the most part, this seemed to be general IHL training with little specific focus on children.

There were, however, exceptions to this. For example, Sweden provided a short lecture specifically on children to all its officers as part of its general IHL training. Uganda and Sierra Leone, both of which had undergone lengthy armed conflicts affecting large numbers of children as combatants and as civilians, were providing training concerning children to at least some sections of their armed forces. In the case of Sierra Leone, this training took place largely after the apparent cessation, in 2001/2002, of the conflict that had lasted for so long and claimed so many lives. In Uganda, the child-specific training did not seem to be integrated into an ongoing programme of military IHL training, and this obviously weakened its impact. Indeed, the admittedly random and unrepresentative testimony of the three interviewed former LRA child soldiers seemed to bear this out. However, steps were being taken to improve UPDF training (as evidenced by the December 2002 human rights workshop), and the research visit indicated that some UPDF staff members and others had put considerable effort into this.

As regards other countries specifically in Category (A) (those with current/recent experience of conflict 'at home') there was wide variation in their practice concerning military training on children.

Some of these countries, such as Colombia and Sri Lanka, seemed to have recently undergone a major shift towards providing widespread IHL training for their armed forces, when formerly little such training had been available. However, in these two cases the information on the positive recent initiatives came from official sources. While no doubt accurate, the information may not have fully reflected the reality and difficulties experienced 'on the ground'. That said, in his letter of 22 August 2001 the Colombian Ambassador to London did frankly acknowledge that 'much remains to be done', and that the Colombian government was 'working on it'.[59]

Regarding Israel, the official information provided by the IDF spokesperson indicated that IHL training was generally provided for IDF personnel. However, it proved difficult to obtain more precise information regarding IDF training concerning children.

The situation in both BiH and South Africa was different again. Neither of those countries was, at the time of writing, actively engaged in armed conflict 'at home' (although they were involved in peace support operations). Both countries were at different stages of restructuring their societies after major periods of instability and conflict. In this context, efforts were being made to provide at least some general IHL training, and in South Africa this training apparently included basic child-specific principles as set out in 1949 GC IV and 1977 GP I.

Regarding countries in Category (B) (those involved mainly in training and peace support activities, and/or in armed conflict 'abroad'), these did all appear to provide IHL training. However, none of these countries, aside from Sweden, provided much training specifically concerning children, although the UK stated that it would so do if the particular mission required this.

In any event, military training in many countries may increasingly take into consideration issues regarding children, under the influence of the relevant information now incorporated into the revised ICRC Teaching File.

Thus, the overall impression is of a patchwork of varied approaches by different national armed forces to military training on children, as regards: whether any such training is provided at all; who provides the training (eg NGOs or governments); what the training covers (eg brief information on 1949 GC provisions, or a week-long IHL or even 'child rights' course), and how it is provided (eg in specific lectures or integrated into general IHL training). That said, some of the country studies, and the information from the ICRC, reveal materials that could be of use across a broad spectrum in other countries and contexts, and these will be highlighted in the concluding Chapter below.

Endnotes

1   Letter from Air Commodore, Director-General Defence Education and Training Policy, 19 Nov 2001.

2   Among others, these were: the 'three fundamental principles' (military necessity, unnecessary suffering and proportionality); the 'significance of combatant and non-combatant status'; 'rules for the treatment of protected persons', and 'individual and command responsibility'.

3   For example, the course on 'Operations Law for the Tactical and Operational Level' contained modules on, *inter alia*: Hague and Geneva Laws; Additional Protocols; Inter-

national Human Rights Impact on Operations; Key Sources of International Law for the ADF; UN Law, and International Tribunals.

4   E-mail from ADF officer, 22 Nov 2001.

5   *Id.*

6   E-mail of 29 Nov 2001 from Swedish officer involved in training.

7   Swedish National Defence College, Department of Civil Security Studies, 'Swedish National Defence College: Course Outline: International Law/Law Studies' (23 April 2001), p 4.

8   E-mail of 29 Nov 2001.

9   Apparently, many international organisations—governmental and non-governmental— participated in these exercises, including eg ICRC/Swedish Red Cross, UNHCR, Save the Children and Amnesty International, as well as experts from the Swedish government (*Id.*). One example of such an exercise was VIKING 01, involving approximately 450 participants from various nations and organisations in a 'Computer Assisted Command Post Exercise' culminating in Dec 2001. See, www.fksc. mil.se/viking01, visited on 9 Sept 2002. Interestingly, the final report on this exercise (p 6) emphasised the importance of participants having 'proven capability of acting and communicating in English', thereby stressing the need for a common language in training (as mentioned above, Chapter Seven).

10   E-mail of 29 Nov 2001.

11   E-mail of 1 Aug 2002, from SC S, attaching SC S outline of 'Training of Peace Keeping Forces in Child Protection' (hereafter SC S 'Training of PKF'). See 'Background Notes', Appendix Four, for further information on SWEDINT.

12   E-mail of 16 Sept 2002, from SC S. According to this e-mail, until 1996 SC S had trained the soldiers, but then 'due to logistical constraints' this was changed to training of officers only. The e-mail points out that the Norwegians, eg, do provide their soldiers generally with training on children.

13   SC S 'Training of PKF' (2002), p 1.

14   *Ibid*, p 2.

15   *Ibid*, p 1.

16   This was training provided for legal officers. All such officers attended IHL courses of different lengths and complexity appropriate to their rank.

17   The training of the officer corps was done by the Army Legal Services, through periods at Sandhurst and the Junior Division of the Staff College as well as individual training within Commands, and through various publications.

18   This training was conducted principally by unit officers, sometimes with the help of legal officers. Such training was mandatory, and formed part of a unit's annual assessment. There was no set training procedure, but training aids such as videos were available.

19   Letter of 29 Jan 2002.

20   This Manual was rather outdated, the most recent edition being published in 1958.

21   MOD, *A Soldier's Guide to the Law of Armed Conflict* (MOD, April 2001).

22   Letter of 10 April 2002.

23   This was to 'protect both combatants and non-combatants; safeguard fundamental human rights, and remove the bitterness and hatred arising from armed conflict, thereby facilitating the restoration of peace.' Presentation, p 2.

24 'Basic principles' were listed as 'military necessity; unnecessary suffering, and proportionality'. Presentation, p 6.

25 'Non-military objectives' were listed as including, *inter alia*, objects indispensable to the survival of the civilian population; civilians and civilian objects; prisoners, and demilitarised zones and non-defended localities. Presentation, pp 11–12.

26 These were summarised as including, *inter alia*, prohibitions on: attacking persons who are '*Hors de Combat*'; starvation and scorched earth policy, attacks on protected zones and non-defended localities, and indiscriminate attacks. Presentation, pp 31–32.

27 'Targeting Considerations' included, *inter alia*, the need to: consider the effect on civilians; take precautions to reduce collateral damage, and observe the rule of proportionality. Presentation, p 48.

28 The arguments presented for compliance are interesting, including: more effective use of military power; breaches attract bad public opinion; compliance encourages enemy compliance, and breaches can result in personal liability for war crimes. Presentation, p 49.

29 These included: 1) Introduction (eg International Law, and Rules of Engagement); 2) The Law of Armed Conflict (eg Basic Principles, and Individual Responsibility); 3) The Status of Individuals (eg Civilians); 4) The Rules of Combat (eg Protection of Combatants; Protection of Civilians; Prohibitions; Protective Zones) 7) Prisoners of War (eg Basic Protection; Conditions of Internment; Repatriation); 8) Protection of Civilians in Enemy Hands (eg Protected Persons, and Occupied Territories); 9) Service Discipline; 10) Internal Armed Conflict, and 11) Peace Support Operations. This Guide also contained various Annexes, including 'An *Aide Mémoire* for Use in Armed Conflict', and it was reviewed and updated annually. (Letter from Army Legal Services, 10 April 2002).

30 As regards the video, the officer also requested, from the author, suggestions on the child-related content of the video transcript for inclusion in the proposed updated version.

31 Indeed, there was clearly some concern within the UK army that greater attention needed to be paid to the issue of child soldiers, as the author was also contacted by a Senior Instructing Officer at the Joint Doctrine and Concept Centre, who was seeking information on child soldiers and the relevant law. This was apparently in order to prepare UK military personnel for 'the inevitability of allied forces having to contend with these units' in opposing forces (eg as happened in Sierra Leone), and to make better provision for under-18 year olds in the UK armed forces. (Letter of 18 Feb 2002).

32 See, http://untreaty.un.org/ENGLISH/bible/englishinternetbible/partI/ChapterXVIII/treaty10.asp, visited on 13 Nov 2002.

33 Col W Hays Parks was the Special Assistant to The Judge Advocate General of the Army and Chief, Law of War branch, International and Operational Law Division, Office of The Judge Advocate General of the Army; Colonel, US Marine Corps Reserve (Retired), and Adjunct Professor of International Law, American University. The paper, 'Law of War Training', was presented at a US Institute of Peace Working Group on IHL in 2001 (W H Parks, 'Law of War Training', *US Institute of Peace Working Group on IHL*, (Washington, US Institute of Peace, 24 May 2001)).

34 Hays-Parks e-mail of 27 Feb 2002.

35 Hays Parks generally used the term 'law of war' in his paper. He argued against use of the term 'international humanitarian law/IHL' (Parks (2001), pp 1–2).

36 *Ibid*, p 9.

37   *Ibid*, p 11.

38   *Ibid*, p 29.

39   *Ibid*, p 11.

40   *Ibid*, pp 10 and 17.

41   *Ibid*, p 15.

42   *Ibid*, p 17. The 'mid-grade judge advocates teach young judge advocates', they in turn teach officers who are non-lawyers and non-commissioned officers, and they then teach the soldiers below them in rank. *Ibid*, p 18.

43   *Ibid*, p 19.

44   Hays Parks commented that 'culture plays a very large part in respect for the law of war, as does leadership', and that a soldier who serves in the armed forces of a nation that does not believe in the rule of law is unlikely to 'recognize an illegal order even if it came up and bit him on the nose'. *Ibid*, p 21.

45   Again, Col Hays Parks gave permission for his name to be used as authority for this information.

46   Hays Parks (2001), pp 8 and 20.

47   The cooperation between the ICRC and the San Remo Institute was formalised by the signing of an agreement on the organisation of military training courses. See, G Blais, 'The International Institute of Humanitarian Law (San Remo) and its International Military Courses on the Law of Armed Conflict', 319 *IRRC* (1997), pp 451–454.

48   See the San Remo Institute's website at, http://www.iihl.org/mdepartment.htm, visited on 14 Jan 2003.

49   The latter session was presented by the author.

50   ICRC, *To Serve and Protect* (Geneva, ICRC, 1998(b)). This manual apparently aims, *inter alia*, to assist instructors to develop new techniques for including the relevant rules in their curricula.

51   The introduction to this chapter emphasises that it was written before the 2000 Optional Protocol on Child Soldiers came into force, and is based largely on the 1989 CRC and the Beijing Rules.

52   This discusses, *inter alia*, the purpose and scope of the relevant measures, and the implications for law enforcement practice.

53   This covers eg general principles; rights on arrest and following arrest, and detention.

54   The emphasis here is that 'the utmost restraint must be exercised in the use of force and firearms against children'.

55   This stresses the need of children for special care, and cites 'protective measures', eg regarding education; reunion of separated families, and minimum age for participation in combat.

56   The file on 'Conduct of Operations—Part A' (p 10) explains the need to include such information thus: 'In a lesson on the conduct of operations, why do we need separate sections on women and children? Are they not covered in the section on civilians? Of course, women and children are protected as civilians. They do, however, also have to be considered separately, for two reasons. First, both categories have *special additional protection* under the law, and secondly, both play an important role in combat—women legally and children illegally.'

57 *Note*: Excerpts are also available at, http://www.icrc.org/Web/Eng/siteeng0.nsf/html/EB75D79539D6A05E41256C630060BF07/$File/ANG03_09_fas_logo.pdf, visited on 23 March 2003.

58 As regards child combatants in opposing forces, the materials acknowledge that they may be ill-trained and under the influence of drugs or alcohol, and may be 'formidable and tough foes' to deal with, but nonetheless they should be handled 'with due regard and sympathy for their plight'. ICRC Teaching File (2002) p 2.

59 See Chapter Eight above.

Part III

Summary and Recommendations

10

Conclusion

Introduction

The Introduction to this book, in Chapter One, raised a number of questions regarding the usefulness of military training concerning children, or indeed traditional military IHL and human rights training generally, given recent world events and other developments (eg in weapon technology). It is undoubtedly true that the face of global politics is constantly changing so that, among other things, at the time of writing the US had become—after years of 'Cold War' deadlock—the only world 'super-power', and new forms of terrorism were evolving and provoking novel military and legal responses.

However, IHL and human rights law and policy relevant to military training on children, as outlined in the text above (Chapters Two to Six), have not been 'overtaken by events'. They remain largely valid and applicable, at least in theory (although they have often been violated in practice, as already discussed). Their validity rests not simply in the fact that the applicable customary norms are universal, and that almost the entire international community has ratified key treaties (especially the 1989 CRC and the 1949 GCs).

The pertinent law and policy also retain their validity in that: 1) the high-profile conflicts involving massive human rights violations and/or powerful actors within the international community (eg Rwanda, the former Yugoslavia, Iraq) still require consideration by military personnel of basic principles such as unnecessary suffering, proportionality, and military necessity, (even if, again, this requirement is often not fulfilled in practice), and 2) while the high-profile conflicts may be more dramatic and publicised, the other, smaller conflicts continue 'on the ground' in the same deadly, messy way that they have done for centuries, and they too (again, in theory at least) do not escape the reach of basic IHL and human rights principles. In both conflict situations—the publicised and the seemingly forgotten—international law and policy for the protection of children may, among other things, serve as the 'thin edge of the wedge' in introducing, first, child-specific, and then more generally applicable IHL and human rights considerations into the conduct of armed conflict.[1]

That said, the aim here—as stated in the Introduction to this book—has been to address the following questions: what are the obligations of officers of national armed forces in relation to children, either civilians or combatants, whom they or those under their command may encounter while participating in situations of armed conflict? How realistic and achievable are these obligations? How can compliance with them be encouraged, monitored, and/or enforced?

In order to respond to these questions, the present work has now:

1) in Part I(A)(1) (Chapters Two to Five), outlined international law and policy relevant to the training of officers in national armed forces as regards the treatment of children at the outset, during, and shortly after situations of armed conflict;
2) in Part I(A)(2) (Chapter Six), summarised the obligations of states to provide such training;
3) in Part I(B) (Chapter Seven), considered training methodology,
4) in Part II (Chapters Eight and Nine), described existing training programmes provided by a range of different countries and the ICRC.

The Conclusion, below, addresses the final task: ie, to summarise key points from the text, and to highlight recommendations regarding the content and/or dissemination of pertinent training programmes. Given the many issues and dilemmas raised by this research, such recommendations do seem both 'appropriate and necessary' (to use the wording in the Introduction to Chapter One). The recommendations themselves will be marked with *, and highlighted.

Key Points, and Recommendations—Part I

a)   *Content of Relevant Law*

i   Obligations of Officers

Part I of this research summarised a wide range of law and policy pertinent to the training of officers of national armed forces regarding children. It considered first: *the obligations of officers, and content of rules relevant to their training (Part I(A)(1))*.

Basic Principles (Chapter Two)
The relevant rules incorporated basic IHL and human rights principles, as outlined above in Chapter Two.

* These basic IHL and human rights principles—including military necessity; proportionality; prohibition of unnecessary suffering; special treatment of children (among others); 'right to life', and prohibition of torture—should be incorporated in all military training of whatever level, as fundamental rules that underpin conduct in armed conflict. At its most simple, conduct regarding children can then be incorporated within such training by stressing that all the above general princi-

ples apply fully to children, along with their entitlement to special treatment.

Officers should of course be familiar with these principles, and ensure that they are adequately conveyed to subordinates. They should also be aware—as a minimum—of the existence of more detailed rules regarding children, including children in specific categories (eg captured child soldiers) or specific situations of armed conflict (eg in occupied territory) (as outlined in Chapters Three and Four).

Note:

– Training should sensitise military personnel as regards the international law entitlement of children to special treatment in situations of armed conflict—while also discussing and taking account of practical problems in implementing this principle.

– Military training should emphasise that the basic human rights principles (eg the 'right to life', and prohibition on torture/inhumane treatment) apply to both adults and children and to all conflict situations, even those (such as internal security operations) that fall below the level of an 'armed conflict'.

Child Civilians and Child Soldiers (Chapters Three and Four)

In addition to the basic principles above, there is a great deal of fairly detailed law and policy that is relevant to the training of military personnel regarding the treatment of children, including rules relating to child civilians and child soldiers in various contexts (Chapters Three and Four). This more detailed information is not generally pertinent to the training of soldiers, unless the specific context so requires. However, depending on the circumstances and on their particular rank and role, officers may require such training concerning the treatment of children.

* **In all national armed forces there should be at least some officers who are familiar with the more detailed principles of law and policy regarding the treatment of child civilians and child soldiers, and/or who know where and how to rapidly access such information when required. In addition to that, officers generally should be familiar with (and should, as appropriate, convey to their subordinates) certain of the main principles concerning child civilians and child soldiers, including:**

a) **regarding child civilians—that they are entitled to protection in the same way as all other civilians, and, in addition, they are entitled to 'special treatment' as child civilians.**

– Such 'special treatment' includes, *inter alia*: protection from abuse (including sexual abuse); priority in receipt of relief; evacuation in certain circumstances; access to 'zones of safety'; family contact; and additional safeguards in relation to detention, due process, and punishment.

b) **regarding child soldiers (ie generally those under 18)—that they should be given special consideration whether they are combatants or *'hors de combat'*.**

– As combatants, certain basic IHL rules should be observed regarding, eg rules prohibiting recruitment and use of those under 15 (to 18, depending on the particular national law). Child soldiers who are members of national armed forces must be trained appropriately for their age, including in IHL and human rights principles. As regards child soldiers in opposing forces, the harsh reality is that, when engaged in combat, they can legitimately be attacked, although minimum force should be used and, where possible, allowance made in decisions regarding, eg, proportionality.

– When they are captured, child soldiers are subject to particular safeguards under both human rights law and IHL (regarding the latter, see Appendix One).

Landmines, Command Responsibility, and War Crimes Trials (Chapter Five)

* **In their general IHL and human rights training, officers of national armed forces should also be trained: a) on the need to avoid the use of landmines, and b) on rules regarding command responsibility and culpability, including c) the role played by war crimes trials. As discussed in Chapter Five, these three topics also merit special attention in military training regarding the treatment of children. Such training should highlight the particular impact of landmines on children, and ways in which military personnel can prevent or limit this. Moreover, the training should point out that rules regarding culpability and command responsibility apply fully to violations committed against children. Further, international courts have put in place special mechanisms to deal with such violations, and are increasingly taking a serious view, in their judgments and sentencing, of offences committed against children (as in the cited ICTY and ICTR cases).**

ii   Obligations of States

Part I(A)(2) of the research then considered the obligation of states to provide IHL and human rights training—incorporating some specific training regarding children—for their military personnel.

State Obligations (Chapter Six)

* **In order to comply with both customary and treaty law obligations concerning the conduct of armed conflict, including rules for limiting the harm inflicted on children, states must necessarily provide appropriate IHL and human rights military training for their armed forces.**[2]

– The military training obligations of states are set out (explicitly or implicitly) in treaties such as the 1949 GCs, the 1977 GPs, and the 1989 CRC.

Further, international organisations such as the UN and the ICRC are increasingly expressing concern at the impact of armed conflict on children, and are urging states to provide military training that can improve the treatment of children in such situations. Of particular significance here are the various UN General Assembly and Security Council resolutions that refer to military training, and the role of the Committee on the Rights of the Child in examining country reports and making recommendations.

* **States should take account of UN pressure—and of initiatives of the ICRC and other international bodies—to provide military training on children for their armed forces, as one way of reducing the impact of armed conflict on children in accordance with international law and policy. States should also take note of specific comments and suggestions on this issue pertaining to them, made by the Committee on the Rights of the Child.**

b) Realistic and/or Achievable Obligations?

Part I(B) of the research then examined the question of the extent to which the legal obligations outlined in Part I(A) seemed to be realistic and/or achievable.

Methodology (Chapter Seven)

Part I(B) argued that it is both realistic and achievable for states and their military trainers to at least provide (very) minimal military training on children, but the more difficult question is how they can provide military training that actually has some impact on the behaviour of those trained. After briefly setting this question in a wider context, Part I(B) focussed on training methodology, in order to identify key factors in the training process itself. A number of recommendations emerged from this analysis, some of which relate to military training generally, and all of which are relevant to military training regarding children. Key recommendations are set out below:

* **in conducting military training, it is worth bearing in mind a working definition of 'learning', eg as 'a relatively permanent change in behaviour that occurs as a result of practice or experience'.**

* **it is necessary to be realistic about the likely impact of military IHL and human rights training, given certain limiting factors inherent in situations of armed conflict.**

  Note: These limiting factors include the fact that: a) military training must frequently be put into practice in extreme circumstances, where fear, anger, etc. can be the overwhelming emotions; b) the military mission is central, and military personnel are therefore juggling competing tasks, in which the requirements of international law—particularly as regards children—may not be considered a priority; c) certain IHL and human rights norms are vague and therefore can be difficult to put into practice; d) in some armed forces, the standard of the available—or selected—personnel may mean that they are not willing or able to behave in accordance with IHL, and e) training can be disrupted eg by rotation or loss of key staff.

* **good, well-prepared, on-going military training can overcome many of the limitations outlined above. Training must therefore be regular, varied, relevant**

to the specific context, and of an appropriate length, level, structure and style to be both comprehensible and effective for the necessary range of personnel and situations. Training that aims to change attitudes, and develop values and instincts broadly in accordance with pertinent legal principles, is likely to be more effective than 'legalistic' training.

Note: Various factors should be considered here, including that:
- Ways should be found of motivating the particular military personnel to learn and comply with the applicable law and policy, eg by relating it to the current mission, and/or by the example of compliance by senior officers.
- Cultural differences should be catered for, and priorities should be established (eg regarding who is to be trained, and on which particular issues).
- Repetition should be used, especially for training the lower ranks, as should simple '*aide-memoirs*'.
- Wherever possible, military training should be evaluated on a continuing basis.

* **Specifically as regards military training concerning children, it is important to place this in a wider context that takes account of the general needs and rights of children and the impact on them of armed conflict, as well as teaching the relevant international law and policy.**

* **Where military training involves civil-military co-operation, attention should be paid to co-ordination between the various bodies involved, and to addressing problems that may arise.**

In this context, account should be taken of factors such as: possible differences in working practices, and difficulties in communication, between civil and military organisations, between the various ranks within a particular armed force, and between the armed forces of different countries.[3]

Key Points, and Recommendations—Part II

Part II of the research, examining *actual practice in 11 selected countries, and the work of the ICRC,* highlighted the somewhat haphazard and inconsistent way in which military training regarding children was (or was not) provided at the time of writing.

Practice in Eleven Countries, and the Role of the ICRC (Chapter Eight)
As regards the 11 countries, it appeared that certain countries with experience of armed conflicts affecting large numbers of children did provide some child-specific training (eg Sierra Leone), while others appeared to do so to a lesser extent (eg possibly Sri Lanka and Israel). Not surprisingly, the child-specific training that was provided seemed to address issues of particular concern in the affected countries.[4]

In relation to the ICRC, their new military Teaching File incorporated within general IHL training some useful materials on children. The research findings regarding the selected countries and the ICRC are summarised at the end of Chapter Nine.

A key aim of this book has been to ascertain whether there are in existence good—or even adequate—military training resources regarding children, and, specifically, materials that were being or could be used to train officers of national armed forces. It transpires that there are indeed such materials.[5] The relevant sections of the new ICRC Teaching File, and some existing child-focussed military training materials (eg, those prepared by, or with the assistance of, Save the Children Sweden for use in Sweden and West Africa), provide a useful model, and extracts are set out in Appendix Five. Such materials can be adapted for use in other countries.

* **The ICRC approach integrates small sections of child-specific materials at different points within the general IHL training, while Sweden incorporates one child-focussed session of a few hours into their military IHL/human rights course, and the Save the Children/ECOWAS West African materials can be adapted to different contexts, including week-long (or longer) sessions specifically focussing on children. The approach selected for training on children may depend on the particular circumstances. Thus, eg, in armed conflict situations where the involvement of children is likely to be minimal, the ICRC approach may suffice (and in any event represents a basic level of training on this issue)—while at the other end of the spectrum, conflicts involving large numbers of children may be best suited to the approach used in the West African materials. These approaches are not mutually exclusive.**

For regular training of national armed forces, the ICRC materials have the merit of integrating child-focussed information within general on-going IHL courses, while, eg, the Save the Children/ECOWAS approach could be used when and if those same armed forces are engaged in a conflict that calls for more detailed information on the treatment of children.

Final Recommendations and Conclusion

* **Accordingly, countries that wish to integrate new materials on children, or to augment existing information in their military training, do not have to 'reinvent the wheel'. There are a number of possible courses of action:**
– **reference could be made to the materials in Appendix Five, and these could be adapted for national use (as outlined above);**
– **the information set out in the text of this book could be similarly adapted, as well as or instead of other existing materials. A self-contained summary of some of the key rules regarding child civilians and child soldiers is set out in Appendix Six (at end) to facilitate such use;[6]**

- contact could be made with countries or organisations that are currently involved in military training concerning children (eg, the ICRC; UNICEF, or Save the Children Sweden), to explore possibilities of their being able to provide advice or assistance;
- requests for such advice or assistance could be made by states through the Committee on the Rights of the Child.

To end more or less where this work began: when it comes to armed conflict, prevention is surely better than cure. Nothing would more effectively protect children from armed conflict than an end to such conflicts themselves. For reasons already discussed in the Introduction to Chapter One, a scenario of global peace seems, at this point in history, as elusive as it ever did, or perhaps even more so (although that in no way negates the need to strive for this).

Given that reality, military training on IHL and human rights law and policy—including such training regarding the treatment of children—remains an essential, if neglected, component in the attempt to limit the havoc wreaked by armed conflict. As has been mentioned in the text above, the ethical conduct of armed conflicts may at least limit their destructive impact, and lessen the urge for revenge and savagery. Further, the more that children are respected and protected from the kind of extremes experienced in armed conflict, the more likely it is that they will mature to become responsible, competent and compassionate adults, able to positively shape the future of the world that they are destined to inherit.

Endnotes

1   In this way, eg, provision of relief supplies for child civilians in situations of armed conflict is likely to also mean provision of supplies for their mothers, and then possibly the wider family and community. Similarly, action taken to protect children—eg establishing cease-fires for immunisation campaigns, or 'zones of safety'—would also incorporate others.

2   It is indeed arguable that the duty to provide such training is, in itself, a customary law obligation, as noted in Chapter Six.

3   Further, it is necessary to be aware of possible civil/military distrust, and ways of addressing this. 'Ownership' of the training should be considered and planned for. Consideration should also be given to questions such as: who will do the training? How will information 'trickle down' the ranks? How will training continuity be ensured? (see Appendix Two.)

4   For example, the training in Uganda was situated mainly in the north of the country, and addressed both child civilians and child soldiers. The specific (UNICEF-backed) training that was planned for Sri Lanka was intended to focus on the treatment by the national armed forces of captured child soldiers of the LTTE.

5   In addition to the selected materials (highlighted in the text below), there are a number of good training materials relevant to the topic under discussion here, but which have only briefly been referred to in this book, as they were not designed primarily for use by officers of national armed forces. These include the ARC materials, and the training materials recently prepared for the use of UN peacekeepers (see McCauley (draft, 2002)).

Appendices

Appendix **1**

Captured Child Soldiers in Non-International and in International Armed Conflict[1]

The information set out below, as previously mentioned (Chapter Four), differs from the rest of this text in that it separately considers rules applicable in international and non-international armed conflict, and contains more detail than would generally be required for military training or reference purposes. However, in some instances officers may require training or guidance on some of the more detailed rules set out in this Appendix.

Detained Children in Non-International Armed Conflict

The general rules already outlined regarding conditions of detention and due process (in text, Chapters Three and Four) form a minimum standard which largely continues to apply to detained children in non-international armed conflicts. In many ways those general rules, drawn primarily from the 1989 CRC and international human rights instruments, provide more protection than the rules to be considered below, which are based in IHL and apply specifically to children in non-international armed conflict.

* **In non-international armed conflict, IHL provides merely that 'a detained child participant remains subject to the local law; there is no prisoner of war status, and no category of protected persons or civilian internee from which to benefit'.** [2]
Thus children can find themselves facing criminal charges under domestic law for their actions committed in the course of the conflict.

* **The manner in which the domestic law applies must be modified to take account of the child's age and circumstances (in accordance with,** *inter alia,* **1989 CRC principles). Basic IHL principles relating to detained persons in non-international armed conflict** (as set out in Common Article 3 of the 1949 GCs, and Article 4 of 1977 GP II) **must also be taken into account. A guiding norm here is that all 'per-**

sons taking no active part in the hostilities' (and this includes 'detained child participants or detained children suspected of participation in hostilities', whether over or under 15 [3]) are, under Common Article 3, entitled to humane treatment and respect for their person, honour, and religious practices.

The *'fundamental guarantees'* contained in 1977 GP II are also relevant. These 'guarantees' augment Common Article 3, by, *inter alia*, reaffirming the entitlement to humane treatment of persons no longer taking part in hostilities (Article 4(1)[4]). Further, they specifically provide, among other things, for children to be provided with education, and removed to safer areas within the country (Article 4(3)).

In addition to these measures, guidelines are set out in 1977 GP II (Article 5) explicitly regarding *conditions of detention* for persons (adult or child) deprived of their liberty for reasons related to the conflict.[5] Article 5 has been described as moving the standard of protection nearer to that applying to POWs,[6] although it falls short of conferring a special status on those detained in internal conflicts. Moreover, Common Article 3(1)(d) and Article 6 of 1977 GP II articulate *due process* guarantees (eg that no sentences or penalties shall be imposed without an independent and impartial court hearing) and these apply equally to detained children.

To simplify matters, it is worth repeating that compliance with the 1989 CRC and related human rights provisions regarding the treatment of children generally, and conditions of detention and due process in particular, as already outlined in Chapters Three and Four, would largely suffice to meet these IHL standards. It is also useful once more to bear in mind Article 41 of the 1989 CRC, providing for the higher standard to prevail where there are a number of applicable rules.

In any event, the basic principle is that children are entitled to humane treatment when detained, and this principle applies equally in situations of non-international armed conflict. Detained children in such situations should also be provided with, *inter alia*, adequate nutrition and accommodation; education; family communication; due process in any legal proceedings, and should have their age and circumstances taken into account in all matters, including sentencing for offences committed.

Detained Children in International Armed Conflict

Under IHL, captured child soldiers in situations of international armed conflict may become POWs, or, eg, civilian internees.

Like adult soldiers in these situations who are captured by an opposing force, captured child soldiers can, in principle, be detained for an indefinite period (eg until the cessation of hostilities) without having to be charged with any particular offence. Their detention should, nonetheless, be in accordance with the principles set out below.

a)   Child Participants in International Armed Conflict Who Are Not Entitled To POW Status

* If children participate in international armed conflict but are not categorised as combatants within the IHL definition,[7] 'they remain subject to the domestic legislation of the countries of which they are nationals'.[8] If they are captured by the opposing force and come within the 1949 GC category of 'protected persons', such children become 'civilian internees'.

> As internees, they are entitled [9] (as mentioned in Chapter Three above) eg to be reunited with their parents; to be given appropriate accommodation, food, education, and exercise, etc (see Articles 82, 85(2), 89(5), and 94 of 1949 GC IV, above), and to be punished only as appropriate, *inter alia*, for their age (1949 GC IV, Article 119).

* In any event, even if captured children who have taken part in hostilities are not entitled to any special status (eg as protected persons), they must (under Article 45(3) 1977 GP I) be granted the general protection offered by Article 75, 1977 GP I (setting out a minimum of protective humanitarian rules, or 'Fundamental Guarantees'). They also, of course, remain entitled to the protection of basic human rights principles (eg the 'right to life', and prohibition of torture, as outlined in Chapter Two above).

b)   Child POWs

* In international armed conflict, IHL provides that children aged 15 to 17 who are considered combatants,[10] 'enjoy prisoner of war status automatically if captured'.[11] Children under 15 who unlawfully (due to their age) participate as combatants can also benefit from this status, as there is '... no age limit for entitlement to prisoner of war status: age may simply be a factor justifying privileged treatment'.[12]

> Thus, in international armed conflict all captured child soldiers (ie those under 18, including those under 15), are entitled to POW status. However, it would generally be good practice to hand all captured child soldiers under 15, at least, to civilian authorities, rather than subjecting them to a military regime.[13]

* In any event, child soldiers under 15 should not be punished for the fact of their participation in the conflict.

> Article 77(2) of 1977 GP I makes it clear that the state must bear responsibility for its under-age soldiers. In other words, '[t]he nature of the obligation is to condemn the conduct of the parties to the conflict, with whom lies responsibility for the breach, not to penalize the participants'.[14] This does not mean that child soldiers can escape liability for violations that they may have committed, but rather it means that they cannot be penalised for the mere fact of being under-age soldiers.

* If detained as POWs, children should once more be treated according to their age and hence given special consideration.[15] They also benefit from rules regarding the treatment of POWs generally as set out in treaties including 1949 GC III,[16] and 1977 GP I.[17]

* Their entitlement to special consideration does not exempt child POWs from penal proceedings if they are alleged to have committed serious breaches of IHL, war crimes and/or offences against the law of the Detaining Power.

* Regarding *conditions of detention*, the IHL and human rights principles concerning all children deprived of their liberty, already outlined (Chapter Three), continue to apply to child POWs. In addition, child POWs again benefit from provisions regarding conditions of detention for POWS in general.

> For example, Article 11 of 1977 GP I provides that the physical or mental health and integrity of persons deprived of their liberty for reasons related to the conflict should not be endangered by unjustified acts or omissions, including unnecessary medical procedures,[18] which would be considered a grave breach of that treaty. Fundamental guarantees for POWs, including children, can also be found in Articles 12-16 of 1949 GC III.[19] Article 16 specifically allows for privileged treatment of certain POWs, according, *inter alia*, to their age. Further, Article 49 of 1949 GC III requires that age must be taken into account by the Detaining Power as regards utilising the labour of POWs.

* In any disciplinary hearing involving child POWs, *due process* provisions applicable to all children deprived of their liberty outlined above (Chapter Four) would apply, in addition to the various rules on 'penal and disciplinary sanctions' for all POWs set out in Section VI, Chapter III of 1949 GC III.

Again, to simplify matters, it is worth pointing out that compliance with the 1989 CRC[20] and related human rights provisions would largely suffice to meet these IHL standards as regards due process and conditions of detention for child POWs.

c)   *Release, Repatriation or Internment in a Neutral Country*[21]

i   Release/Repatriation

POWs

Repatriation of child soldiers is not expressly provided for in the relevant law, and they are therefore subject to general rules regarding this.

* As regards *repatriation of child POWs during hostilities*, Article 109 of 1949 GC III can be interpreted as encouraging the repatriation of particularly vulnerable POWs (ie the sick and wounded). Arguably, this interpretation could be expanded to include other vulnerable categories of people, such as children.

In any event, when early repatriation is to take place, the consent of the child should be obtained, as Article 109(3) of 1949 GC III states that repatriation during ongoing hostilities may not take place against the will of the person being repatriated (and under Article 12 of 1989 CRC the child should in any event be consulted). Once repatriated, children must not be allowed to re-enlist and fight (Article 117, 1949 GC III).

* **Concerning *repatriation at the end of hostilities*, child POWs, like all POWs, must be repatriated at this time** (Article 118, 1949 GC III)**, unless they are involved in criminal proceedings** (Article 119(5), 1949 GC III).

Internees

* **As regards children who participate in hostilities and then become civilian internees, they (like all internees)) must be released 'as soon as possible after the close of hostilities', unless, again, they are involved in certain penal proceedings** (1949 GC IV, Article 133)**. Moreover, even during the continuation of hostilities, parties to the conflict should try to agree the release and repatriation of, *inter alia,* child internees** (Article 132(2), 1949 GC IV).

ii   Internment in a Neutral Country

An alternative to the traditional system of detention for POWs is their internment in a neutral country, and this is encouraged by Article 111 of 1949 GC III.

***Specifically as regards children detained as POWs, they (like all POWs) can be interned in a neutral country, but it is good practice to do so in accordance with the safeguards set out in Article 78, 1977 GP I.**
Article 78, 1977 GP I, (now the prevailing standard (see Chapter Three above)), modifies Article 24, 1949 GC IV[22] in that it allows for internment of children in a neutral country, but 'only for reasons relating to safety or health of the child,[23] and only with agreement of all parties, including a representative of the child',[24] (unless no such representative can be found). Again, the child's views should also be taken into account (Article 12, 1989 CRC).

In summary: although the rules set out above regarding captured child soldiers in situations of international and non-international armed conflict are rather detailed (and hence in this Appendix rather than in the main text), officers of national armed forces (and perhaps particularly legal officers) may on occasion have to make decisions on the status and treatment of captured children who have been participating in such situations. Questions may arise such as: 'Are these children entitled to POW status? Should they be treated differently from captured adult combatants? Can they be repatriated?'.

Without guidance on such questions, the temptation may be to improvise solutions. The rules summarised above provide useful information for resolving these questions without succumbing to that temptation, and they should be available at least for reference purposes.

Endnotes

1   Although, strictly speaking, 1977 GP I or 1977 GP II respectively may not apply to particular international or non-international armed conflicts (eg due to non-ratification by parties to conflicts), relevant principles from these treaties will be included in this Appendix in order, once more, to consistently express the higher standard.

2   Goodwin-Gill and Cohn (1994), p 128.

3   See Goodwin-Gill and Cohn (1994), p 128.

4   Art 4(1) explicitly includes, in this category, those whose liberty has been restricted.

5   Provision is made for matters such as the health, nutrition, hygiene and labour conditions of persons in detention. (Art 5(1)). Further, those responsible are also obliged, where possible, to ensure separate accommodation of men and women, (except where families are accommodated together); family correspondence; location out of the combat arena, and protection of physical and mental integrity (Art 5(2)).

6   Goodwin-Gill and Cohn (1994), p 128.

7   Those considered combatants are persons enrolled in the armed forces, or who take part in a mass uprising of the civilian population. See Art 43(2), 1977 GP I, and Art 2, 1907 Hague Convention IV, Regulations.

8   M T Dutli, 'Captured Child Combatants', 278 *IRRC* (1990), p 428.

9   Subject to 1949 GC IV, Art 5, regarding eg spies and saboteurs.

10 See n 7 above, regarding 'combatant' status.

11 Goodwin-Gill and Cohn (1994), p 127. And see Art 43, 1977 GP 1, and Art 4, 1949 GC III.

12 Dutli (1990), p 427. See also S Singer, 'The Protection of Children during Armed Conflict Situations', 252 *IRRC* (1986), pp 133–167. She argues, *inter alia*, (pp 153–154) that children under 15, even if recruited into the armed forces, should be considered civilians once captured, although they can be categorised as POWs. They should in either case be given special treatment.

13 This is arguably particularly the case now that the use of children under 15 as combatants is categorised as a war crime by the ICC (see Chapter Four above).

14 Goodwin-Gill and Cohn (1994), p 127.

15 In addition to eg 1977 GP I, Art 77 and the 1989 CRC generally, various articles of 1949 GC III (re POWs) seem to confirm that age should be a criterion for special consideration. See eg, Art 16 (in text below), Art 49 (in text below), and Art 45, (that, *inter alia*, POWs other than officers and the equivalent are to be 'treated with the regard due to their rank and age').

16 For example, Art 5, (providing for a presumption in favour of POW status, where the status of a combatant has not yet been established by a competent tribunal), and Art 87 (forbidding corporal punishment).

17 For example, Art 45, (further elaborating on circumstances in which POW status can be presumed).

18 Thus it prohibits, *inter alia*, mutilation, experimentation, removal of organs, involuntary or forced donation of blood, skin or organ.

19 Among other things, Art 12 provides for POWs to be the responsibility of the Detaining Power; Art 13 stresses their entitlement to humane treatment; Art 14 provides for respect for their persons and honour, with particular mention of the regard due to women, and Art 15 specifies their right to free maintenance and medical attention.

20 Once more, this includes Art 41, encouraging the highest applicable standard.

21 The provisions on repatriation etc traditionally relate to international armed conflicts, although to some extent they could be extended, by analogy, to internal conflicts.

22 As already mentioned (Chapter Three above), Art 24 of 1949 GC IV provides for the reception of orphaned or unaccompanied children aged under 15 in a neutral country, subject to certain safeguards.

23 Under 1949 GC IV, Art 132(2) sick children are, in any event, to be hospitalised in a neutral country during hostilities.

24 Dutli (1990), p 432.

Appendix **2**

Civil-Military Cooperation:[1] Save the Children, West Africa

As already mentioned in Chapter Seven above, a great deal of military training relevant to the treatment of children (whether on IHL in general, or specifically focussing on children) involves civil-military co-operation, in that it is conducted by, or with input from, the ICRC and/or various NGOs and others such as UNICEF.[2]

Save the Children has established a programme of military training that is probably the most well-documented and detailed initiative of this kind that focuses specifically on children. This work has, to the time of writing, been located particularly in East and West Africa, and in Sweden. Their work in West Africa will be discussed briefly below, by way of example.

As regards the West Africa initiative, Save the Children describe their aim as putting 'child rights and child protection on to military training curricula in the region' with the ultimate goal of bringing about 'a change in military behaviour towards children'.[3] They emphasise that soldiers must be informed of this aim, and be reassured that the purpose of the training is not to pursue soldiers for abuses of child rights.[4]

Save the Children argue that:

> [c]ivilians, and women and children in particular, are increasingly the victims of armed conflict. In West Africa children constitute the majority of the population and their rights have been hugely abused in recent conflicts. Interaction between children and military personnel (from both governmental and non-state entities) has increased in recent and existing conflicts. This growing interface is not monitored or integrated into military strategic planning in any way. Recognition of the need to introduce children's issues into the regional military agenda on a systematic basis comes from a combined understanding of the impact of conflict on children and the ever-increasing interaction that members of armed forces have with children and their communities.[5]

Specifically as regards the relationship between armed forces and humanitarian organisations, Save the Children comment that:

[a]s armed forces and humanitarian agencies not only share the language of co-operation but also, and ever more frequently, share their physical working environment they also begin to share mandates that overlap. The protection of children and the observance of their rights is no exception to this increasing trend in the new working environment ....[6]

The Save the Children training programme in West Africa envisages that national armed forces:

pilot the curriculum and further develop it based on local and national experiences. The target is an adaptable ECOWAS-approved training module on Child Rights and Child Protection Before, During and After Conflict, which will be used by national armed forces in the region and by military organisations and schools preparing regional military personnel for peacekeeping missions. A smaller booklet for senior military personnel, a cartoon training book and illustrated pocket cards will complement the manual and enable trainers to better target training objectives at different levels in the military hierarchy ....[7]

Many of their general findings have already been referred to in Chapter Seven, and, in addition, Save the Children has outlined a number of relevant issues particularly regarding civil-military cooperation. These include the fact that there are often *different working styles between civilians and the military*, including as regards 'training/teaching methodologies, hierarchical perceptions of teaching, and training based on learning rules and regulations versus flexibility and participatory approaches'.[8] Further, they comment on *variations within armed forces*, noting that, eg, 'there are often clashes of how different generations think, and the ability to adapt to the wider and increasingly important world of civil military cooperation varies.'[9] Save the Children also point out that different armed forces have different approaches as regards, *inter alia*, training, and that this is 'particularly clear in a region where armed forces are modelled on different colonial systems' (eg French, British, Portuguese).[10]

Save the Children stress that the *support and participation in the training of 'the most senior' officers is crucial*, as 'this will not only increase the knowledge base but will also ensure support to the program by the senior officers'[11] They have found that training aimed at *changing attitudes* is more effective than rule-based teaching, but caution that it requires more time.[12] Thus they emphasise the need to teach military personnel about child development, and children's needs and rights, and about the impact of armed conflict on children (including through the direct involvement of children in the training, as already mentioned (Chapter Seven)), in addition to providing teaching on international law, and on civil-military cooperation.

Further, Save the Children comment that there can be '*suspicions* on both the part of armed forces and humanitarian agencies of each other's roles' (emphasis added). Thus, eg, on occasion:

military collaboration with a training project is based on buying respectability or bargaining chips. Armed forces known for abuses can offer to "buy into" a project to gain international credibility or to be able to bargain with children's rights ...'.

On the other hand, 'at times military personnel may feel NGOs are abusing children's rights, using child abuse issues and figures for fundraising purposes'.[13]

One aim of the Save the Children work on military training is ultimately to transfer '*ownership*' of the child-focussed training from themselves to the military. They note the risk that NGOs and others in civil society can 'take over governments' responsibilities for including children's welfare in their military agenda'.[14] Thus, it is part of the work of the NGOs and others involved in military training to ensure that any resources are allocated for specific and limited purposes, and that they have an 'exit strategy' that is planned from the outset.[15] Accordingly, part of Save the Children's perceived role is to identify and train military personnel who can take over the training of other 'trainers', (a 'pyramid' structure of training). In this context, they employ various selection criteria for participation in the 'training of trainer' programmes. One such criterion for selection as a trainer is that the person concerned should hold 'the rank of Major (Anglophone military structures), Commandant or Captain (Francophone military structures) ...'.[16] However, Save the Children comment that:

> [i]n addition to identifying trainers of trainers among ranking officers it is also important to try to identify potential trainers among the soldiers because they know the issues and they talk the same languages as those who will be/are deployed on the ground and have primary contact with children.[17]

In summary: the above outline of certain key issues regarding civil-military co-operation—in this case specifically as regards military training concerning children—indicates that such co-operation requires considerable planning and sensitivity if it is to function smoothly. Attention must be paid to issues such as possible mutual distrust, variations in working styles of the different players (eg, NGOs and the armed forces) and the need for clarity as regards division of labour and ultimate responsibility for the various tasks involved.

Endnotes

1   McCauley and Ransquin (2001(a), p 4) define civil-military cooperation as '[a]ll actions and measures under any circumstances that concern the organised relationships between the military and the civil entities and individuals.' (Quoting Dennis Vandi, Ministry of Defence, Sierra Leone).

2   McCauley and Ransquin (*ibid*, p 7) stress the importance of co-operation among the various agencies that can be involved in training, in order to ensure 'that each agency is aware of the messages being passed and the military do not have to convene several times for similar workshops.' In this context, one experienced ICRC military trainer points out that the ICRC expertise is in teaching IHL, and that they therefore call on 'local specialists in human rights law to cover this topic' (Roberts (1997), p 8).

3   McCauley and Ransquin (2001(b)), p 21.

4   *Ibid*, p 20. Nonetheless, it is possible that in any disciplinary proceedings for subsequent violations committed against children, the fact that a soldier had received and ignored relevant training could count against him or her.

5   *Ibid*, p 4.

6   McCauley and Ransquin (2001(a)), p 4. However, perhaps this observation is most accurate as regards peace support operations.

7   McCauley and Ransquin (2001(b)), pp 7–8.

8   McCauley and Ransquin (*ibid*, p 15) comment that: 'There is a continued dialogue about whether soldiers should be given the 'rules' and laws governing armed conflict before being introduced to substantive information about child development and the impact of conflict on children. Again military personnel asked to comment insisted that legal standards should be the first section of the manual while most people coming from a humanitarian or training background felt that this should be the final section'.

9   McCauley and Ransquin (2001(a)), p 10.

10 *Id*.

11 *Ibid*, p 6.

12 U McCauley and C Ransquin, *Report of Workshop on Experiences of Training Members of Armed Forces on Child Rights and Child Protection, Before, During and After Conflict* (Abidjan, 23–26 Oct 2001), (Save the Children, 2001), hereafter McCauley and C Ransquin (2001(c)), p 10. This report notes the 'inappropriate attitudes of soldiers' on some occasions: 'Some soldiers' attitudes concerning the abuse of children, particularly the sexual abuse and use of children in armed forces as non-combatants, confirm the need to emphasise a change of behaviour and attitudes of military personnel.' The Save the Children trainers were apparently not surprised by these attitudes, but rather by how openly they were expressed. 'At the beginning of the training it was clear that many soldiers did not see that these attitudes were inappropriate. This sensitive problem was dealt with mainly as an internal matter between military participants and military trainers from the training team …'. McCauley and Ransquin (2001(b)), p 13.

13 *Ibid*, p 31.

14 McCauley and Ransquin (2001(b)), p 18.

15 McCauley and Ransquin (2001(a)), p 21. The authors emphasise here that 'the issue of ownership and how humanitarian organisations withdraw from doing the training themselves is extremely important …'.

16 *Ibid*, p 21.

17 *Ibid*, p 20.

Appendix **3**

Charts: I) Child-Related Training Materials—Eleven Selected Countries, and II) Summary of Comments—San Remo Institute

I)   Eleven Selected Countries

Note:
1) The Charts below summarise only information on military training specifically concerning children, and they do not address training on more general legal and policy measures, eg regarding landmines and culpability.
2) In the Charts below, a definite 'yes' or 'no' is indicated by an 'x' in the appropriate column. However, where there is some uncertainty, eg 'possibly yes', this is indicated by '?x' in the 'yes' column.

a)   Category (A)—Countries Currently or Recently Involved in Armed Conflict 'At Home'

i   Bosnia and Herzegovina (BiH)

In the absence of any concrete information about BiH military training concerning children, it has not been possible to complete a Chart on this subject. As discussed in the text, however, the ICRC was offering some general IHL training in BiH, and others were also providing this (eg the Lieutenant Colonel cited). Accordingly, basic information on children may have been incorporated, as part of the general IHL military training in BiH.

ii   Colombia

Again, in the absence of sufficient information for this purpose, it has not been possible to complete a Chart summarising Colombian military training on the treatment of children. However, the ICRC apparently conducted much of the general CAF training, and the new ICRC Teaching File encourages at least some reference to issues concerning children. Further, the 1999 law prohibiting recruitment of under-18 year olds has presumably had an impact—reflected in training—on the composition and consciousness of the CAF.

iii   Israel

Once more, in the absence of sufficient information on this issue, there is no Chart below regarding IDF training on the treatment of children. However, according to official sources, some such training was conducted, in addition to general IHL training.

iv   Sierra Leone

SUBJECT	YES	NO	NOTES
Mention of children	x		This Chart is compiled on the basis that training of the RSLAF officers incorporated material from the Save the Children Sweden (SC S)/ECOWAS 'Child Rights and Child Protection Before, During and After Conflict: Booklet for Senior Military Personnel' (hereafter 'the Booklet') (Jan 2001).[1] See also 'Comment' below.
Impact of armed conflict on children	x		In the Booklet, Unit 2 addresses 'Child development and basic needs', including discussion of 'Concepts of childhood' and 'How conflict affects child development' (pp 21–24). Unit 3 then focusses on the 'Effects of armed conflicts on children'. Topic 2 in this Unit specifically addresses, *inter alia*, issues such as the 'effects at different levels' (eg on the individual child; the child in the family, the child in the community) (p 31).
			Child civilians
– special treatment principle (including prohibition on ill-treatment and sexual assault)	x		Unit I of the Booklet (Legal Standards on Child Rights and Child Protection), in Topic I (Major Legal Instruments) briefly summarises the provisions of the 1989 CRC as well as, *inter alia*, relevant provisions of the 1949 GCs. It specifically refers to 1977 GP I (Article 77) and 1977 GP II (Article 4) as among the 'major legal standards' (pp 7–10). Further, the Child Protection Code of Conduct for Soldiers (hereafter the Child Protection Code),[2] at the end of Unit 3, states: 'Ensure safety and protection of civilians. Pay special attention to women and children' (p 58).

– provision of relief/ food/necessities	x	The Booklet refers to this principle, eg, 1) in Unit 2, where it emphasises that the basic needs of children include 'well balanced diets' as well as adequate water, shelter, health care, etc (p 22), and the Child Protection Code reaffirms this: 'Respect the basic needs of children …' (p 58); and 2) in Unit 3, Topic 4 (The role of military personnel in preventing and minimising the worst impacts of conflict on children), where, *inter alia*, 'Military interventions to reduce impacts of war on individual child' include: 'Facilitating work of humanitarian organisations …; Ensuring that provisions and basic needs of children are met' (p 46).
– zones/removal	x	Unit 3, in a chart on 'Alleviating impacts of conflict on children', contains a module, under the heading of 'Action' that provides for 'control of zones' to be undertaken during conflict for the purpose of restoring security (p 45).
– evacuation	x	Again, the Unit 3 chart on 'Alleviating impacts of conflict …' contains a module on 'Evacuation of threatened populations' to be undertaken during conflict, in collaboration with UNHCR (p 45).
– family contact	x	The Child Protection Code states: 'Do not separate children from their parents' (p 58). The Booklet also makes reference to family contact, eg, in Unit 2, describing the basic needs of children as including 'Trusting relationships' (with their main carer, usually the mother); 'Positive guidance' (eg by parents), and 'A stable environment' (p 22). In Unit 3, 'family reunification' is described as one way of reducing the impact of conflict on children (pp 51–52).
– punishment (including conditions of detention and due process)	?x	The principle of humane treatment of children is indirectly included in the Booklet via its summary of the main provisions of 1989 CRC (pp 9–10 and 19), and Common Article 3 of the 1949 GCs (p 8). However, specific reference is not made to punishment, detention, etc.
Child Soldiers		
Generally	x	Unit I contains a section on 'International legal standards governing child soldiers' (pp 14–15).
– age of participation	x	Unit I summarises the 1977 GP provisions concerning child soldiers, including those regarding the age of participation. Mention is also made of relevant provisions in the 1989 CRC, the 1990 African Charter, the 1998 Statute of the ICC and 1999 ILO Convention No. 182 (pp 14–15).

– age of recruitment	x		As immediately above. Mention is made of the age of recruitment.
– punishment (including conditions of detention and due process)		?x	See 'punishment' (above), as regards 'Child Civilians'. In relation to detention, the Booklet states in Unit I (regarding child soldiers) that 'Detained children must be kept apart from other prisoners and must be given special treatment' (p 14).
As combatants	x		
– in own forces	x		Unit 3, Topic 2, of the Booklet, on the 'Impacts of conflict on children', includes a section focussing on child soldiers (pp 33–35). As such, it is relevant to child soldiers in own and opposing forces. The Child Protection Code states: 'Children should not be used in armed forces. Protect them, do not use them' (p 58).
– in opposing forces	x		See again Unit 3, Topic 2, as immediately above. Also, the section of Unit I dealing with child soldiers states: 'When confronted with a child combatant, soldiers should use minimum force in self-defence' (p 14), and the Child Protection Code reiterates this (p 58).
Repatriation/internment	?x		Unit I, Topic 3 (Integrating legal standards … into Military Operations) does not address this issue directly regarding eg child POWs, but states that, after conflict, military personnel should 'participate in activities which help normalise the situation', including return of displaced populations, and rehabilitation (p 19).
Comment			According to the information set out in Chapter Eight above, the RSLAF conducted training on children based on the SC S/ ECOWAS materials, which are fairly comprehensive. However, it was not possible in the course of this research to obtain a copy of the actual materials adapted for use in Sierra Leone, so the information in this Chart is based on the contents of the main 'proforma' Booklet prepared for use in West Africa. The SC S/ECOWAS materials come in the form of two main publications: a larger 'Manual for Military Personnel' and a 'Booklet for Senior Military Personnel', which is intended to complement the Manual (both already cited in text above, eg in Chapters Three and Seven). The information in this Chart is based on the Booklet for Senior Personnel. Since the SC S/ ECOWAS material is comprehensive, it can be used for training programmes lasting for as long as two weeks, or adapted for shorter sessions.

> In keeping with the philosophy of SC S on this issue, the
> SC S/ECOWAS materials pay much attention to 'sensitising'
> military personnel regarding, eg, the development and needs
> of children, and the impact of armed conflict on them. As well
> as summarising many of the main relevant legal principles, it
> also contains sections on mechanisms (including the ICC) for
> punishing violations against children, and on the importance
> of reporting violations by military personnel. Further, as is
> appropriate for materials prepared for use in Africa, the Booklet
> contains information specifically on the African context,
> and on the 1990 African Charter. The Booklet, in addition,
> contains a number of useful materials for use in case studies, eg
> 'testimonies' of child soldiers, etc.

Note:

1) There were other Save the Children Sweden/ECOWAS materials that could be used in addition to 'the Booklet'. Such materials included: a) the 'Manual for Military Personnel', already mentioned; b) a cartoon booklet featuring 'The Good Soldier',[3] and c) a laminated pocket card summarising the 'Child Protection Code'.

2) A short extract from the Save the Children Sweden/ECOWAS 'Manual for Military Personnel', including the 'Child Protection Code' (which contains a useful summary of basic rules concerning military conduct towards children) is set out in Appendix Five below.

v   South Africa

SUBJECT	YES	NO	NOTES
Mention of children	x		As indicated in Chapter Eight above, children were mentioned in the general LOAC training (Lecture IV, summarised in the Chart below).
Impact of armed conflict on children		x	As far as could be ascertained, this was not specifically addressed in the training.
Child civilians			
– special treatment principle (including prohibition on ill-treatment and sexual assault)	?x		1977 GP I Article 77 was not specifically referred to in Lecture IV, although there was reference to other provisions in this treaty. However, under the heading 'Child Welfare', 1949 GC IV (Article 24) was cited to the effect that parties 'are to care for children under 15 years of age who are orphaned or who are separated from their families. They are not to be subjected to political propaganda.'

– provision of relief/ food/necessities	x		Under 'Free Passage of Relief Supplies', Lecture IV summarised 1949 GC IV, Article 23 and 1977 GP I, Article 70 in general terms, to the effect that 'parties to the conflict shall allow and facilitate rapid and unimpeded passage of all relief consignments and equipment meant for the civilian population' etc. Further, parties 'shall protect relief consignments and facilitate their rapid distribution'.
– zones/removal	x		Under 'Localities and Zones under Special Protection', Lecture IV stated (referring to 1949 GCs I (Article 23) and IV (Article 14 and Annex 1)) that hospital and safety zones 'may be set up in peacetime' for various persons including 'infants, children under 15 years of age, expectant mothers and mothers with children under 7 years of age'. Further, at 'the outbreak and during the course of hostilities' the parties may conclude agreements on recognition of the zones and localities created.
– evacuation	x		Under 'Evacuation', Lecture IV cited 1949 GCs I (Article 15); II (Article 18), and IV (Article 17) to the effect that local ceasefires can be arranged for removal from besieged or encircled areas of various categories of person, including children. Further, evacuations can be ordered 'for military reasons or for the security of the population'.
– family contact	x		Under 'Family News', 1949 GC IV (Articles 25 and 26) and 1977 GP I (Article 74) were cited, stating that parties 'are to assist members of families to keep in touch with each other and, if possible, to reunite families'.
– punishment (including conditions of detention and due process)		x	

Child Soldiers

Generally		x	
– age of participation		x	
– age of recruitment		x	
– punishment (including conditions of detention and due process)		x	
As combatants		x	
– in own forces		N/ A	Not applicable to South Africa
– in opposing forces		x	
Repatriation/internment		x	

Comment	The SANDF training included many of the basic provisions regarding the treatment of child civilians, although apparently not the underlying principle as stated in Article 77, 1977 GP I. However, child soldiers were not mentioned. Some relevant principles as regards the treatment of children may also have been included in the 'civic education programme' mentioned in Chapter Eight above, eg under the headings of 'gender issues', 'military professionalism' and 'civilian control'.

vi   Sri Lanka

As stated in Chapter Eight, the information from Sri Lanka indicated that there were at least two lectures regarding children for officers and senior officers of the SLA within the general training on Human Rights Law (2001 and 2002), and there was the proposed UNICEF-backed training on captured (LTTE) child soldiers. However, in the absence of more detailed information on the contents of such training, it was not possible to complete a Chart regarding Sri Lanka.

vii   Uganda

There is no Chart prepared on Uganda, as the UPDF officer training was apparently based on the Save the Children Sweden/ECOWAS 'Child Rights and Child Protection Before, During and After Conflict: Booklet for Senior Military Personnel' ('the Booklet'), and its accompanying materials (eg, the 'Manual for Military Personnel'). Since the training of officers in the RSLAF (Sierra Leone) was also based on these documents, the Sierra Leone Chart above applies equally to the UPDF.

That said, information from the Booklet and Manual has been adapted as needed for specific training sessions in different countries and contexts, and the Chart does not attempt to summarise the latter more particular materials.[4]

Specifically as regards Uganda, there was also a pocket-sized booklet 'Children, Our Future: A handbook on Child Rights Protection during peace and war time', (prepared for the UPDF by Save the Children Sweden and Save the Children Denmark in March 2000). This contained a few basic principles as guidelines for the treatment of children by military personnel, and a brief discussion of these.[5]

b)   *Category (B)—Countries Substantially Involved in Armed Conflict 'Abroad', and/or in Training, and/or in Peace Support Operations*

i   Australia

Note:
The italicised information in the Chart below indicates uncertainty regarding inclusion of Australian Red Cross materials into ADF training.

SUBJECT	YES	NO	NOTES
Mention of children	x		Letter from the ADF (see Chapter Nine above) confirmed that children were included, at least under the heading of 'civilians in conflict'.
Impact of armed conflict on children	?x		*The Red Cross materials contained statistics and general information on the physical and psychological impact of armed conflict on children.*
Child civilians			
– special treatment principle (including prohibition on ill-treatment and sexual assault)	?x		This concept may have been mentioned in the training provided on 'civilians in conflict', referred to in the ADF letter (Chapter Nine). *The Red Cross materials cited 1977 GP I, Article 77(1).*
– provision of relief/ food/necessities	?x		*Under the heading 'Essential Supplies', the Red Cross materials referred to the role of states to provide necessities, while also stating that the ICRC often intervened for this purpose.*
– zones/removal		x	
– evacuation		x	
– family contact	?x		*Again, under 'Reuniting Families' the Red Cross materials mentioned state responsibility, and outlined the role of the Red Cross in maintaining family contact (and see immediately below, regarding 'punishment').*
– punishment (including conditions of detention and due process)	?x		*Under 'The ICRC and Children in Captivity', the Red Cross materials summarised the main provisions regarding children who are arrested, detained or interned, including that they should be kept separately from adults, unless with family members, and that they should be given additional food and allowed contact with family members.*
Child Soldiers			
Generally	?x		*Under 'Child Soldiers', the Red Cross materials quoted 1977 GP I, Article 77 as regards recruitment and participation of under 15 year olds. Brief information was also given regarding the causes and effects on children of participation in armed conflict.*
– age of participation	?x		See immediately above.
– age of recruitment	?x		Ditto
– punishment (including conditions of detention and due process)		x	
As combatants		x	
– in own forces		x	
– in opposing forces		x	

Repatriation/internment		x	
Comment			The impression of the ADF training for officers is that it was quite thorough as regards general IHL training (see Chapter Nine). However, there appeared to be a minimal amount of training on child civilians, and probably none on child soldiers (according to the official information provided, and given that it was unlikely that the Red Cross materials were used in training).

ii   South Africa

See Chart above, in Category (A).

iii   Sweden

Note:

The Swedish training module referred to in Chapter Nine and summarised in this Chart is set out more fully in Appendix Five (below).

SUBJECT	YES	NO	NOTES
Mention of children	x		As indicated in Chapter Nine, child-focussed training was provided for Swedish officers, with the assistance of SC S. In addition to referring to the 1949 GCs and the 1977 GPs, the training included specific instruction on the 1989 CRC, particularly Article 38. However, it emphasised that the relevant legal principles were generally ignored in practice, and that children suffered accordingly (p 3).
Impact of armed conflict on children	x		The training divided information on the impact of armed conflict into four areas: 1) children as targets; 2) children as actors; 3) children as victims; 4) children losing their childhood (p 3).
			Child civilians
– special treatment principle (including prohibition on ill-treatment and sexual assault)	x		The training implicitly conveyed this principle in that it focussed entirely on children, although the special treatment principle as such did not appear to be emphasised. However, it set out a basic 'Do and Do Not User's Guide', including (13) 'Do not hit children or commit other violent acts against children', and (14) 'Do not have sexual relations with minors'. It also focussed on the prohibition of child prostitution, and awareness of risks of STDs and HIV/AIDS and their impact on children.
– provision of relief/ food/ necessities	x		For example, the 'Do and Do Not' rule (7) stated: 'Assist humanitarian organisations in distribution of food, non food items and escorts'.

– zones/removal		?x	Apparently there was no specific mention of this issue. (However, depending on the particular circumstances, this topic may not be relevant to peace support operations.)
– evacuation		?x	As immediately above (re 'zones/removal').
– family contact	x		For example, the 'Do and Do Not' rule (8) was 'Assist families and communities ...'.
– punishment (including conditions of detention and due process)		?x	Again, as above regarding 'zones/removal'.
Child Soldiers			
Generally	x		As part of this training, it was emphasised that 'child soldiers' included not only the armed soldier, but also children with other roles in the military environment. It was also stated that the responsibility for using children as soldiers rested with the adults involved (p 4).
– age of participation	x		The training specifically included study of Article 38.
– age of recruitment	x		As immediately above. Further, the training stressed that voluntary recruitment is a 'myth', as no child really understands the consequences of recruitment (p 4).
– punishment (including conditions of detention and due process)	?x	?x	See item above regarding 'zones/removal'.
As combatants			
– in own forces	N/A		Not applicable to Sweden.
– in opposing forces		?x	See item above regarding 'zones/ removal'.
Repatriation/internment		?x	Again, as above regarding 'zones/removal'.
Comment			This Swedish army/SC S training on children included a number of other key elements. For example: – it raised some of the larger questions for discussion, such as asking participants to consider 'what happens to human dignity and values' in a context of continuing armed conflict and violations of children's needs (p 4); – it summarised steps that could be taken to improve protection of children in armed conflict, including: 'Make children visible; Keep the focus on' their special need for protection; 'Help to restore as normal conditions for children as possible ...'; 'Mobilise all possible resources for their protection, survival and development; Make the international laws ... known and assist in their implementation';

– it involved participants in discussion of appropriate action, based on the schema STOP ('Structure' (support in creating structures to normalise life for children); 'Talking and Time' (talk with children and give them time to talk); 'Organise Play and Recreational Activities'; 'Protection and Parent Support' (protect children and prevent violations, and support families in providing care for their children) (p 5);
– it emphasised the importance of reporting violations and abuse of children (including as regards recruitment) (pp 5 and 6);
– finally, it generally seemed to encourage awareness of the needs of children and the impact of armed conflict on them— ie 'consciousness raising'—rather than focussing on detailed rules.[6]

iv   United Kingdom

SUBJECT	YES	NO	NOTES
Mention of children	x		As mentioned in Chapter Nine, child civilians were referred to in the UK general LOAC training (and see below).
Impact of armed conflict on children		?x	There did not appear to be specific training on this.
Child civilians			
– special treatment principle (including prohibition on ill-treatment and sexual assault)	x		This principle was briefly referred to in the LOAC training video ('Particular care should be taken of … young children'), and the LOAC presentation ('… there are special provisions relating to the protection of women and children'). However, the underlying principle set out in 1977 GP I (Article 77(1)) was not mentioned in *A Soldier's Guide to the Law of Armed Conflict* (hereafter *A Soldier's Guide*), although some child-specific measures were summarised therein (see below). Chapter 8 (Protection of Civilians in Enemy Hands) of *A Soldier's Guide*, under 'child welfare' (p 8–1) cited 1949 GC IV (Article 24) and 1977 GP I (Articles 77 and 78) regarding duty of parties to the conflict to care for 'children under 15, orphans and those separated from their families'.
– provision of relief/ food/ necessities	x		Chapter 8 of *A Soldier's Guide*, under 'Free Passage of Relief Supplies' (p 8 – 1), cited 1949 GC IV (Articles 18– 20) and 1977 GP I (Article 71) regarding, *inter alia*, passage of '… food and clothes for children, expectant mothers and maternity cases.'

– zones/removal	x		Chapter 8 of *A Soldier's Guide*, under 'Safety Zones' (p 8-1), cited 1949 GC IV (Article 14) regarding 'safety zones' for, *inter alia*, children under 15, expectant mothers, and mothers of children under seven. Chapter 4 (Rules of Combat) (*Ibid* p 4-6) also cited various provisions in 1949 GC IV (eg Article 15) and 1977 GP 1 (Articles 59 and 60) regarding, *inter alia*, neutralised and demilitarised zones, and non-defended localities.
– evacuation	x		Chapter 8 of A Soldier's Guide, under 'evacuation' (p 8-1) cited 1949 GC IV (Article 17) regarding evacuation of, *inter alia*, children and maternity cases from besieged and encircled areas.
– family contact	x		Chapter 8 of *A Soldier's Guide*, under 'family news' (p 8– 1), cited 1949 GC IV (Articles 25 and 26), and 1977 GP I (Article 74), regarding family contact and reunion.
– punishment (including conditions of detention and due process)		?x	There was no direct reference in *A Soldier's Guide* to special provision regarding punishment of children. However, the obligation to treat all 'protected persons' humanely was cited under 'Protected Persons' (Chapter 8 of *A Soldier's Guide*, pp 8–1 and 8–2). Chapter 10 also cited Common Article 3 of the 1949 GCs (p 10–1).
Child Soldiers			
Generally		?x	Although there was no specific reference to child soldiers in the training materials provided, the letter of 10 April 2002 from Army Legal Services, (cited in Chapter Nine above), stated that context-specific training on this would be provided when necessary.
– age of participation		x	
– age of recruitment		x	
– punishment (including conditions of detention and due process)		?x	No specific information was contained in the materials provided, but *A Soldier's Guide* did address the issue of POWs generally (Chapter 7), including the duty to treat them humanely and with respect (citing 1949 GC III, Articles 13 and 14) (p 7–2), and provisions regarding 'Conditions of Internment' (p 7–3) and 'Discipline' (p 7–5).
As combatants			
– in own forces		x	
– in opposing forces		?x	Again, no specific mention of this, but context-specific training could be provided (letter of 10 April 2002 from Army Legal Services (Chapter Nine)).

Repatriation/internment	?x	No mention of relevant provisions regarding children, but *A Soldier's Guide*, Chapter 7, set out basic rules regarding repatriation of POWs generally (citing 1949 GC III, Article 118).
Comment		IHL training of UK officers apparently made reference to child civilians and specific provisions concerning them, but training on child soldiers was mission-specific. From the materials provided, it was difficult to assess whether account was taken of the particular training requirements of under 18s in the British armed forces.

v   United States

There is no Chart below on US military training regarding children, since there appeared to be no such training specifically provided. Children were subsumed under general rules concerning, eg, the treatment of civilians and the principle of distinction between combatants and non-combatants.

II)   San Remo Institute, 2001—Comments on Military Training Regarding Children

Note:

Most of the officers interviewed at the San Remo Institute in 2001 replied in writing to a questionnaire, and all of them discussed this questionnaire in small group meetings with the author. Some therefore replied in writing and verbally, while others replied only verbally. Accordingly, the information in the Chart below is set out in two columns: one for written answers and additional oral comments, and one for oral answers.

Further, some countries had more than one representative present at the San Remo Institute on this occasion, and in those cases the replies are numbered, eg Belgium 1 and Belgium 2. The contributors generally requested anonymity so that they could freely express their personal opinions.

The answers in the Chart below were given in response to one question of key importance here (as mentioned in Chapter Nine): *In your personal opinion, is it necessary or useful to focus any training on specific groups such as women or children?*

Countries	Written answers	Oral answers
Belgium	**Belgium 1**: Yes, but these specific groups are already 'incorporated' in our legal framework. ***Additional oral comments***: Special protection should not be necessary at all in theory, as *de facto* there should anyway be more protection of women and children. But recently we have read about women and girls being more and more victims of aggression etc. The image of children is changing—they are not so protected by society anymore. There is a contradiction between law and real situations. Children can be both victims and perpetrators of terrible crimes. However, it is not realistic to give soldiers the mission of educating about children. It is more to do with general social attitudes.	**Belgium 2**: My personal opinion is that it is not necessary to have specific training on children. This is a matter of command responsibility. It must be a combination of command responsibility and training in the field.

Countries	Written answers	Oral answers
Burkina Faso	Because of the nature of conflicts today, with grave violations of women and children's rights, it is important to put the emphasis on these specific groups. ***Additional oral comments***: There are two aspects to this problem: (1) regarding women and children in my country; (2) regarding operations with particular exposure to women and children. Regarding 1) in our traditions we don't pay special attention to women and children. No special legal protection. Most of our soldiers are illiterate and they come from an environment where modern rights of women and children, based on law, are practically non-existent. And we have had a kind of colonial spirit in our army … and for a long time we had military regime, when military personnel could do as they pleased. So, for us specific training on women and children is essential. 2) Regarding our experiences in operations in Liberia—the soldiers there included children, and we did not know what to do with them. And, often with women, soldiers thought they had a special right to them. So we have put in place special training on rights of the child. Our module is very recent (since 2000). There will be a meeting of 32 officials from ECOWAS countries and Save the Children Canada to put that training in place. The only aspect I disagree with is that this training on children is not incorporated into the general IHL training. I think it should be integrated. In Burkina we will incorporate it into IHL training.	

Countries	Written answers	Oral answers
Burundi	**Burundi 1**: Absolutely necessary. Aside from physical weakness, women's disappearance means the disappearance of their offspring, and children are the future working population of our country. ***Additional oral comments***: Due to the nature of women and children they have protected status in normal life. But the training in international law is to teach personnel in combat to have the reflex to apply the law. To get that reflex … it is necessary to have specific training regarding women and children. There must be a way of organising specific training on women and children, so the army has the appropriate reflexes. **Burundi 2**: Yes. ***Additional oral comments***: Protection of women and children is necessary. Totally indispensable, as we have seen violations in the field. We work on an ethnic basis in Burundi. The army must train, eg, to protect civilians. If the national army harms civilians, the population will turn to the rebels. So, we must educate our troops.	
Chile	No. ***Additional oral comments***: We are now teaching the Chilean navy (which I am part of) about the law of armed conflict. We have been doing so for the last 10 years. In that framework it is useful every time to learn about children and women, but it is not necessary to have a specific course.	

Countries	Written answers	Oral answers
Egypt		There is a national committee in Egypt starting to study how to put humanitarian law material in all levels of education—including civilian schools. The military have a humanitarian law package that they are disseminating, with actual training in theory and practice. It gives real situations, case studies on how to include the law. We have lectures in humanitarian law, and basic materials at all levels.
France	**France 1**: On a practical level, now in the French academy they are teaching this legal aspect through the GCs etc—but nothing specific on women and children aside from that. Focus on GC IV. I think that is sufficient. It is particularly important to have easy and practical training on GCs. We need that, but not anything more detailed. **France 2**: It is very important to focus on this kind of training, especially when in peace support operations we have to deal with civilians in a hostile atmosphere. ***Additional oral comments***: Sometimes it is not easy to distinguish between combatants and non-combatants. It can be even more difficult to distinguish between adult and child. We can talk, eg, of children 12–16, and then 16–18—just judging from appearance. They may well not have any ID. There is a problem at specific situations, eg at checkpoints. Children are more dangerous, they can't tell reality from a game. Not only do they need special protection, they need special caution! One can negotiate with adults but not children.	

Countries	Written answers	Oral answers
Greece	It is both necessary and useful to update the officers corps on the new developments concerning IHL about women and children and vulnerables in an armed conflict. In Greece, human rights of women and children have a special treatment from the primary education to the secondary education and the military training establishment. There are courses taught embodied in the weekly school schedules, concerning the issue both in peacetime and during armed conflict. ***Additional oral comments***: I agree with what has been said about Chile and naval training (since I am in the Greek navy). But—what about when, eg, you fire and capture a ship with refugees from an enemy country? Or drug trafficking vessels with refugees inside? There is law on this in the GCs but most soldiers don't know about it. We need to discuss this—that we must treat vulnerable people in specific ways.	
Italy		It is useful to know some of the law about women and children—but not mandatory to focus on them in a special course. I think they should just be included in general IHL training.
Lebanon	Yes, that is because of the development of the international crisis and the nature of the internal conflicts.	
Madagascar		We don't see the utility for the moment as we work with the civil population, teaching them rules of conduct and of behaviour in case of armed conflict.

Countries	Written answers	Oral answers
Pakistan	No, because these aspects are adequately covered under Islamic teachings, Geneva Conventions and basic moral values. *Additional oral comments*: Where do you draw the line? There are specific rules already, and some things are common sense. In addition to IHL, every army has disciplinary rules. If, eg, someone maltreated women or children—that is already covered. Every army respects certain things—if you add a whole training on specific groups that would be too much. The soldier already is supposed to know so much. So, military personnel should have an awareness of general issues regarding women and children. Legal military personnel need more detailed information. In any training on this I would also include the elderly. Women, children and the elderly require special protection. A mixture of 1949 GCs etc, and Islamic injunctions.	
Romania	According to me, this course is not necessary. *Additional oral comments*: Women and children are included within training under GC IV. I don't think it is necessary to do more.	
Singapore		1 - no one can say there is no need, or it is not useful, to have special protection of women and children. It is both of these things, but 2 - we don't want to burden foot soldiers with too much information 3 - in our training we do mention women and children, but a lot of this is common sense. No soldier can argue that it is acceptable for their own conscience and compatible with IHL to abuse women and children. So, it is useful to include some information on this in general training. But fuller information is necessary for specific missions only.

Countries	Written answers	Oral answers
South Africa	**S.A. 1**: Very much so. Women and children are the first victims in a situation of armed conflict. ***Additional oral comments***: There is a need for specific focus on women and children. Lectures currently given to soldiers are not enough.	**S.A. 2**: If we are not going to try specific military training on children, then we will never know if it can make a difference. There is room to try. Even if we don't know how much it will help. In SA we are moving towards women being trained as operators. They are soldiers, not women. They are combatants—the same applies to children in combat. Personally—I think that if they are big enough to carry a gun and fight, they are old enough to be a soldier and be treated as such. Maybe they should be given different treatment after capture. SA is not yet up to that standard—to be honest this is a new subject.
Sudan	**Sudan 1**: Yes. **Sudan 2**: Yes.	**Sudan 3**: GC IV is covered in our training, regarding civilians generally. I think it would be of use if we had something specific on women and children. How to deal with them. It would give more emphasis to this. Everything that enhances humanity in the world is good. Every religion has something on this. In Islam, there are statements clearly saying not to use children in the battle area—same for women. Islam forbids this. This prohibition is part of behaviour in the field.

Countries	Written answers	Oral answers
UK	Not in general but perhaps for specific units or troops deploying on specific operations. ***Additional oral comments***: In combat, I'm not sure that children should have special treatment. For example, in Sierra Leone UK forces were taken hostage. There was a firefight to release them—some quite young people were killed. That is legitimate. No difference if they are 10 or 40, in my opinion. However, once child soldiers are captured—eg in Sierra Leone—I think they would be treated differently. UK army is overstretched. Training is at a premium, and this would be a small part of a training programme. What would one try and get across?? Small bits on this and that are unrealistic. It is better to concentrate on general protections—but emphasise, eg, children if the specific situation requires this.	
Zambia	It is necessary as these are the most vulnerable groups in any armed conflict and they require special protection.	Women and children are relatively new in our courses. Most of the courses have not paid much attention to this. We know they are more vulnerable. We have not had the experience of armed conflict involving children in our homeland—but have seen it in, eg, Sierra Leone. We know that child soldiers can be very nasty and dangerous.

Endnotes

1   For an overview of the materials in this Booklet, the contents outline is summarised here: *Unit I: Legal Standards on Child Rights and Child Protection. Key Concepts; Topic 1*: Major legal instruments; *Topic 2*: Rules of Engagement and Codes of Conduct; *Topic 3*: Integrating legal standards and Codes of Conduct into military operations. *Unit 2: Basic Rights and Needs of Children. Key Concepts; Topic 1*: The concept of childhood; *Topic 2*: Development and basic needs of children. *Unit 3: Effects of Armed Conflict on Children. Key concepts; Topic 1*: Types of conflict and interaction of military forces with children; *Topic 2*: Impact of conflict on children; *Topic 3*: Preventing/alleviating impact and monitoring abuses. *Unit 4: Collaboration with Humanitarian Organisations/Civil Authorities. Key Concepts; Topic 1*: Humanitarian organisations and civil authorities: structure and mandates; *Topic 2*: Interrelation between humanitarian and civil structures and points of collaboration with military forces.

2   This code is set out in Appendix Five below.

3   SC S and ECOWAS/CEDEAO, 'Child Rights and Child Protection Before, During and After Conflict: The Good Soldier' (nd, Abidjan). This reiterates the 'Child Protection Code' (mentioned in the Chart above), as well as providing information on 'the good soldier' in various contexts, eg as regards: separated children, child soldiers, landmines, and the duty to combat 'the bad use of children'.

4   One example of such materials was the SC S Regional Office for Eastern and Central Africa, 'Rights of Children in Armed Conflict and Displacement: A training manual for military personnel' (SC S, Ethiopia, Nov 1999). This contained: I) *Introduction* (introducing the participants and facilitators, and the organisation of the training); II) *Concept of Childhood* (in traditional, national and global contexts; and discussion of factors in child growth and development); III) *Effects of armed conflict and displacement on children* (overview and information on helping affected children and the role of the military); IV) *Childrens' rights in situations of armed conflict* (legal provisions, monitoring violations, and training of military personnel) and *Appendices* containing, eg, case studies; examples of practical implementation of the rights of children, and a summary of relevant provisions of the 1989 CRC.

5   SC S and SC D in collaboration with the UPDF, 'Children, Our Future: A handbook on Child Rights Protection during peace and war time' (Np, Sept 1999). This starts by stating that children have the right to special protection and its contents include: 'Who is a child? Why discuss about children? Experience of children in armed conflict; International legal provisions; Children should not be recruited as fighters; The soldier as role model; Moral and ethical dilemmas; Making children visible in situations of peace and security'.

6   As mentioned above regarding methodology (Chapter Seven), SC S generally find this approach more effective.

Appendix **4**

'Background Notes' to Country Studies—Category (A) and Category (B)

Introduction

Chapter Eight above has already outlined the reasons for placing in this separate Appendix the 'Background Notes' to the 11 selected countries. Before proceeding with these, it is important to acknowledge once more that a few of the 11 selected countries have been strongly criticised for the treatment of children by their armed forces, and some readers may find it frustrating that little mention is made of this in the 'Background Notes'. Again, it must be emphasised this is a very conscious omission. One of the main aims of this book is to encourage national armed forces in general to pay greater attention to training concerning the treatment of children. Criticism in this book of specific armed forces may undermine that aim, and in any event such information can be found in other sources.

The 'Background Notes' will therefore include only basic relevant information on each particular country (since WW II), including pertinent information regarding children. They will deliberately not discuss in any detail the impact on children of the conduct of the pertinent armed forces either at home or abroad, and they will endeavour to be politically neutral. However, footnote references will generally be provided for sources of further information regarding children in relation to the various armed forces under discussion. Also, see 'Concluding Observations' of the Committee on the Rights of the Child (summarised above, Chapter Six), which highlight pertinent concerns of the Committee about some of the selected countries.

Finally, a word of caution: the 'Background Notes' on each country are based on reputable sources, and were checked for accuracy, but nonetheless the author does not claim to be an expert on the history of the 11 selected countries,[1] and apologies are made in advance for any inadvertent inaccuracies or political bias.

a)   *Category (A)—Countries Currently or Recently Involved in Armed Conflict 'At Home'*

i   Bosnia and Herzegovina (BiH)

The origins of the 1992–1995 Bosnian conflict were complex, being at the same time ethnic, economic, territorial and political. Between 1945 and 1991, BiH was one of the six Federal Republics of the Socialist Federal Republic of Yugoslavia, held together and ruled until his death in 1980 by Josep Broz, better known as General 'Tito'. One of the characteristics of Bosnia was that none of the ethnic or religious groups present—the Serbs, the Croats and the Muslims—had a majority status. This, as well as other factors, led to difficulties when the Republic of Yugoslavia collapsed with the declarations of independence of the Republics of Slovenia and Croatia in 1991, and the refusal of the Bosnian Croats and Muslims to stay in a Serb-dominated Yugoslavia. In early 1992, a referendum, boycotted by the Serbs, supported the independence of Bosnia. Soon after Bosnian independence was officially declared (April 1992), a largely non-international armed conflict broke out between the various ethnic and religious groups.[2]

The Bosnian conflict involved many different actors – particularly government and non-government armed forces, and paramilitary groups. It claimed thousands of lives, including those of children.[3] Estimates of the exact number of casualties vary according to the source, but an official figure released by the Bosnian government in 1994 set the number of deaths at 140,000.[4] There was also widespread rape of women and children.[5] Furthermore, the conflict displaced two million of the 4.3 million pre-war population of BiH,[6] and it was said that the Bosnian conflict created the largest number of refugees and displaced people in Europe since WW II, and also the 'largest global dispersement of children'.[7] Moreover, between 3000 and 4000 children were reported to have taken part as combatants in the conflict in the former Yugoslavia, the majority in BiH and Croatia.[8]

Much of the conflict involved 'ethnic cleansing' operations, aimed at eliminating specific ethnic groups from particular territorial locations[9] (including some UN-mandated 'safe havens'), and again affecting large numbers of children, among others.

The UN and others in the international community[10] undertook various interventions in attempting to resolve the crisis in the former Yugoslavia. Some commentators described this as the most complicated conflict in which the UN had been involved since its inception.[11]

The Bosnian conflict ended in December 1995 with the General Framework Agreement for Peace (also known as the Dayton peace agreement), signed by the BiH Republic, the Federal Republic of Yugoslavia and the Republic of Croatia. This agreement retained BiH international borders and national government but established two states entities: the Republika Srpska (Serbian Republic) and the Federation of BiH (itself divided into Croatian and Muslim entities).[12]

Each entity had its own army but that of the Federation of BiH was separated into Bosnian Muslim and Bosnian Croat components.[13] According to some, there were in fact three separate armies.[14] In 2002 the Bosnian armed forces were facing large cuts, estimated at about 50 percent of existing personnel.[15]

In 2002, BiH was involved in a UN peace support operation in Ethiopia/ Eritrea.[16]

ii   Colombia

Colombia had, to the time of writing, been affected by more or less continual non-international armed conflict for over 50 years. The main parties to the conflict were: the Colombian Government; Revolutionary Armed Forces of Colombia (FARC); National Liberation Army (ELN) (the latter two both armed opposition groups), and United Colombian Self Defence (AUC, a national organisation of paramilitary groups).

This conflict had grown in complexity over time, and the nature of the conflict and the actors involved had changed. Between the late 1940s and the late 1950s, ('la Violencia'), the conflict was largely political, opposing the Liberals to the Conservatives, and causing casualties mainly among the rural poor. 'La Violencia' was resolved in 1958, with a pact signed between the Liberals and Conservatives. However, another type of conflict then developed, involving the Colombian government; the various guerrilla and paramilitary groups; and drug traffickers,[17] all alleged at certain periods to have committed human rights abuses and/or violations of IHL.[18] By 2002 the conflict affected all sectors of society.[19] It had been complicated by substantial involvement of certain factions in the production of cocaine.[20]

At the time of writing, the conflict in Colombia was intense, resulting in many thousands of casualties,[21] and a large part of the country was said to be occupied either by guerrillas or paramilitary groups. The conflict apparently caused significant population displacement, especially of women and children.[22] Children were also particularly affected in this conflict as victims of kidnappings[23] and landmines,[24] and through being used as child soldiers by the guerrillas and the paramilitary groups.[25]

Further, until 1999 the Colombian armed forces had been enrolling children from the age of 15 in military schools,[26] and had been recruiting, among others, those aged under 18. However, legislation enacted in that year had begun to change recruitment practices. This legislation formed part of a series of legislative and other reforms aiming to make the CAF more accountable, and to improve their IHL and human rights training (see Chapter Eight).

Peace talks had continued very sporadically for 20 years, to the time of writing. On 1 November 2002, the UN Secretary-General's Special Adviser on Colombia was formally appointed, with the mandate of maintaining the peace talks.[27]

As regards peace support operations, Colombia had participated in several of these (eg, in Angola,[28] BiH,[29] Central America,[30] and El Salvador[31]), but was not participating in any such operations in 2002.

iii   Israel

By the end of 2002, Israel had been more or less consistently embroiled in conflict with the Palestinian people since its creation in May 1948,[32] (and it had also been engaged in hostilities at different times with various Arab states). This conflict was largely rooted in competing historical claims over the same land, Palestine. The international community had, in various capacities, been involved in the conflict from its beginnings, and the UN had intervened through the adoption of many resolutions, including numerous Security Council resolutions.

The conflict escalated once again in 2001, after a Palestinian uprising (Intifada) against Israeli occupation of the West Bank and Gaza Strip broke out in September 2000. Amnesty International warned that the rate at which children were being killed increased significantly in 2002.[33] Both sides in this conflict had been accused of human rights violations, (although see statistics below regarding child deaths and injuries of the Palestinians in particular).

The question of whether the situation in the 'Occupied Territories' since September 2002 amounted to an armed conflict, and if so what type of armed conflict, had been a matter of some controversy.[34] That said, Israel had on occasion classified this situation as an 'armed conflict'.[35]

As regards recruitment practices: at the time of writing, the Israeli Defence Forces (IDF) recruited volunteers from the age of 17 with parental consent, and IDF recruits below the age of 18 had apparently been seen carrying weapons.[36] There was mandatory conscription for Jewish Israelis, and recruitment procedures started at the age of 16, with military service beginning at 18.[37] By 2002, however, the IDF had announced that they would end the deployment of under 18s, and cease to accept conscripts under the age of 18, apart from volunteers.[38]

Israeli children (as with Israeli civilians generally) were most directly affected by the conflict as victims of Palestinian suicide bombers. In 2001, eg, Palestinian armed groups or individuals killed 187 Israelis in this way, including 154 civilians of whom 36 were children.[39] Young people were apparently sometimes targeted by suicide bombers operating in locations where the young people congregated.[40]

However, at the time of writing, many more Palestinian than Israeli children had suffered death or injury during this conflict.[41] The statistics, while differing to some extent from source to source, all indicated a high casualty rate, which had provoked criticism of Israeli military policy in some circles.[42]

One source stated in September 2002 that 7000 Palestinian children had been injured since September 2000 as a result of the conflict.[43] Other statistics reported that 33.8 percent of Palestinians injured in the West Bank between September 2000 and April 2001 were between the ages of 10 and 19, and 2.7 percent were under 10 years old. During that period in the Gaza strip, 53.2 percent of Palestinians injured were apparently aged between 10 and 19, and 3.8 percent were under the age of 10.[44]

As regards deaths of Palestinian children in this conflict, it was said that between 29 September 2000 and 15 July 2002, 250 Palestinian children under 18 were killed.[45] According to other figures, 409 children under the age of 17 were killed by Israeli security forces in the Occupied Territories between 1991 and 31 January 2002, including 101 under the age of 13.[46]

Israel was not a contributor to UN peace support operations.

iv   Sierra Leone

A few years after its independence from the UK in 1961, Sierra Leone entered a period of 30 years of one-party military rule.[47] During those years, Sierra Leone had a highly centralised and inefficient government,[48] with only a small number of Sierra Leoneans having access to the country's plentiful resources.[49] For the majority of Sierra Leoneans this resulted in poverty, social exclusion, a high unemployment rate, collapsing institutions and social services,[50] and it led ultimately to conflict.

The ensuing lengthy non-international armed conflict in Sierra Leone,[51] involving government forces, armed opposition groups, mercenaries,[52] and international peace support personnel, was fuelled by a complex combination of internal and external factors.[53] It erupted in March 1991 when a small armed opposition group, the Revolutionary United Front (RUF), launched several attacks in Eastern Sierra Leone.[54] The lack of a concerted governmental response to these attacks enabled the RUF to gather momentum, and the confrontation turned into a brutal armed conflict.[55] The main parties to the conflict remained the government armed forces and the RUF, but the Civil Defence Force was an important third force.

In the course of this conflict, thousands of civilians in Sierra Leone suffered serious human rights and IHL violations, and the impact of the conflict on Sierra Leone's children was described as catastrophic.[56] Violations were committed particularly by armed opposition forces, but also apparently by government forces—on both sides including children, who became victims and also perpetrators of abuses.[57]

During the armed conflict in Sierra Leone many thousands of children served as soldiers (often forcibly recruited), either for the RUF,[58] the Civil Defence Force, or for the government. Some estimates stated that there were some 5000 such child soldiers,[59] half of them aged between eight and 14. However, other estimates were much higher.[60]

Moreover, the conflict in Sierra Leone resulted in considerable internal displacement of the population and a huge number of refugees, which placed a heavy burden on neighbouring countries.[61] According to Save the Children, more than three million people were displaced at some point during the conflict, of whom 1.8 million were children, often separated from their parents.[62]

The international community (through the UN, ECOWAS and the OAU, as well as some individual states (eg Nigeria, the UK and the US)), was involved in seeking an end to the conflict in Sierra Leone.[63] After a number of failed initiatives,[64] a ceasefire was signed in November 2000 and consolidated in May 2001. The elections held in May 2002 gave Ahmed Tejan Kabbah (the Peoples Party) 70.6 percent of the votes, leading one commentator to state that these elections were a 'final confirmation that the war officially declared over in January has actually ended'.[65]

In September 2002, work was underway to bring to trial before a war crimes tribunal some of those responsible for major violations of international law in the Sierra Leone conflict, while others, including children forcibly conscripted as soldiers, were to give evidence before a truth and reconciliation commission.[66] Efforts were also underway to provide IHL and human rights training, including some training specifically on children, to the newly reconstituted Sierra Leoneon armed forces (see Chapter Eight).

At the time of writing, Sierra Leone had not contributed to UN operations since the 1960s.[67]

v   South Africa

While South Africa was not involved, at the time of writing, in armed conflict 'at home', it had, particularly during the apartheid era, been engaged intermittently in international and non-international armed conflict, involving mainly government armed forces and armed opposition groups, within South Africa and in neighbouring countries.

The South African Defence Force (SADF) played an important role in maintaining the apartheid regime, which has been described as conducting a 'dirty war', a regime of political oppression.[68] The apartheid government:

> destabilized surrounding states,[69] routinely engaged in torture of political opponents, engaged in political killings, supported factions that undermined peace and security, and sought to control every aspect of society in responding to threats against the apartheid regime.[70]

Although human rights abuses and/or IHL violations were committed predominantly by the government, they were also allegedly committed by others involved in these conflicts.[71] Certainly, the apartheid regime caused extreme suffering to many millions of people, including children. For example, it was said in this context that 24,000 children as young as 12 were detained incommunicado in South Africa between 1985 and 1989, and some were tortured.[72]

With the end of apartheid on Nelson Mandela's election in 1994, the different components of the South African military forces were blended into the South African National Defence Force (SANDF). The SANDF had a very different mandate and composition from that of the SADF, and had to rethink its role, and deal with major restructuring and budget cuts.[73] As a result, SANDF faced a number of challenges, including the fact that training was limited by lack of resources.[74] However, the ICRC was conducting some IHL training for the SANDF.[75] Further, there were apparently no persons under 18 in these armed forces, as the minimum age of recruitment in the SANDF was 18.[76]

South Africa had been involved in a number of peace support operations. For example, in June 2002 it was contributing 147 troops to UN operations and ranked 43rd in the list of countries contributing military and civilian police to UN operations.[77] At the time of writing, the SANDF was involved in UN peace support operations in the Democratic Republic of the Congo and in Ethiopia/Eritrea. Moreover, in October 2001 South Africa deployed 700 soldiers in Burundi, as part of a non-UN mandated peace support operation.[78] SANDF had also been militarily involved in attempts to restore peace in Lesotho (under an operation mandated by the South-ern African Development Community), after instability following the Lesotho May 1998 elections.[79]

vi   Sri Lanka

After the independence of Sri Lanka (then Ceylon) [80] from the UK in 1948, various tensions in the country propelled it towards a fierce non-international armed conflict, erupting in 1983. The conflict continued (with sporadic interruptions) to 2002. The main parties involved were: (Sinhala) government forces, and various Tamil military groups, of which only the Liberation Tigers of Tamil Eelam (LTTE) remained as a force opposed to the government.[81] The LTTE were primarily seeking independence of part of Sri Lanka for the Tamil population.[82] India also became involved in the 1980s.[83] However, conflict developed between the LTTE and the Indian Peacekeeping Force (IPKF) after negotiation of the Indo-Lanka Accord in 1987,[84] and India withdrew in 1990.

There were also other dimensions to the conflict, including clashes between different Tamil military groups, and tensions between various elements within the Tamil minority.[85] Also, there was violent opposition to government actions from sections of the Sinhala population.[86]

It was estimated that the Sri Lankan conflict claimed more than 64,000 lives from among both combatants and the civilian population.[87] It also left thousands of civilians injured and caused significant displacement and emigration. All sides of the conflict were said to have been responsible at certain times for human rights and/or IHL abuses, 'including indiscriminate suicide bombings by the LTTE, and torture and "disappearances" by government security forces and affiliated para-military'.[88] Children were also the victims of these abuses, eg they were apparently among those who 'disappeared',[89] and a quarter of victims of land mines were said to be children.[90] Moreover, children were used as soldiers by paramilitary groups and by the LTTE,[91] and critics of the LTTE claimed that they relied heavily on such soldiers.[92] It was alleged that some of these LTTE child soldiers who were captured by the Sri Lankan Special Task Force and the Terrorism Investigation Division of the police had been ill-treated by their captors.[93]

In 2001 the Sri Lankan government launched a major IHL training programme for their armed forces, with plans to include one component specifically aiming to improve their treatment of captured child soldiers (see Chapter Eight).

Numerous attempts were made to reach a peaceful resolution to the conflict in Sri Lanka,[94] and on 22 February 2002 the parties signed the most recent (at the time of writing) ceasefire agreement.[95] Direct talks between the parties commenced on 16 September 2002, although a final peace accord was not, at that stage, anticipated until 2004.[96]

At various times, Sri Lanka had also been involved in peace support operations.[97] In 2002 Sri Lanka was not contributing troops to UN operations, but was contributing civilian police and military observers.

viii   Uganda

Uganda became independent of the UK in October 1962, with A Milton Obote's party, (the Uganda's Peoples Union), and a traditional leader, the Kabaka Yekka (the Kabaka), forming the first post-colonial government. Obote broke his alliance with the Kabaka in 1966, and conflict ensued. In securing his position, Obote eliminated many of his opponents and gave the armed forces an important political role. Obote's first period in office lasted until January 1971, when it was terminated by a *coup d'etat* by General Idi Amin Dada. Amin ruled for the next eight years, and his regime caused the deaths of huge numbers of people (estimated at 300,000— including many children). The regime also expelled most of the Ugandan Asian community. Uganda's infrastructures and economy largely collapsed, and in 1979 Amin fled the country.

Obote won the ensuing elections in 1980, but the results were contested. Internal conflict persisted, and in the early 1980s Obote's government was responsible for the deaths of thousands of Ugandans, and many more fled the country. Obote was overthrown in 1985 by General Tito Okello and Brigadier Bazilio Okello, who were in turn overthrown, in January 1986, by Yoweri Museveni's National Resistance Army/Movement (NRA/M).[98] When the NRA/M took power in 1986, more than 3,000 children aged under 16 (called 'kadogos'—Swahili for 'little ones') were in its ranks. Most of them had been orphaned in conflicts during Obote's rule, and they were said to be disciplined, reliable and trustworthy.[99] Museveni remains in power at the time of writing.

The on-going non-international armed conflict affecting Northern Uganda[100] started when the NRM/A took power and, at the time of writing, it had continued from 1986 to 2002. Although the main parties to this conflict were the Ugandan government and the Lord's Resistance Army (LRA),[101] its causes lay in Uganda's history, and it has been described as resulting from ethnic, religious, political, economic, social and regional divisions. [102]

From 1986 until 1997, conflict in Uganda was mostly confined to the north and north west. In 1997, however, the internal conflict expanded to other regions of Uganda, as on-going tensions worsened between the Ugandan government and the Allied Democratic Forces in the south-western part of the country.[103]

Killing, rape, torture and abduction were widely perpetrated by the armed opposition groups against civilians in the Ugandan zones of conflict. The conflicts had also caused substantial population displacement. In Gulu in the north, eg, 80 percent of the population had been displaced and lived in camps in 1999.[104] Moreover, landmines had been laid by the LRA and the Allied Democratic Forces, killing and injuring civilians.[105] Children had also been particularly affected by the conflict, especially in Northern Uganda, since, by 2001, most of the LRA fighters and camp followers were children or had been children when they were abducted.[106]

UNICEF and various NGOs stated that between 1986 and 1999, 10,000 children had been abducted by the LRA.[107] According to Olara Otunnu (SRSG/CAC), some of these children were as young as five.[108] The Allied Democratic Forces were also responsible for abducting and maltreating children.[109]

The situation was further complicated by the fact that the government armed forces – the Ugandan People's Defence Forces (UPDF)—had themselves allegedly been responsible for human rights abuses and/or IHL violations at certain times.[110] The UPDF also recruited those aged under 18,[111] although at the time of writing it was expected that there would be changes in recruitment practice, following Ugandan accession to the 2000 Optional Protocol on Child Soldiers. In any event, the UPDF had, since about 1999, periodically provided some military training specifically on children for certain personnel (see Chapter Eight).

Attacks by the LRA and the Allied Democratic Forces on civilians continued throughout 2002. In that year, the Ugandan and Sudanese governments joined forces in 'Operation Iron First', aiming to eliminate LRA bases in the Sudan. The situation regarding human rights in Northern Uganda—and the particular impact of this conflict on children—was considered so serious by the SRSG/CAC that he recommended the appointment of a Special Rapporteur for Northern Uganda in his 2002 report.[112]

Uganda had apparently not participated in UN peacekeeping operations.

b) Category (B)—Countries Substantially Involved in Armed Conflict 'Abroad', and/or in Training, and/or in Peace Support Operations

i Australia

Since WW II, Australia had participated in various armed conflicts, including in Korea (1950–1953), Malaya (1950–1960), Indonesia (1964–1966), Vietnam (1962–1972) and Iraq (1990–1991). At the time of writing, Australia was involved in Afghanistan, as a contributing member of the 'international coalition against terrorism',[113] and was preparing to support a possible US and UK-led attack on Iraq.

As regards Australian recruitment policy, in June 2002 the Department of Defence issued 'Defence Instructions (General)',[114] aiming to bring Australian law into compliance with the 2000 Optional Protocol on Child Soldiers. According to these Instructions, the minimum voluntary recruitment age in the Australian Defence Force (ADF) would continue to be 17 years (with some limited exceptions, including for military schools) (paragraph 4). Persons wishing to join the ADF were required to present their birth certificate as proof of age (paragraph 5), and, if under-age, to obtain the written consent of their parents or guardians (paragraph 6). The Instructions stated that the 'ADF will take all feasible measures to ensure that minors do not participate in hostilities' (paragraph 10),[115] with certain exceptions, including naval operations in some circumstances (paras. 13–14).[116]

There were several ways of entering the ADF army, navy and air force, depending on the grade and the specialisation. Training (including for peace support operations) was conducted in a range of institutions. [117]

In 1999–2000, 17 percent of Australian recruits were apparently under the age of 18. At that time, the number of recruits aged under 18 was said to be rising and seemed unlikely to decrease since, according to one source, the ADF was then planning to expand its armed forces and was encountering difficulties regarding recruitment and retention.[118] On occasion the ADF had been criticised, eg, for its treatment of recruits, but these were apparently isolated incidents.[119]

Since 1947 Australia has had a significant involvement in UN 'peace operations',[120] sometimes including the provision of military training. The ADF had—by 2002—participated in some 34 missions, involving 36,000 personnel.[121] In June 2002, Australia contributed 1,150 troops to 'peace operations' and it was 10th in the ranking of military and civilian police contributions (observers, police and troops) to UN operations.[122] It ranked 9th (in June 2002) if troop contributions alone were taken into account.[123]

ii   South Africa

As mentioned in Chapter Eight, South Africa is included as one of the countries in this category, Category (B). Since it is also included in Category (A) (Countries Currently or Recently Involved in Armed Conflict 'At Home'), the 'Background Notes' regarding South Africa can be found in this Appendix above.

iii   Sweden

Since 1815, Sweden had avoided participating as a party to armed conflict, its foreign policy being founded on the premise that the most effective way to safeguard national security was to preserve its neutrality by avoiding entry into military alliances. In 2002, Sweden revised this security doctrine to state that Sweden might in future enter into military alliances in response to threats against international peace and security.[124]

In 2001, Sweden had 52,700 active members in its armed forces.[125] There was compulsory recruitment at the age of 19, and no voluntary recruitment. Accordingly, no person under the age of 18 was involved in the Swedish armed forces.[126]

Swedish overseas forces had, since 1948, contributed to about 30 peace support operations, in countries including Afghanistan, Sierra Leone, the (then) Republic of the Congo, East Timor, Cambodia, Croatia, Eritrea/Ethiopia, Georgia, Guatemala, India/Pakistan, Korea, Kuwait and the Middle East. At the time of writing, Sweden was contributing military and other personnel to two operations under NATO's lead: the SFOR operation in BiH and the KFOR operation in Kosovo, and it was also contributing military personnel to the International Security Assistance Force (ISAF) in Kabul. In June 2002, Sweden was listed as 46th in the ranking of military and civilian police contributions to UN peace support operations, which included supplying troops, observers and police.[127]

Sweden—through the Sweden Armed Forces International Centre (SWED-INT)[128]—had been involved in providing training for peace support operations to military and police forces; Red Cross delegates; aid workers, etc from over 65 countries. SWEDINT was also responsible for some of NATO's 'Partnership for Peace' (PfP) activities, such as military staff training courses and PfP exercises, which aimed, *inter alia*, to facilitate international cooperation, and provide training for peace support operations.[129]

In respect of all its military activities, international law advisers apparently counsel Swedish military commanders on the way that legal rules apply to particular situations, and on the way that military staff should be trained regarding such rules.[130]

iv   United Kingdom

The UK has been involved in many armed conflicts since WW II, as a party to international armed conflicts (eg the Falklands War and the 1991 Gulf War), a member of NATO, and as a major participant in peace support operations (eg in BiH, and see below). It has also been involved in (periodically high-intensity) civil unrest in Northern Ireland.[131]

At the time of writing, the UK was supporting the US in preparing for a possible war against Iraq.[132] Further, UK armed forces were, among other things, involved in Afghanistan, as part of the US-led 'war against terrorism' that began in October 2001 (1,700 UK troops deployed between March and June 2002).[133] The UK was also one of 19 countries contributing troops to ISAF in Kabul (2,000 troops contributed).[134]

In addition, UK armed forces had participated fairly recently in NATO operations in Kosovo and BiH.[135] They had also been substantially involved, *inter alia*, in Iraq,[136] and Sierra Leone[137] (where they provided some military training, (see above, Chapter Eight)). UK armed forces had also been present, on an on-going basis, in Cyprus, Gibraltar, the Falkland Islands and, as already mentioned, in Northern Ireland.[138] (In relation to the latter, some had voiced concerns regarding the treatment of children.[139])

As regards recruitment, UK law, at the time of writing, permitted those aged under 18 to enter the armed forces, the minimum age for entry generally being 16, and, for officers, 17.[140] Recruitment procedures could be started at the age of 15.[141] The Ministry of Defence required parental consent for entry of those under 18.[142] Recruitment of those aged under 18 decreased between 1990 and 1996,[143] although from 1997 it had been rising: 4529 under 18s were recruited in 1997, and 7676 in 1999.[144] In total, 40 percent of UK military personnel in 1999 joined the armed forces at the age of 16 or 17,[145] and, at the time of writing, apparently one third of recruits were under 18.[146] The commitment was normally to stay in the armed forces for 4–6 years.[147]

UK 16 and 17-year olds had sometimes been deployed in conflict situations.[148] However, in March 2002 the UK Ministry of Defence declared that it would no longer send those aged under 18 to situations of armed conflict.[149]

Since 1971, there had, to the time of writing, been seven deaths in active service of UK military personnel aged under 18.[150] As regards injuries, ten under-18 military personnel were seriously injured in armed conflicts between January 1980 and March 2000.[151] Apparently a larger number of this age group had been killed or injured during military training.[152]

UK armed forces had participated in many UN missions. In December 2002, eg, the UK was contributing military observers and troops to missions in Afghanistan, Cyprus, the Democratic Republic of the Congo, Ethiopia/Eritrea, Georgia, Iraq/Kuwait, Kosovo and Sierra Leone.[153] The UK also provided training to military personnel from a number of other countries, either in those countries or in UK-based institutions such as the Royal College of Defence Studies.[154]

v   United States

The US had been directly and indirectly involved in a very large number of armed conflicts since WW II, including in Vietnam, Somalia, Iraq, Haiti, Kosovo, Colombia and Panama. Some commentators had criticised the actions of the US and its allies in certain of these conflicts, but others rejected these criticisms.[155]

As already mentioned (Chapter Nine), the US initiated widespread IHL training for its armed forces in the aftermath of the conflict in Vietnam, apparently at least in part as a response to violations they had committed.

At the time of writing, the US was involved in a 'war against terrorism' in Afghanistan (Operation Enduring Freedom), and was (with the UK and others) preparing for a possible attack on Iraq to oust the government of Saddam Hussein, depending on the outcome of renewed UN-backed weapon inspections in that country.[156]

The US has one of the largest armed forces in the world.[157] On 30 September 2002, eg, there were 1,181,150 military personnel based in the US and 230,484 based in foreign countries, making a total of 1,411,634.[158] The active-duty military personnel strength level reached its peak during the Korean conflict (1950–1953) and the Vietnam war (1965–1973). It had apparently been decreasing since.[159]

The US was also, in 2002, providing military training and assistance to 'virtually every country but Cuba, Iraq, Iran and the other countries on the terrorist list'.[160]

As regards recruitment, in 2001 the voluntary age of recruitment for the US armed forces was set at 17, with parental consent required for those under 18. Apparently 23 percent of recruits were aged 17 at the time of signing the enlistment contracts, and 6 percent of new recruits were aged 17 when they commenced their training.[161] Some US 17 year olds did serve in Somalia, in BiH and in the 1991 Gulf War.[162] According to official data, there had been 78 deaths of 17 year olds, out of a total of 32,151 deaths in the US armed forces between October 1979 and September 1998.[163]

On 30 June 2002, the US was contributing 33 military observers, 646 police and one officer to UN peace support operations.[164] Its overall ranking as a contributor to such operations was 19th in June 2002.[165] The US also contributed to NATO operations in BiH (IFOR and SFOR) and in Kosovo (Kosovo Force—KFOR).

Endnotes

1   The author's Research Assistant was also not a historian, but nonetheless her work in preparing the initial drafts of the 'Background Notes' was greatly appreciated. In any event the 'Notes' were also sent, to be checked for accuracy, to various experts on each country. Any inaccuracies, however, of course remain the responsibility of the author.

2   See eg, X Bougarel, *Bosnie: anatomie d'un conflit* (Paris, La Découverte, Les dossiers de l'Etat du monde, 1996), and S. Woodward, *Balkan tragedy: chaos and dissolution after the Cold War* (Washington, DC, Brookings Institution, 1995).
    The categorisation of this conflict as non-international is complicated particularly by alleged Serbian involvement.

3   See eg, E Daly, 'Grief and Rage over Playground Massacre', *The Independent* (26 June 1995), and see ICTY cases cited in Chapter Five above.

4   Bougarel (1996), pp 11-12. Casualty estimates for this conflict varied from 25,000 to 250,000 persons (S Dickey et al, 'Bosnia and Herzegovina', *Worldmark Encyclopaedia of the Nations*, 10th ed, (Detroit, Gale Group, 2001), p 76). Moreover, in the post-conflict period the number of victims of landmines in BiH remained very high. See ICRC, *The Silent Menace: Landmines in Bosnia and Herzegovina* (Geneva, ICRC, 1997), available at http://www.icrc.org, visited on 10 June 2002.

5   See eg, UN Doc A/RES/49/205 (23 Dec 1994), Rape and abuse of women in the areas of armed conflict in the former Yugoslavia. Apparently, boys were also victims of rape in this conflict (Machel, (1996), para 93).

6   UN Press Release 11/31, 17 Jan 1996.

7   Woodward (1995), p 2.

8   Some of the children involved were apparently as young as 10 (CSC (2001), p 95). See also, A Cataldi, 'Child Soldiers' in R Gutman and D Rieff (Eds.) *Crimes of War: What the Public Should Know* (New York/London, WW Norton & Company, 1999).

9   See eg, Bougarel (1996), p 13.

10 In particular, the bodies involved were the European Community, NATO, the Organisation for Security and Cooperation in Europe (OSCE) and the UN. The Security Council established the UN Protection Force (UNPROFOR) in Feb 1992 with the general mandate of creating conditions of peace and security to facilitate the resolution of the Yugoslav crisis (see UN Doc S/RES/743 (21 Feb 1992)). Its mandate was enlarged several times (see eg, UN Docs. S/RES/761, (29 June 1992); S/RES/776 (14 Sept 1992); S/RES/781 (9 Oct 1992) and S/RES/824 (6 May 1993)). In 1994 and 1995 the UN co-operated with NATO in a number of air strikes against Serbian forces (see eg, http://www.un.org/Depts/dpko/ dpko/co mission/unprofb.htm, visited on 11 Dec 2002, and, eg, P Malanczuk, *Akehurst's Modern Introduction to International Law*, seventh revised edn (London, Routledge, 1997), p 414).

11 For example, see D A Leurdijk, 'Background Paper: United Nations Protection Force (UNPROFOR): Report and Recommendations of the International Conference, Singapore, February 1997', in N Azimi et al (eds.) *Humanitarian action and peace-keeping operations: debriefing and lessons* (London, Kluwer Law International, 1997), p 69. The complexity of this operation has been attributed, *inter alia*, to its scale, the flagrant violations of humanitarian principles, the lack of clarity over the UN mandate, and the hostile environment in which UN troops and humanitarian agencies had to operate.

12 A large multinational military implementation force, (IFOR), was deployed to implement and monitor the military aspects of the Dayton peace agreement. A smaller NATO-led Stabilisation Force (SFOR) later replaced it (see generally, http://www.nato.int/sfor, visited on 17 Jan 2003). The UN mission in BiH, UNMIBH, was established on 21 Dec 1995 and, at the time of writing, its mandate had been extended until 31 Dec 2002 (UN Doc S/RES/ 1423 (12 July 2002)).

13 See eg, US Department of State, 'Country Reports on Human Rights Practices' (Washington DC, US Department of State, 1996).

14 See eg, CSC (2001), p 94.

15 S Bose, 'Mostar, 1994-2001: Nationalist Partition and International Intervention in a Bosnian Town', *Lecture*, (London, LSE's Crisis States Programme, DESTIN Research Seminar Series, 11 Feb 2002). According to Bose, in 2001 joint military exercises were held, under international supervision, involving all elements of the armed forces: Serbian, Muslim and Croat. He also observed that BiH was becoming demilitarised, and the police were more important as regards internal security.

16 UNMEE started in July 2000. See http://www.un.org/Depts/dpko/missions/unmee/facts.html, visited on 11 Dec 2002.

17 See generally, HRW, *War Without Quarter: Colombia and International Humanitarian Law* (New York, HRW, 1998). Regarding the two main active guerrilla forces in Colombia, FARC and ELN, see eg, LeGrand, C C, 'The Colombian Crisis in Historical Perspective', *Colombia in Context*, (University of California, Berkeley, 2 March 2001), available at, http://socrates.berkeley.edu:7001/colombia/ workingpapers.html, visited on 13 Feb 2003, p 7. As regards the AUC, see eg, ICHRP (2000), p 7; AI, *Amnesty International Report 2001* (London, AI, 2001) and U.S. Department of State, 'Country Reports on Human Rights Practices' (Washington DC, US Department of State, 2001).

18 The US was also involved through Plan Colombia, (an aid package, the stated aim of which was to 'defend Colombia's democracy' and combat drug cultivation), which included, *inter alia*, the provision of military training and equipment to the Colombian Armed Forces (CAF). The US had contributed $1.8 billion to Plan Colombia by Dec 2002 (Press Conference, Secretary of State Colin L Powell, 4 Dec 2002, Bogotá, Colombia, available at http://usinfo.state.gov/regional/ar/colombia/, visited on 12 Feb 2003). This aid was conditional on, *inter alia*, the CAF agreeing to suspend and punish 'military officers credibly alleged to have committed gross violations of human rights or to have aided…paramilitary groups'. (See, http://www.state.gov/r/pa/prs/ps/2002/13332.htm, visited on 4 Nov 2002). Plan Colombia was controversial (see eg, http://www.amnesty-usa.org/news/2000/ colombia07072000.html, visited on 18 April 2002).

19 See eg, LeGrand (2001), pp 11-12.

20 Colombia was, in 2001, said to be the source of 80% of the global coca production. M. Lemoine, 'Cultures illicites, narcotrafic, et guerre en Colombie', *Le monde diplomatique*, (Jan 2001), p 18.

21 According to one authority, '[s]ince 1985, there have been 25,000 violent deaths per year, a total of 300,000 murders over the past decade and a half. Homicide is the leading cause of death for men between the ages of 18 and 45, and the second leading cause for women. In 2000, 1,800 people died in massacres and more than 3,500 were kidnapped for ransom …. Close to two million people, mostly the rural poor, have been displaced and are now refugees inside the country …'.(LeGrand (2001), p 1.)

22 A 2002 UNICEF report on Colombia stated that 45% of the two million displaced over the previous 15 years were children under 18 (UNICEF, 'Humanitarian Action: Colom-

bia, Donor Update' (29 May 2002), available at, http://www.unicef.org/emerg/ Country/ Colombia/020529.PDF, visited on 18 Sept 2002). Men were apparently more affected by political killings (HRW (1998), p 19).

23 LeGrand (2001), p 6.

24 For example, apparently an average of 200 people were killed each year by landmines between 1998 and 2001, of whom 40% were under 18 (UNICEF (2002)).

25 CSC (2001), pp 126-127.

26 *Ibid*, p 124.

27 UN News service, 'James LeMoyne appointed as Annan's Special Adviser on Colombia' (1 Nov 2002).

28 UNAVEM II, from May 1991 to Feb 1995 (see, http://www.un.org/Depts/DPKO/ Missions/ Unavem2/UnavemIIF.html, visited on 15 Sept 2002).

29 UNPROFOR, from Feb 1992 to March 1995 (see, http://www.un.org/Depts/dpko/ dpko/ comission/unprofb.htm, visited on 15 Sept 2002).

30 ONUCA, from Nov 89 to Jan 92 (see, http://www.un.org/Depts/DPKO/Missions/ onuca.htm, visited on 11 Dec 2002).

31 ONUSAL, July 1991 to April 1995 (see, http://www.un.org/Depts/dpko/dpko/ comission/ onusal.htm, visited on 15 Sept 2002).

32 Israel was founded in 1948 after agreement could not be reached between Jews and Arabs on a UN-backed plan to divide Palestine into a Jewish state and a Palestinian one. (See UN Doc GA resolution 181 (II) of 29 Nov 1947. See also UN summary of the history of the conflict at http://www.un.org/Depts/dpa/ngo/history.html, visited on 10 Dec 2002.)

33 AI, 'Israel, the Occupied Territories and the Palestinian Authority: Killing the Future: Children in the line of fire' (London, AI, 2002); P Graff, 'Amnesty warns of child victims', *The Guardian* (1 Oct 2002), and S Goldenberg, 'The War of the Children', *The Guardian* (*G2*), (27 Sept 2001).

34 See eg, for opinions of several international legal experts on this and related issues: S Sullivan, 'Israel and the Palestinians: What Laws Were Broken?' Report of the Crimes of War Project, 8 May 2002, http://www.crimesofwar.org/expert/me-intro.html, visited on 16 April 2003.

35 See, eg Israel's submission in a Supreme Court case, *HCJ 769/02 The Public Committee Against Torture et al. v. State of Israel et al*, Additional Submission by the State Attorney's Office, 2 Feb 2003, paras. 11-12. See also: Consideration of reports submitted by States Parties under Art 40 of the Covenant, Second Periodic Report, Addendum: Israel, UN Doc CCPR/C/ISR/2001/2, 4 Dec 2001, para 8.

36 SC S, 'Children at Risk in Israel/Palestine', 3:4 *Children of War* (2000), p 3.

37 See eg, CSC (2002), p 53.

38 HRW, *World Report* (New York, HRW, 2002).

39 AI, *Annual Report 2002* (London, AI, 2002).

40 See eg, Graff, (*The Guardian*,1 Oct 2002).

41 It was said that the high number of child casualties could be attributed, *inter alia*, to the fact that 53% of the population in the 'Occupied Territories' was under 18; children had to pass through checkpoints on their way to school, and housing overcrowding meant that children were frequently outside in the streets (SC S (2000), p 3). According to some commentators, this situation was exacerbated by the despair and anger felt by much of Palestinian population, often leading to, eg, confrontations (frequently involving chil-

dren) with IDF soldiers, and/or the wish for martyrdom (see eg, C. Hedges, 'The New Palestinian Revolt', 80:1 *Foreign Affairs* (2001), pp 124-138). At the same time, some Israelis argued that Palestinian children were indoctrinated from a very young age to hate Israelis (see eg, BBC News, 'Baby bomber shocks Israel', 28 June 2002).

42   Regarding some of the controversial Israeli actions, and criticism of these, see *inter alia*: HDIP '857 Palestinians killed (Shuhada) between Sept 29th 2000 and Nov 27th 2001' (Ramallah, HDIP, 2002), available at http://www.hdip.org/reports/Martyrs_statistics.htm, visited 29 July 2002; BBC news, 'Peres "regrets Gaza Bombing Mistake"' (24 July 2002), available at http://news.bbc.co.uk, visited on 3 Aug 2002; UN Wire, 'Settlers Kill Palestinian Girl' (29 July 2002); HRW, 'Israel, the Occupied West Bank and Gaza Strip, and the Palestinian Authority Territories; Jenin: IDF military operations' (New York, HRW, May 2002); Watchlist on children and armed conflict, 'The Impact of Conflict on Children in Occupied Palestinian Territory and Israel' (New York, Watchlist on children and armed conflict, 2002); R. Dudai, 'Trigger Happy: Unjustified Shooting and Violation of the Open-Fire Regulations during the al-Aqsa Intifada' (Draft) (Jerusalem, B'Tselem, March 2002); Y Stein, 'Death in Custody: the Killing of Murad Awaisa, 17, in Ramallah, 31 March 2002', Case Study No. 14 (Jerusalem, B'Tselem, May 2002); HDIP, 'Health Care under Siege II, The Health Situation of Palestinians During the First 7 Months of the Intifada (September 28th 2000-April 28th 2001)' (Ramallah, HDIP, May 2001), p 3, and AI, 'Israel and the Occupied Territories Shielded from Scrutiny: IDF violations in Jenin and Nablus', (London, AI, Nov 2002).

43   Watchlist on children and armed conflict, (2002), p 6.

44   HDIP (May 2001), p 5. Those figures were based on 8,073 Palestinians injured in the West Bank and 3,761 Palestinians injured in the Gaza Strip and treated in health facilities.

45   See, http://www.jmcc.org/banner/banner1/childaqsa.htm, visited on 29 July 2002. Further, 11 Palestinian children were recorded as having been killed by landmines and unexploded ordnance in 2002 (Watchlist on children and armed conflict, (2002), p 3).

46   Defence for Children International (DCI), Israel Section, in consultation with the Israeli Children's Rights Coalition, 'NGO Comments on the Initial Israeli State Report on Implementing the UN Convention on the Rights of the Child: A Mixed Bag: Lawmaking to Promote Children s Rights, Ongoing Discrimination, and Many Serious Violations: Prepared for the Presessional Working Group UN Committee on the Rights of the Child, 31st Session', (Jerusalem, DCI, April 2002), pp 269-270.

47   J L Hirsch, *Sierra Leone: Diamonds and the Struggle for Democracy* (Boulder, Lynne Rienner Publishers, 2001), pp 28-30, and F M Hayward, 'Sierra Leone', in J Krieger (Ed.) *The Oxford Companion to the Politics of the World* (Oxford, OUP, 1993) 827-828. One-party rule effectively began in 1967, although there was an elected government at that time.

48   Hirsh (2001), pp 28-31; A Ayissi and R E Poulton, 'Peace Building and Practical Disarmament: Beyond States, with Civil Society', in A Ayissi and R E Poulton (eds) *Bound to Cooperate: Conflict, Peace and People in Sierra Leone* (Geneva, UNIDIR, 2000), p 3, and J A D Alie, 'Background to the Conflict (1961–1991): What Went Wrong and Why?' in Ayissi and Poulton (2000), p 18.

49   Sierra Leone is very rich in natural resources, possessing some of the world's most lucrative diamond fields. (Alie (2000), p 30).

50   In 1989 Sierra Leone was classified as one of the poorest countries in the world (UNDP Human Development Report 1992, Global Dimensions of Human Development (New York, UNDP, 1992), p 98), and in 1990 Sierra Leone was the third lowest country in

the human development index (UNDP, Human Development Report 1990, Concept and Measurement of Human Development (New York, UNDP, 1990)).

51 Despite being a largely non-international armed conflict, it was 'internationalised' to some extent by Liberian support for the Revolutionary United Front (RUF).

52 On mercenaries in Sierra Leone, see eg, D J Francis, 'Mercenary Intervention in Sierra Leone: Providing National Security or International Exploitation?' 20:2 *Third World Quarterly* (1999), p 319–338.

53 See eg, Francis (1999), p 324, and Alie (2000), pp 34-35.

54 As stated in the Basic Document of the RUF, The Second Liberation of Africa, 1989: 'We can no longer leave the destiny of our country in the hands of a generation of crooked politicians and military adventurists who, everyday since independence, have proved beyond all reasonable doubt that they are inefficient, irresponsible and corrupt. ...It is our right and duty to challenge and change the present political system in the name of salvation and liberation.' (Available at, http://www.sierra-leone.org/footpaths .html, visited on 16 May 2002).

55 Alie (2000), pp 15-16.

56 SC UK, 'War Brought us Here: Protecting Children Displaced within Their Own Countries' (London, SC UK, 2000), p 93.

57 Thousands of Sierra Leoneans, regardless of age, were the victims of killings, rape, abduction, and amputation of limbs (the latter had become the trademark of the RUF) (see eg, P Veerman, 'The Children's Rights Crisis in Sierra Leone', *Monitor* (1999), p 10). Such abuses were apparently still continuing into 2001.

58 The RUF generally abducted children and forced them—usually under threat, or under the influence of drugs and alcohol—to fight and to commit abuses (see eg, AI (2000(a)), p 1 and Zack-Williams (2001), pp 79-80). Thousands were also estimated to have been used by the RUF in non-combat roles, eg carrying goods, being used as sex slaves, etc (see eg, AI (2000(a)), p 1). In addition, the RUF was allegedly responsible for the forced labour of children in diamond fields. (D Farah, 'Sierra Leone rebels still take a shine to diamonds', *Guardian Weekly* (30 Aug-5 Sept 2001), p 29). According to some, the conflict was fuelled by the desire to control the diamond industry (Hirsh (2001), p 15. See also, D Keen, 'Sierra Leone: War and its Functions', in F Stewart, V Fitzgerald and Associates (eds) *War and Underdevelopment* (Oxford, OUP, 2001)).

59 AI, 'Sierra Leone: Childhood—a Casualty of Conflict' (London, AI, 2000(a)), p 1. According to the CSC, 'up to 30 percent of government-sponsored Citizens Defence Force in some areas are children between 7 and 14, despite government promises to the contrary' (CSC (2001), p 30).

60 Zack-Williams (2001), p 74. According to SC, between 15,000 and 17,000 Sierra Leonean children in total served as soldiers (SC UK (2000), p 93).

61 HRW, 'Forgotten Children of War: Sierra Leoneon Refugee Children in Guinea' (New York, HRW, 1999(a)) Chapter IV, p 3.

62 SC UK (2000), p 98.

63 See in general, UN, ABC des Nations Unies (New York, UN, 2001), pp 102-103.

64 In June 1998, the UN Security Council established UNOMSIL (UN Observer Mission in Sierra Leone) to monitor and advise on disarmament, restructure the security forces, and document human rights abuses. However, UNOMSIL left when conflict resumed in Jan 1999. Various diplomatic initiatives followed, leading finally to the Lomé peace agreement (July 1999). In Oct 1999, the Security Council established UNAMSIL (UN

Mission in Sierra Leone – replacing UNOMSIL), which became, in 2000, the largest ever peace support force (A Roberts and R Parker, 'Human Cost of Civil War', July/August *Amnesty Magazine* (2000), p 7). At the time of writing, UNAMSIL was still in Sierra Leone, although with reduced capacity.

65 C McGreal, 'Kabbah elected as Sierra Leone rejects rebels', *The Guardian* (20 May 2002), p 15.

66 R Dowden, 'Justice goes on trial in ravaged Sierra Leone', *Guardian Weekly* (10-16 Oct 2002), and see Ch 4 above, n 31.

67 It had, eg, contributed troops in what was then the Congo, as part of UNOC, between 1960 and 1964. (See, http://www.un.org/Depts/DPKO/Missions/onuc.htm, visited on 28 Oct 2002).

68 There were in fact several independent military forces that were active in South Africa during apartheid (G Mills, 'Armed Forces in Post-Apartheid South Africa', 35:3 *Survival* (1993), pp 78-79).

69 In the 1980s, South Africa supported insurgencies and raids in neighbouring countries (eg Angola and Namibia). See eg, N M Stultz, 'South Africa in Angola and Namibia', in T G Weiss and J G Blight (eds) *The Suffering Grass: Superpowers and Regional Conflict in Southern Africa and the Caribbean* (London, Lynne Reiner Publishers, 1992), pp 79–99.

70 A Ugalde, P Richards and A Zwi, 'Health Consequences of War and Political Violence', in L. Kurtz (ed) *Encyclopaedia of Violence, Peace, and Conflict* (San Diego, Academic Press, 1999), p 109. Evidence of these and related activities was also gathered during the proceedings of South Africa's much-publicised Truth and Reconciliation Commission.

71 Furthermore, human rights abuses were committed in the context of later internal South African conflicts such as the ANC-Inkatha violence of the early 1990s.

72 D Summerfield, 'The Social Experience of War', in Bracken and Petty (1998), p 11. Moreover, as a result of these various conflicts, 25 children were said to have died every hour during this period (see, UNICEF, African-European Institute and Southern African Research and Documentation Centre, *Transcending the Legacy of Apartheid: Children in the New South Africa* (New York, UNICEF, 1996), available at http://www.unicef.org/trans/, visited on 15 Sept 2002)—and Mozambique, eg, apparently had the highest infant mortality rate in the world (Summerfield (1998), p 11).

73 See eg, G Kynoch, 'The "Transformation" of the South African Military', 34:3 *The Journal of Modern African Studies* (1996), pp 442–443; R J Griffiths, 'South African Civil-Military Relations in Transition: Issues and Influences', 21:3 *Armed Forces and Society* (1995), pp 395–407, and more generally, Ministry of Defence—South Africa, 'Defence in a Democracy: White Paper on National Defence for the Republic of South Africa', (May 1996). The latter stated, among other things, that all SANDF activities were to be carried out in accordance with IHL (Chapter 2, para 21).

74 For example, there was restricted availability of certain weapons systems (e-mail of 3 March 2003, from ISS). In 2002, the BBC claimed that SANDF was undergoing a crisis: it was said that only 3,000 out of 76,000 soldiers could be deployed and training had more or less stopped (BBC news, 'South Africa's army "unfit"', 16 July 2002). The South African Ministry of Defence refuted this claim.

75 For example, there was an ICRC seminar for members of the Ministry of Defence, the army, the air force, the navy and medical services, in Oct 2001, which covered, *inter alia*, the obligations of states to include IHL in military training of the armed forces. The

entire top military command was said to have attended this seminar (ICRC (2002(a)), p 150).

76 CSC (2001), p 336.

77 See, http://www.un.org/Depts/dpko/dpko/contributors/index.htm, visited on 12 Aug 2002.

78 See, HRW, World Report (2002). The aim of this operation was apparently to protect the transitional government.

79 With the approval of the Lesotho government, South Africa sent 600 troops to Lesotho in Sept 1998 (of whom nine were said to have died in the operation). This intervention was controversial. See eg, BBC News, 'Africa Chaos in Lesotho' (23 Sept 1998), available at http://news.bbc.co.uk, visited on 13 Nov 2002, and BBC News, 'Lesotho King denied radio access' (25 Sept 1998), available at http://news.bbc.co.uk, visited on 13 Nov 2002.

80 Ceylon changed its name to Sri Lanka in 1972.

81 M Haug, 'The Intervention Strategies of Humanitarian Agencies in a Complex Political Emergency: the Case of Sri Lanka' (London, LSE, PhD Thesis, 2001), p 22.

82 A Jeyaratnam Wilson and A Joseph Chandrakanthan, 'Tamil Identity and Aspirations', 4 *Accord: An International Review of Peace Initiatives* (1998), available at http://www.c-r.org/acc_sri/tamil_identity.htm, visited on 28 April 2002, p 4.

83 Haug (2001), p 48.

84 E Nissan, 'Historical Context', 4 *Accord: An International Review of Peace Initiatives* (1998), available at http://www.c-r.org/acc_sri/background.htm, visited on 28 April 2002.

85 J D Rogers, 'Sri Lanka', in J Krieger (ed) *The Oxford Companion to Politics of the World* (Oxford, OUP, 1993), p 873.

86 In particular, the Sinhala JVP (Janatha Vimukthi Peramuna, a political party) campaigned strongly against the government (*ibid*). During the 1980s, government forces harshly suppressed two violent uprisings of this party, and many thousands were killed.

87 US Department of State, (2001), Sri Lanka.

88 HRW, *World Report* (2002), Sri Lanka. Human rights violations were also apparently perpetrated by the IPKF (Nissan (1998)).

89 See eg, AI, 'Children in South Asia' (London, AI, April 1998), pp 37-38.

90 BBC News, 'Sri Lanka's Children at War' (22 June 1998).

91 See eg, CSC (2001), pp 341-342.

92 See eg, Machel (2001), p 10. It was said that the LTTE had two armed units composed of children, the 'Baby Brigade' and the 'Leopard Brigade', *id*. Some children, including girls, had apparently been recruited with the specific goal of training them to become suicide bombers (R Brett and M McCallin, *Children: the Invisible Soldiers* (Stockholm, SC S, 1998), p 64). Moreover, children were said to have been used in the frontline of battles (*ibid*, pp 98, 93 and 114), as well as being forced, eg, to act as porters (*ibid*, p 94). In June 2002, the LTTE stated (not for the first time) that it would no longer recruit children under 18 (UNICEF Press Center, 'UNICEF officials negotiate with LTTE on the release of recruited children' UNICEF News Notes (20 June 2002)). However, according to some sources, their recruitment of under-18s continued thereafter (BBC News, 'Tigers Still Recruiting Children' (22 July 2002)).

93 See eg, Brett and McCallin (1998), p 114.

94 For example, in 1989, a cease-fire was agreed between the Government and the LTTE but fighting resumed in 1990. Another cease-fire agreement was reached in 1994, but in 1995 the conflict resumed. (Haug (2001), p 46). See also, eg, HRW, *World Report 2002*, on Sri Lanka.

95 The agreement was perceived as somewhat fragile, and had been the subject of protests. See eg, BBC News, 'Anti-peace rally in Sri Lanka', (24 April 2002).

96 UN Wire, 'Sri Lanka: Annan Welcomes Launch of Direct Peace Talks' (17 Sept 2002).

97 For example, between Dec 1992 and Dec 1994 Sri Lanka contributed military personnel to the UN operation in Mozambique (ONUMOZ). See http://www.un.org/Depts /dpko/ dpko/comission/onumozF.html, visited on 28 Oct 2002.

98 For pre-1986 history as summarised above, see eg, E A Brett, 'Neutralising the Use of Force in Uganda: the Role of the Military in Politics', 33:1 *Modern African Studies* (1995), pp 134-144; O Otunnu, 'Causes and Consequences of the War in Acholiland', 11 *Accord: An International Review of Peace Initiatives* (2002); P Mutibwa, *Uganda since Independence: A Story of Unfulfilled Hopes* (Kampala, Fountain Publishers, 1992), and http: //memory.loc.gov/cgi-bin/query/r?frd/cstdy:@field(DOCID+ug0020, visited on 13 March 2003.

99 See eg, Goodwin-Gill and Cohn (1994), p 34.

100 The areas particularly affected were the districts of Gulu and Kitgum, in Acholiland (home to the Acholi people). This conflict was to some extent 'internationalised' by the involvement of Sudan.

101 The United Democratic Christian Movement/Army (UDCM/A), later renamed the LRA, emerged from the Uganda's People Defence Army (UPDA) after the latter made peace with Museveni. A key figure initially connected with these groups was a 'spiritual leader', Alice Aluma 'Lakwena' (T Allen, 'Understanding Alice: Uganda's Holy Spirit Movement in context' 61:3 *Africa* (1991), pp 370-399). After various upheavals, the LRA was, to the time of writing, led by another 'spiritual leader', Joseph Kony. At its inception, the UDCM/A apparently had a political agenda, but was later said to have lost this. 95% of LRA fighters were from Acholiland, many of them originally abducted. See eg, B Nyeko and O Lucima, 'Profiles of the Parties to the Conflict', 11 *Accord: An International Review of Peace Initiatives* (2002).

102 See eg, O Otunnu (2002), p 2. Otunnu proposed four main factors to explain why the conflict in Northern Uganda had lasted so long: widespread human rights violations committed by the LRA against civilians and the fact that the LRA had refused to take an alternate political view; the existence of regional and international power struggles; the fact that the conflict was lucrative for some members of the population and, finally, the reluctance of the Ugandan government to pursue in good faith a negotiated solution to the conflict. *Ibid*, p 4.

103 See eg, ICRC News, 'Update No. 97/01 on ICRC activities in Uganda' (11 Nov 1997). The Allied Democratic Forces were a multi-ethnic guerrilla force dominated by Muslim fundamentalists, and had been opposing Museveni's government since 1986. They apparently relied heavily on support from the Sudan (K Nezan, 'Power Struggle in Kivu', *Le monde diplomatique* (July 1998)).

104 AI Press Release, 'Uganda: the full picture-uncovering human rights violations by government forces in the northern war' (17 March 1999). Regarding displacement in southwestern Uganda, see eg, ICRC News, 'Update No 97/45. Uganda: Aid to 80,000 people displaced in the south-west' (13 Nov 1997).

105 US Department of State (2001).

106 Rights of the Child—Report of the United Nations High Commissioner for Human Rights on the mission undertaken by her Office, pursuant to Commission resolution 2000/60, to assess the situation on the ground with regard to the abduction of children from northern Uganda. UN Doc E/CN4/2002/86 (9 Nov 2001), p 5.

107 UN Doc E/CN4/1999/69 (27 Jan 1999), Rights of the Child: Abductions of Children from Northern Uganda, Report of the Secretary General, para 4. This statistic has, however, been queried

108 *Ibid*, para 17. By 2001, one-third of the 26,365 reported cases of abductions in Northern Uganda apparently involved children under 18 (Statement of the High Commissioner for Human Rights Pursuant to Resolution 2000/60, on the Abduction of Children from Northern Uganda, Commission on Human Rights, 57th session, Geneva, 19 April 2001).

109 See eg, AI, *Report 2001* on Uganda. See also *HRW World Report* (New York, HRW, 1999), regarding an Allied Democratic Forces attack on a school in which an estimated 50 to 80 students died and others were abducted. Both armed opposition groups generally abducted children from their homes, schools, or from refugee camps. Once abducted, these children usually endured severe maltreatment (see eg, UN Doc E/CN.4/2002/86, pp 5-6, and AI, 'Uganda: Stop child abductions for slave soldiering', (1999)). Girls were generally sexually abused and given as 'wives' to the armed opposition fighters. Moreover, children who attempted to escape or who could not or would not follow orders were beaten or killed, often by other children (frequently under duress) (see eg, UN Doc E/CN4/2002/86, pp 5-6).

110 See eg, AI Press Release, (17 March 1999).

111 CSC (2001), p 370.

112 UN Doc E/CN4/2002/86, p 4.

113 See, http://www.defence.gov.au/terrorism/, visited on 2 Sept 2002. The stated aim of this coalition was to track down the Al Qaida network, following the 11 Sept 2001 terrorist attacks on the US.

114 'Defence Instructions (General)', Department of Defence, Canberra ACT 2600, 28 June 2002.

115 Para 11 explains further that 'to the maximum extent possible, and where it will not adversely impact on the conduct of operations, minors should not be deployed into areas of operations where there is a likelihood of hostile action'.

116 Under-18s did apparently take part in the Sept 1999 Australian peace support operation in East Timor, although obviously this was prior to the 2002 Defence Instructions (see CSC (2001), p 74).

117 The Australian Defence Force Academy, the College of Defence and Strategic Studies, the Australian Defence Force Warfare Centre, and the Royal Military College were, among others, responsible for training. See, http://www.defencejobs.gov.au/armysite.htm for the training required to enter the army, http://www.defencejobs.gov. au/navysite.htm to enter the navy, and http://www.defencejobs.gov.au/airsite.htm to enter the air force (visited on 13 Nov 2002). A separate ADF Peacekeeping Centre was established in 1993 (see, http://www.defence.gov.au/adfwc/peacekeeping/index.htm, visited on 2 Sept 2002).

118 CSC (2001), pp 73 and 74.

119 *Ibid*, p 75. There have also been some alleged violations committed by the ADF in operations. See eg, ADF investigation regarding incidents in East Timor (UN Wire, 'East Timor: Australia Probing Claims of War Crimes by its Troops' (3 Oct 2002)).

120 Apparently this term is preferred by the ADF to 'peace support operations'. E-mail from ADF officer, 27 Feb 2003.

121 P Copeland, 'Australian Defence Force Involvement in Peacemaking and Peacekeeping Operations 1947-Present' (Australia, Australian Peacekeepers and Peacemakers Association), available at http://www.peacekeepers.asn.au/start.htm, visited on 7 April 2002.

122 See, http://www.un.org/Depts/dpko/dpko/contributors/index.htm, and http://www.un.org/Depts/dpko/dpko/contributors/30062002.pdf, visited on 12 Aug 2002.

123 Only 'developing countries' contributed more substantially (Bangladesh, Ghana, India, Kenya, Nigeria, Pakistan, Ukraine, and Uruguay) (*id*).

124 See, http://www.utrikes.regeringen.se/inenglish/frontpage/security_eng.htm, visited on 12 Aug 2002.

125 CSC (2001), p 350.

126 *Id*.

127 See, http://www.un.org/Depts/dpko/dpko/contributors/30062002.pdf, visited on 12 Aug 2002. In June 2002 Sweden was apparently only contributing one active officer (the Force Commander for the UN Disengagement Observer Force in the Syrian Golan Heights) to UN peace support operations, although it was contributing 87 members to the UN police force, and 33 military observers. See, http://www.un.org/Depts/dpko/dpko/contributors/index.htm, visited on 12 Aug 2002.

128 SWEDINT is an international centre responsible for bringing together the skills and resources of the Swedish armed forces in the field of peace support (http://www.swedint.mil.se/article.php?id=1742, visited on 2 Sept 2002).

129 See http://www.nato.int/docu/facts/2001/part-coop.htm, visited on 2 Sept 2002. Sweden has participated in PfP since 1994. In July 1997 Sweden set up its own PfP training centre (see http://www.swedint.mil.se/article.php?id=1766, visited on 1 Sept 2002). See Swedish PfP-exercises at http://www.fksc.mil.se/viking03 or www.nordicpeace02.mil.se.

130 Swedish Armed Forces Headquarters, *Facts and Figures, Swedish Defence: 2000-2001* (Stockholm, Swedish Armed Forces, 2001), Chapter I, p 12, available at, http://www2.mil.se/article.php?id=1672, visited on 1 Sept 2002.

131 Some commentators have characterised the Northern Ireland conflict as reaching the level of a non-international armed conflict (see eg, http://www.birw.org), but this view is disputed by the UK government.

132 BBC News, 'Timetable: Next steps on Iraq' (5 Dec 2002). See also, UN Doc S/RES/1447 (4 Dec 2002).

133 United Kingdom Cabinet Office, 'The United Kingdom and The Campaign against International Terrorism, Progress Report' (London, Cabinet Office, Sept 2002), available at, http://www.cabinet-office.gov.uk/reports/sept11/coi-0809.pdf, visited on 3 Oct 2002, pp 4-5.

134 See, http://www.operations.mod.uk/, visited on 22 July 2002. (The mandate of ISAF had been extended to Dec 2003 (UN Doc S/RES/144 (27 Nov 2002))). And see UK Cabinet Office (Sept 2002), p 5.

135 Some commentators have criticised the conduct of NATO operations in Kosovo (see eg, BBC News, 'Bombs missed Kosovo Targets' (14 Aug 2000), and HRW, 'Cluster Bomb Memorandum' (New York, HRW, April 2001)), but this view is contested.

136 See eg, http://www/guardian.co.uk/Iraq/Story/0,2763,419224.html, regarding on-going UK military involvement in Iraq.

137 UK troops in Sierra Leone, operating independently of the UN, supported the government of Sierra Leone in its conflict with the RUF. See eg, E MacAskill, 'Annan urges

Britain to don blue beret in Sierra Leone' *Guardian Weekly* (29 March 4 April 2001), and see Sierra Leone 'Background Notes' above.

138 See, http://www.mod.uk/aboutus/factfiles/operations.htm, visited on 22 July 2002.

139 For further information on concerns about UK armed forces treatment of children in N Ireland, see eg Committee on the Rights of the Child, CRC/C/15/Add34, 15 Feb 1995, para 10, and the 2002 Concluding Observations of the Committee (Chapter Six above). See also, eg, more generally, the official web site of the 'Bloody Sunday' enquiry at http://www.bloody-sunday-inquiry.org.uk/.

140 AI, *United Kingdom U-18s: Child Soldiers at Risk* (London, AI, 2000(b)), p 4. See also R. Harvey, 'Article 38—Living Commentary: Children and Armed Conflict' (publication pending 2003, Children and Armed Conflict Unit on behalf of the Children's Rights Alliance England, 2002), p 14, for specific minimum ages for recruitment in the UK army, the Royal Navy, the Royal Marines, the Royal Air Force and the volunteer reserves.

141 AI (2000(b)), p 4.

142 Regarding concerns about parental consent in this context, see eg, *ibid* p 6.

143 *Ibid*, p 4.

144 CSC (2001), p 376. Some recruitment strategies were specifically designed for under-18s. See, eg, MOD website (http://www.army.mod.uk/careers/index.htm, visited on 23 July 2002). See also CSC (2001), pp 377-378.

145 AI (2000(b)), p 4.

146 UN Doc CRC/C/15/Add.188 (9 Oct 2002), Concluding Observations of the Committee on the Rights of the Child: United Kingdom of Great Britain & Northern Ireland, para 51.

147 This period was longer than that required of adults—but revision of this anomaly had been under consideration. See UN Doc CRC/C/83/Add3 (14 Sept 1999), Second periodic report of the United Kingdom of Great Britain and Northern Ireland to the Committee on the Rights of the Child, p 208, and UN Doc CRC/C/15/Add188 (9 Oct 2002), para 51.

148 For example, more than 200 personnel aged under-18 served in the 1991 Gulf War; about 50 such personnel participated in the peace support operation in Kosovo, and ten under-18 Royal Navy personnel served on ships supporting operations in East Timor. (CSC (2001), p 378. See also AI (2000(b)), p 1, and Harvey (2002), p 8.)

149 See, BBC News, 'Boy soldiers banned from conflict' (29 March 2002).

150 CSC (2001), pp 377-378.

151 *Id*.

152 Since Jan 1982, 88 under-18s in the UK armed forces had died while not in situations of armed conflict (Harvey (2002), p 9), and between 1996 and 1999, 407 were injured (AI (2000(b), pp 27-29). See also CSC (2001), pp 376-377, regarding allegations concerning the treatment of some UK recruits.

153 See http://www.un.org/Depts/dpko/dpko/contributors/December2002Summary.pdf, visited on 27 Jan 2003.

154 As regards the latter, see http://www.mod.uk/rcds/background.htm, visited on 21 Jan 2003.

155 See eg, HRW, 'Needless deaths in the Gulf War: Civilian Casualties During the Air Campaign and Violations of the Laws of War' (New York, HRW, 1991). In certain of these conflicts, and particularly in Vietnam, US military personnel had been found guilty of, *inter alia*, war crimes, including some committed against children (see eg *United States v Calley* (1973) (above, Ch 5, n 38)). See also, eg, *Military and Paramilitary Activities in*

and against Nicaragua (*Nicaragua v United States of America*) Merits, Judgment, ICJ. Reports 1986.

156 BBC News, 'Timetable: Next steps on Iraq' (5 Dec 2002). See also, UN Doc S/RES/1447 (4 Dec 2002).

157 CSC (2001), p 381.

158 See, http://www.dior.whs.mil/mmid/m05/hst0902.pdf, visited on 28 March 2003.

159 See, http://www.dior.whs.mil/mmid/military/ms9.pdf, visited on 12 Aug 2002.

160 Barbara Burfeind, Defence Department spokeswoman, cited in UN Wire, 'U.S.: Washington Links International Criminal Court Immunity to Military Aid' (12 Aug 2002). US assistance was often conditional. At the time of writing it was, in relation to certain countries, conditional on the signing of bilateral agreements exempting US troops from the jurisdiction of the ICC. For further comment on these agreements, see eg, *id*. See also, http://www.iccnow.org/documents/otherissuesimpunityagreem.html, visited on 13 Nov 2002.

161 CSC (2001), p 381. Regarding allegations concerning the ill-treatment of some young recruits in the US armed forces, see *ibid*, p 382.

162 *Ibid*, p 382.

163 See, http://www.dior.whs.mil/mmid/casualty/table7.htm, visited on 12 Aug 2002.

164 See, http://www.un.org/Depts/dpko/dpko/contributors/index.htm, visited on 12 Aug 2002. The US apparently had a policy of not generally sending military personnel on UN peace support operations after the deaths, in Oct 1993, of 18 US military personnel in Somalia during an operation supporting UNOSOM II (United Nations Operation in Somalia II) (see eg, http://www.cdi.org/terrorism/nation-building-pr.cfm, visited on 17 Nov 2002).

165 See, http://www.un.org/Depts/dpko/dpko/contributors/30062002.pdf, visited on 12 Aug 2002.

Appendix 5

Sample Training Materials

I)   Save the Children Sweden—*Training for the Swedish National Armed Forces* (2002)

II) Extracts from: ECOWAS/CEDEAO and Save the Children Sweden, West Africa Regional Office—*Child Rights and Child Protection Before, During and After Conflict: Training Manual for Military Personnel* (Abidjan, Dec 2000)

III) ICRC: Discussion Paper for FAS Delegates Concerning the Protection of Children in Armed Conflicts and Disturbances—*Excerpt from the Teaching File* (2002)

Note: The materials in Appendix Five are copies of existing training materials taken directly from electronic sources, and reprinted with the appropriate permissions. They are unedited, aside from corrections of small typing and spelling errors, and formatting adjustments.

I
Save the Children Sweden: *Training for the Swedish National Armed Forces— sample presentation—2002*

Note: As already mentioned (Chapter Nine), although the material in (I) below was prepared for peacekeeping forces, it could be adapted for other types of forces and operations.

TRAINING OF PEACE-KEEPING FORCES IN CHILD PROTECTION

1)   Introduction
Why, what and how to address Peace-Keeping Forces

When the proportion of armed conflicts and number of civilians killed escalated during the last decade, the importance of Peace-keeping Forces (PKF) became obvious and emphasized. Even though these forces do not constitute operational aid organisations, their role and mandate is to protect civilians who are not taking part in the conflict. More and more Peace-keepers have been given the task of supporting and assisting humanitarian work, stressing the need and demand for civil-military cooperation. When it is estimated that more than 50% among the civil population are children, awareness of international law on Children's Rights is fundamental in order to undertake the duties during assignments where the protection and monitoring of Human Rights are increasingly featuring in the mandate of a Peace-keeping operation.

Peace-keeping soldiers meet many children, in their missions, suffering from war-trauma. Highlighting and explaining psychological consequences of war for children will increase the understanding and committment of soldiers, as well as an understanding of their own reactions when confronted with violations.

Girls are particularly at risk during armed conflict, facing various threats such as rape and forced prostitution. Previous experience has shown that the need for training of PKF is evident in order to prevent violations, in particular sexual abuse, committed by international soldiers.

The training will provide practical guidance to soldiers, within their mandate, to identify activities and appropriate steps for prevention, protection and reporting of violations of children during and after conflict.

The methodology used in the training comprises lectures involving a dialogue between the trainer and the participants. Each section is illustrated by case studies from the current mission area and actual events. The training session lasts for 3 hours as an integral part in the general PKF preparatory training before the mission.

2) Training Concept

a) *Why do we want to reach you—why are you important actors for children*

– Your UN assignment has a humanitarian aspect—you should make sure that human rights are respected and valued
– You are important resources and actors in the international system
– You can prevent violations of rights
– You can report on violations of rights
– You are going to meet children whatever position you have—you can be good role models for children.

b) *The aims of the training*

– To create understanding of how armed conflict influences children's lives
– To clarify how children's roles may change during war and conflict and how children experience armed conflicts
– To provide insight into the UN Convention on the Rights of the Child as it relates to children affected by armed conflict and to make the participants aware that protection of children's rights according the CRC is a part of their mandate.
– To discuss how UN peace-keeping personnel can protect children and be good role models for children

c) *Contents of the training*

Short presentations of the aims and contents of the training

The character of the war and conflict situations of today
From "traditional state-to-state wars" with soldiers fighting against each other to civil wars where most of the victims are civilians and where civilians become actors and targets.

Up to 80–90% of the victims of today's conflicts are civilian—more than half of the civilians are children under 18.

International Conventions and Guidelines
Short presentation of some of the international conventions and guidelines regulating the conduct of armed forces in war, aimed at protecting the civilian population / children:

- The Geneva Conventions from 1949 and the additional protocols from 1954 and 1977 represent some of the most important international laws in relation to the protection of civilian rights during wartime. Concerned with human rights for all parties involved in and affected by the conflict.
- Refugee Children. Guidelines on Protection and Care. UNHCR 1994.

Presentation of the United Nations Convention on the Rights of the Child
General information
- Adopted by the General Assembly of the United Nations in 1989.
- Almost universally ratified except by Somalia and USA (2000).
- The CRC , once ratified by a state, cannot be waived by that state under circumstances of armed conflict.

Short presentations of the contents of the CRC
- Principles and application
- The four main areas of rights:
    1   The right to survival.
    2   The right to develop one's full potential.
    3   The right to protection.
    4   The right to participate.

What does the CRC say about the child's right to protection in armed conflict
- Presentation of the CRC Article 38, part 4.
- In spite of the protection afforded to civilians in armed conflict by these international laws, there is overwhelming documentation that the Conventions are totally ignored and that civilians continue to suffer unimaginable brutalities.
- The child's right to protection is not honoured.
- The United Nations Report "The impact of armed conflict on children" prepared by Graca Machel in August 1996 was the very first comprehensive human rights assessment of war-affected children and pointed to special risks regarding protection of children.
- The report resulted in a comprehensive agenda for action to improve the protection and care of children in situations of conflict.
- The need for a special adviser under the UN Secretary General to follow up the situation for children in armed conflicts.
- The report has been followed up and reviewed and a book is being prepared to provide a glossary of achievements since 1996 and to give recommendations on new strategies to increase the protection of children in armed conflicts. (Report presented by Graca Machel at the International Conference on War-affected Children in Winnipeg, Canada in September 2000).
- The report from Winnipeg presents a new and expanded focus to five areas:
    1   Small arms and weapons.

2   Women's role in peace-building.
3   Peace and security.
4   HIV/AIDS.
5   Media and communications.

The Consequences of War for Children
Presented under four headings:
1   Children as targets.
2   Children as actors.
3   Children as victims.
4   Children losing their childhood.

Children as targets
–   Ethnic cleansing.
–   Genocide.

Examples/cases from relevant/ actual situations

Children as actors
CRC article 38.3
  Child soldiers:
–   Why use children as soldiers?
–   How are they recruited? (Forced recruitment/ abduction. Stress that voluntary recruitment is a "myth"—does not exist—because no child really understands the consequenses of recruitment.)
–   Child soldiers, children in military services, not only the armed soldier. Children with other roles in the military environment than fighters: cooking, cleaning, care for wounded soldiers, lovers, "wives" . . .
–   Responsibility: The responsibility of using children as soldiers and the responsibility for what they are doing lies with the adults, not the child.

Examples/case stories.

Children as victims
–   Loss of parents—family—friends.
–   Witnessing killing/torture/abuse of close persons.
–   Victims of violence/torture/abuse.
–   Experiencing their parents and other adults' inability to protect them.
–   Destruction of infrastructure or prevention of use of the existing infrastructure due to ethnic/religious conflicts, because of war or poverty.
–   No normal daily life for children—cannot get access to school or recreational activities.
–   Living in continual anxiety and fear.

Children as victims of social and economic deprivations brought about by war.

CRC—Article 32.1

Children as victims of sexual exploitation—trafficking.
CRC—Article 34
- Child prostitution with emphasis on UN soldiers' abuse and potential for exploiting children in this context.
- STD and HIV/AIDS. Consequences for the child.

Examples/case stories visualising the consequences for the child.

Children losing their childhood
- Children who have never experienced life without war.
- Children who grow up with parents who never have experienced life without war.
- Children whose future perspective is a life under armed conflict.
- The growth of fear, insecurity, violence, aggression.

A pessimistic vision of tomorrow's world if the wars and conflicts go on and the child's needs for protection and care are not taken seriously:
- What happens to human dignity and values?
- How is it possible to cope with the traumatic experiences when neither adults nor children feel they have any hope for a future without war?

What can be done to improve the protection of and the situation for children in war and conflict
- Make children visible.
- Keep focus on the special needs of children and adolescents for protection.
- Help to restore as normal conditions for children as possible, even under abnormal conditions.
- Mobilise all possible resources for the protection, survival and development of children.
- Make the international laws, guidelines and CRC known and assist towards their implementation.

What can you do?
Brainstorming of what the participants think they can do.
If relevant: discussion of the "List of ideas" prepared by the trainers.
What can you do related to "STOP":
Structure: Support in making structures that make it possible to create as normal daily life situation for children as possible. (Safe roads to school, safe and secure school buildings and kindergardens, safe and secure playgrounds, protection of vulnerable children so they get access to school).
Talking and time: Talk with children and give them time to talk. Do not be afraid of talking with children about serious matters and listen to their stories, but remember, you are not their therapist. Humor and kindliness is important, every time

you are able to bring a smile to a child's face you are supporting the child's mental recovery process.

Organise play and recreational activities: Help to clean and organise playgrounds, sport grounds and parks for recreational activities for children and their families. Play football with the children, support the local football team or other local organisations and institutions working with recreational activities for children. Make a "Children's Day", provide books and toys for children, etc.

Protection and Parent Support: Protection of children, prevention of violation of children's rights. Act in a supportive way to the parents and families in the raising of their children. Do not "add new burdens". (Prostitution, giving money to begging children, neglecting of cultural conduct, etc.) Training of children and parents in, eg, mine awareness and other relevant subjects.

Reporting
NB! Follow the reporting line of the UN system.
Contact with NGOs regarding special concerns.

"Do and Do Not" User's Guide

1. Organise a protected playground area.
2. Organise games, eg football, tournaments.
3. Escort children to school when in need of protection in insecure areas.
4. Organise a "Children's Day".
5. Distribute toys, sports-equipment eg footballs, school-materials or children's books at hospitals, schools or institutions. Contact relevant NGOs for information and material either prior to departure or at the mission area.
6. Talk to, listen to and socialise with children, eg tell jokes but do not try to act as a therapist.
7. Assist humanitarian organisations in distribution of food, non-food items and escorts.
8. Assist families and communities, eg clearing of roads, reparations.
9. Maintain your integrity and impartiality. Assist all involved groups.
10. Assist in the dissemination of mine awareness.
11. Do not "favour" only one child.
12. Do not give money or cigarettes. Put sound limits on what to accept or not in a firm but kind manner when confronted with beggars.
13. Do not hit children or commit other violent acts against children.
14. Do not have sexual relations with minors. Respect the culture and traditions.
15. Do not take photos without asking and receiving agreement.
16. Report violations and abuse of children.
17. Report recruitment of children as soldiers.

Remember: You are the Protector of Children and Children are the
            future in our World!

II

Extracts from: ECOWAS/CEDEAO and Save the Children Sweden, West Africa Regional Office—*Child Rights and Child Protection Before, During and After Conflict: Training Manual for Military Personnel* (Abidjan, Dec 2000)

Note:

– As an example of the approach used in the ECOWAS/Save the Children Manual, the Appendix below contains: A) its *Unit 2*, regarding *Child Development and Basic Needs'*. This topic was selected for use here as it is not addressed at length in the text of this book, yet it is an important subject that should be included, in addition to rules of IHL and human rights law, in military training regarding children.

– Each Unit in this Manual is followed by a suggested lesson plan and accompanying materials (see eg, 'Overhead 2.1', below).

– The Appendix below also contains B) *The Child Protection Code of Conduct for Soldiers* (already mentioned), developed in June 2000 by soldiers from 13 West African Countries, and later adopted by ECOWAS. This is an example of a useful basic summary of the relevant rules.

A) MANUAL, UNIT 2

UNIT 2: CHILD DEVELOPMENT AND BASIC NEEDS

Introduction—Key concepts

Main topics

Topic 1: Concepts of childhood, child development and basic needs

Sample programmes

Training materials

– Handouts
– Checklists
– Overheads
– Visuals

Unit 2

Child Development and Basic Needs

Introduction—Key Concepts

– Perceptions of childhood are relative, though fundamental development stages of children remain the same. Childhood can be perceived differently at local, regional, national and global levels.
– The United Nations Convention on the Rights of the Child (UNCRC) defines a child as any individual below the age of 18 years, and as such gives people who are under 18 special rights and protection.
– The four categories of Children's Rights developed in the UNCRC are closely linked to the fundamental basic needs of children.
– As children develop, they pass through different stages. The child has specific needs, reactions and capacities at each stage. For a child to develop well he or she needs to be in a trusting, caring and stable environment. Any disruption of the environment will affect the child's development.
– The changing nature of conflict means that soldiers play an increasingly important role in the community. On the ground, soldiers often form part of the community over a long period of time and interact with children.
– It is important for military personnel to acquire a basic understanding of children's fundamental needs. Armed forces have a role to play in ensuring that these fundamental needs are met and that there is minimum disruption to development during conflict situations.
– In order to have an impact on ensuring that fundamental needs are met and there is minimum disruption of development, it is important for members of armed forces to have a basic understanding of the needs and priorities of the children that they meet in the field.

Unit 2

Child Development and Basic Needs

Topic 1: Concepts of Childhood, Child Development, and Basic Needs

Contents

1. The concept of childhood
2. Child developments and basic needs
3. Fundamental rights linked to children's needs
4. How conflict affects child development

Key Learning Points

- The concept of childhood is understood differently in different contexts. The United Nations Convention on the Rights of the Child (UNCRC) considers a person to be a child until he or she reaches the age of 18 years.
- In the theatre of operations, soldiers often live with communities and interact with children. It is necessary to be aware that there are universal needs and rights afforded to all children.
- All children pass through developmental stages in the process of growing up.
- Stages of child development are linked with specific physical and emotional needs. Because children are less mature than adults they are particularly vulnerable to change. Conflict disrupts a child's normal development environment, and therefore his or her development may be affected both in the short and the longer term.
- It is important for military personnel to acquire a basic understanding of children's fundamental needs. Armed forces have a role to play in ensuring that these fundamental needs are met and that there is minimum disruption to development during conflict situations.

Objectives

Objectives for Commissioned and Non-Commissioned Officers:

– Establish how the concept of childhood is understood in different contexts e.g. community, local, national and legal understandings
– Identify different stages of child development and their characteristics
– Understand how conflict can affect child development
– Recognize how the fundamental Rights of the Child relate to children's basic needs

Training materials

Type	Title	Reference
Handouts	Child development key messages	H/O unit 2.1
Overhead	Four categories of basic Child Rights	OHP unit 2.1

1)   *The Concept of Childhood*

There are many different understandings of the concept of childhood. It is important for the trainer to understand what soldiers understand by childhood in their own culture and see how those ideas can be complemented by global and standard definitions of childhood.

The understanding of what childhood is, is based on many factors. These vary from community to community and in different countries. Soldiers serving in communities and countries that are not their own need to understand the different ways in which the concept is understood.

Different understandings of childhood can be defined by some of the following: age, relationship with elders or family, marital status, parenthood, initiation, level of economic responsibility, level of education, the possession of legal rights, e.g. the right to vote, meeting criteria for recruitment, etc.

Nearly all countries have a legal definition of the age of majority, reflected in the age of majority established for voting, recruitment into the military and the age of criminal responsibility, among others.

There are various rights and several obligations associated with the concept of childhood. The different perceptions we may have of childhood will influence the way we behave towards children when we have to interact with them.

The UNCRC defines the child as 'every human being under the age of 18' unless national law has defined the age of majority as lower. This international definition was agreed and endorsed by the ratifying States of the UNCRC, making it one of the most commonly agreed definitions in the world. The international definition of childhood ensures maximum protection of young people and sets a standard against which other measures for their well-being and protection can be measured.

2) Child development and basic needs

Most people are already aware of what we call children's basic needs. However, it is important to underline how these needs, and subsequently the healthy development of the child, can be disrupted in times of conflict.

As armed forces have a role to play in ensuring that these basic needs are met and that there is minimum disruption to development during times of conflict, it is important to identify some of the major factors contributing to a child's development.

Five important examples are given here. Many others can be suggested:
- **Basic needs**. Children need well-balanced diets to feed their developing minds and bodies. They need clean water, adequate shelter and access to primary health care facilities. Children in the first years of their lives are the most vulnerable to childhood diseases and other infections which threaten their very survival.
- **Trusting relationships**. The relationship of an infant with its main carer, usually the mother, should be built on trust and security. This continues to develop into childhood, adolescence and adulthood. Adult behaviour is largely determined by childhood relationships and experiences. This implies that every person in the developing child's environment influences how they are likely to develop as adults.
- **Positive guidance**. Parents, parental figures and authority figures in a child's life provide guidance, which is expected to help the child grow up into a responsible adult and citizen. The process of 'socialisation' is often helped by schools and religious institutions. In conflict, when the social environment is disrupted, children often seek other forms of guidance. Military personnel can be among the groups children refer to and can provide either a positive or negative role model.
- **A stable environment**. A stable environment is the most desirable one for children to grow up in. Stability in the environment encourages children to explore, to develop their potential and to feel secure.
- **Play and leisure**. Play is essential to the development of children because it provides an opportunity for physical development. Play is also an important tool for learning and for understanding the environment. It is common to see children imitating parents, teachers or friends, as a way of learning acceptable types of behaviour. During conflict children are often restricted from playing, and their development can be badly affected by this.

3)   *Fundamental rights and needs of children*

A child is a person who has rights. It is important to outline how the fundamental rights of children closely relate to their basic needs. The four fundamental categories of rights defined in the UNCRC are:
–   **Survival**
All children need provision for survival – to have basic needs such as food, shelter, healthcare and education fulfilled.
–   **Development**
To experience the world is to develop. All children need to be brought up in a supporting environment, which helps them to reach their full potential.
–   **Protection**
All children need to be shielded from harmful acts or practices such as physical or mental abuse, commercial or sexual exploitation and the experience of engagement in warfare.
–   **Participation**
All children have a right to be heard on decisions affecting their lives, according to their age and level of maturity.

4)   *How conflict affects child development*

The UN Convention on the Rights of the Child states that a child is any person who is under the age of 18. In the period leading up to the age of 18, children go through several stages of development, during which their needs evolve. In a situation of conflict the 'protection' needs of children, at the different stages, will also differ. Some examples of how conflict can affect child development are given below:
–   Babies and very small children are vulnerable to childhood diseases, which can kill or disable them. They can be made even more vulnerable if conflict interrupts vaccination programmes. Breastfeeding babies are made vulnerable by conflict when mothers are separated from their babies, killed or severely shocked so that their milk dries up. Often there are no safe alternatives to breast milk for these young babies.
–   Children under 5 years of age are extremely vulnerable to malnutrition (although older children can also die from severe malnutrition), especially when there are several small children in the family competing for limited amounts of food. During conflict families often have less food for their children than usual. Displaced people often have to wait for a long period of time before they can access food. Malnutrition stunts children's physical and mental development.
–   Young children who are unable to play or who do not get suitable guidance from adults are likely to grow up without fully exploring or understanding how their communities should work. Children whose development has been disrupted by violence and conflict may imitate the wrong types of adult behaviour and find it difficult to fit into normal social structures when they are older.
–   Adolescent children, while physically more developed than younger children, are still vulnerable and need to be included in protection efforts. Their opin-

ions and views are taking shape, and without proper guidance, these views can become distorted. This distortion can have long term effects on the socialisation of future generations.

–   Adolescents of 15 years and over are still legally allowed to take part in hostilities, despite the fact that they are not yet considered adults. Adolescents, over and under the age of 15, are vulnerable to forced recruitment practices. Children are often used in conflict in the most dangerous roles, and their participation has serious effects on their physical and mental development.

–   Adolescents and young girls may be particularly vulnerable to rape and other forms of sexual abuse. This has harmful physical and psychological effects on them. It can lead to early and unwanted pregnancy, rejection by communities and the rapid spread of sexually transmitted diseases and HIV/AIDS in communities.

The trainer should emphasise that children at different stages of childhood, who are at different levels of physical and mental development, will be in need of different forms of protection. Their basic needs may vary.

Unit 2

Child development and basic needs

Sample programme

Preparation

To facilitate training sessions on the subject matter of the unit, the facilitator should be familiar with concepts of childhood in his or her community.

The facilitator must also be aware of major principles of the UNCRC, and if possible, national laws concerning children.

It is recommended that the facilitator becomes familiar with concepts of child development.

a) Contents

b) Sample programme 1

- Coverage: Unit 2
- Level: Commissioned Officers and Non-Commissioned Officers
- Duration: 1 hour 30 minutes

c) Learning objectives

- Involve participants in recognizing that everyone is concerned about children
- Establish how childhood is understood in different contexts
- State the international definition of a child
- Identify different stages of development and their characteristics
- Discuss major factors in child development
- Understand how conflict can affect child development

– Recognize how the fundamental Rights of Children relate to their basic needs

d) Trainer's notes

Introduction

5 mins	Introduce the concept that children are everyone's concern. Ask open questions to the group about their children: their ages, names, etc. Relax participants during this short brainstorm. If you have brought some, make reference to pictures of children in / out of conflict situations.	(Optional photographs of children)

Cultural concepts of childhood

10 mins	If the group is large, divide it into smaller ones and ask them to discuss what they think childhood is for five minutes then feedback as one group. If the group is small, facilitate a brainstorm on the same question. Discuss and analyse the different concepts of childhood that are prevalent in the country or communities the participants come from, using three questions: – How would you describe childhood in your community? – What obligations and entitlements are part of childhood? – Is the concept of childhood changing in your communities? Ensure that group discussions are based on personal experiences and the participants' own culture.	CRC definition
10 mins	Through this discussion, help participants to draw up a common definition of childhood. Encourage them to create a definition similar to that of the United Nations Convention of the Rights of the Child (UNCRC). Present the UNCRC definition of a child.	

Development and needs of children

5 mins	Briefly describe the different stages of development of a child. Underline the child's vulnerability.	
10 mins	Brainstorming. Ask participants to identify what they think the basic needs of children are, in respect to the different stages of development. Write all ideas on a flipchart.	Flipcharts

15 mins	Review the outcomes by grouping them on a table or in columns, according to the four categories of rights in the UNCRC: provision, development, protection, participation. Note that participation is rarely taken into account. Explain how it should be understood.	OHP unit 2.1

How conflict can affect child development

10 mins	Display a flipchart listing some of the major factors in child development. Participants can be invited to bring up additional factors that they believe may be significant in child development.	
15 mins	After input by the facilitator, participants can be divided into small groups to discuss the ways in which children may be affected during war and displacement with regard to the factors identified above.	
	For each aspect, ask participants to suggest how, as members of armed forces, they can play a role in helping ensure needs are met and disruption is minimal. Record outcomes for a potential session on Unit 3 at a later date.	

UNIT 2

CHILD DEVELOPMENT AND BASIC NEEDS

Training Materials

Overheads

OHP unit 2.1   Four Categories of Basic Child Rights

> Overhead: Unit 2.1
> Four categories of rights defined in the CRC

A Child is a person who has rights to:

Survival

> *The right to life and to benefit from the most basic provisions for survival and an adequate standard of living, such as shelter, nutrition, clean water and primary health care. Protection from life-threatening violence*

Development

> *The rights required for children to reach their fullest potential, such as: education, play and leisure, access to information, care and a supportive environment*

Protection

> *Necessary for safeguarding children against all forms of abuse, violence, neglect and exploitation. Special care for refugee children, protection against involvement in armed forces, child labour, sexual exploitation, torture and drug abuse*

Participation

> *All children have a right to be heard on decisions affecting their lives, according to their age and level of maturity.*

B) MANUAL, CHILD PROTECTION CODE

Child Protection Code of Conduct for Soldiers

- Ensure safety and protection of civilians. Pay special attention to women and children

- Respect the basic needs of children (clean water, food, shelter, health care)

- Do not separate children from their parents

- Do not rape or sexually abuse children

- Protect children from landmines

- Children should not be used in armed forces. Protect them, do not use them

- In self-defence, use minimum force against children

- Co-operate with humanitarian organisations

- Always report Child Rights abuses

- Be firm, fair and friendly; remember "the child belongs to everybody"

Soldiers should be proud to protect those who cannot protect themselves!

III

ICRC: Discussion Paper for FAS Delegates Concerning the Protection of Children in Armed Conflicts and Disturbances

ITEM 2: EXCERPTS FROM THE TEACHING FILE

2.1 In the *lessons on the conduct of operations* the subject is covered as follows:

Civilians—By children we generally mean people who are not yet 18 years old. In the law of armed conflict, however, different provisions apply to those under 15 years of age and those between 15 and 18. In our discussion, 'children' means those under 15 years of age. Children are entitled to special treatment and must be protected against any form of indecent assault. Every effort must be made to provide them with the special care and aid they require.

Combatants—A particularly tragic aspect of modern conflict is the active participation in hostilities of children, both boys and girls. This would seem to have less to do with cultural traditions and more to do with expediency or the shortage of soldiers—often it is simply an excuse or abuse by those in power, in other words getting a child to do an adult's job These child soldiers operate with little or no training and are often fed a diet of alcohol and drugs. Of course they can be formidable and tough foes to deal with. Deal with them you must, but with due regard and some sympathy for their plight.

The law prohibits the direct participation in hostilities of children under the age of 15 years, who must not be recruited into the armed forces. In recruiting those who have reached the age of 15 years but are not yet 18 years old, priority should be given to those who are the oldest.

If children are recruited into armed forces or take a direct part in hostilities, they must, if captured, be guaranteed treatment and conditions of captivity which take their age into consideration, whether they are POWs or not. Certainly in no circumstances should the standard of treatment given to them be lower than that given to POWs. In particular, such child soldiers must be held separately from adults, unless in a family unit.

In the case of children aged between 15 and 18 years the more their treatment can be assimilated to that of those under 15, the better.

In international armed conflicts, persons who were under the age of 18 years when they committed an offence punishable by the death penalty may be sentenced to death, but the sentence must not be carried out. In non-international armed conflicts such persons may not even be sentenced to death.

GC IV, Art. 24
P I, Art 77

Child combatants taken as POWs are entitled to POW status and must be given treatment at least as favourable as that granted to POWs. This means in particular that they may not be prosecuted for having taken part in hostilities. They must be protected against any form of indecent assault. They should be held in separate accommodation from adult POWs.

GC III, Art.16
P I, Art 77

2.2   In the *lesson on internal conflicts*, emphasis is placed on Article 3 common to the four Geneva Conventions and Additional Protocol II.

Children must of course be protected in any armed conflict and, as we have seen, the law does indeed provide the necessary protection. In non-international armed conflicts, children tend to be more vulnerable and are often separated from their parents or other member of their family. One tragic example was Rwanda and the subsequent exodus of the Hutu population into what was then Zaire in the mid-1990s.

The provisions on children in Additional Protocol II take greater vulnerability into account. They stipulate that children must be provided with the care and aid they require. In particular, they must receive an education, including religious and moral education, in keeping with the wishes of their parents or guardians.

All appropriate steps must be taken to facilitate the reunification of families temporarily separated. Many will recall the efforts made by humanitarian organizations such as Save the Children, UNHCR and the ICRC on behalf of separated family members during the crises in Rwanda and Kosovo.

Where necessary, measures must be taken to remove children temporarily from the conflict area to a safer area within the country, whenever possible with the consent of their parents or guardians, and ensure that they are accompanied by persons responsible for their safety and well-being.

Children under the age of 15 years must not be recruited into the armed forces or groups or allowed to take part in hostilities. (Note that this language is stronger than that used by the rules governing international armed conflicts, which state that "all feasible measures" must be taken to ensure that children under the age of

15 years do not take part in hostilities). If, despite this rule, children do take a direct part in hostilities and are captured, they remain fully protected by the law.

P II, Art.4.3

2.3 In the *lessons dealing with internal security operations in connection with internal disturbances*, where the main international legal instruments belong not to international humanitarian law but to human rights law, the emphasis is on the latter.

Use of firearms against children. Unlawful gatherings inevitably attract children, who usually do nothing more than throw stones at the security forces. Of course they should not do this, but in real terms the threat they pose is minimal. Soldiers armed with the range of protective clothing and defensive equipment described above can stand in front of a crowd of stone-throwing children (and indeed adults) all day and probably come to no harm. If the military do not react, then the children usually soon get bored and disperse—the military will therefore have achieved their aim. Firing live ammunition at children who are throwing stones indicates a complete breakdown in the soldiers discipline and a complete lack of command and control by their superiors. It shows they cannot distinguish a military threat from a slight inconvenience or annoyance. Such a response is therefore unnecessary and utterly disproportionate.

Special rules for the arrest of children:
We have already dealt with the law applicable to children and child soldiers in armed conflict. International human rights law tends to reinforce these rules and in some areas enhances the protection given to children. It is important for soldiers to know these rules. In armed conflicts contact with juveniles tends to be a relatively rare occurrence. The opposite holds true for internal security operations: almost all such operations undertaken by the armed forces, in particular in response to demonstrations or riots will bring them into contact with children. Soldiers must therefore be familiar with the applicable law.

Key law: there is an emerging consensus in international law that a child is anyone under the age of 18 years. Therefore, anyone under the age of 18 years is entitled to special protection if arrested or detained.

The Convention on the Rights of the Child defines a child as anyone below the age of 18 years unless, under national law majority is attained earlier. The United Nations Rules for the Protection of Juveniles Deprived of their Liberty define a juvenile as 'every person under the age of 18'. The age of majority is determined by States, but must not deviate greatly from international norms.
The minimum age of criminal responsibility varies from country to country. You will need to seek the advice of your legal branch to know what that age is in your country.

Convention on the Rights of the Child, Art.1
Rules for the Protection of Juveniles Deprived of their Liberty, Rule11(a)

These two instruments, together with the International Covenant on Civil and Political Rights and the United Nations Standard Minimum Rules for the Administration of Juvenile Justice (the Beijing Rules) provide guidance for the arrest or detention of children. The important points for soldiers to know are set out below. Children retain all the rights already covered above for adults if arrested. In addition:

Last Resort. Arrest (and, as we will see detention or imprisonment) of children should be avoided whenever possible and is a measure of last resort. When children are arrested and detained, their cases are to be given the highest priority and handled as fast as possible to ensure the shortest possible period of detention prior to trial.

ICCPR, Art. 10. 2(b), Convention on the Rights of the Child, Arts. 37 and 40, Rules for the Protection of Juveniles Deprived of their Liberty, Rules and 17, Beijing Rules, Rules 13 and 19

Notification of next-of-kin. When a child suspected of breaking the law is arrested or apprehended, his or her parents or guardian are to be notified immediately, unless doing so would be detrimental to the interests of the child. If immediate notification is not possible, the parents or guardian are to be notified within the shortest possible time thereafter.

Convention on the Rights of the Child, Art. 9.4, Rules for the Protection of Juveniles Deprived of their Liberty, Rule 22, Beijing Rules, Rule 10.1

Separation from adults. Children arrested and detained pending trial must be segregated from adults, except where this would not be in the best interests of the child. For example, if the child's parents are being held then it might be in the child's best interests to be held with them rather than separately.

ICCPR, Art. 10. 2(b), Convention on the Rights of the Child, Art. 3 (c), Rules for the Protection of Juveniles Deprived of their Liberty, Rule 29, Beijing Rules, Rule 13.4

Respect for special status. Contacts between military personnel and children must be conducted in a manner which respects the legal status of the child, avoids harming children and promotes their well-being.

Beijing Rules, Rule 10.3

Appendix 6

Summary: Key Rules Regarding Child Civilians and Child Soldiers[1]

1) Basic Principles—Background

Note

Customary rules of international humanitarian law (IHL) and/or human rights law—in this Section (1)—apply to children (and adults) in conflict situations, in addition to the more detailed specific rules regarding child civilians and child soldiers in situations of armed conflict (Sections (2) and (3) below). In general, IHL rules apply in situations of armed conflict, and human rights rules apply in situations that are not categorised as such (eg internal security operations), although these two bodies of law sometimes overlap. It is therefore important to note that **in all conflict situations and security operations at least the basic human rights principles apply, to children as well as adults**—until the threshold is crossed to IHL application.

a) Human Rights Law

i   Special Treatment of Children

* A guiding human rights norm regarding children is that they are, as children, entitled to special treatment. The term 'special treatment' here has a positive construction, meaning the entitlement of children to additional assistance and protection.

*   The entire 1989 CRC[2] can be seen as a detailed expression of the principle that children are entitled to special treatment, and it applies in all situations, including armed conflict.

ii   'Right to Life'

* As regards general human rights law applicable to all persons, both adult and child, the 'right to life' is of primary importance, including in conflict situations (*see eg, Article 6, 1989 CRC*). This right can be more accurately described as the right not to be *arbitrarily* deprived of life.

iii   Prohibition of Torture

* Another basic precept, relevant to the treatment of children as well as adults in all situations including armed conflict, is the absolute human rights prohibition on torture and other cruel, inhuman or degrading treatment or punishment (*see eg, Article 37(a), 1989 CRC*).

> *Note*:
> The three main principles above are also found in IHL, although they are expressed in a different way (eg under IHL, deprivation of life is prohibited if it is 'disproportionate' or otherwise unlawful, rather than 'arbitrary', as under human rights law).[3]

b)   *International Humanitarian Law (IHL)*

* Belligerents are limited by IHL in their choice of methods or means of conducting armed conflict (*see eg 1977 GP I*,[4] *Article 35(1) and 1907 Hague Convention IV*,[5] *Article 22*), and they are particularly prohibited from using such means and methods as will cause 'superfluous injury or **unnecessary suffering**' either to combatants or civilians (*see eg 1977 GP I, Article 35(2)*). Moreover, combatants should use only the minimum degree of force that is both necessary and lawful in order to achieve their mission, in accordance with, *inter alia*, the principles of **military necessity** and humanity. These laws therefore aim to establish a framework for limiting certain methods of armed conflict, as well as for protecting those involved in or affected by armed conflict.

* The challenge of complying with IHL often amounts, in essence, to finding the balance between military necessity and humanitarian considerations.

* This difficult balancing act finds expression in the principle of **proportionality**, which was first set out in treaty form in 1977 GP I, and is generally accepted as a customary norm, binding on all parties to an armed conflict.

> See, eg, 1977 GP I (Article 51(5)(b)), which expresses the proportionality principle in prohibiting indiscriminate attacks, defined as 'an attack which may be expected to cause incidental loss of civilian life, injury to civilians, damage to civilian objects, or a combination thereof, which would be excessive in relation to the concrete and direct military advantage anticipated'.

2)   Child Civilians

> *Note:*
> –   It is worth emphasising first that, under IHL, child civilians are entitled to protection: a) as members of the civilian population generally; b) as children, due to their particular vulnerability within the civilian population, and c) as child civilians in specific categories (eg enemy aliens) if they qualify as

such. The information below will be presented under these three sub-headings.

– In general, the rules in Section (2) below, and those concerning child soldiers (Section (3)) set out the highest relevant legal standard, in the interests of good practice and simplicity, even if the particular rule does not strictly apply. (Thus, eg, no distinction is made here between rules regarding international or non-international armed conflict—and generally the rules applicable to international armed conflict, which tend to establish a higher standard, are presented.)

a)   Civilians Generally

* As regards civilians generally, the **fundamental principle** in IHL is that civilians in the power of a party to the conflict are to be respected and protected in all circumstances, and treated humanely (*see eg 1949 GC IV,*[6] *Article 27*).

* Measures should also be taken to **minimise harm** to civilians in or near the theatre of military operations (*see, eg, 1977 GP I, 48 and 51*).

* A **concise guide** to and summary of fundamental IHL rules regarding the treatment of civilians and other non-combatants is contained in Article 3 of the 1949 GCs (Common Article 3). This provides for humane treatment of 'persons taking no active part in the hostilities'. In relation to such persons, it prohibits 'at any time and in any place whatsoever …: a) violence to life and person …, b) taking of hostages …, c) outrages upon personal dignity …, d) the passing of sentences and the carrying out of executions' without due process.

> *Note*:
> Common Article 3 applies explicitly to situations where the conflict takes place in the territory of one State Party to the 1949 GCs (ie non-international armed conflicts), but it applies implicitly to all situations of armed conflict as a minimum standard.

b)   Child Civilians Generally

* Children in armed conflict are entitled to **special treatment** and must be provided with the care and aid they require. (*See eg: Article 77(1) of 1977 GP I, and, to a lesser extent, Article 4(3) of 1977 GP II,*[7] *both incorporated within Article 38, 1989 CRC, and human rights provisions already outlined*).

* Children should **not be ill-treated**, and this includes, *inter alia*, a prohibition on indecent assault (ie any assault of a sexual nature, including the use of child prostitutes). (*See eg: Articles 77(1) of 1977 GP I; Article 4(3) of 1977 GP II; 1989 CRC, (eg Article 6, 19, 34, 37(a) and 38(1) and (4)), and the 2002 Optional Protocol on the Sale of Children,*[8] *as well as human rights provisions already outlined*).

* Children, expectant mothers and maternity cases should be granted priority in receiving **relief consignments**. Free passage of **essential foods, clothing and tonics** for them must also be granted, subject to certain security conditions. *(See eg: Article 23 of 1949 GC IV, Article 70(1) of 1977 GP I, and Articles 24 and 38(4) of 1989 CRC)*.

* **Zones** should be established to protect child civilians (among others) from hostilities. (*See eg: Articles 14 and 15 1949 GC IV, and Articles 59 and 60 of 1977 GP I*).

* Children and maternity cases (among others) who are in **besieged or encircled areas** should be allowed access to medical and religious facilities, and removed from those areas if possible. (*1949 GC IV, Article 17*).

* No party to the conflict may arrange for the **evacuation** of children, other than its own nationals, to a foreign country, unless this is essential for the health or safety of the children. Where they can be found, parents or guardians must consent to such evacuation. In these situations, evacuated children must have an identification card, sent to the Central Tracing Agency of the ICRC. (*See Article 78 of 1977 GP I, which has largely superseded Article 24 of 1949 GC IV regarding evacuation*). Where children are **removed temporarily** to a safer area within the same country, parental or equivalent consent is again desirable, and they should be accompanied by a responsible person. (*See Article 4 (3)(e) 1977 GP II*). In addition to obtaining parental etc. consent, the views of the children themselves should, where possible, be taken into account. (*See Article 12, 1989 CRC*).

* Children should be kept with their **families and communities** whenever possible. (*See eg: Articles 27, 49 and 82 of 1949 GC IV; among others, Articles 5, 7, 8, 16 of 1989 CRC; Article 23 of 1966 ICCPR and Article 10 of 1966 ICESCR*[9]).

* Children should not be subject to the **death penalty** for offences related to the conflict which were committed when they were under 18 (*Article 68, 1949 GC IV; Article 77(5), 1977 GP I, and Article 6(4), 1977 GP II*). Article 37(a) 1989 CRC has now extended this prohibition to forbid the death penalty for offences committed by children under 18 in any circumstances ((*as does Article 6(5) of the 1966 ICCPR*[10]), and it also forbids the imposition of a sentence of **life imprisonment** without possibility of release.

c) Child Civilians in Specific Categories

It is important to bear in mind that, in addition to the rules above, there are more precise rules that specifically provide for child civilians in the five categories set out below. These rules are too detailed to be summarised here, but can be found in other sources.[11]

– children in occupied territory generally,

- children who are deprived of their liberty (detained or interned), including in occupied territory,
- children who are orphaned or separated from their parents
- children who are considered enemy aliens,
- expectant mothers, maternity cases and babies.

3) Child Soldiers

Note:
- It is good practice, in accordance with the current higher standard in international law, to refrain from recruitment or use of soldiers under the age of 18.
- However, national armed forces can recruit and use 'child' soldiers aged 15-17, since it remains lawful (although in contravention of the current higher standard) to incorporate this age-group in national armed forces, depending on the applicable legal regime in the particular country (see below). In fact, some national armed forces may unlawfully use child soldiers under the age of 15, as do many armed opposition groups.
- As with adult soldiers, there are different rules that apply to child soldiers as combatants and as prisoners. Rules concerning the latter are not set out here, but can be found elsewhere.[12]
- Regarding child soldiers as combatants, there are separate rules regarding: a) child soldiers generally; b) child soldiers in own armed forces; c) child soldiers in opposing armed forces.

Child Soldiers as Combatants

a)   Rules Regarding Child Soldiers As Combatants Generally

* **children under 15 should never participate** in armed conflict (*Article 77(2), 1977 GP I; Article 4(3), 1977 GP II, and Article 38(2), 1989 CRC*). This standard is now being steadily raised to the age of 18 (see below).

* when, in contravention of the law, children under 15 (although for many countries the norm is, or is becoming, 18 (see below)) do participate in hostilities and are then **captured**, they are entitled to special treatment in the same way as are child civilians (*Article 77(3), 1977 GP I; Article 4(3)(d), 1977 GP II*).

* children under 15 should never be **recruited** as combatants, and this includes voluntary recruitment (*Article 77(2), 1977 GP I; Article 4(3)(c), 1977 GP II, and Article 38(3), 1989 CRC*). Voluntary recruitment of those over 15 is permitted, subject to national legislation (see below).

* when recruiting among persons between the ages of 15 and 18, **priority** should be given to those who are oldest (*Article 77(2), 1977 GP I and Article 38(3), 1989 CRC*).

* (as with child civilians), no-one should be subject to the **death penalty** for offences related to the conflict which were committed when they were under 18 (*Article 68, 1949 GC IV; Article 77(5), 1977 GP I, and Article 6(4), 1977 GP II*). Article 37(a) of 1989 CRC has now extended this prohibition to forbid the death penalty for offences committed in any circumstances by persons under 18 (*as does Article 6(5) of the 1966 ICCPR*), and it also forbids the imposition of a sentence of **life imprisonment** without possibility of release.

> *Note:*
> The rules above are taken primarily from the 1977 GPs and the 1989 CRC. Those set out below cover more recent developments, since the 1989 CRC came into force.

* For governments that have ratified it, the **2000 Optional Protocol on Child Soldiers**[13] establishes 18 as the minimum age for conscription by, and direct participation in hostilities with, government forces (*Articles 1 and 2*). As regards the voluntary recruitment of those under 18, it requires governments to raise the minimum age beyond the current minimum of 15, and to make a binding declaration stating the minimum age they will respect (*Article 3 (1) and (2)*). Countries must ensure safeguards are in place for the proper regulation of voluntary recruitment (*Article 3(3)*). In relation to non-governmental forces, this Optional Protocol goes further and prohibits any recruitment or use in hostilities of children under 18, requiring states to criminalise such practices (*Article 4*).

* Prior to this, the **1998 Statute of the ICC**[14] did specifically make it a war crime to conscript or enlist children under 15 into armed forces, or to use them to participate actively in hostilities (*Article 8(2)(b)(xxvi) and Article 8(2)(e)(vii)*).

* Moreover, the **1999 ILO Convention No. 182**,[15] concerning the prohibition and elimination of the worst forms of child labour, included a prohibition on 'all forms of slavery or practices similar to slavery, such as ... forced or compulsory labour, including forced or compulsory recruitment of children for use in armed conflict' (*Article 3(a)*). Under this Convention, children are defined as those under 18 (*Article 2*).

> *Note:*
> To summarise, as regards developments since the 1989 CRC: the 1998 Statute of the ICC makes participation in armed conflict of children under 15 a war crime; the 1999 ILO Convention prohibits forced recruitment of children under 18, and the 2000 Optional Protocol on Child Soldiers, *inter alia*, establishes 18 as a minimum age for conscription and direct participation in armed conflict. It therefore seems that a shift is underway towards a comprehensive ban on the participation in armed conflict of child soldiers under the age of 18, although this has not yet been achieved.

b)   Child Soldiers in Own Armed Forces

* Officers of national armed forces could encounter child soldiers either in their own or in opposing forces. If in their **own forces**, child soldiers (ie generally those aged 15-17, as already mentioned) should, in accordance with good practice and the higher standard in current IHL (see above), only be in training as voluntary recruits, and should not be directly engaged in combat. If a particular army does in fact use child soldiers under the age of 18 in combat, they should, like any other soldier, be trained to observe at least the fundamental IHL and human rights rules.

* On the **training process**—as opposed to the content of the training—it is important to mention the practice in some armed forces of 'initiation ceremonies' ('hazing' of recruits etc). On occasion these can include, eg, beating, bullying, and general humiliation of recruits under 18. Such practices constitute inhuman and degrading treatment, and—as regards recruits who are under 18—they are strictly illegal under Arts. 34 and 37(a) of 1989 CRC, as well as under other international law.[16]

* Regarding **recruitment**—as mentioned above, international law increasingly discourages conscription, and prohibits forcible recruitment, of those under 18.

c)   Child Soldiers in Opposing Armed Forces

* A guiding principle here is the **proportionality** principle. A soldier or officer whose life is in imminent danger is entitled and indeed trained to take necessary measures in self-defence—using minimum force—whether his or her opponent is an adult or a child. Moreover, since the purpose of military operations is generally to defeat the opposing armed forces, in some circumstances combatants confronted by child soldiers may need to prioritise their mission, and will therefore not necessarily be limited to acting solely in self-defence.
However, when realistically possible, **additional restraint** should be exercised when soldiers are aware that child soldiers are present in an opposing armed force.

> The presence of child soldiers in opposing forces should arguably affect, eg, the assessment of proportionality in decisions regarding tactics and strategy, so that a particularly stringent test should be applied to the balance between humanitarian considerations and military necessity.

In summary: Specialist officers, such as military lawyers, should be aware of the more detailed rules, in Sections (2) and (3) above, concerning the treatment of children in situations of armed conflict.

At the other extreme, soldiers 'on the ground', especially in situations where there is a low level of literacy and/or training, need to know only the most simple principle: that IHL and human rights rules for the protection of adults apply equally to children, and arguably should be applied to children with particular diligence, due to their vulnerability and entitlement to 'special treatment'.

Endnotes

1   The more detailed rules—in Sections (2) and (3)—would be most useful for specialist officers, such as military lawyers.

2   1989 Convention on the Rights of the Child.

3   Similarly, in the context of an armed conflict the prohibition on torture etc. can be translated into the IHL prohibition on 'inhumane' treatment.

4   1977 Protocol Additional to the Geneva Conventions of 12 Aug. 1949 and Relating to the Protection of Victims of International Armed Conflicts (Protocol I).

5   1907 Hague Convention IV Respecting the Laws and Customs of War on Land.

6   1949 Convention (IV) Relative to the Protection of Civilian Persons in Time of War.

7   Protocol Additional to the Geneva Conventions of 12 Aug 1949, and Relating to the Protection of Victims of Non-International Armed Conflicts (Protocol II).

8   2002 Optional Protocol to the Convention on the Rights of the Child on the Sale of Children, Child Prostitution and Child Pornography.

9   1966 International Covenant on Economic, Social and Cultural Rights.

10   1966 International Covenant on Civil and Political Rights.

11   See Chapter Three below.

12   For rules concerning child soldiers as prisoners, see Chapter Four and Appendix One, below.

13   2000 Optional Protocol to the Convention on the Rights of the Child on the Involvement of Children in Armed Conflict.

14   1998 Rome Statute of the International Criminal Court.

15   1999 Convention Concerning the Prohibition and Immediate Elimination of the Worst Forms of Child Labour (No. 182).

16   For example, such practices are unlawful under Article 7 of the 1966 ICCPR, and under the 1984 CAT (Convention Against Torture and other Cruel, Inhuman or Degrading Treatment or Punishment) generally.

Bibliography

Books, Articles, and Selected Reports Cited

AI, 'Children in South Asia' (London, AI, 1998).

___, 'Uganda: Stop child abductions for slave soldiering' (London, AI, 1999).

___, 'Sierra Leone: Childhood—a Casualty of Conflict' (London, AI, 2000(a)).

___, 'United Kingdom U-18s: Child Soldiers at Risk' (London, AI, 2000(b)).

___, *Annual Report 2001* (London, AI, 2001).

___, *Annual Report 2002* (London, AI, 2002).

___, 'Israel and the Occupied Territories Shielded from Scrutiny: IDF violations in Jenin and Nablus', (London, AI, 2002).

___, 'Israel, the Occupied Territories and the Palestinian Authority: Killing the Future: Children in the line of fire' (London, AI, 2002).

ALDRICH, G H, 'Compliance with the Law: Problems and Prospects', in H Fox and M A Meyer (eds) *Effecting Compliance* (London, BIICL, 1993) 3–13.

ALFREDSON, L, 'Sexual Exploitation of Child Soldiers', 2 *Child Soldiers Newsletter* (2001) 7.

ALIE, J A D, 'Background to the Conflict (1961–1991): What Went Wrong and Why?' in A Ayissi and R E Poulton (eds) *Bound to Cooperate: Conflict, Peace and People in Sierra Leone* (Geneva, UNIDIR, 2000) 15–35.

ALLEN, T, 'Understanding Alice: Uganda's Holy Spirit Movement in Context' 61:3 *Africa* (1991), 370–399.

ALLEN, T and J SEATON, (eds) *The Media of Conflict: War Reporting and Representations of Ethnic Violence* (London, Zed Books, 1999).

ALSTON, P, (ed) *The Best Interests of the Child: Reconciling Culture and Human Rights*, (Oxford, OUP, 1994).

AN-NA'IM, A, 'Human Rights in the Muslim World: Socio-Political Conditions and Scriptural Imperatives: a Preliminary Inquiry', 3 *Harv Hum Rts J* (1990) 13–52.

___, *Human Rights in Cross-Cultural Perspectives: A Quest for Consensus* (Philadelphia, University of Pennsylvania Press, 1992).

ARENDT, H, *On Violence* (New York, Harcourt Brace and Company, 1969).

AYISSI, A and R E POULTON, 'Peace Building and Practical Disarmament: Beyond States, with Civil Society', in A Ayissi and R E Poulton (eds) *Bound to Cooperate: Conflict, Peace and People in Sierra Leone* (Geneva, UNIDIR, 2000) 1–13.

BALANDIER, G, 'An Anthropology of Violence and War', 110 *International Social Science Journal* (1986) 499–511.

BANTEKAS, I, 'The Interests of States Versus the Doctrine of Superior Responsibility', 838 *IRRC* (2000) 391–402.

BLACK, M, *Growing up Alone: Childhood Under Siege* (London, UNICEF UK, 2001).

BLAIS, G, 'The International Institute of Humanitarian Law (San Remo) and its International Military Courses on the Law of Armed Conflict', 319 *IRRC* (1997) 451-454.

BOS, C S and S VAUGHN, *Strategies for Teaching Students with Learning and Behaviour Problems* (Needham Heights, MA, Allyn & Bacon, 1991).

BOUGAREL, X, *Bosnie: anatomie d'un conflit* (Paris, La Découverte, Les dossiers de l'Etat du Monde, 1996).

BOYDEN, J, 'Social Healing in War-Affected and Displaced Children' (Oxford, Refugee Studies Centre, University of Oxford, 2002).

BOYDEN, J and S GIBBS, *Indicators and Perceptions of Psycho-social Vulnerability and Coping Mechanisms in Cambodia* (Geneva, UNRISD, 1997).

BRACKEN, P and C PETTY, (eds) *Rethinking the Trauma of War* (London, SC and Free Association Books, 1998).

BRETT, E A, 'Neutralising the Use of Force in Uganda: the Role of the Military in Politics', 33:1 *Modern African Studies* (1995) 129–152.

BRETT, R and M McCALLIN, *Children: the Invisible Soldiers* (Stockholm, SC Sweden, 1998).

BRETT, R, 'Recruiting Child Soldiers: The Link between Displacement and Recruitment', 1:122 *Refugees* (2001) 19.

___, 'Girl Soldiers: Challenging the Assumptions', 6 *Child Soldiers Newsletter* (December 2002) 7–10.

CATALDI, A, 'Child Soldiers' in R. Gutman and D. Rieff (eds) *Crimes of War: What the Public Should Know* (New York/London, WW Norton & Company, 1999).

CHINKIN, C, 'Women's International Tribunal on Japanese Military Sexual Slavery', 95:2 *AJIL* (2001) 335–341.

CICC, *The International Criminal Court and Child Victims of Genocide, War Crimes and Crimes Against Humanity* (New York, CICC, 2001).

CMA, *CMA Training Skills Pack* (London, CMA, 1995).

COHN, I, 'The Convention on the Rights of the Child: What it Means for Children in War', 3:1 *Int'l. J. Refugee L.* (1991) 100–111.

CSC, *Child Soldiers Global Report* (London, CSC, 2001).

___, *Child Soldiers 1379 Report* (London, CSC, 2002).

___, 'Displacement and Child Soldiering', 4 *Child Soldiers Newsletter* (2002) 6–8.

DAVIS, M, *Late Victorian Holocausts: El Nino Famines and the Making of the Third World* (London, Verso, 2001).

DCI (Israel section) in consultation with the Israeli Children's Rights Coalition, 'NGO Comments on the Initial Israeli State Report on Implementing the UN Convention on the Rights of the Child: A Mixed Bag: Lawmaking to Promote Children's Rights, Ongoing Discrimination, and Many Serious Violations: Prepared for the Presessional Working Group UN Committee on the Rights of the Child, 31st Session' (Jerusalem, DCI, April 2002).

DE MULINEN, F, 'The Law of War and the Armed Forces' 202 *IRRC* (1978) 18–43.

___, *Handbook on the Law of War for Armed Forces* (Geneva, ICRC, 1989).

___, 'The Law of War and the Armed Forces', updated 1995 version of the 1978 article available at http://www.icrc.org, *IRRC* (1995).

DETRICK, S, (ed) *The United Nations Convention on the Rights of the Child: a Guide to the "Travaux préparatoires"* (Dordrecht, Martinus Nijhoff, 1992).

DICKEY, S *et al.*, 'Bosnia and Herzegovina', *Worldmark Encyclopedia of the Nations*, 10th edition, (Detroit, Gale Group, 2001).

DUDAI, R, 'Trigger Happy: Unjustified Shooting and Violation of the Open-Fire Regulations During the al-Aqsa Intifada' (Draft) (Jerusalem, B'Tselem, March 2002).

DUFOUR, G, 'La défense d'ordres supérieurs existe-t-elle vraiment?' 82:840 *IRRC* (2000) 969–992.

DUTLI, M T, 'Captured Child Combatants', 278 *IRRC* (1990) 421–434.

ECOWAS/CEDEAO and SC-SWEDEN, WEST AFRICA REGIONAL OFFICE, *Child Rights and Child Protection Before, During and After Conflict: Training Manual for Military Personnel* (Abidjan, SC-Sweden West Africa Regional Office, Dec 2000).

___, *Child Rights and Child Protection Before, During and After Conflict: Booklet for Senior Military Personnel* (Abidjan, SC-Sweden West Africa Regional Office, Jan 2001).

EL-HAJ, T A, 'The Impact of Armed Conflict on Children', 122 *Childright* (1995) 12.

FANON, F, *The Wretched of the Earth* (London, Penguin, 1963).

FERIA-TINTA, M, 'Commanders on Trial: The Blaskic Case and the Doctrine of Command Responsibility Under International Law', XLVII:3 *Netherlands Int'l L. Rev.* (2000) 293–322.

FIRKIN, P, *Training Skills and Methodologies* (UK, Contolearn, 1999).

FLECK, D, (eds) *The Handbook of Humanitarian Law in Armed Conflicts* (Oxford, OUP, 2000).

FOTTRELL, D, (ed) *Revisiting Children's Rights: 10 Years of the UN Convention on the Rights of the Child* (The Hague, Kluwer Law International, 2000).

FOUCAULT, M, *Discipline and Punish: The Birth of the Prison* (Harmondsworth, Penguin Books, 1977).

FRANCIS, D J, 'Mercenary Intervention in Sierra Leone: Providing National Security or International Exploitation?' 20:2 *Third World Quarterly* (1999) 319–338.

FRANK, T M, 'Are Human Rights Universal?' 80:1 *Foreign Affairs* (2001) 191–204.

GALEANO, E., *Open Veins of Latin America: Five Centuries of the Pillage of a Continent* (New York, Monthly Review Press, 1973).

GANTZEL, K J, 'War in the Post World War II World: Some Empirical Trends and a Theoretical Approach', in D Turton (ed) *War and Ethnicity: Global Connections and Local Violence* (Rochester, University of Rochester Press, 1997) 123–44.

GARDAM, J G, (ed) *Humanitarian Law* (Aldershot, Dartmouth/Ashgate, 1999).

GARDAM, J G, *Non-Combatant Immunity as a Norm of International Humanitarian Law* (Dordrecht, Martinus Nijhoff, 1993).

GNAEDINGER, A, 'Security Challenges for Humanitarian Action' 841 *IRRC* (2001) 171–82.

GOODWIN-GILL, G S and I COHN, *Child Soldiers: the Role of Children in Armed Conflict* (Oxford, OUP, 1994).

GREEN, L C, *The Contemporary Law of Armed Conflict* (Manchester, Manchester University Press, 2000).

GREENWOOD, C, 'Customary International Law and the First Geneva Protocol of 1977 in the Gulf Conflict', in P Rowe (ed) *The Gulf War 1990–91 in International Law and English Law* (London, Routledge, 1993(a)).

___, 'Command and the Laws of Armed Conflict' (Camberley, SCSI, 1993(b)).

___, 'The Development of International Humanitarian law by the International Criminal Tribunal for the Former Yugoslavia', 2 *Max Planck Yearbook of United Nations Law* (1998) 97–140.

GREPPI, E, 'The Evolution of Criminal Responsibility under International Law', 81:835 *IRRC* (1999).

GRIFFIN, M, 'Ending the Impunity of Perpetrators of Human Rights Atrocities: A Major Challenge for International Law in the 21st Century', 838 *IRRC* (2000) 369–389.

GRIFFITHS, R J, 'South African Civil-Military Relations in Transition: Issues and Influences', 21:3 *Armed Forces and Society* (1995) 394–410.

GURR, T R, M G MARSHALL and D KHOSLA, *Peace and Conflict 2001: A Global Survey of Armed Conflicts, Self Determination Movements, and Democracy* (University of Maryland, Center for International Development and Conflict Management, 2001).

HAMPSON, F, 'Fighting by the Rules', 269 *IRRC* (1989) 111–24.

___, 'Human Rights and Humanitarian Law in Internal Conflicts', in M. Meyer (ed) *Armed Conflict and the New Law: Aspects of the 1977 Geneva Protocols and the 1981 Weapons Convention* (London, BIICL, 1989) 55–80.

___, 'Using International Human Rights Machinery to Enforce the International Law of Armed Conflicts', 19:117 *Revue de Droit Militaire et de Droit de la Guerre* (1992).

___, *Legal Protection Afforded to Children under International Humanitarian Law: Report for the Study on the Impact of Armed Conflict on Children* (Essex, University of Essex, 1996).

HARVEY, R, 'Article 38—Living Commentary: Children and Armed Conflict' (publication pending 2003, Children and Armed Conflict Unit on behalf of the Children's Rights Alliance England, 2002).

HAUG, M, *The Intervention Strategies of Humanitarian Agencies in a Complex Political Emergency: the Case of Sri Lanka* (London, LSE, PhD Thesis, 2001).

HAYWARD, F M, 'Sierra Leone', in J. Krieger (ed) *The Oxford Companion to the Politics of the World* (Oxford, OUP, 1993) 827–28.

HDIP, 'Health Care under Siege II, The Health Situation of Palestinians During the First 7 Months of the Intifada (September 28th 2000–April 28th 2001)' (Ramallah, HDIP, May 2001).

___, '857 Palestinians killed (Shuhada) between Sept 29th 2000 and Nov 27th 2001' (Ramallah, HDIP, 2002).

HEDGES, C, 'The New Palestinian Revolt', 80:1 *Foreign Affairs* (2001) 124–138.

HIGGINS, R, *The Development of International Law Through the Political Organs of the United Nations* (London, OUP for the Royal Institute of International Affairs, 1963).

___, 'Derogations under Human Rights Treaties', 48:281 *BYIL* (1976–7) 281–320.

___, *Problems and Process: International Law and How We Use It* (Oxford, Clarendon Press, 1994).

HIRSCH, J L, *Sierra Leone: Diamonds and the Struggle for Democracy* (Boulder, Lynne Rienner Publishers, 2001).

HRW, *Needless Deaths in the Gulf War: Civilian Casualties During the Air Campaign and Violations of the Laws of War* (New York, HRW, 1991).

___, 'Peru, Presumption of Guilt: Human Rights Violations and the Faceless Courts in Peru', 8:5(B) *HRW Reports* (1996).

___, *War Without Quarter: Colombia and International Humanitarian Law* (New York, HRW, 1998).

___, *World Report* (New York, HRW, 1999).

___, 'Forgotten Children of War: Sierra Leoneon Refugee Children in Guinea' (New York, HRW, 1999).

___, 'The "Sixth Division": Military-Paramilitary Ties and U.S. Policy in Colombia' (New York, HRW, 2001).

___, 'Israel, the Occupied West Bank and Gaza Strip, and the Palestinian Authority Territories. Jenin: IDF military operations' (New York, HRW, May 2002).

___, *World Report* (New York, HRW, 2002).

HUNT, E B, 'Human Abilities: An Information Processing Approach,' in R J Steinberg (ed), *Human Abilities: An Information Processing Approach* (New York, Freeman, 1985).

IBHAWOH, B, 'Cultural Relativism and Human Rights: Reconsidering the Africanist Discourse', 19:1 *Netherlands Int'l L Rev* (2001) 43–62.

ICHRP, *Ends and Means: Human Rights Approaches to Armed Groups* (Geneva, ICHRP, 2000).

ICRC, 'Fundamental Rules of Humanitarian Law Applicable in Armed Conflict', 206 *IRRC* (1978) 247–249.

___, *The Silent Menace: Landmines in Bosnia and Herzegovina* (Geneva, ICRC, 1997).

___, 'ICRC Special Report: Stemming the Tide of Violence: ICRC Activities in Relation to the International Community's Prevention Strategies' (Geneva, ICRC, 1998).

___, *To Serve and Protect* (Geneva, ICRC, 1998).

___, 'Plan of Action for the Years 2000–2003, 27th International Conference of the Red Cross and Red Crescent', 836 *IRRC* (1999) 880–95.

___, *Special Report: Mine Action* (Geneva, ICRC, 1999).

___, *Fight it Right: Model Manual of the Law of Armed Conflict for Armed Forces* (Geneva, ICRC, 1999).

___, *Children and War, Summary Table of IHL Provisions Specifically Applicable to Children* (Geneva, ICRC, 2001).

___, *Legal Protection of Children in Armed Conflict* (Geneva, ICRC, 2001).

___, *ICRC Annual Report 2001* (Geneva, ICRC, 2002(a)).

___, 'Sierra Leone: Promoting International Humanitarian Law', 2:7 *ICRC News* (2002).

___, 'Colombia: ICRC operations in 2002' (Geneva, ICRC, 9 Sept 2002).

IGNATIEFF, M, *The Warrior's Honor: Ethnic War and the Modern Conscience* (New York, Metropolitan Books, 1998).

___, *Virtual War: Kosovo and Beyond* (New York, Metropolitan Books, 2000).

INDEPENDENT INTERNATIONAL COMMISSION ON KOSOVO, *The Kosovo Report: Conflict, International Response, Lessons Learned* (Oxford, OUP, 2000).

INTERNATIONAL INSTITUTE OF HUMANITARIAN LAW, *Seminar on International Humanitarian Law and Future Wars* (San Remo, 24–27 Oct. 2001).

JEYARATNAM WILSON, A and A JOSEPH CHANDRAKANTHAN, 'Tamil Identity and Aspirations', 4 *Accord: An International Review of Peace Initiatives* (1998).

JOCHNICK, C and R NORMAND, 'The Legitimation of Violence: A Critical History of the Laws of War', 35:1 *Harv Int'l LJ* (1994 (a)) 49–95.

___, 'The Legitimation of Violence: A Critical History of the Laws of War', 35:2 *Harv Int'l LJ* (1994(b)) 387–416.

KALDOR, M, *New and Old Wars: Organized Violence in a Global Era* (Cambridge, Polity Press, 1999).

KALSHOVEN, F and L ZEGVELD, *Constraints on the Waging of War: An Introduction to International Humanitarian Law* (Geneva, ICRC, 2001).

KAPLAN, R D, 'The Coming of Anarchy', *San Remo Seminar, Future Wars* (2001).

KEEN, D, *The Economic Functions of Violence in Civil Wars* (Oxford, OUP, International Institute for Strategic Studies, 1998).

___, 'Incentives and Disincentives for Violence', in M Berdal and D Malone (eds) *Greed and Grievance: Economic Agendas in Civil Wars* (Boulder, Lynne Rienner Publishers, 2000) 19–41.

___, 'Sierra Leone: War and its Functions', in F Stewart, V Fitzgerald and Associates (eds) *War and Underdevelopment* (Oxford, OUP, 2001).

KEEVA, S, 'Lawyers in the War Room', 77 *ABA Journal* (1991) 52–59.

KLENNER, D, 'Does International Humanitarian Law Still Stand a Chance? Reflections on Instruction and Training for the Military and Armed Groups and on the Role of the International Red Cross (ICRC), on the Occasion of the 50th Anniversary of the Four Geneva Conventions in August 1999' (Geneva, ICRC, 1999).

___, 'Training in International Humanitarian Law', 82:839 *IRRC* (2000) 653–661.

KUPER, J, 'Reservations, Declarations and Objections to the 1989 Convention on the Rights of the Child', in J P Gardener (ed) *Human Rights as General Norms and a State's Right to Opt Out: Reservations and Objections to Human Rights Conventions* (London, BIICL, 1997(a)) 104–119.

___, *International Law Concerning Child Civilians in Armed Conflict* (Oxford, Clarendon Press, 1997(b)).

___, 'Children and Armed Conflict: Some Issues of Law and Policy', in D Fottrell (ed) *Revisiting Children's Rights: 10 Years of the UN Convention on the Rights of the Child* (The Hague, Kluwer Law International, 2000) 101–113.

KYNOCH, G, 'The 'Transformation' of the South African Military', 34:3 *The Journal of Modern African Studies* (1996) 441–457.

LATTIMER, M and P SANDS, *Justice for Crimes Against Humanity* (Oxford, OUP, 2001).

LEGRAND, C C, 'The Colombian Crisis in Historical Perspective', *Colombia in Context*, (University of California, Berkeley, 2 March 2001).

LEURDIJK, D A, 'Background Paper: United Nations Protection Force (UNPROFOR): Report and Recommendations of the International Conference, Singapore, February 1997', in N. Azimi, Institute of Policy Studies of Singapore, United Nations Institute for Training and Research and National Institute for Research Advancement of Japan (eds) *Humanitarian action and peace-keeping operations: debriefing and lessons* (London, Kluwer Law International, 1997) 69–79.

LEVINE, I, 'Promoting Humanitarian Principles: the Southern Sudan Experience' (London, ODI Relief and Rehabilitation Network, 1997).

LILLY, D, 'From Mercenaries to Private Security Companies: Options for Future Policy Research' (London, International Alert, 1998).

MACHEL, G, *The Impact of Armed Conflict on Children* (New York, United Nations, 1996).

___, 'The Impact of Armed Conflict on Children: A Critical Review of Progress Made and Obstacles Encountered in Increasing Protection for War-Affected Children', *International Conference on War-Affected Children*, (Winnipeg, Canada, Sept 2000).

___, *The Impact of War on Children* (London, Hurst and Co, 2001).

MALANCZUK, P, *Akehurst's Modern Introduction to International Law*, seventh revised edition (London, Routledge, 1997).

MARTINS, M S, 'Rules of Engagement for Land Forces: A Matter of Training, Not Lawyering', 143 *Military L. Rev.* (1994) 3–160.

MATHEWS, D, *Fifty Stories of People Resolving Conflicts* (Oxford, Oxford Research Group, 2001—reprint 2002).

MCCAULEY, U, *Training Manual for UN Peacekeepers Regarding Children* (forthcoming—draft provided by the author, 2002).

MCCAULEY, U and C RANSQUIN, *Experiences of Training Members of Armed Forces on Child Rights and Child Protection, Before, During and After Conflict: Draft Lessons Learned Working Document* (Stockholm, Save the Children Sweden (forthcoming—draft provided by the authors), 2001(a)).

___, *Putting Children on the Military Agenda in West Africa: Documentation of the Process to Date* (Stockholm, Save the Children Sweden (forthcoming—draft provided by the authors), 2001(b)).

___, *Report of 'Workshop on Experiences of Training Members of Armed Forces on Child Rights and Child Protection, Before, During and After Conflict* (Abidjan, (23-26 Oct. 2001), Save the Children Sweden (forthcoming—draft provided by the authors), 2001(c)).

MCCONNAN, I and S UPPARD, *Children - Not Soldiers: Guidelines for Working with Child Soldiers and Children Associated with Fighting Forces* (London, SC, 2001).

MCCOUBREY, H, 'Jurisprudential Aspects of the Modern Law of Armed Conflict', in M Meyer (ed) *Armed Conflict and the New Law* (London, BIICL, 1989) 23–54.

MERON, T, *Human Rights in Internal Strife: Their International Protection* (Cambridge, Grotius, 1987).

___, 'War Crimes in Yugoslavia and the Development of International Law', 88 *AJIL* (1994) 78–87.

___, 'The Humanization of Humanitarian Law', 94:2 *AJIL* (2000) 239–278.

MERTUS, J, 'Judgment of Trial Chamber II in the Kunarac, Kovac and Vukovic Case', *ASIL Insights* (2001).

MILLER, G A, 'The Magical Number Seven, Plus or Minus Two: Some Limits on Our Capacity for Processing Information', 63 *Psychol Rev* (1956) 81–97.

MILLS, G, 'Armed Forces in Post-Apartheid South Africa', 35:3 *Survival* (1993) 78–96.

MINISTRY OF DEFENCE—SOUTH AFRICA, 'Defence in a Democracy: White Paper on National Defence for the Republic of South Africa', (1996).

MINISTRY OF DEFENCE—UK, 'Nanotechnology: Its Impact on Defence and MOD' (London, Ministry of Defence, 2001).

___, *A Soldier's Guide to the Law of Armed Conflict* (London, Ministry of Defence, April 2001).

MITCHELL, A, 'Failure to Halt, Prevent or Punish: The Doctrine of Command Responsibility for War Crimes', 22:3 *Sydney L. Rev.* (2000) 382–410.

MUTIBWA, P, *Uganda since Independence: A Story of Unfulfilled Hopes* (Kampala, Fountain Publishers, 1992).

NIOD, *Srebrenica, a 'Safe Area': Reconstruction, Background, Consequences and Analyses of the Fall of a Safe Area* (Amsterdam, Boom Publishers, 2002).

NISSAN, E, 'Historical Context', 4 *Accord: An International Review of Peace Initiatives* (1998).

NYEKO, B and O LUCIMA, 'Profiles of the Parties to the Conflict', 11 *Accord: An International Review of Peace Initiatives* (2002).

ORAÁ, J, *Human Rights in States of Emergency in International Law* (Oxford, Clarendon Press, 1992).

OSIEL, M, 'Obeying Orders: Atrocity, Military Discipline, and the Law of War', 86:5 *California L Rev* (1998) 939–1129.

___, *Obeying Orders: Atrocity, Military Discipline and the Law of War* (N.J., Transaction Publishers, 1999).

OTUNNU, O, 'Causes and Consequences of the War in Acholiland', 11 *Accord: An International Review of Peace Initiatives* (2002).

PALWANKAR, U, 'Measures Available to States for Fulfilling their Obligations to Ensure Respect for International Humanitarian Law', 298 *IRRC* (1994) 9–25.

PARKS, W H, 'Law of War Training', *US Institute of Peace Working Group on IHL*, (Washington, US Institute of Peace, 24 May 2001).

PICKLES, T, *Toolkit for Trainers* (Brighton, Pavilion, 1995).

PICTET, J, (ed) *Commentary: IV Geneva Convention Relative to the Protection of Civilian Persons in Time of War* (Geneva, ICRC, 1958).

PULKOL, D, 'Proliferation of Small Arms and the Problem of Child Soldiers', in E. Reyneke (ed) *Small Arms and Light Weapons in Africa: Illicit proliferation, circulation and trafficking* (Pretoria, ISS, 2000) 73–79.

RATNER, S R and J S ABRAMS, *Accountability for Human Rights Atrocities in International Law* (Oxford, OUP, 2001).

REPUBLIC OF COLOMBIA, Ministry of National Defense, *Annual Human Rights and International Humanitarian Law Report 2000* (Colombia, Jan 2001).

RESSLER, E M, M EVERETT, J M TORTORICI and A MARCELINO, *Children in War: A Guide to the Provision of Services* (New York, UNICEF, 1993).

ROBERTS, A and R GUELFF, *Documents on the Laws of War* (Oxford, OUP, 2000).

ROBERTS, A and R PARKER, 'Human Cost of Civil War', July/August *Amnesty Magazine* (2000) 6-9.

ROBERTS, D L, 'Internal Security Operations', *Lecture for Human Rights Course* (San Remo Institute, June 2002).

___, 'Training the Armed Forces to Respect International Humanitarian Law: The Perspective of the ICRC Delegate to the Armed and Security Forces of South Asia', 319 *IRRC* (1997) 433–446.

RODLEY, N, 'Soft Law, Tough Standards', 43:7.3 *Interights Bulletin* (1993) 41–46.

ROGERS, A P V, *Law on the Battlefield* (Manchester, Manchester University Press, 1995).

ROGERS, J D, 'Sri Lanka', in J. Krieger (ed) *The Oxford Companion to Politics of the World* (Oxford, OUP, 1993) 873–874.

SC, *HIV and Conflict: A Double Emergency* (London, SC, 2002).

SC and UNHCR, 'Action for the Rights of Children: Facilitator's Toolkit', CD-Rom (Geneva, UNHCR, Aug 2001).

SC—DENMARK, 'Briefing Pack: Strengthening the Child Protection Unit, UPDF Fourth Division Gulu' (Copenhagen, SC—Denmark, Jan 2001).

___, 'Project Progress Report: Mainstreaming Child Rights into the Uganda People's Defence Forces (UPDF)' (Copenhagen, SC—Denmark, Jan–June 2002).

SC—SWEDEN Regional Office for Eastern and Central Africa, 'Rights of Children in Armed Conflict and Displacement: A training manual for military personnel' (Ethiopia, SC—Sweden, Nov. 1999).

SC—SWEDEN, 'Children at Risk in Israel/Palestine', 3:4 *Children of War* (2000).

___, 'Rwanda: 'Children of Genocide' Released from Prison', 2/01:2 *Children of War* (2001).

SC—SWEDEN and ECOWAS/CEDEAO, 'Child Rights and Child Protection Before, During and After Conflict: The Good Soldier' (nd, Abidjan).

SC—SWEDEN and SC—DENMARK in collaboration with the UPDF, 'Children, Our Future: A handbook on Child Rights Protection during peace and war time' (N.p., Sept 1999).

SC—UK, *War Brought us Here: Protecting Children Displaced within Their Own Countries* (London, SC—UK, 2000).

SCHMITT, M N, 'The Principle of Distinction in 20th Century Warfare', *San Remo Seminar, Future Wars* (2001) 24-44.

SHAW, M N, *International Law* (Cambridge, CUP, 1999).

SINGER, S, 'The Protection of Children during Armed Conflict Situations', 252 *IRRC* (1986) 133–167.

SMITH, D, 'Center for Defence Information Finds Wars on the Increase', 3:1 *Weekly Defence Monitor* (1999).

STEIN, Y, 'Death in Custody: the Killing of Murad Awaisa, 17, in Ramallah, 31 March 2002', Case Study No 14 (Jerusalem, B'Tselem, May 2002).

STEINBERG, R J, (ed) *Human Abilities: An Information Processing Approach*, (New York, Freeman, 1985).

STULTZ, N M, 'South Africa in Angola and Namibia', in T G Weiss and J G Blight (eds) *The Suffering Grass: Superpowers and Regional Conflict in Southern Africa and the Caribbean* (London, Lynne Reiner Publishers, 1992) 79–99.

SUMMERFIELD, D, 'The Social Experience of War', in P. J. Bracken and C. Petty (eds) *Rethinking the Trauma of War* (London, Free Association, 1998) 9–35.

SWEDISH ARMED FORCES HEADQUARTERS, *Facts and Figures, Swedish Defence: 2000–2001* (Stockholm, Swedish Armed Forces, 2001).

THE CHALLENGES PROJECT, 'Challenges of Peace Operations: Into the 21st Century: Concluding Report 1997–2002' (Stockhom, Elanders Gotab, 2002).

THE OFFICE OF THE VICE PRESIDENT OF COLOMBIA, *Policy on Human Rights and International Humanitarian Law Progress Report: March 2000* (Bogota, 2000).

TYLER, J and A BERRY, *Time to Abolish War! A Youth Agenda for Peace and Justice* (Geneva, Hague Appeal for Peace, 2000).

UGALDE, A, P RICHARDS and A ZWI, 'Health Consequences of War and Political Violence', in L Kurtz (ed) *Encyclopedia of Violence, Peace, and Conflict* (San Diego, Academic Press, 1999) 103–121.

UNITED KINGDOM CABINET OFFICE, 'The United Kingdom and The Campaign against International Terrorism, Progress Report' (London, Cabinet Office, Sept 2002).

UN, *ABC des Nations Unies* (New York, UN, 2001).

___, *United Nations Conference on the Illicit Trade in Small Arms and Light Weapons in All Its Aspects* (New York, UN, 9–20 July 2001).

UNDP, *Human Development Report 1990, Concept and Measurement of Human Development* (New York, UNDP, 1990).

___, *Human Development Report 1992, Global Dimensions of Human Development* (New York, UNDP, 1992).

UNHCR, *The State of the World's Refugees 1997–1998: A Humanitarian Agenda* (Geneva UNHCR, 1997).

___, 'Action for the Rights of Children: Facilitator's Toolkit', CD-Rom (Geneva, UNHCR, 2001).

UNHCR and SC—UK, *Note for Implementing and Operational Partners on Sexual Violence and Exploitation: The Experience of Refugee Children in Guinea, Liberia and Sierra Leone* (London, SC - UK, 2002).

UNICEF, *The State of the World's Children 2001* (New York, UNICEF, 2001).

UNICEF, AFRICAN-EUROPEAN INSTITUTE and SOUTHERN AFRICAN RESEARCH AND DOCUMENTATION CENTRE, *Transcending the Legacy of Apartheid: Children in the New South Africa* (New York, UNICEF, 1996).

US DEPARTMENT OF STATE, 'Country Reports on Human Rights Practices' (Washington DC, US Department of State, 1996).

___, 'Country Reports on Human Rights Practices' (Washington DC, US Department of State, 2001).

VAN BUEREN, G, *The International Law on the Rights of the Child* (The Hague, Kluwer Law International, 1998).

VAN DONGEN, Y, *The Protection of Civilian Populations in Time of Armed Conflict* (Amsterdam, Thesis Publishers, 1991).

VEERMAN, P, 'The Children's Rights Crisis in Sierra Leone', *Monitor* (1999) 10–15.

WATCHLIST ON CHILDREN AND ARMED CONFLICT, 'The Impact of Conflict on Children in Occupied Palestinian Territory and Israel' (New York, Watchlist on children and armed conflict, 2002).

WCRWC, *Making the Choice for a Better Life: Promoting the Protection and Capacity of Kosovo's Youth* (New York, WCRWC, 2001).

WILLIAMS, J, *The Protection of Children Against Landmines and Unexploded Ordnance* (Washington DC, Viet Nam Veterans of America Foundation, 1996).

WOODWARD, S, *Balkan tragedy: chaos and dissolution after the Cold War* (Washington, D.C, Brookings Institution, 1995).

WRIGHT, S, 'A Worse Fate Still to Come?' 3 *Landmine Action Campaign* (2001) 4–5.

ZACK-WILLIAMS, A B, 'Child Soldiers in the Civil War in Sierra Leone', 28:87 *Review of African Political Economy* (2001) 73–82.

Treaties, Case Law, and UN Documents

Selected Treaties and Other International Instruments

1868 St Petersburg Declaration Renouncing the Use, in Time of War, of Explosive Projectiles Under 400 Grammes Weight, 18 Martens Nouveau Recueil (ser 1) 474, 138 Consol TS 297.

Hague Convention IV Respecting the Laws and Customs of War on Land, 3 Martens Nouveau Recueil (ser 3) 461, 187 Consol TS 227.

Geneva Declaration on the Rights of the Child, Records of the Fifth Assembly, Supplement no 23 League of Nations Official Journal (1924).

Charter of the International Military Tribunal, (Agreement for the Prosecution and Punishment of the Major War Criminals of the European Axis (London Agreement)), 8 Aug 1945, 58 Stat 1544, EAS No 472, 82 UNTS 280.

Charter of the United Nations, 26 June 1945, 59 Stat 1031, TS 993, 3 Bevans 1153.

Universal Declaration of Human Rights, GA res 217A (III), UN Doc A/810 at 71 (1948).

Convention on the Prevention and Punishment of the Crime of Genocide, 78 UNTS 277.

Convention (I) for the Amelioration of the Condition of the Wounded and Sick in Armed Forces in the Field, 75 UNTS 31.

Convention (II) for the Amelioration of the Condition of Wounded, Sick and Shipwrecked Members of Armed Forces at Sea, 75 UNTS 85.

Convention (III) relative to the Treatment of Prisoners of War, 75 UNTS 135.

Convention (IV) relative to the Protection of Civilian Persons in Time of War, 75 UNTS 287.

Convention relating to the Status of Refugees, 189 UNTS 150.

European Convention for the Protection of Human Rights and Fundamental Freedoms, 213 UNTS 222 (as amended by Protocols Nos. 3, 5, 8, and 11).

Declaration of the Rights of the Child, UN Doc A/1386(XIV), 20 Nov 1959.

Protocol Additional to the Geneva Conventions of 12 August 1949, and relating to the Protection of Victims of International Armed Conflicts (Protocol I), 1125 UNTS 3.

Protocol Additional to the Geneva Conventions of 12 August 1949, and relating to the Protection of Victims of Non-International Armed Conflicts (Protocol II), 1125 UNTS 609.

International Covenant on Civil and Political Rights, GA res 2200A (XXI), 21 UN GAOR Supp (No 16) at 52, UN Doc A/6316 (1966), 999 UNTS 171.

International Covenant on Economic, Social and Cultural Rights, G A res 2200A (XXI), 21 UN GAOR Supp (No 16) at 49, UN Doc A/6316 (1966), 993 UNTS 3.

ILO Convention No 138 Concerning the Minimum Age for Admission to Employment, 1015 UNTS 297 (1976).

1979 Convention on the Elimination of All Forms of Discrimination Against Women, G A res 34/180, 34 UN GAOR Supp (No 46) at 193, UN Doc A/34/46.

Convention on Prohibitions or Restrictions on the Use of Certain Conventional Weapons which may be Deemed to be Excessively Injurious or to have Indiscriminate Effects, and Protocols, UN Doc A/Conf.95/15, Annex I (1980).

African [Banjul] Charter on Human and Peoples' Rights, OAU Doc CAB/LEG/67/3 Rev 5, 21 ILM 58 (1982).

1984 Convention Against Torture and Other Cruel, Inhuman or Degrading Treatment or Punishment, G A res 39/46, [annex, 39 UN GAOR Supp (No 51) at 197, UN Doc A/39/51 (1984)].

Convention on the Rights of the Child, G A res 44/25, annex, 44 UN GAOR Supp (No 49) at 167, UN Doc A/44/49 (1989).

Second Optional Protocol to the International Covenant on Civil and Political Rights, aiming at the abolition of the death penalty, G A res 44/128, annex, 44 UN GAOR Supp (No 49) at 207, UN Doc A/44/49 (1989).

Protocol on Prohibitions or Restrictions on the Use of Mines, Booby-Traps and Other Devices, as amended on 3 May 1996, (Protocol II to the 1980 Convention as amended on 3 May 1996), G A res 51/89.

Cape Town Principles and Best Practice on the Prevention of Recruitment of Children into the Armed Forces, and Demobilization and Social Reintegration of Child Soldiers in Africa, (Symposium on the Prevention of Recruitment of Children into the Armed Forces, and Demobilization and Social Reintegration of Child Soldiers in Africa) Cape Town, 30 April 1997.

Convention on the Prohibition of the Use, Stockpiling, Production and Transfer of Anti-Personnel Mines and on their Destruction, 36 I.L.M. (1997) 1507–19.

Rome Statute of the International Criminal Court, UN Doc A/CONF.183/9, 17 July 1998.

Convention concerning the Prohibition and Immediate Action for the Elimination of the Worst Forms of Child Labour (ILO No 182), 38 ILM 1207 (1999).

Accra Declaration on War-Affected Children in West Africa, (West African Ministerial Conference on War-Affected Children) (Accra, Ghana, 27–28 April 2000).

Optional Protocol to the Convention on the Rights of the Child on the Involvement of Children in Armed Conflict, UN Doc A/54/L84.

Optional Protocol to the Convention on the Rights of the Child on the Sale of Children, Child Prostitution and Child Pornography, UN Doc A/RES/54/263.

Case Law

International Court of Justice

Military and Paramilitary Activities in and against Nicaragua (Nicaragua v United States of America) Merits, Judgment, ICJ Reports 1986.

Case concerning Application of the Convention on the prevention and punishment of the crime of genocide (Bosnia and Herzegovina v Yugoslavia (Serbia and Montenegro)), Request for the indication of provisional measures, ICJ Reports 1993.

Legality of the Threat or Use of Nuclear Weapons, Advisory Opinion, ICJ Reports 1996.

International Criminal Tribunal for the Former Yugoslavia

The Prosecutor v Dusko Tadíc, Case No IT–941–AR72, Appeals Chamber, 2 October 1995.

The Prosecutor v Dusco Tadíc, Case No IT–94–1–T, Trial Chamber, Sentencing Judgement, 14 July 1997.

The Prosecutor v Zejnil Delalic, Zdravko Mucic also known as "Pavo", Hazim Delic, Esad Landzo also known as 'Zenga' ('Celebici Case'), Case No IT–96–21–T, Trial Chamber, 16 November 1998.

The Prosecutor v Dusko Tadíc, Case No IT–94–1–A, Appeals Chamber, 15 July 1999.

The Prosecutor v Zoran Kupreskic, Mirjan Kupreskic, Vlatko Kupreskic, Drago Josipovic, Dragan Papic, Vladimir Santic, also known as 'Vlado', Case No IT–95–16–T, Trial Chamber, 14 January 2000.

The Prosecutor v Tihomir Blaskic, Case No IT–95–14–T, Trial Chamber, 3 March 2000.

The Prosecutor v Anto Furundzija, Case No IT–95–17/1–T, Trial Chamber, 10 December 1998, confirmed in Case No IT–95–17/1-A, Appeals Chamber, 21 July 2000.

The Prosecutor v Zejnil Delalic, Zdravko Mucic also known as "Pavo", Hazim Delic, Esad Landzo also known as 'Zenga' ('Celebici Case'), Case No IT–96–21–A, Appeals Chamber, 20 February 2001.

The Prosecutor v Dragoljub Kunarac, Radomir Kovac, and Zoran Vukovic, Case No IT–96–23–T and IT–96–23/1–T, Trial Chamber, 22 February 2001.

The Prosecutor v Dario Kordic and Mario Cerkez, Case No IT–95–14/2–T, Trial Chamber, 26 February 2001.

The Prosecutor v Radislav Krstic, Case No IT-98-33-T, Trial Chamber, 2 August, 2001.

The Prosecutor v Milosevic 'Croatia', Initial indictment, Case No IT–50–I, 8 October 2001.

The Prosecutor v Milosevic et al. 'Kosovo', Second amended indictment, Case No IT–99–37–PT, 29 October 2001.

The Prosecutor v Zoran Kupreskic, Mirjan Kupreskic, Vlatko Kupreskic, Drago Josipovic, Dragan Papic, Vladimir Santic, also known as 'Vlado', Case No IT–95–16–A, Appeals Chamber, 23 October 2001.

The Prosecutor v Dusko Sikirica et al., Case No IT-95-8-T, Trial Chamber, 13 November 2001.

The Prosecutor v Milosevic "Bosnia and Herzegovina", Initial indictment, Case No IT–51–I, 22 November 2001.

International Criminal Tribunal for Rwanda

The Prosecutor v Jean-Paul Akayesu, Case No ICTR–96–4–T, Trial Chamber, Judgement, 2 September 1998.

The Prosecutor v Jean-Paul Akayesu, Case No ICTR–96–4–T, Trial Chamber, Sentence, 2

October, 1998.

European Court of Human Rights

Bankovic and Others v Belgium and 16 Other Contracting States (application No 52207/99), 19 December 2001.

Domestic Case Law

United States v Calley, US Court of Military Appeals (1973) 22 USCMA 534, 48 CMR 19.

Elvin Kyle Brown v Her Majesty the Queen, Court Martial Appeal Court of Canada, Judgment, 6 January 1995, (CMAC 372).

HCJ 769/02 The Public Committee Against Torture et al. v State of Israel et al., Additional Submission by the State Attorney's Office, 2 February 2003.

UN Documentation

Security Council

UN Doc S/RES/808 (22 Feb 1993), on the Establishment of an International Tribunal for the Former Yugoslavia.

UN Doc S/RES/955 (8 Nov 1994), on the Establishment of an International Tribunal for Rwanda and Adoption of the Statute of the Tribunal.

UN Doc S/PRST/1998/18 (29 June 1998), Statement of the Security Council on Children and Armed Conflict.

UN Doc S/RES/1260 (20 Aug 1999), on the Situation in Sierra Leone.

UN Doc S/RES/1261 (25 Aug 1999), on Children and Armed Conflict.

UN Doc S/RES/1265 (17 Sept 1999), on the Protection of Civilians in Armed Conflict.

UN Doc S/RES/1279 (30 Nov 1999), on the Situation Concerning the Democratic Republic of the Congo.

UN Doc S/RES/1296 (19 Apr 2000), on the Protection of Civilians in Armed Conflict.

UN Doc S/RES/1314 (11 Aug 2000), on Children and Armed Conflict.

UN Doc S/RES/1379 (20 Nov 2001), on Children and Armed Conflict.

UN Doc S/RES/1422 (12 July 2002), on United Nations Peacekeeping.

UN Doc S/RES/1447 (4 Dec 2002), on the Situation between Iraq and Kuwait.

General Assembly

– Resolutions

UN Doc A/RES/49/205 (23 Dec 1994), Rape and abuse of women in the areas of armed conflict in the former Yugoslavia.

UN Doc A/RES/51/77 (20 Feb 1997), on the Rights of the Child.

UN Doc A/RES/52/107 (13 Feb 1998), on the Rights of the Child.

UN Doc A/RES/53/25 (19 Nov 1998), on the International Decade for a Culture of Peace and Non-Violence for the Children of the World (2001–2010).

UN Doc A/RES/53/128 (23 Feb 1999), on the Rights of the Child.

UN Doc A/RES/54/149 (25 Feb 2000), on the Rights of the Child.

UN Doc A/RES/54/263 (26 June 2000), on the Optional Protocols to the Convention on the Rights of the Child on the involvement of children in armed conflict and on the sale of children, child prostitution and child pornography.

UN Doc A/RES/55/79 (22 Feb 2001), on the Rights of the Child.

–	Reports

UN Doc A/53/482 (12 Oct 1998), Protection of children affected by Armed Conflict.

UN Doc A/54/430 (1 Oct 1999), Protection of children affected by Armed Conflict.

UN Doc A/55/442 (3 Oct 2000), Protection of children affected by Armed Conflict.

UN Doc A/55/163-S/2000/712 (19 July 2000), Children and Armed Conflict.

UN Doc A/55/985-S/2001/574 (7 June 2001), Prevention of Armed Conflict.

UN Doc A/56/342-S/2001/852 (7 Sept 2001), Children and Armed Conflict.

Secretary-General

UN Doc ST/SGB/1999/13 (6 Aug 1999), Secretary General's Bulletin on the Observance by United Nations Forces of International Humanitarian Law.

UN Doc A/S–27/3 (4 May 2001), Report of the Secretary-General, We the Children: End-decade review of the follow-up to the World Summit for Children.

UN Doc S/2002/1300 (26 Nov 2002), Report of the Secretary-General to the Security Council on the Protection of Civilians in Armed Conflict.

UN Doc S/2002/1299 (26 Nov 2002) Report of the Secretary-General on Children and Armed Conflict.

Committee on the Rights of the Child

UN Doc CRC/C/SR.39 (12 Oct 1992), Summary Record of the 39th meeting, General Discussion on Children in Armed Conflict.

UN Doc CRC/C/15/Add30 (15 Feb 1995), Concluding Observations of the Committee on the Rights of the Child: Colombia.

UN Doc CRC/C/15/Add40 (21 June 1995), Concluding Observations of the Committee on the Rights of the Child: Sri Lanka.

UN Doc CRC/C/Q/Mya.1 (19 June 1996), List of issues to be taken up in connection with the considerations of the initial report of Myanmar.

UN Doc CRC/C/15/Add79 (10 Oct 1997), Concluding Observations of the Committee on the Rights of the Child: Australia.

UN Doc CRC/C/15/Add80 (21 Oct 1997), Concluding Observations of the Committee on the Rights of the Child: Uganda.

UN Doc CRC/C/83/Add3 (14 Sept 1999), Second periodic report of the United Kingdom of Great Britain and Northern Ireland to the Committee on the Rights of the Child.

UN Doc CRC/C/15/Add110 (10 Nov 1999), Concluding Observations of the Committee on the Rights of the Child: Russian Federation.

UN Doc CRC/C/15/Add122 (28 Jan 2000), Concluding Observations of the Committee on the Rights of the Child: South Africa.

UN Doc CRC/C/15/Add115 (23 Feb 2000), Concluding Observations of the Committee on the Rights of the Child: India.

UN Doc CRC/C/15/Add116 (24 Feb 2000), Concluding Observations of the Committee on the Rights of the Child: Sierra Leone.

UN Doc CRC/C/15/Add137 (16 Oct 2000), Concluding Observations of the Committee on the Rights of the Child: Colombia.

UN Doc CRC/C/100 (14 Nov 2000), Report on the twenty-fifth session, Thematic Discussion Day on Violence against Children, paras. 666–88.

UN Doc CRC/OP/AC/1 (12 Oct 2001), Guidelines regarding initial reports of States Parties to the Optional Protocol to the Convention on the Rights of the Child on the involvement of children in armed conflict.

UN Doc CRC/C/15/Add188 (9 Oct 2002), Concluding Observations of the Committee on the Rights of the Child: United Kingdom of Great Britain and Northern Ireland.

UN Doc CRC/C/15/Add195 (9 Oct 2002), Concluding Observations of the Committee on the Rights of the Child: Israel.

UN Doc CRC/C/70/Add17 (19 Nov 2002), Second Periodic Report of Sri Lanka to the Committee on the Rights of the Child.

Economic and Social Council

UN Doc E/CN.4/Sub.2/1989/58 (1 Sept 1989), Resolution 1989/31 of the Sub-Commission, appointing Mary Concepción Bautista as Special Rapporteur.

UN Doc E/CN.4/Sub.2/1991/24 (2 July 1991), Resolution 1990/21 on the Application of International Standards Concerning the Human Rights of Detained Juveniles.

UN Doc E/CN.4/Sub.2/1992/20 (3 June 1992), Resolution 1992/20 on the Application of International Standards Concerning the Human Rights of Detained Juveniles.

UN Doc E/CN.4/1999/69 (27 Jan 1999), Rights of the Child, Report of the Secretary General on the abductions of children from Northern Uganda.

UN Doc E/CN.4/2000/71 (9 Feb 2000), Rights of the Child, Additional Report of the Special Representative of the Secretary-General for Children and Armed Conflict, Olara Otunnu.

UN Doc E/CN.4/2001/76 (25 Jan 2001), Rights of the Child, Additional Report of the Special Representative of the Secretary-General for Children and Armed Conflict, Olara Otunnu.

UN Doc E/CN.4/2001/121 (16 March 2001), Question of the violation of human rights in the occupied Arab territories, including Palestine, Report of the human rights inquiry commission established pursuant to Commission resolution S–5/1 of 19 October 2000.

UN Doc E/CN.4/2002/85 (7 Feb 2002), Rights of the Child, Additional Report of the Special Representative of the Secretary-General for Children and Armed Conflict, Olara Otunnu.

UN Doc E/CN.4/2002/86 (9 Nov 2001), Rights of the Child, Report of the High Commissioner on the abduction of children from northern Uganda.

UN Doc E/CN.6/2002/4 (18 Dec 2001), Commission on the Status of Women, Report of the Secretary-General on the Release of women and children taken hostage, including those subsequently imprisoned, in armed conflicts.

UN Doc E/CN.6/RES/46/1 (25 March 2002), Commission on the Status of Women, Resolution on the Release of women and children taken hostage, including those subsequently imprisoned, in armed conflicts.

Human Rights Treaty Bodies

UN Doc HRI/GEN/1/Rev5 (26 April 2001), Compilation of General Comments and General Recommendations Adopted by Human Rights Treaty Bodies.

Human Rights Committee

UN Doc CCPR/C/21/Rev1/Add11 (31 August 2001), General Comment No 29, States of Emergency (Article 4).

UN Doc CCPR/C/ISR/2001/2 (4 December 2001), Consideration of reports submitted by States Parties under Article 40 of the Covenant, Second Periodic Report, Addendum: Israel.

Conferences and Special Sessions

UN Doc A/CONF.192/15 (20 July 2001), Report of the UN Conference on the Illicit Trade in Small Arms and Light Weapons in all its Aspects.

UN Doc A/S–27/19/Rev1 (10 May 2002), Outcome document of the Special Session, 'A World Fit for Children'.

UNICEF

UN Doc E/ICEF/1986/CRP2, (1986), Children in Situations of Armed Conflict.

Index

A

Accra Declaration on War-Affected Children
in West Africa, 95n
adolescents, 9, 245, 252-253
see also under-18
age
    ascertaining, 46
    birth registration and, 46
    child and definition of a, 9, 118n, 248,
        251, 261
    child soldiers of, 4, 9, 45-50, 53n, 54n, 64,
        67, 76n, 193, 196, 200, 202, 267-269
    combatant and, 4, 45-50, 171, 181, 184n,
        267-269
    conscription and, 47, 48, 268
    criminal proceedings and, 51-53, 64-65
    criminal responsibility and, 51, 57n, 64,
        181, 261
    death penalty and, 37, 47, 53, 56n, 260,
        266, 268
    detention and 179-182, 184n
    deprivation of liberty and, 38-39, 43, 182
    international law and, 9, 46, 47, 48, 104,
        261
    recruitment and, 91, 194, 196, 198, 200,
        202, 217, 218, 220, 223, 224, 225, 226,
        259
aims of book, vii, 1, 6-8, 10, 17n, 21, 99,
    121, 124, 169-170, 175, 215
air force, 22, 149n, 224, 232n, 235n, 237n
anti-personnel mines, 60, 61, 74
    see also landmines
armed conflict
    changes in nature of, 1-3, 5, 11n, 16n,
        29n, 248
    Committee on the Rights of the Child
        and, 88-91
    conduct of, 3, 16n, 23, 30n, 31n, 34, 40n,
        42n, 46, 51, 62, 82
    decline in, 3
    definition of, 10, 23
    deprivation of life and, 26
    disturbances which are not armed
        conflict, 7, 21, 75n, 83, 161, 261-262

ECHR and, 28n
    impact on children of, 2-4, 85-86, 192,
        195, 198,199, 201, 219, 223, 243
    international, 2, 13-14n, 22, 28-29n, 50,
        56n, 180-181, 265
    non-international, 2, 12n, 14n, 21-22,
        28-29n, 34, 50, 54n, 64, 75n, 179, 216,
        219-220, 222, 227, 231, 236, 260, 265
    perpetuation of, 6
    prevention of, 5-6, 15n, 176
    preventing involvement of children in, 5
    protection of children in, 1, 4, 24, 25, 33,
        35, 56n, 86
    right to life and, 26, 29n, 55n, 84, 170-
        171, 181, 257, 263
    treatment of children in, 1, 3, 10, 22, 25-
        27, 34, 39, 84, 86
    women and girls in, 33-35, 38, 40-43n,
        54n, 70-73, 77n, 79n, 86, 95n, 118n,
        160, 205, 227, 235n, 241, 253
armed opposition groups, 7-8, 10, 16n, 45,
    49, 89, 217, 219-220, 223, 235n, 267
arms, 2, 6, 7, 33n, 54n, 95n, 131, 135, 147,
    160, 161, 165n, 244, 261
    see also weapons
    industry, 6
    firearms, 7, 160-161, 165n, 261
    small arms, 2, 11n, 95n, 243
Australia, 151-153, 197-199, 223-224
    Committee on the Rights of the Child
        and, 90, 96
    involvement in armed conflict, 132
    involvement in peace support operations,
        7, 144n, 224, 235n, 236n
    involvement in training of foreign armed
        forces, 223
    participation of children in hostilities,
        223-224
    recruitment, 223
    relevant treaties signed, ratified, etc., 152
Australian Defence Force
    training chart, 197-199
    training concerning children, 145n,152-
        153, 198-199

training, general, 30-31n, 55n, 116n,
    152, 198-199, 235n
treatment of recruits, 224
Australian Red Cross, 153, 197

B
babies, 37, 39, 72, 150n, 252, 267
impact of conflict on, 252
    special protection of, 37, 39, 267
birth registration, 46
bombardment, 22
border, 35, 40-42n, 55n
Bosnia and Herzegovina (BiH), 125-126,
    191, 216-217
    see also ICTY
    ethnic cleansing, 216
    impact of conflict on children, 67, 68,
        69-70, 216
    involvement in armed conflict, 162, 216
    involvement in peace support operations,
        122, 162, 217
    NATO and, 28n, 145n, 224-228n
    participation of children in hostilities in,
        216
    peace support operations in, 217, 224-
        225, 228n
    rape of women and children, 216
    refugees, 216
    relevant treaties signed, ratified, etc., 125
Bosnia and Herzegovina, Armed Forces of
    training chart and, 191
    training, concerning children, 126
    training, general, 125-126, 145n, 192
bullying, 48, 55n, 91, 269

C
camps, 35, 49, 55n, 222, 235n
Cape Town Principles and Best Practices,
    53-54n
child
    see also, armed conflict, impact on
        children *and* age
    age of criminal responsibility, 51, 57n,
        250, 261
    arbitrary deprivation of life, 26, 46, 84
    arrest, detention and imprisonment of,
        51, 67, 137, 160, 161, 166n, 198, 261-
        262
    as competent survivors, 9, 31n
    as hostages, 40n

as internees, 38, 39
as passive victims, 31n
as refugees, 14n, 34, 40n, 49, 209, 216,
    219, 235n, 243, 257
best interests, 38, 49, 57n, 118n, 262
civilians, 33-43, 264-265
    arrest, detention and imprisonment
        of, 43n, 52, 83, 137, 161, 165n, 198,
        261-262
    babies, 37, 39, 252, 267
    besieged, 36, 196, 202, 266
    enemy aliens, 33, 37, 39, 264, 267
    evacuation of, 36, 41-42n, 156, 171,
        193, 196, 198, 200, 202, 266
    family contact, 35, 38, 135, 171,
        193,196, 198, 200, 202, 266
    in occupied territories, 37, 43n, 131
    military training regarding, 33-43
    orphaned or separated from their
        parents, 37, 39, 195, 267
    protection, 34-40, 61, 171, 264-267
    provision of relief, 36, 135, 156, 171,
        176n, 193, 196, 198-199, 201, 266
    punishment, 27, 38, 43n, 53, 57n, 171,
        184n,193-194, 196, 198, 200, 202,
        264
    removal, 36, 42n, 161, 193, 196, 198,
        200, 202, 266
    sexual abuse of, 35, 38, 171
    zones of protection, 35-36, 39, 41n,
        135, 149n, 156, 164n, 171, 176n,
        193, 198, 200, 202, 266
criminal proceedings against, 51
death penalty and, 26, 37, 47, 53, 56n,
    260, 268
definition of, 9
deprived of their liberty, 37, 38-39, 50,
    51-53, 180, 182, 261-262, 267
development, 188, 190, 192, 195, 245,
    247-257
disabled, 2, 35, 42
due process and, 38, 43, 51-53
HIV/AIDS and, 35, 41n, 199, 244, 245,
    253
in conflicts on land, 22
in occupied territory, 37-38, 42n, 51,
    266-267
injured/disabled by conflict, 2, 74n, 129,
    218
internally displaced, 34, 40n, 49

kept with their families, 36, 42n, 266
killed by conflict, 2, 11n, 60n, 67, 217,
    241
labour, 3, 38, 48, 70, 182, 231, 257, 268
landmines and, 2, 14n, 59-79, 172, 213n,
    217, 230n, 258
made homeless by conflict, 2
orphaned/separated from their parents,
    37, 39, 185n, 195, 201, 222, 267
participation in armed conflict, 17n, 48,
    54n, 198, 268
participation in decisions, 17n, 36, 42n,
    43n, 52, 183, 266
positive obligations of military personnel
    to assist, 35
protection, 1, 4, 17n, 25, 26, 35, 48, 49,
    62, 83, 85, 86, 87, 96n, 160, 169, 188,
    200, 242, 243, 246, 259-262
Protection Code, 192-195, 213, 247, 258
Protection Officer(s), 133, 147-148n
prostitutes, 35, 41n, 265
protection from torture of,26-27, 38, 39,
    46,53, 55n, 83, 84, 93n, 170, 171, 181,
    257, 264, 270n
protection from enslavement of, 25, 35,
    84
punishment of, 43n, 53, 57n, 171, 193,
    194, 196, 198, 200, 202
questioning of, 52
refugees, 14n, 17n, 34-35, 40-41n, 49,
    55n, 209, 216, 220, 228, 232, 235, 243,
    257
soldiers
    age of participation and, 193, 196, 198,
        200, 202
    age of recruitment, 194, 196, 198, 200,
        202
    arrest, detention and imprisonment
        of, 51
    as combatants, 46-47, 194, 196, 198,
        200, 202, 267-268
    ban on forced recruitment of, 48-49
    basic rules relating to, 46
    captured, 51-52
    demobilising, 17n, 45, 51, 56n, 116n
    disciplinary proceedings against, 51
    entitlement to fair hearing, 52
    forcible conscription, 53
    girl, 45n, 54n, 235n, 259
    in opposing armed forces, 49, 269

    in own armed forces, 48, 269
    initiation ceremonies, 48
    internment, 183, 194, 198, 200, 202
    POWs, 50, 53, 56n, 92n, 180-185, 194,
        202, 203, 259-260
    punishment, 194, 196, 198, 200, 2
    repatriation, 182-183, 194, 196, 198,
        200, 202
    recruiting, 27, 46-49, 53, 55n, 88, 89,
        91, 111, 127-129, 140, 143, 148n,
        150n, 161, 171, 192, 194, 196, 198,
        200, 201, 203, 217, 218, 219, 223,
        225, 226, 244, 253, 259, 260, 267-
        268
    sexual abuse of, 45, 54n,190n
    training of, 111
slavery, 27, 48, 268
special needs of, 35, 156, 245
special treatment principle, 25, 27, 31n,
    34, 38, 46, 50, 55n, 66, 83-84, 86, 99,
    104, 129, 161, 170-171, 184n, 192,
    194-195, 198-199, 201, 209, 212, 259,
    263, 265, 267, 269
trafficking of, 3, 64, 70, 76n, 95n, 245
witnesses, 65, 70, 77n
childhood, 9, 192, 199, 212n, 244, 247, 248,
    249-253, 254, 255
beginning of, 9
upper age limit, 9
children
    see child
civilian courts, 51, 56n
    see also military courts
civilians
    IHL rules concerning, 34, 265
    treatment of, 34, 203, 265
civil-military cooperation, 101, 112, 143,
    174, 187-190, 241
Colombia, 126-129, 191-192, 217
    Committee on the Rights of the Child
        and, 89-90
    military academies in, 145n, 217
    involvement in armed conflict, 217
    involvement in peace support operations
        in, 217
    participation of children in hostilities,
        217
    population displacement, 217
    recruitment, 217
    relevant treaties signed, ratified, etc.,

126-127
Colombian Armed Forces
  implicated in human rights violations/
    breaches of IHL, 129, 146n
  training chart and, 191-192
  training, concerning children, 129, 191
  training, general, 127, 128
command responsibility, 59-79, 149n, 162n,
  172, 205
Committee on the Rights of the Child, 88,
  93n, 113n, 123, 144, 172-173
  'Day of discussion', 4, 89
  encouraging states to ensure training in
    child rights, 89
  encouraging states to raise awareness
    about violence against children, 89
  guidance for states, 88-89
  limiting the impact of armed conflict on
    children, 88
  monitoring of military training on
    children, 91
  Reports
    Australia, 90
    Colombia, 89-90
    Israel, 91
    Sierra Leone, 90-91
    South Africa , 90
    Sri Lanka, 90
    Uganda, 90
    United Kingdom, 91
  role in military training, 88-89
conscripts, 23, 218
  see also volunteers
conduct of operations, 92n, 137, 161, 165n,
  235n, 259-260
crimes against humanity, 69, 70, 72, 76n,
  77n, 88
criminal responsibility, 51, 57n, 63, 64, 75n,
  250, 261
culture, relevance of, 5, 9, 15n, 106, 107,
  111, 158, 165n, 174, 250, 255
customary international law, 12n, 30n, 81
  see also customary law
customary law, 3, 13n, 23, 25, 30n, 31n, 33,
  38, 62, 82, 83, 92n, 176n

D

death penalty, 26, 31n, 37, 47, 53, 56n, 260,
  266, 268
deprivation of life, 26, 31n, 46, 84, 264

  see also right to life
derogation, 31n, 55-56n, 83-84
detention, 51-52, 83, 138, 161, 165n, 171,
  183, 262
  conditions of, 38, 39, 43n, 51, 180, 182,
    184n, 193, 194, 196, 198, 200, 202
  due process and, 51-52, 56n, 179-180,
    182, 193, 194,196, 198, 200, 202
detained children, 38, 43n, 50-57, 180-185,
  194
  see also children, deprived of their liberty
  in international armed conflict, 180-181
    as civilian internees, 181
    as non-combatants, 181
    as POWs, 180-183
  in non-international armed conflict,
    179-180
    fundamental guarantees, 180
    humane treatment, 180
    IHL rules and, 179
    protected person category, 179
discrimination, prohibition of, 25, 45
distinction, principle of, 34, 159, 203
disturbances not constituting an armed
  conflict, 7, 21, 75n, 83, 161, 261-262
due process, 27, 34, 38, 43n, 51-53, 63, 171,
  179, 180, 182, 193, 194, 196, 198, 200,
  202, 265

E

ECOWAS, 133-134, 144n, 148n, 175, 188,
  192, 194-195, 197, 206, 219
  training manual for military personnel,
    115n, 133, 194, 195, 197, 247-258
  The Child Protection Code of Conduct for
    Soldiers, 258
education, 3, 25, 37, 38, 39, 40n, 41n, 42n,
  43n, 61, 76n, 91, 165n, 180, 181, 209,
  252, 257, 260
enemy aliens, 33, 37, 39, 264, 267
expectant mothers, 35, 36, 39, 43n, 196,
  201, 202, 266, 267
  see also mothers

F

family, 25, 33, 36, 37, 42n, 110, 180, 244,
  250
  contact, 36, 38, 135, 171, 193, 196, 198,
    200, 202
  news, 36, 156

reunification, 161, 193
food, 35, 39, 70, 78n, 142, 181, 193, 196,
    198, 201, 246, 252
    see also nutrition

G

genocide, 26, 31n, 57n, 63, 64, 72, 73, 76n,
    77n, 88, 93n, 244
girls
    as soldiers, 45n, 54n, 235n, 259
    gratuitous discrimination against, 45
    particular health needs of, 45
    sexual abuse of, 35, 38, 241, 253
guardian, 36, 52, 223, 260, 262, 266

H

health, 3, 25, 34, 36, 37, 38, 39, 45, 49, 61,
    127, 182, 183, 193, 251, 252, 257, 258,
    266
HIV/AIDS, 35, 41n, 149n, 199, 244, 245, 253
Human Rights Committee, 57n, 84, 292
human rights
    basic principles , 25-27, 170-171, 181
        prohibition of arbitrary killing, 25
        prohibition of enslavement, 25
        prohibition of torture, 26, 181, 264
        right to life, 181, 263
        special treatment of children, 263
    derogation from, 83-84
    law, 21-22, 25-27, 83-85, 169, 176, 261,
        263
    rules regarding child civilians, 33-40,
        171-172
    rules regarding child soldiers, 46-54,
        171-172
    training obligations of officers, as
        regards, 59, 61, 62, 102, 172
    training obligations of states, as regards,
        81-85, 89, 90, 172-173
humanity
    principle of, 23, 30n
hygiene
    see also health

I

imprisonment, 3, 51, 83, 262
    life, 37, 47, 266, 268
    conditions of, 38-39, 43n, 51, 180, 182,
        184n, 193, 194, 196, 198, 200, 202,
        259

internal disturbances, 7, 75n, 161, 261-262
internally displaced persons, 34, 40n, 49
International Children's Day, 85
International Committee of the Red Cross
    (ICRC)
    child-specific materials, 110, 126
    Discussion Paper Concerning the
        Protection of Children in Armed
        Conflicts
    and Disturbances, 259-262
    Central Tracing Agency, 36, 266
    military training regarding children, 108,
        135, 159-161, 173, 174-175, 176
    mine-awareness programmes, 75n
    plans of action referring to children in
        armed conflict, 86-87
    practice of training officers, 7, 125-126,
        130, 132, 136-137, 139
    reforms of international law and policy,
        15n
    Teaching File, 160, 162, 166, 175, 191,
        259-262
    training of military personnel on their
        legal obligations, 4, 82, 92n, 103, 105,
        108, 116n, 125, 146n, 232n
    training of military personnel in
        traditional values, 107
    training of trainers, 125
    training programmes, 15n
International Criminal Court (ICC),12n,
    29n, 39, 48, 64-65, 76n, 77n, 125, 127,
    130, 132, 134, 136, 138, 145n, 147n, 151,
    153, 155, 157, 184n, 193, 194, 238n, 268,
    270n
    Victims and Witnesses Unit, 65
international humanitarian law (IHL)
    changing context of, 2
    rules regarding child civilians, 23-24, 33-
        40, 171-172, 264-267
    rules regarding child soldiers, 9, 23-24,
        45-53, 171-172, 179-184, 267-270
    training obligations of officers, as
        regards, 59-74, 170-172
    training obligations of states, as regards,
        81-91, 172-173
    validity of, 2, 169
International Tribunal for Rwanda (ICTR),
    12n, 21, 26, 59, 64, 65, 66, 76n, 172
    The Prosecutor v Akayesu, 71-73, 79n
        girls, 72

Hutu, 72
   reference to child civilians, 72
   reference to child soldiers, 72
   Tutsi, 72-73
International Tribunal for the Former
   Yugoslavia (ICTY), 12n, 22, 26, 59, 64,
   65, 66, 76n, 172
   The Prosecutor v Blaskic, 77n
   reference to aggravating circumstances,
      67
   reference to child civilians, 67
   reference to child soldiers, 67
   reference to command responsibility, 67
   *The Prosecutor v Kunarac, Kovac and
      Vukovic,* 69-71, 78n
      convictions of rape and enslavement
         as crimes against humanity, 70
      girls, 70, 71
      rape, 69-70
      reference to aggravating
         circumstances, 70
      reference to child civilians, 69-70
      reference to child soldiers, 69
      responsibility, 71
   *The Prosecutor v Kupreskic, Kuprescik,
      Kuprescik, Jasipovic, Papic, Santic
      (aka Vlado),* 68-69
      reference to aggravating
         circumstances, 68
      reference to child civilians, 68
      reference to child soldiers, 68
      reference to military training, 68
internees, 38, 39, 43n, 159, 180, 181, 183
internment, 50, 92n, 194, 196, 199, 200,
   202, 203
   in a neutral country, 182-184
Ireland, 91, 96, 225, 236n, 237n
Israel, 130-131, 192, 218-219
   Committee on the Rights of the Child
      and, 91, 96n
   conflict with Palestinian people, 2, 42n,
      113n, 218-219, 229n-230n
   impact of conflict on children, 218
   involvement in armed conflict, 192, 218
   involvement in peace support operations,
      219
   Occupied Territories, 218
   participation of children in hostilities in,
      193-194
   recruitment, 218

   relevant treaties signed, ratified, etc.,
      130, 147n
Israeli Defence Forces
   Ethical Code, 131
   ICRC training, 130-131
   recruitment, 218
   training chart and, 192
   training concerning children, 131, 174,
      192-195
   training, general, 162
issues excluded from study, 6-8

J
jus ad bellum, 11n
jus in bello, 11n

K
Kosovo, 2, 17n, 74n, 224, 225, 226, 236n,
   237n, 260

L
land, 39, 82
   operations on, 22
landmines, 2, 14n, 59-62, 74-75n, 172, 191,
   213n, 217, 222, 227n, 229n, 258
   see also anti-personnel mines
   alternative weapons, 60
   prohibition on use of, 59
law and policy, implementation of in
   selected countries
   countries involved in armed conflict 'at
      home'
      Bosnia and Herzegovina, 121, 125-126
      Colombia, 121, 126-129
      Israel, 121, 130-131
      Sierra Leone, 121, 132-134
      South Africa, 121, 134-136
      Sri Lanka, 121, 136-138
      Uganda, 121, 123, 138-144
   countries involved in peace support or
      other military activities 'abroad'
      Australia, 121, 151-153
      South Africa, 121, 153
      Sweden, 121, 153-155
      United Kingdom, 121, 155-157
      United States, 121, 157-159
law of armed conflict (LOAC), 125, 132-133,
   135, 152, 155-156, 195, 201
Lord's Resistance Army, 49, 139
   child soldiers, 143

children abducted by, 141
Kony, Joseph, 234n
Ugandan People's Defence Army, 234n
United Democratic Christian Movement/
Army, 234n

M
Machel, Graca, 14n, 53n, 243
Machel Reports, 4, 60, 75n, 89
landmines, 60, 75n
protection of children in armed conflict,
4
media, 45, 79n, 100, 104, 244
medical, 27n, 29n, 36, 39, 61, 131,155, 182,
185n, 232, 266
mercenaries, 219, 231n
maternity cases, 29, 35, 36, 37, 41n, 201,
202
special protection of, 39, 266, 267
methodology, 99-113
military training, methodology, 102-113
military commanders, 71, 82, 111, 158, 225
criminal responsibility, 62, 64
responsibility for crimes committed by
subordinates, 73
military courts, 51, 56n, 66
see also civilian courts
military necessity
principle of, 23-24, 162n, 169, 170
military personnel
definition of, 9-10
dissemination and awareness of
standards on the rights of the child, 86
legal obligations, 1, 4
quasi-legal obligations, 1
regional training programmes for, 86
reporting of violations by, 41n, 195
responsibilities to civilians, 86
sexual abuse and, 41n, 142
training on the treatment of children, 4,
5, 35, 87
training for peace support, 4, 7, 87
training in IHL/human rights, 14n, 21-
22, 27, 82-83, 86-87
aim of, 4,103
content, 106
context, 104
cultural differences, 107
ensuring protection of children, 86
evaluation, 109

motivation, 103
proportionality, 104
punishment, 104
regarding child civilians, 171-172
regarding child soldiers, 171-172
regarding protection of children and
women in armed conflict, 86
regarding treatment of children, 86,
171-172, 176
style of, 103, 106
techniques, 107-108
timing of, 105
military training
see also military personnel *and* training
of soldiers *and* training of officers
balancing demands of military
effectiveness and 'ethics', 104, 112
basic questions, 5-6
child-focussed, 65, 110, 174
child soldiers, 110-112
concerning children
Australia, 197-199
Bosnia and Herzegovina, 191
Colombia, 191, 192
Israel, 192
Sierra Leone, 192-195
South Africa, 197-197, 199
Sri Lanka, 197
Sweden, 199-201
Uganda, 197
United Kingdom, 201-203
United States, 203
concerning children, evaluation of, 112
cultural differences, 111
effectiveness of, 100
for participants including combatants
and civilians, 111
good practice, 122
international law, 5
'legalistic', 105
methodology and children, 110-113
national, 124
obligations of officers, 10, 170-172
obligations of states, 8, 10, 31n, 47, 81-
96, 172-173
obligations towards children, 35
pre-deployment training, 111
preventive law, 105
standard of in particular countries, 122
Toolkit of training techniques, 101-102,

109, 117n
weapons training and tactics, 5
minimum force, 49, 50, 141, 172, 194, 258,
    269
mothers of children, 36, 39, 43n, 176n, 196,
    202, 252

N

NATO, 2, 28n, 145n, 154, 224, 225, 226,
    227n, 228n, 236n
national armed forces
    obligations of officers of,1, 10, 34, 60,
        109, 169-172
    provision of basic instruction on law and
        policy to, 99
    training of, 1, 100, 175
naval
    forces, 22
    operations, 29n, 158, 160, 223
necessities, 131, 193, 196, 198, 199, 201
non-governmental forces, 2
non-governmental organisations (NGOs),
    6, 15n, 36, 101, 109, 110, 123, 133, 134,
    142, 143, 162, 187, 189, 223, 246
nutrition, 37, 43n, 75n, 1180, 184n
    see also food

O

occupied territory, 37, 38, 39, 42n, 43n, 51,
    131, 147, 171, 218, 219, 229, 266, 267
Occupying Power, 42n
officer
    definition of, 9
officer training
    basic general, 59
    culpability and command responsibility,
        59, 62-66, 74, 172
    guidance on legal problems, 21
    IHL and human rights training, 23-27,
        59, 102-109, 170-171
    international law relevant to, 21, 59, 81,
        97-102
    regarding children, 33-74, 110-113
Otunnu, Olara, 4, 65, 85, 89, 93n, 123, 223

P

Palestine, 2, 113n, 147n, 218, 229n
    Palestinian Authority, 147n
parents, 36, 37, 39, 52, 110, 111, 142, 181,
    193, 219, 223, 244, 245, 246, 251, 258,

260, 262, 266, 267
paramilitary forces, 2
peace negotiations
    involvement of children in, 8
peace support
    operations, 14n, 16n, 87, 92n, 121-122,
        135, 151, 153, 190n, 197, 200, 208,
        217, 219, 220, 221, 222, 223, 224, 225,
        226, 235n, 236n, 237n, 238n, 241
    personnel, 7, 41n, 87, 95n, 188, 219, 225,
        242
    training for, 7, 87, 107,115n, 135,
        139,148n, 154, 155, 158, 188, 224, 241
prisoners of war (POWs),14n, 50, 53, 56n,
    92n, 180, 181-183, 184n, 185n, 194, 202,
    203, 259, 260
'proportionality' principle, 24, 52, 162n,
    169-170
prosecutions
    for crimes against humanity, 8
    for genocide, 88
    for war crimes, 8

R

rank, 24, 27, 71, 73, 106, 107, 109, 111, 124,
    134, 145n, 158, 159, 163n, 165n, 171,
    174, 184n
rape, 41n, 69-70, 72, 76n, 78n, 79n, 142,
    216, 222, 227, 231, 241, 253, 258
regional treaties, 8
religion, 36, 39, 147n, 180, 211, 216, 222,
    244, 251, 260, 266
release/repatriation of children, 183
Republic of Sierra Leone Armed Forces,
    132-134
    ECOWAS West Africa, 134
    recognition of need for child-focussed
        training, 134
    Save the Children – Sweden, 133-134
    training chart, 192-195
    training concerning children, 133-134
    training, general, 132-133
    UNICEF, 133
right to life, 27, 83-84, 170-171
    see also deprivation of life
Rules of Procedure and Evidence
    ICTY, 65
    ICTR, 65
    ICC, 65
Rwanda, 2, 22n, 55n, 56n, 57n, 64, 71, 72,

73, 79n, 169, 260
Rwandan massacres, 72-73

S

sanctions, 14n, 15n, 63, 88, 106, 146, 182
San Remo Institute, 117n, 123, 125, 128, 134, 139, 159-162, 165n
chart of comments, 204-212
Save the Children
and military training on children, 110, 114n, 126, 133, 140, 154, 175-176, 189, 190n
civil-military cooperation, 187-190
Colombia, 129
East Africa, 187
mine-awareness work, 75n
Denmark, 123, 139, 140, 141, 197
training for Ugandan army, 123, 139-144
South Africa, 135, 148n
Sweden, 122, 133, 134, 154-155, 175, 176, 192, 194-195, 197, 241
training of peace-keeping forces in child protection, 241-246
training manual for military personnel, 247-258
West Africa, 42n, 112, 187, 247
training programmes, 75, 188-189
schools, 34, 42n, 61, 235n, 246, 251
security forces, 89, 90, 136, 137, 160, 219, 221, 231n, 261
self-defence, 49, 50, 194, 258, 269
sexual abuse, 35, 38, 45, 48, 54n, 76n, 96n, 142, 146n, 171, 190n, 241, 253
Sierra Leone, 192-195, 219-220
see also Republic of Sierra Leone Armed Forces
Committee on the Rights of the Child and, 90-91, 96n
impact of conflict on children, 219
international community and, 219
involvement in armed conflict, 219
involvement in peace support operations, 220
non-international armed conflict, 219
participation of children in hostilities, 219
population displacement, 219
recruitment, 219-220
relevant treaties signed, ratified, etc., 132
Revolutionary United Front (RUF), 219,

231n
truth and reconciliation commission, 220
war crimes trial, 56n, 220
slavery
prohibition of, 27, 48, 268
'soft' law, 38, 43n, 50, 56n, 81-95
military training, and, 84-85
soldier
definition of, 9
Somalia, 13n, 66, 77n, 95n, 117n, 226, 238n, 243
South Africa, 195-197, 199, 220-221
Committee on the Rights of the Child and, 90, 96n
impact of conflict on children, 195-196, 220
involvement in armed conflict, 220, 232n, 233n
involvement in peace support operations, 153, 220-221
participation of children in hostilities, 196, 220
recruitment, 196, 220
relevant treaties signed, ratified, etc., 134
South African Defence Force, 220
Truth and Reconciliation Commission, 232n
South African National Defence Force
ICRC cooperation with, 135-136
LOAC, 135
Save the Children - South Africa, 135
training chart, 195-197, 199
training concerning children, 135-136
training, general, 134-135
Special Rapporteur on the Sale of Children, 89
special treatment of children, 25, 27, 31n, 34, 38, 83-84, 99, 104, 170-171, 192
see also 'child, special treatment principle'
Sri Lanka, 136-138, 197, 221-222
Committee on the Rights of the Child and, 90, 96n
human rights/IHL abuses, 221-222
IHL training programme, 136-138, 161, 221
impact of conflict on children, 221
involvement in armed conflict, 22, 221
involvement in peace support operations, 222

Liberation Tigers of Tamil Eelam, 16n,
    136, 137, 149n, 176n, 197, 221, 233n,
    234n
  participation of children in hostilities,
    95n, 221
  recruitment, 221
  relevant treaties signed, ratified, etc., 136
Sri Lankan Army
  ICRC and, 136-138
  training chart and, 197
  training concerning children, 137-138,
    221
  training, general, 136-137
  treatment of children, 221
  UNICEF training, 137, 176n
states
  civil-military cooperation, 174
  conduct of armed conflict, 86,88, 172
  dissemination obligations of, 82
  ICRC, and, 86-87, 151-166, 172-175
  military training obligations of, 86, 172
  provision of military training on children
    and, 83, 84-85, 91n, 172-174
  UN and, 172-173,
statistics, 11n, 54n, 75n, 198, 218, 236n
Sweden, 153-155, 199-201, 224-225
  impact of conflict on children, 199
  involvement in armed conflict, 224
  involvement in peace support operations,
    224-225
  involvement in training of foreign armed
    forces, 225
  neutrality of, 224
  participation of children in hostilities,
    200
  recruitment, 224
  relevant treaties signed, ratified, etc., 153
SWEDINT, 154, 155, 225, 236n
Swedish National Armed Forces
  Save the Children Sweden and, 133, 134,
    154, 155, 175, 176, 187, 192, 195, 241-
    247, 247-258
  training chart, 199-201
  training concerning children, 154-155,
    161, 162, 241-247
  training, general, 153-154
Sudan, 16n, 95n, 111, 116n, 118n, 211, 223,
  234
supplies, 135, 156, 176, 196, 198, 201

T
terrorism, 169, 223, 225, 226,
    terrorist attacks, 2, 235n
torture
  of children, 27, 72, 90, 220, 244
  prohibition of, 24, 25, 26-27, 31n, 38,
    46, 53, 55n, 57n, 83-84, 93n, 170-171,
    181, 264, 270n
  protection from, 43n, 55n, 84, 257
  other gratuitous or degrading treatment,
    27, 38, 48, 52, 264, 269
  requirement of humane treatment, 27,
    34, 56n, 180, 185n, 193, 265
training of armed opposition groups, 7-8,
  16n
training of officers, 1, 2, 5, 6, 7, 8, 10, 17n,
  21-118, 125-150, 152-166, 170, 199, 203,
  250, 254
training of peace support personnel, 7, 87,
  107,115n, 135, 139,148n, 154, 155, 158,
  188, 224, 241
training of police, 8, 89, 90, 128, 225
  see also security forces
training of private companies, 8, 16n
training of soldiers, 2, 6-7, 171

U
Uganda, 138-144, 197, 222-223
  Committee on the Rights of the Child
    and, 90, 96n
  impact of conflict on children, 90, 123,
    140, 161, 222-223
  involvement in armed conflict, 121, 161,
    222
  involvement in peace support operations,
    223
  Lord's Resistance Army, 49, 222-223
  participation of children in hostilities,
    95n, 140, 222
  recruitment, 223
  relevant treaties signed, ratified, etc., 138
Ugandan Human Rights Commission, 139-
  141
Ugandan People's Defence Forces
  Child Protection Units, 140, 142, 148n
  human rights and IHL violations, 222-
    223
  ICRC and, 139
  monitoring and evaluation of training,
    143

recruitment, 223
Save the Children - Denmark, 123, 139-141, 143
sexual abuse of children and, 142
training chart and, 197
training concerning children, 40. 139-142, 161, 176n, 223
training, general, 139
under-18, 129, 164n, 192, 226, 233n, 235n, 237n
UNHCR, 36, 41n, 55n, 193, 260
UNICEF, 2, 41n, 56-57n, 89, 148n
  IHL training techniques, 116n
  military training on children, 16n, 176, 187, 197
  mine-awareness work, 75
United Kingdom, 155-157, 201-203, 225-226
  Committee on the Rights of the Child and, 91
  impact of conflict on children, 201
  involvement in armed conflict, 225-226
  involvement in peace support operations, 122, 226
  involvement in training of foreign armed forces, 226
  participation of children in hostilities, 202, 225
  recruitment, 202, 225
  relevant treaties signed, ratified, etc., 155
United Kingdom Armed Forces
  LOAC, 155-157
  mission-specific training, 155
  training chart, 201-203
  training, general, 155
  training regarding children, 156-157, 201-203
United Nations (UN)
  Charter, 93n
  Child Protection Advisors, 87
  Committee on the Rights of the Child, 4, 56n, 87-88, 99, 144n
  Convention on the Rights of the Child, 3, 243-244, 248, 249, 252, 254, 255, 256, 261
  General Assembly, 86
  peace support operations, 4, 7, 8, 41n, 122, 154, 164n, 217, 219, 220, 222, 223, 224, 226, 236n, 238n
  Security Council, 41n, 85, 86, 87, 88, 93n, 227n, 231n

Special Rapporteur, 42n
United States, 157-159, 203, 226-227
  involvement in armed conflict, 226-227
  involvement in peace support operations, 121, 226
  involvement in training of foreign armed forces, 128, 226, 228n
  participation of children in hostilities, 227
  recruitment, 226
  relevant treaties signed, ratified, etc., 13n, 157, 243
United States Armed Forces
  training chart, 203
  training concerning children, 122, 159
  training, general, 116n, 158-159
'unnecessary suffering' principle, 24, 162n, 169, 170

V
volunteers, 23, 218
  see also conscripts

W
war crime(s), 12n, 13n, 14n, 15n, 41n, 47, 48, 56n, 88, 104, 145n, 164n, 182, 184n, 220, 237n, 268
war crimes trials, 15n, 59-79, 99
  role played by, 172
weapons
  see also arms
  booby traps, 61, 75n
  firearms, 7, 160-161, 165n, 261
  landmines, 2, 14n, 59-79, 172, 191, 213n, 217, 222, 227n, 229n, 230n, 258
  small arms, 2, 11n, 95n, 243
women, 33, 40n, 41n, 43n, 67, 69, 70, 72, 77n, 86, 95n, 107, 128, 137, 146n, 160, 165n, 185n, 187, 192, 201, 205, 206, 207, 208, 209, 210, 211, 212, 216, 217, 227n, 228n, 244, 258

Y
Yugoslavia, the former, 2, 21, 32n, 64, 74n, 77n, 169, 216-217, 227n
  see Bosnia and Herzegovina

Z
zones, 35-36, 39, 41n, 135, 149n, 156, 164n, 171, 176n, 193, 196, 198, 200, 202, 266